COMPUTER
BOOK SERIES
FROM IDG

VRML & 3D on the Web For Dummies®

Cheat Sheet

Navigating with the mouse in your VRML browser

All five browsers we discuss (Live3D, VRML Add-In, Voyager, VR Scout, and Pioneer) let you navigate with the mouse in similar ways.

Charge and retreat

Drag up the screen to go forward and down the screen to go backward. Exception: In Live3D's Fly mode, pressing the mouse button without a drag moves you forward, and you can't go backward with the mouse.

Screen motion

Screen motion (a.k.a. sliding) works by dragging while pressing something extra. The extra "somethings" are as follows:

Live3D	Alt key
VRML Add-In	Slide button on the screen (click once, don't hold)
Voyager	Option key (Mac), Ctrl key (Windows)
VR Scout	Shift key
Pioneer	Right mouse button

Head motion

Turn right or left by dragging right or left.

Tilt up or down by pressing something extra and dragging up or down (in regular mode) or down or up (in joystick mode). The extras and modes are as follows:

Live3D	Ctrl key (walk mode regular, fly mode joystick)
VRML Add-In	Tilt button on the screen (click once, don't hold) (joystick)
Voyager	Shift key (regular)
VR Scout	Ctrl key (regular)
Pioneer	Both mouse buttons (joystick, adjustable to regular)

The Voyager exception

Voyager doesn't use a mouse drag. Instead of the "drag up/down/left/right" routine in the preceding instructions, use the mouse to position the cursor up/down/left/right and then press the mouse button.

IDG
BOOKS
WORLDWIDE

D1299723

...For Dummies: #1 Computer Book Series for Beginners

FOR
DUMMIES

COMPUTER
BOOK SERIES
FROM IDG

VRML & 3D on the Web
For Dummies®

Cheat
Sheet

Using VRML Builders

	Walkthrough Pro	Pioneer / Pioneer Pro
Navigate		
Walk/Fly	Walk only: Click and hold in walk view	Walk (feet icon): Click and drag to move
		Fly (plane icon): Click and drag to start
Charge/Retreat	Click and hold above/below	Click and drag forward/backward crosshairs
Turn left/right	Click and hold right/left of crosshairs	Click and drag to left/right
Slide left/right/up/down	Add Ctrl key (Option key on Mac)	Click and drag with right mouse button
Turn or Look up/down	Add Shift key, click above/below crosshairs	Press both buttons, drag back or forward
Display		
Turn rendered view on	Always on	3DR button (variant of wire-frame button)
Add views	View⇨New View	Small House icon
Create/Edit a shape		
Create a shape	Design View toolpad, 3rd row	Primitives panel (click Sphere, Cube, or Cone icon)
	Window⇨Depth Window for depth	
Change size	Scale tool (center, 2nd row of toolpad)	Scale tool (variant of Move and Rotate)
		Drag with both buttons to scale uniformly
Fiddle with shape	Drag corner points in Design View	Click "Orange-Face" tool; click face; drag
	Use skew tool (behind scale tool)	Click sweep tool to extend face
	Use tumble editor (cube with slice)	Left button = X, Y; Right button = Z
Position objects		
Select axis for motion	Choose a Design View	Left button = X, Y; Right button = Z
		Choose axes at far right of help bar
Move object	Click selection tool; drag in a Design View	Choose Object Move tool; drag
Rotate object	Click rotate tool, drag a handle from any point on object, and move the handle	Choose Object Rotate tool; drag
Change appearances		
Paint selected object	Click and hold on bar, center of toolpad; choose color	Click "Funnel" icon (right-click to set appearances)
Paint a surface	Click Wall-with-Door-and-Window icon, then surface	Click "Paintbrush" icon (right-click to set appearances); click surface
Apply a texture	Window⇨Textures; double-click texture	Right-click any paint tool; right-click checkered ball; left-click same ball
Save VRML file		
Command	File⇨Export⇨VRML	File⇨Scene⇨Save
Check these checkboxes	Export Textures Links	Marked Objects, LOD children, Textures

References for the Rest of Us! ®

COMPUTER BOOK SERIES FROM IDG

Are you intimidated and confused by computers? Do you find that traditional manuals are overloaded with technical details you'll never use? Do your friends and family always call you to fix simple problems on their PCs? Then the *...For Dummies*® computer book series from IDG Books Worldwide is for you.

. . .For Dummies books are written for those frustrated computer users who know they aren't really dumb but find that PC hardware, software, and indeed the unique vocabulary of computing make them feel helpless. *. . .For Dummies* books use a lighthearted approach, a down-to-earth style, and even cartoons and humorous icons to diffuse computer novices' fears and build their confidence. Lighthearted but not lightweight, these books are a perfect survival guide for anyone forced to use a computer.

> *"I like my copy so much I told friends; now they bought copies."*
>
> **Irene C., Orwell, Ohio**

> *"Quick, concise, nontechnical, and humorous."*
>
> **Jay A., Elburn, Illinois**

> *"Thanks, I needed this book. Now I can sleep at night."*
>
> **Robin F., British Columbia, Canada**

Already, hundreds of thousands of satisfied readers agree. They have made *...For Dummies* books the #1 introductory level computer book series and have written asking for more. So, if you're looking for the most fun and easy way to learn about computers, look to *...For Dummies* books to give you a helping hand.

IDG BOOKS WORLDWIDE™

2/96

VRML & 3D ON THE WEB FOR DUMMIES®

by David Kay and Douglas Muder

IDG Books Worldwide, Inc.
An International Data Group Company

Foster City, CA ♦ Chicago, IL ♦ Indianapolis, IN ♦ Braintree, MA ♦ Southlake, TX

VRML & 3D On The Web For Dummies®

Published by

IDG Books Worldwide, Inc.

An International Data Group Company
919 E. Hillsdale Blvd.
Suite 400
Foster City, CA 94404

Library of Congress Catalog Card No.: 96-75748

ISBN: 1-56884-611-8

Printed in the United States of America

10 9 8 7 6 5 4 3 2 1

1A/RX/QW/ZW/IN

Distributed in the United States by IDG Books Worldwide, Inc.

Distributed by Macmillan Canada for Canada; by Contemporanea de Ediciones for Venezuela; by Distribuidora Cuspide for Argentina; by CITEC for Brazil; by Ediciones ZETA S.C.R. Ltda. for Peru; by Editorial Limusa SA for Mexico; by Transworld Publishers Limited in the United Kingdom and Europe; by Academic Bookshop for Egypt; by Levant Distributors S.A.R.L. for Lebanon; by Al Jassim for Saudi Arabia; by Simron Pty. Ltd. for South Africa; by Pustak Mahal for India; by The Computer Bookshop for India; by Toppan Company Ltd. for Japan; by Addison Wesley Publishing Company for Korea; by Longman Singapore Publishers Ltd. for Singapore, Malaysia, Thailand, and Indonesia; by Unalis Corporation for Taiwan; by WS Computer Publishing Company, Inc. for the Philippines; by WoodsLane Pty. Ltd. for Australia; by WoodsLane Enterprises Ltd. for New Zealand. Authorized Sales Agent: Anthony Rudkin Associates for the Middle East and North Africa.

For general information on IDG Books Worldwide's books in the U.S., please call our Consumer Customer Service department at 800-762-2974. For reseller information, including discounts and premium sales, please call our Reseller Customer Service department at 800-434-3422.

For information on where to purchase IDG Books Worldwide's books outside the U.S., contact IDG Books Worldwide at 415-655-3078 or fax 415-655-3295.

For information on translations, contact Marc Jeffrey Mikulich, Director, Foreign & Subsidiary Rights, at IDG Books Worldwide, 415-655-3018 or fax 415-655-3281.

For sales inquiries and special prices for bulk quantities, write to the address above or call IDG Books Worldwide at 415-655-3200.

For information on using IDG Books Worldwide's books in the classroom, or ordering examination copies, contact the Education Office at 800-434-2086 or fax 817-251-8174.

For authorization to photocopy items for corporate, personal, or educational use, please contact Copyright Clearance Center, 222 Rosewood Drive, Danvers, MA 01923, or fax 508-750-4470.

 is a trademark under exclusive license to IDG Books Worldwide, Inc., from International Data Group, Inc.

About the Authors

David C. Kay

Dave Kay is a writer, engineer, and aspiring artist, combining professions in the same way as his favorite store, Acton Muffler, Brake, and Ice Cream. This is Kay's ninth computer book. They include multiple editions of *Microsoft Works For Windows For Dummies, WordPerfect For Windows For Dummies, MORE WordPerfect For Windows For Dummies,* and *Graphics File Formats.*

In his other life, as the Poo-bah of BrightLeaf Communications, he creates promotional copy, graphics, and Web sites for high-tech firms. In his spare time, he studies human and animal tracking, munches edible wild plants, makes strange blobs from molten glass, hikes in whatever mountains he can get to, and longs to return to New Zealand and track kiwis and hedgehogs in Wanaka. He hates writing in the third person like this and will stop now.

Douglas J. Muder

Doug Muder is a mathematician who spent ten years writing impenetrable papers about such important topics as the number of ping-pong balls that can fit into a very big cardboard box. He finally cracked under the pressure of taking his own work seriously and became a *Dummies* author.

This is his first complete computer book, though he did have a hand in the updating of Dave's *Microsoft Works For Windows For Dummies* and wrote small portions of *MORE Internet For Dummies* and *Internet E-Mail For Dummies.*

In his spare time, he writes short fiction, plays the stock market, and studies all varieties of esoterica. His ambition is to simplify his life to the point where he and his wife Deb can fit all their possessions into a small car and drive around the United States visiting everyone they know. He would also like to return to Wanaka, New Zealand and become a hiking bum in Mount Aspiring National Park. His motto is "Have Internet connection, will travel."

Welcome to the world of IDG Books Worldwide.

IDG Books Worldwide, Inc., is a subsidiary of International Data Group, the world's largest publisher of computer-related information and the leading global provider of information services on information technology. IDG was founded more than 25 years ago and now employs more than 7,700 people worldwide. IDG publishes more than 250 computer publications in 67 countries (see listing below). More than 70 million people read one or more IDG publications each month.

Launched in 1990, IDG Books Worldwide is today the #1 publisher of best-selling computer books in the United States. We are proud to have received 8 awards from the Computer Press Association in recognition of editorial excellence and three from Computer Currents' First Annual Readers' Choice Awards, and our best-selling ...*For Dummies*® series has more than 19 million copies in print with translations in 28 languages. IDG Books Worldwide, through a joint venture with IDG's Hi-Tech Beijing, became the first U.S. publisher to publish a computer book in the People's Republic of China. In record time, IDG Books Worldwide has become the first choice for millions of readers around the world who want to learn how to better manage their businesses.

Our mission is simple: Every one of our books is designed to bring extra value and skill-building instructions to the reader. Our books are written by experts who understand and care about our readers. The knowledge base of our editorial staff comes from years of experience in publishing, education, and journalism — experience which we use to produce books for the '90s. In short, we care about books, so we attract the best people. We devote special attention to details such as audience, interior design, use of icons, and illustrations. And because we use an efficient process of authoring, editing, and desktop publishing our books electronically, we can spend more time ensuring superior content and spend less time on the technicalities of making books.

You can count on our commitment to deliver high-quality books at competitive prices on topics you want to read about. At IDG Books Worldwide, we continue in the IDG tradition of delivering quality for more than 25 years. You'll find no better book on a subject than one from IDG Books Worldwide.

John J. Kilcullen

John Kilcullen
President and CEO
IDG Books Worldwide, Inc.

Authors' Acknowledgments

A special order of sainthood is reserved for authors' wives. Katy Weeks and Deb Bodeau have earned their places.

Thanks also to . . .

The congenial editors at IDG: Project Editor Tim ("Oh, Never Mind") Gallan, Copy Editor Christa Carroll, Product Development Manager and General Factotum Mary Bednarek, Permissions Editor and Tenacious Goad of Software Vendors Joyce Pepple.

Technical Editor and CD compiler John Gwinner.

Our helpful contacts at software vendors: Roman Ormandy and Erik Johnson of Caligari, Ashley Sharpe of Virtus, Dan Greening of Chaco, Phil Utykanski of Viewpoint, and Alan Walford of Eos Systems.

All the people who allowed us to show off their VRML creations and gave us helpful hints about where to find other wonderful stuff: D. Owen Rowley, C. Scott Young, Glenn Crocker, Robert M. Free, Adrian and Christine Clark, Franz Buchenberger, Dan Greening, Adrian Scott, Marke Pesce, Tony Parisi, Gavin Bell, all the fun-loving folks at Netscape and Planet 9, and of course, Supreme Commander Patchouli.

The patient people who allowed Doug and his laptop to use their space as an office-away-from-office: Lynn Stone, Sean Nolan, Bob Levine, Steve and Sara Gross, Don and Lois Muder, and Yelena Khazatsky, the strudel lady.

Family cheerleader Karen ("Hey, My Brother-in-Law's an Author") Weeks and Procurer of Macintoshes John Weeks.

Oh, yes . . . and Rusty the Wonder Dog.

Dedication

We would like to dedicate this book to Doug's parents, Don and Lois Muder, and to Dave's wife, Katy Weeks.

Publisher's Acknowledgments

We're proud of this book; please send us your comments about it by using the Reader Response Card at the back of the book or by e-mailing us at feedback/dummies@idgbooks.com. Some of the people who helped bring this book to market include the following:

Acquisitions, Development, & Editorial

Project Editor: Tim Gallan

Assistant Acquisitions Editor: Gareth Hancock

Product Development Manager: Mary Bednarek

Permissions Editor: Joyce Pepple

Copy Editor: Christa Carroll

Technical Reviewer: John Gwinner

Editorial Manager: Kristin A. Cocks

Editorial Assistant: Constance Carlisle, Chris Collins

Production

Associate Project Coordinator: Debbie Sharpe

Layout and Graphics: E. Shawn Aylsworth, Cheryl Denski, Anne Malani, Anna Rohrer, Kate Snell

Proofreaders: Jenny Kaufeld, Nancy Price, Rob Springer, Carrie Voorhis, Karen York

Indexer: Liz Cunningham

General & Administrative

IDG Books Worldwide, Inc.: John Kilcullen, President & CEO; Steven Berkowitz, COO & Publisher

Dummies, Inc.: Milissa Koloski, Executive Vice President & Publisher

Dummies Technology Press & Dummies Editorial: Diane Graves Steele, Associate Publisher; Judith A. Taylor, Brand Manager; Myra Immell, Editorial Director

Dummies Trade Press: Kathleen A. Welton, Vice President & Publisher; Stacy S. Collins, Brand Manager

IDG Books Production for Dummies Press: Beth Jenkins, Production Director; Cindy L. Phipps, Supervisor of Project Coordination; Kathie S. Schnorr, Supervisor of Page Layout; Shelley Lea, Supervisor of Graphics and Design

Dummies Packaging & Book Design: Erin McDermit, Packaging Coordinator; Kavish+Kavish, Cover Design

◆

The publisher would like to give special thanks to Patrick J. McGovern, without whom this book would not have been possible.

◆

Contents at a Glance

Cartoons at a Glance

By Rich Tennant • Fax: 508-546-7747 • E-mail: the5wave@tiac.net

page 346

page 91

page 177

page 9

page 289

page 317

page 229

Table of Contents

Introduction

Maybe you've heard of VRML. Or maybe not.

Maybe you've heard that 3D modeling has come to the World Wide Web, but the exact four-letter combination has never stuck in your head.

Maybe you've seen "VRML" in print, or maybe you've heard somebody talking about "vermil," which is how VRML is pronounced.

Maybe you were looking over the shoulder of a coworker, friend, or housemate when you saw cool 3D images running around on a computer screen. When you asked, your coworker/friend/housemate said, "It's VRML," as if that were supposed to mean something.

Maybe you were reading one of those pretentious newsweeklies (you know the ones we mean) when you saw an article filled with buzzwords like VRML and Java and Internet agents. The article didn't explain anything but left the vague impression that those who don't already know are doomed to be slaves of the techno-elite.

Maybe you ran across VRML in a breathless article in one of those technology fan magazines. And you learned that it's cyberspace from *Neuromancer*. It's the metaverse from *Snow Crash*. It's here. It's now. It's cool. It's hot. It's real. It's happening — whatever it is.

Or maybe you were just wandering around in a bookstore when you saw this book and said, "3D on the Web? Sounds like fun, but what the heck is VRML?"

What the Heck VRML Is

VRML is the Virtual Reality Modeling Language. It's a computer language for describing three-dimensional scenes. But don't panic: This book is not about writing a computer language. It's about exploring and building 3D worlds.

Like any computer language, VRML uses text and numbers — ordinary characters that appear on every computer keyboard in the world. As a result, both humans and computers can read and write it — but only if by "human" you mean "computer wizards." Fortunately for the rest of us humans, the wizards have been busy building computer programs that do almost all the work and leave us the fun. Now ordinary mortals don't have to read or write VRML to build or explore 3D worlds.

Why VRML Exists

VRML was made to be used on the World Wide Web so that people all over the world can create and share three-dimensional objects and spaces. In fact, its authors envision using it to create one big stitched-together virtual world. They intended VRML to be a worldwide standard, so they didn't tie it to any particular software company, chip, or operating system. An Appalachian with an Apple can combine a VRML throne (created by a Crimean with a Cray) with a VRML castle (constructed by a Columbian with a Compaq) — and send the synthesis to someone with a Sun in Sudan. With today's VRML world-building tools, it's almost easier done than said.

Why You Might Care

The simplest and most obvious reason to care about VRML is that it's fun. You'll enjoy seeing all the cool 3D stuff that other people have made (and maybe even make cool 3D stuff yourself). Go look at the pictures in the color section. (You don't have to read the pages of this book in order. We won't tell anybody.) Every one of those pictures comes from a 3D scene that is just sitting there on the Web, waiting for you to wander around in it for free. If none of those pictures raises a smile on your face, just put this book back and go on about your very serious business. We're sure that the bookstore has plenty of glum, dour, tedious books you can buy instead.

But if you did smile, and if that smile isn't already reason enough to get into VRML, consider the following rationalizations:

- ✔ Adding a jazzy 3D logo to your Web page will draw more attention to your business or your résumé.
- ✔ Rearranging the VRML model of your dream house is cheaper than having the blueprints redrawn.
- ✔ People who check out your Web site may stick around to play with 3D models of your products, such as houses, toys, or machines. And then they might buy them.
- ✔ Your kids will understand atoms, DNA, solar systems, and geometrical objects much better if they can see them modeled in 3D.
- ✔ You (or your kids, or somebody) will learn a lot more about the Web if you have something fun to look for — like 3D scenes.
- ✔ If you have to explain or illustrate something horribly complicated, a 3D scene is sometimes worth a thousand 2D pictures (or a million words).
- ✔ You don't want to be enslaved by the techno-elite.
- ✔ You want to join the techno-elite and enslave others.

And besides, it's cool, it's hot, and it's happening.

What We Do For You

We do two very simple things in this book:

> ✔ Give you tools.
>
> ✔ Teach you how to use them.

The tools are programs for your computer that we have put on a CD in the back of the book. The teachings are spread throughout the next three or four hundred pages. If you have a not-too-old PC or Mac, a CD-ROM drive, Internet access, and a Web browser, then this book and its CD are all you need to:

> ✔ Look at 3D scenes and objects on the World Wide Web.
>
> ✔ Build your own 3D scenes and objects in VRML.
>
> ✔ Put your VRML creations out on the Web for other people to look at.

Just how new and jazzy should your computer be? A 66MHz 486 PC running Windows 3.1 or 95, or a Power Mac with 8MB of memory will do the job. A graphics accelerator card will help but isn't a requirement.

What's on the CD?

We've assembled a good collection of VRML tools on the CD, which is both PC- and Mac-readable. Some of the software on the CD is available free on the Web — if you know where to look, and if you know what you want. Some of the other tools will cost you hundreds of dollars if you bought them in a store, but you get to try them out here for the price of a book. And we've thrown in a book for free.

What do the tools do? They read and write VRML so that you don't have to. Tools that read VRML are called *browsers*. Tools that write VRML are called *builders*. VRML itself doesn't care what kind of machine you have, but the browsing and building tools do. So we've put together a collection that gives both Mac users and Windows users a full range of capabilities.

Browsers

VRML describes a 3D scene with text and numbers. But you don't want to see the text and numbers; you want to see the 3D. That's what a VRML browser is for: It reads the VRML description of a scene, does a mind-boggling calculation, and then displays what you would see if you were inside the scene. Every time you give a command to move, the browser recalculates your view.

VRML browsers work hand-in-glove with Web browsers, and some are specifically designed for a particular Web browser. We have included four VRML browsers on the CD in order to cover as many Web browser/operating system combinations as possible. The four are

- ✔ Microsoft Internet Explorer VRML Add-In
- ✔ Chaco VR Scout
- ✔ Caligari Pioneer (also a builder)
- ✔ Virtus Voyager

We cover Netscape's Live3D in the book, and though it isn't on the CD, we tell you where you can download it. We've also included Pueblo, a special tool for sharing multimedia stuff (3D being one of the media) over the Web — and chatting about your experiences.

And when newer, jazzier versions of these programs come out, you'll be able to download them free over the Web. We tell you how.

Builders

You might wonder how the 3D ideas in your head can get translated into VRML. That's what builders are for. If you've ever used a 2D drawing program (like PowerPoint or MacDraw), you'll see a lot of analogies between drawing programs and VRML builders. Both give you toolbars of shapes and colors which allow you to construct complicated structures without worrying about the details of any computer language.

In this book, we show you in detail how to use builders from two vendors:

- ✔ Caligari, which makes Pioneer and Pioneer Pro (for Windows 95 only)
- ✔ Virtus, which makes Walkthrough Pro (for the Mac and Windows)

Evaluation copies of these applications are on our CD. For fun, we've also included an evaluation copy of Caligari's trueSpace, which is their professional software for creating and animating 3D scenes that are too jazzy even for VRML.

By the way, Walkthrough Pro expires 90 days after installation. Pioneer expires after 30 hours of use (or 60 days). Pioneer Pro expires after 10 hours of use (or 30 days). trueSpace 2 expires 90 days after installation. For more information, see both the "About the CD" Appendix and the OUR_CD file (which comes in both HTML and text formats) on the CD itself. You should also read the license agreements that come with each program. The upshot here is that you should install an individual piece of software from the CD only when you plan to spend some time working with it. Don't install one of the programs on your hard drive and let it sit there unused. In the case of Walkthrough and trueSpace, the software will eventually expire. In the case of Pioneer and Pioneer Pro, someone else may decide to use your computer, innocently discover the software, and start playing with it, which ultimately wastes *your* time with the software.

The frosting on the cake is that you'll find actual video demonstrations of how to use the VRML builders. Building 3D objects on a 2D screen is tricky, and trying to describe it in words on paper is even trickier, so we've captured the moves in a few short demonstrations.

Other VRML-related stuff

If we had to build our houses starting from trees and sand, caves would still look pretty attractive. To help you avoid a similar situation in VRML, we've included a few pre-fab parts and tools on the CD as well:

- ✔ Object libraries from ViewPoint Data Labs, a leading commercial source for 3D objects
- ✔ Sample *textures* (images that can be pasted onto 3D objects)
- ✔ Example models and building materials by the authors
- ✔ A few other useful tools

Also, because we ran out of room in the book, the CD is where you will find the nitty-gritty official details of VRML: the actual specification, reproduced here for all the die-hard technoids (and technoid wannabes) in the audience.

What's in the book?

We don't think it's enough just to give you a bunch of VRML tools and say, "Have fun." (If you think it is enough, hey, the CD's in the back. Have fun. Buy the book, though; the bookstore owner is watching.) We've tried to find tools that are as easy to use as possible, but none of them are exactly obvious — at least not to us. So we've run them through their paces, banged our heads against a few virtual walls, and now we're happy to share with you what we've learned.

The book splits into seven parts (as our heads have — after banging them against the wall):

Part I: Cruising 3D Hyperspace

Part I covers the fine art of exploring 3D worlds with VRML browsing tools. It begins with a general description of what browsers do, gives you instructions on how to use the browsers on the CD (and Live3D), and concludes with a tour of the fun VRML sites we've found on the Web. Even if this part is as far as you get, you'll still be able to find all the stuff in our color pictures.

Part II: Building Tools and Materials

Part II starts with some perspective on building tools and — just to show you why you don't want to write VRML yourself — an introduction to VRML programming. Part II then gives you a detailed reference chapter (in the usual *Dummies* style) for each tool. We finish up Part II with a guide to finding, using, and recycling VRML building materials.

Part III: World Building 101

Part III is our walk-before-you-run part. It shows you how to make simple shapes and move them around; how to build rooms with doors and windows; how to paint and add lights and cameras; and how to fill your rooms up with furniture conveniently made by somebody else (and conveniently provided on the CD).

Part IV: Making a Better World

By Part IV, we figure that you're starting to pick up a little confidence in your abilities, and you're ready to unleash a little creativity. Want to sculpt fancy virtual shapes, build your own furniture, or add a nice wood-grain finish to your virtual den? Get serious about world building with a little terraforming and landscaping: Add mountains, lakes, caves, and trees. Go wild.

Part V: Worlds on the Web

If you read up to Part V, then you've got it, but how are you going to flaunt it? Stake out some virtual real estate and put your creations out where 20 million people can find them! Too shy? Hey, the '90s are more than half over, folks. Modesty is *so* retro. But it takes more than just sticking your world on the Web to make it in the big time. Part V gives you the tricks of the trade that make your worlds work on the Web.

Part VI: The Part of Tens

In this part, we discuss the future of VRML, mainly the addition of sound and animation to 3D worlds. As we explain in the introduction to this part, all *Dummies* books have a "Part of Tens" where the author provides top-ten lists. We, however, want to give you useful information, stuff that you can use to make your 3D world a better place. We're sure that each of the chapters in this part contain at least ten useful bits of information, so that's one of the reasons why we feel that we can call this part "The Part of Tens" (thus making our publisher happy).

Web page? What Web page?

Our Web page is `http://www.brightleaf.com/VRML4dum/`. Look there to find late-breaking news about:

- ✔ Mistakes we made in the book (Mistakes? Us?)
- ✔ Things that have changed since we wrote the book
- ✔ Where to find the latest updates of the free software on our CD
- ✔ Lists of great VRML sites on the Web

✔ Any weird or cool models we've made

✔ When we're appearing on *Letterman* (well, maybe not)

What we don't do

Windows (the glass kind).

We've tried to make this book useful for people with a wide range of backgrounds, but it's not all things to all people. If you want to become a hard-core VRML hacker who can take advantage of all the little nuances of the language, you can probably find a better book than ours — though you may want to buy this book for the software.

If you've never used a computer or the Internet before, you should read some other book first. (*PCs For Dummies, Macs For Dummies,* and *The Internet For Dummies* are fine books written by good, honorable authors who doubtlessly will feel obligated to recommend our books now.) We assume that you have a computer (and know the basics of using it), a means of accessing the Internet, and a Web browser (and you know how to tell this Web browser to go fetch our Web page). If that doesn't sound like rocket science, you and this book should get along just fine.

We can't promise you that the software is bug free. It isn't. (Believe us, we know.) Most of the programs on the CD are what the software companies call "beta versions" — which is their way of saying that they haven't tested everything yet. We think it all works well enough to be interesting and useful. And we know just how frustrating it is to trip across something that doesn't work the way it's supposed to. (Oh, do we know. We wish we didn't.) But don't reprogram your computer with a baseball bat and don't tear this book into little pieces. Take a walk, have a cup of hot chocolate, and check our Web page (or the software company's Web page) to see if anybody has found a way around the bugs yet.

One convention you should know about: When we refer to commands in pull-down menus, we use a little right-pointing arrow (⇨) to indicate the command in the given menu. So if we want you to choose the Save command in the File menu, we say, "Choose File⇨Save." It's just easier that way.

We thought you should know that just before presstime, Caligari changed the name of its builder from Fountain to Pioneer. We've made what changes we could, but a few of the illustrations may still say "Fountain." Don't let the name confuse you: Fountain is Pioneer, not something new and different (it's actually old and similar) that we haven't told you about.

The icons we use

Occasionally, you'll see little drawings in our margins. No, we didn't get bored and start doodling. These drawings are icons that tell you what the nearby chunk of text is up to. If you've read other . . . *For Dummies* books, you may recognize some of them.

The Note icon flags anything important we want you to remember (or take *note* of).

We use the Tip icon to flag tricks and shortcuts that will save you time, money, energy, and possibly your sanity.

Whenever you might be in danger of losing data or screwing up in a big way, we let you know with the Warning icon.

The tool designers have anticipated *almost* everything you might want to do with VRML, but not *absolutely* everything. The Deep VRML icon points out the places where we have rolled up our sleeves and are mucking around tool-lessly with the VRML code itself.

We use this icon whenever we refer to software you can find on our CD.

What Now?

If you're still standing furtively in the bookstore, buy the book already! Then pull the CD out of the slot in the back of the book and get ready to have some serious fun. If you're new to VRML and 3D on the Web, start by installing a VRML browser and wandering through some of the scenes in Chapter 5, "Oh, the Places You'll Go". See Part I to help you choose and use a browser. When you've seen enough to convince you to build your own 3D world, turn to Part II and read how to join the party. Afterward, drop us a line at `vrml@dummies.com` and tell us where to find your own cool Web world! We'd love to hear from you.

Part I
Cruising 3D Hyperspace

The 5th Wave   By Rich Tennant

"WHAT CONCERNS ME ABOUT THE INFORMATION SUPERHIGHWAY IS THAT IT APPEARS TO BE ENTERING THROUGH BRENT'S BEDROOM."

In this part . . .

Solar system models, bizarre architectural wonders, virtual sculptures — people have left all kinds of neat 3D stuff lying around on the Web. You can look around in their strange new worlds for free, after you discover how to use one of the VRML browsers we provide on our CD.

Chapter 1

Blasting Off for 3D Worlds:
The Browser

● ●

In This Chapter

▶ What a VRML browser does

▶ The types of VRML browsers: plug-ins, helpers, and browser/builders

▶ Basic moves you can make with any VRML browser

▶ Extra features that many VRML browsers have

▶ Advanced features that anticipate VRML 2.0

▶ Which VRML browsers run on your computer

▶ Which VRML browsers work with your Web browser

▶ How to choose which VRML browser is best for you

● ●

*V*RML is a language for describing three-dimensional scenes and objects, but if you're like us, it's not the kind of language you like to sit down and read for entertainment. Most of the time, we'd rather not read a VRML file at all — we just want to look at the world it describes.

That's what a VRML browser is for. It reads the VRML so that we don't have to, and then it displays on our computer what we would see if we were in the scene. Figure 1-1 shows some VRML code from `diner.wrl` (which you can find in the Samples folder on the CD); Figure 1-2 shows you what the code produces.

New VRML browsers come out every month or so, and new, souped-up versions of old VRML browsers come out even more often. They all look a little bit different, and you tell them what to do in different ways, but fundamentally, they are all doing the same thing: translating VRML into images on your computer screen.

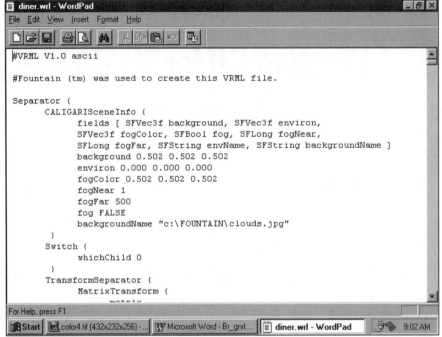

Figure 1-1:
What a
VRML
browser
reads: A
chunk of
code from
diner.wrl.

```
#VRML V1.0 ascii

#Fountain (tm) was used to create this VRML file.

Separator {
        CALIGARISceneInfo {
                fields [ SFVec3f background, SFVec3f environ,
                SFVec3f fogColor, SFBool fog, SFLong fogNear,
                SFLong fogFar, SFString envName, SFString backgroundName ]
                background 0.502 0.502 0.502
                environ 0.000 0.000 0.000
                fogColor 0.502 0.502 0.502
                fogNear 1
                fogFar 500
                fog FALSE
                backgroundName "c:\FOUNTAIN\clouds.jpg"
        }
        Switch {
                whichChild 0
        }
        TransformSeparator {
                MatrixTransform {
```

Figure 1-2:
What a
VRML
browser
shows you:
Dave's
Diner, as
displayed by
Pioneer.

The purpose of this chapter is to give you an overview of what VRML browsers do, the different kinds of browsers, the basic moves they all have to let you make, what extra features you might look for, and how you might choose which browser you want to learn to use.

A Browse around the Browser

By now, computers have 2D motion down pat. Whether you have a mouse, a trackball, a glide-point, or whatever, they all work pretty much the same way: You move your hand forward/backward or left/right, and that moves the cursor up/down or left/right on the screen. Or you use the arrow keys on the keyboard. It's standard. You don't have to learn it from scratch every time you get a new application.

As long as the Web was made up of 2D documents, standardizing Web browsers was easy. If you know Netscape's Navigator, Microsoft's Internet Explorer is no mystery, and vice versa. Even the Web browsers on the big commercial services like AOL and Prodigy have the same basic commands in more-or-less the same places: There's a button to go back to the previous page, a window to type a Web address (URL) into, a list of bookmarks you can jump to, and so on.

Someday 3D motion will be just as standardized, but it hasn't happened yet. VRML is a step in the right direction because it at least gets all the geeks speaking the same language. But even so, learning how to use one VRML browser can leave you clueless about how to use any other one.

Worse, because a VRML browser produces a 3D experience that you don't have to be an Einstein to appreciate, VRML browsing has become a battlefield in the Software Wars. Netscape has its special VRML browser (Live3D), and so does Microsoft (VRML Add-In). Companies that make expensive 3D modeling software have VRML browsers that look a lot like their upscale cousins. Every software company hopes that an eye-catching VRML browser will tempt you to look at the rest of its products.

The CD contains versions of several browsers: Microsoft's VRML Add-In, Chaco's VR Scout, Virtus' Voyager, and Caligari's Pioneer. In Chapter 2, we tell you how to download another browser, Netscape's Live3D. We got the most recent versions we could, but the field is moving so fast that more recent versions are probably out by the time you read this. Think of the CD as a sampler: Take a look at the programs to see what you like. When you decide you like something and want the most up-to-date version, the *VRML For Dummies* Web page (http://www.brightleaf.com/VRML4dum/) will tell you where to look on the Web to download it. (We can update the home page in a minute. Putting out a new version of the CD takes a little longer.)

What VRML browsers do

At its most basic level, VRML is just a way of using text and numbers to describe a 3D scene: "There's a blue cube over there; it's three inches long" — that sort of thing, only much more structured and technical. (Check out Figure 1-1 to see what VRML looks like.) What a VRML browser does, then, is to read this description and figure out what you would see if you were inside of it.

The VRML browser also interprets your mouse and keyboard commands as moving orders: go forward, turn left, look up, and so forth. With each motion, it recomputes what you would see from the new perspective: If you turn your head left, the scene should swing to the right. If you look up, the brick wall won't block your view any more, so you'll see the road on the other side.

The VRML browser has a huge computational job. It keeps track of all the objects in the scene and all their relative positions. It figures out how big an object appears from a given distance and what it looks like from a given angle. An advanced browser even keeps track of the lighting: Where are the light sources? Where are the shadows? What does this color look like with this amount of light?

For this reason, processor speed is a big factor in the quality of your VR experience. Some VRML browsers won't run on anything less than a fast workstation that costs $10,000 or more. Most require a high-end personal computer of some sort — a 486DX or higher in the Windows/Intel world or a Power Mac or fast 68040 in the Apple world. Even so, some VRML worlds are just too big for a home computer to keep track of. Or if you do run them on your home machine, you need to make undemanding choices to maintain a sense of realism.

In this book, we assume that you don't have the $50,000 Silicon Graphics workstation. We assume that you have either a PC with at least a 486DX chip or a Macintosh PowerPC. If you have better, fine. Everything will work just the same way, only a little faster — or maybe a lot faster.

The types of VRML browsers

A VRML file (which is called a *world* and looks like `filename.wrl`) containing a 3D scene can live anywhere (your hard disk is as good a place as any), but VRML was created for the purpose of putting 3D worlds out on the World Wide Web where anybody can experience them. For that reason, VRML browsers are designed to work with Web browsers.

We've provided examples of three different types of VRML browsers on the CD:

- ✔ **Plug-ins.** A plug-in VRML browser is designed with a particular Web browser in mind, and the two work so closely together that you may have a hard time figuring out where the Web browser ends and the VRML browser begins. VRML worlds can appear on a Web page surrounded by text, pictures, or anything else that commonly shows up on a Web page.

- ✔ **Helper applications.** These VRML browsers work with a variety of Web browsers. A Web browser calls in a helper application as a specialist when it sees something it doesn't know how to display. The VRML browser then opens its own window on your screen to display a VRML world.

- ✔ **Browser/builders.** Some VRML helper applications have extra capabilities. Not only can you view VRML worlds created by others, but you can build your own VRML worlds with the same tool.

Plug me in

Some VRML browsers are designed to plug in to a particular Web browser so that VRML worlds can be displayed inside the Web browser's window the same way that, say, photographs are. These VRML browsers are known as *plug-ins*.

The plug-in is a fairly new idea (even in the VRML world, where six months ago is ancient history), and so far, plug-ins have been written only for Netscape Navigator and Microsoft Internet Explorer. (Even the one for Internet Explorer is only approximately a plug-in, since it doesn't do VRML-embedded-in-HTML.) Others may exist by the time you read this.

Plug-ins have many advantages. The biggest is that they allow VRML worlds to be part of a larger picture. With a plug-in, a 3D VRML world can sit on the same page with a paragraph of text, a photograph, a map, a button to play a piece of music, or any of the other things that peacefully coexist on a Web page.

The major disadvantage of a plug-in is that it only works with the Web browser it was designed for. If you're the kind of person who likes to play the field and doesn't like being tied down to Netscape, Internet Explorer, or some other Web browser, having a VRML-browsing plug-in may be more of a commitment than you're ready for. (You could maintain several Web browsers, each with its own VRML browser, but that begins to eat up a lot of disk space.)

A Web browser and its plug-ins work so closely together that the plug-in may not work any more after you install a new version of the Web browser. You may have to install a new version of the plug-in at the same time.

If you use the Web browser that comes with one of the major Internet services such as AOL or CompuServe, you have no choice — no one has written a plug-in for them yet. Recently, however, most services have been making either Netscape or Internet Explorer available to their users. Check with your service for the latest news.

The CD contains two plug-in VRML browsers: VR Scout (for Netscape) and VRML Add-In (for Internet Explorer).

Help! Give me an application

When a Web browser (without a plug-in) comes across a VRML file, it calls for help. AOL's call looks like Figure 1-3.

Figure 1-3:
How a Web browser calls for help with a VRML file.

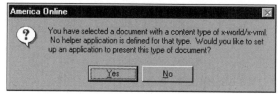

We'll tell you exactly how to answer the call in Chapter 3, but for the moment, all you need to know is that any good Web browser realizes when it's in over its head, and it asks you what to do.

What to do is to call in a specialist application and let it handle things. A VRML browser that connects to a Web browser in this way is called a *helper application*. Most VRML browsers (other than plug-ins) can be set up to work as a helper application with almost any Web browser (including Netscape or Internet Explorer).

Helper applications don't work as closely with a Web browser as a plug-in would, so you don't get some of the special effects, like VRML worlds sitting on an ordinary Web page. As compensation, you get the versatility of being able to work with any Web browser you want.

Among the browsers on the CD, Virtus' Voyager and Chaco's VR Scout work as helper applications with your Web browser, whatever it is. VR Scout comes in both a helper application version and a Netscape plug-in version. Caligari's Pioneer (which we're categorizing as a browser/builder) also works as a helper application for Netscape or Mosaic.

Browser/builders

If nobody ever built VRML worlds, there wouldn't be anywhere to browse. In Part III, you'll start learning how to build your own worlds using applications called *builders*. It's natural for a builder to have some browsing capabilities as well — after all, you want to be able to see what you're doing and what your world will look like to the people who browse through it. You want to be able to move around in it and see what it looks like from a lot of angles.

With that notion in mind, a simple idea develops: Why not have one piece of software that does everything? The advantages are obvious:

✔ You only have to learn one set of commands.

✔ You can be sure that your browser and builder are compatible.

✔ You only have one program to install, update, and store on your hard drive.

So far this idea has not taken off. The only true browser/builder we have been able to find is Caligari's Pioneer. The prerelease version (Pioneer .96) has a lot of potential, but it's far from perfect as a browser. It has two major deficiencies:

✔ Motion is slow compared to other browsers. When it slows down too much, Pioneer compensates by not fully animating the scene — you move through a wire-frame world until you stop, and then the program fills in the surfaces and colors.

✔ So far, Pioneer can be configured as a helper application only with Netscape or Mosaic. With any other browser, you need to save the VRML file to your disk and then open it with Pioneer. (Caligari is working on this problem. By the time you read this book, versions of Pioneer may be available that work with a wider range of browsers.)

Caligari's competitor Virtus has the next best thing to a browser/builder. Its Walkthrough Pro builder and Voyager browser share a number of features, so the skills you learn with one often carry over to the other.

Both Caligari's Pioneer and Virtus' Voyager and Walkthrough Pro are on the *VRML & 3D On The Web For Dummies* CD.

Learning the Moves

Three-D motion may be new to your computer, but it's old stuff to you. Like the guy who was amazed to discover he'd been speaking in prose all his life, you've been moving in 3D for a long, long time now. So none of the 3D moves should be the least bit strange to you — the only thing you will need to learn is how to tell the browser what move to make next.

In this section, we describe the basics of motion in 3D. (Well, at the end, we also throw in a couple of special features that aren't basic, but we think they're cool.) These basic motions are so fundamental that every browser has to give you some way to do them. In Chapters 2 through 4, we will discuss the individual browsers on the CD and describe how you tell each of them to perform these basic motions.

Basic motions

When you navigate through a 3D landscape, you want to be able to do the following things:

- ✔ Move forward and backward. We'll call this *charge* and *retreat.*
- ✔ Move in the plane of the screen so that your viewing position moves up/ down and left/right. We'll call this *screen motion.* It's also sometimes called *sliding.* The game *Doom* calls it *strafing mode,* but don't expect to blow up your VRML models!
- ✔ Turn your head so that you look up/down or left/right without changing your position in space. We'll call this *head motion.*

Once you've decided what kind of motion you want, you want to be able to control

- ✔ When you start moving
- ✔ When you stop
- ✔ How fast you go

Charge, retreat, screen motion, head motion, start, stop, and speed — any VRML browser has to let you control these things somehow. The commands may vary from one to the other, but 3D is 3D no matter what program you're running.

Typically, you make the basic moves with a mouse command, though most browsers provide an alternate keyboard command. (Some commands combine the two: You move the mouse while holding down a key like Shift or Alt.) The mouse moves are intuitive for the most part. For instance, in every browser, you move forward by dragging the cursor up the screen and backward by dragging it down. The only confusing movement is tilting your head up or down. If you think of the motion as a mouse drag (combined with a keyboard command), it makes sense to tilt your head up by dragging up and down by dragging down. But if you think of the way that joysticks work in airplanes, the opposite way makes sense. Different browsers do it opposite ways, and Pioneer allows you to choose between the two.

Standard extra features

Most VRML browsers give you powers and options beyond the basic moves. The particular package of extra features varies from browser to browser, but (like power steering and cruise control) the same general ideas show up again and again.

Some objects have connections

In ordinary Web browsing, some words show up in a different color from the rest. Your cursor changes shape when it passes over them, and if you click on them, you're transported somewhere else on the Web (you hope somewhere related to the word you clicked).

Something similar happens in VRML browsing. Certain objects are *hotlinks*. They don't change color, but your cursor changes shape as it passes over them. If you click (or double-click, depending on your VRML browser) a hotlinked object, you are transported somewhere else on the Web — sometimes to a Web page, sometimes to a VRML world. For example, Figure 15 in the color section shows a VRML model of the Earth floating in space. The continents on that globe are hotlinked to current satellite photos of those continents.

You can't link to the Web if you aren't online. Your browser will still show you which objects are hotlinked, but it can't connect you to the linked Web sites.

Moving in for a close-up

Sometimes you get annoyed with having to tell the browser things like "Go left. Go right. Back up. Tilt your head." What you'd really like to do is point at something and say, "Go there." Most VRML browsers, including Live3D, VRML Add-In, and Pioneer, will take you in for a closer view of whatever part of the scene you click on.

As the world turns

When you're looking at Asia on a globe, and you decide to look at America, you don't walk around to the other side of the globe, you spin it. Live3D, VRML Add-In, and VR Scout allow you to "spin" a VRML world to see the other side.

A good way to check out the big picture in a VRML world is to back away and then spin the world slowly.

Changing your point of view

You can do a few things in VRML that you can't do in real life. One of them is to jump to a new viewpoint instantly. (A new physical viewpoint, that is. A politician can jump to a new viewpoint whenever a new poll comes out, but even so, his or her body stays in the same place.)

The people who build VRML worlds (watch out, you may become one of them if you read Part III) can designate certain preferred viewpoints — sort of like the places in the national parks where they put the coin-operated binoculars. In any VRML browser, there has to be some place where you can click the mouse and get a menu of all the built-in viewpoints. Once you see that menu, you can click on one of the choices and see that view immediately.

Most of the VRML worlds we've looked at so far don't take advantage of this feature, but every world or object has to have at least one predetermined viewpoint, called the Entry View. This view is what you see when you first open the file.

Because VRML doesn't give you any peripheral vision, it's easy to get lost. You're out in space looking down at the Earth, and then you look away for a second (or you hit some button by mistake), and now all you see is star-dotted blackness. Earth must still be out there somewhere, but you can't find it. Or you're looking around a room when you unexpectedly smash your nose against a blue wall, and now the whole screen is just blue, without a hint as to why, or which direction you need to turn your head. When this happens, you can always bail out by returning to Entry View.

Web controls

When you're looking at something on the Web, your Web browser has a convenient little window that tells you where you are (and allows you to type a new address to go to). It also has buttons to go forward or back, or to stop downloading something that is taking too long. You need the same capabilities when you're browsing VRML files on the Web as well.

Plug-ins inherit the buttons and windows of the Web browsers they plug into. But other VRML browsers have to provide their own URL windows and Forward/Back/Stop buttons.

Don't curse the darkness

The lighting in VRML worlds tends to be inconsistent, so many browsers provide you with a headlight. You can turn it on or off, and some browsers let you adjust its brightness.

Collision detection

The early VRML browsers let you crash through walls without any consequences — no headaches, no broken walls, nothing. It's fun, for a while. Like Superman, you can't be stopped.

Flattering as that thought is, in reality, one of these browsers has no idea that you have gone through a wall. It just knows that at one moment, you have your nose pressed up against a blank wall (which is easy for it to display), and at the next moment, you are on the other side of the wall, looking at whatever is there. It doesn't think you're Superman; it just doesn't understand walls. Eventually, almost everybody finds that crashing through walls stops being fun and starts to detract from the reality of the virtual reality experience.

A browser with collision detection, on the other hand, knows about walls and trees and other solid objects (if the designer of the world has designated certain objects as solid). When you try to run through a wall, it won't let you. You just stand there with your nose pressed against the wall until you catch on and turn around.

And if you find yourself longing to be Superman again, you can just turn Collision Detection off.

Seeking professional help

Help files are usually available, if you know where to look. They're usually written by the same people who wrote whatever confused you in the first place, so they're not always helpful. But when you're desperate, anything is worth a try.

Borrowing from the future

Various companies (especially Netscape) have tried to jump the gun on the next version of VRML (VRML 2.0) by incorporating proposed VRML 2.0 features like animation and sound into their browsers. Some new browsers even allow online chatting between people visiting the same VRML world on the Web. (The early versions of these browsers had a lot of problems, so we haven't included any on the CD. But we'll tell you in Chapter 5 how to download their most recent versions, which — by the time you read this — may be more reliable.)

Sound

Some worlds now have sound in them — and not just in the background. The sounds have definite locations and get louder or softer as you move closer or further away.

Animation

In VRML 1.0, worlds are static and you move through them. But VRML 2.0 will allow certain limited forms of motion (which we'll describe in more detail in Chapter 19). Figures 10 and 16 in the color section are pictures of VRML worlds in motion.

Animated textures

In VRML, texture is what keeps a surface from being just a blank wall or flat floor. When you define a wall to look like brick or stone, you've given it a texture. *Animated* texture is one step (maybe several steps) cooler than that — the texture can actually move. A world that takes advantage of animated texture can, for instance, have a water surface that ripples.

Why do scenes look different in different browsers?

No two VRML browsers display a world in exactly the same way. (Compare the various views of our welcome message in the next two chapters.) Why? Three reasons: Competition, making do with limited processing power, and freedom to interpret the standards. (All these reasons are covered in more detail in "The Reality behind the Scenery" in Chapter 6.)

In the old days (you have to be a geezer of almost 30 to remember them clearly), each software company had its own way of doing things, and if you wanted to read its files, you had to use its software. But the whole point of VRML (like HTML before it) is to have a standard so that everybody can look at everything on the Web.

That standardization is great for us users, but it gives the software companies all kinds of headaches. How do you make your browser stand out when everybody's browser does a standard thing, and your competitors are giving theirs away for free?

The Netscape solution, which was soon copied by nearly everyone else who makes software for the Web, was to take what you might call a *standards plus* approach. In other words, you write your software so that it implements the standard, plus it has a few other cute features. If people are tempted into using those cute features and putting their work out on the Web, then suddenly your standard browser has an advantage — it displays those scenes better than anybody else's standard browser.

To fully render a large VRML world and move through it at a reasonable speed requires more processing power than almost anyone has. In order to function at all, a VRML browser has to cheat a little by taking some short cuts rather than showing everything. For example, some browsers may speed things up by showing spotlights as only white lights; others might use a richer, slower color-displaying technology. How each browser does these short cuts will give each a distinctive look. In particular, colors will often look completely different from one browser to the next.

Finally, the standards don't specify everything. The standards define what a light source is, for example, but each browser has its own interpretation of what this implies for shadows and shading.

Do you want to look good or go fast?

Most VRML browsers let you give up a little in the appearance department in order to pick up some speed. You'll want to use these features if you're looking at a very big or complicated VRML world that is giving your processor a hernia or making your hard drive sound like it's grinding coffee. What follows are a couple of the standard speed-enhancing features:

View in wireframe

If a VRML world looks like a cartoon ordinarily, switching to wireframe view turns it into a line drawing. (Check out the contrast between Figures 1-4 and 1-2.) The browser can stop worrying about color, texture, shading, objects that block your view of others, and so on, which means that it can go a lot faster.

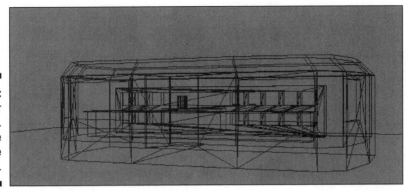

Figure 1-4:
Dave's Diner
in wireframe.
Compare
with Figure
1-2.

Turn off options

A less drastic way to trade appearance for speed is to turn off whatever special options your VRML browser has. Any feature that has texture or shading in its name is probably dragging down your speed.

Which Browsers Can You Use?

The greatest VRML browser in the world won't do you any good unless you can run it. Not all VRML browsers run on all computers or work with all Web browsers. We've chosen the browsers on the CD to try to cover all the bases.

Many perfectly fine VRML browsers are not on the CD. (By the time you read this, even the browsers that are on the CD may not be the latest versions.) Some of them, such as Intervista's Worldview and SGI's WebSpace (adapted by TGS for Windows and the Mac), are getting good reviews. In a field that is as young and fast-moving as VRML, any day could see a new browser come out that blows the doors off of every previous browser. Check out our Web page to see where to download the latest, hottest browsers.

With your computer?

Browsing through a VRML world requires a lot of computation. In the early days of VRML, you needed a high-powered workstation to run any of the browsers, and while that's no longer true, you still need a pretty powerful chip. The reason is more than just snobbishness. Even if someone wrote a VRML browser for, say, a 386, it would be a VRML browser in name only. (In theory, Virtus Voyager will run on a 386, but we haven't tried it, and Virtus doesn't recommend it.) If you tried to move through a VRML world on a 386, the new frames would come up so slowly that the illusion of animation would be lost. You would see a series of still images, not virtual reality.

PCs

All the PC-compatible browsers on our CD need a 486 or Pentium chip. Even the low-end 486s are problematic. We have managed to install Live3D on a machine with only a 486SX, for instance, but it didn't work very well.

If you do have a 486DX or Pentium chip in your computer, any of the VRML browsers on the CD will run on your machine.

Macs

So far, VRML software developers haven't done very well by the Macintosh community. Mac versions of the most popular browsers tend to come out months later than the PC versions, if they come out at all.

At the moment, no plug-in VRML browsers are available for the Mac. Live3D has been promising a Mac version for some while now, but as of press time, it hadn't appeared. Microsoft has recently released a Mac version of its Web browser, Internet Explorer 2.0, but at the moment, there is no VRML Add-In for the Mac. Either or both of these may be out by the time you read this. (You can check our Web page for instructions on how to get them if they are available.)

Virtus is the exception to the rule: It writes Mac versions first and PC versions come out later. Virtus' Voyager is the only browser on the CD that will run on a Macintosh. As with PCs, though, you need a powerful chip. Voyager runs on a Power Mac, PowerBook, Centris, or Quadra with 8 megabytes of RAM running version 6.05 of the Mac operating system. But Virtus recommends at least a 68040 chip with 16 megabytes of RAM running version 7.1 or later.

UNIX workstations

Silicon Graphics has been one of the leading forces behind VRML, so the best and fastest VRML applications of all sorts run on the SGI machines and other UNIX workstations. In this book, we are focusing on the lower end of the market, so we won't cover the workstation applications. (We're just jealous of people with better hardware than ours.)

With your Web browser?

Which Web browser you use affects which VRML browsers are available to you.

Netscape Navigator

Because Netscape is the most popular Web browser, it is a rare VRML browser indeed (other than a plug-in for something else) that won't run with Netscape.

Live3D and VR Scout are plug-ins specifically for Netscape. Both Virtus Voyager and Caligari Pioneer can be configured as helper applications for Netscape.

Microsoft Internet Explorer

VRML Add-In is a plug-in for Internet Explorer, but only if you are using the Windows 95 version. Voyager and VR Scout can be configured as helper applications, but Pioneer cannot.

Among the VRML browsers not on the CD, many can be set up as helper applications for Internet Explorer.

Other Web browsers

Oracle's Power Browser is set up for plug-ins, but so far we know of no VRML-browsing plug-ins that have been written for it. The AOL, CompuServe, and Prodigy Web browsers have no plug-ins but can work with helper applications like Voyager or VR Scout. Current versions of Pioneer will not work with these Web browsers.

What to Look for and How to Choose

More than a dozen VRML browsers are already out there (four of them are on our CD), and it seems like a new version of one-or-another of them comes out almost every day. How do you choose one? A few simple questions should cut the field down to size.

- ✔ **Can you use it at all?** Your hardware and other software may limit your choices. Silicon Graphics has been one of the leaders in developing VRML, so the hottest, slickest VRML products usually come out first for Silicon Graphics machines. If you're like us, you can't afford one. (If we could, we'd be drinking mai tais on the beach in Tahiti, not sitting in front of a console writing a book.) If you have an Intel processor less powerful than a 486DX, your choices are limited. If you have a Mac, your choices are limited. See the section, "Which Browsers Can You Use?"

- ✔ **Does the interface feel natural to you?** You'll have to answer this question for yourself. The coolness of VRML fades quickly if you can't control where you're going or if you have to keep pulling out the instructions to figure out what to do next. Every browser requires a little learning, just as every car does. But before long, you should be able to stop paying attention to the way the controls work and just think about moving through the world. The controls of the four browsers on the CD are described in Chapters 2 through 4.

- ✔ **How fast is it?** Speed is an essential factor in making virtual reality seem real. With a slow browser, you begin to see through the illusion of animation and realize that you are looking at a series of still images. Which browser is fastest depends on your hardware. Pioneer (and older versions of VR Scout) are based on Intel's 3DR rendering software. 3DR is like lightning if you have a graphics accelerator in your computer but slow if you don't.

✓ **Which worlds can it show you?** Standardization is a goal that is still not fully achieved. Most browsers can open most worlds, but not all.

✓ **How does it look?** Some browsers can open a world but not show you all the features of it. The builder half of Pioneer, for instance, allows you to build in some very nice lighting effects — unfortunately, the early versions of most browsers couldn't see them.

✓ **What special features does it have?** Live3D (known as WebFX until Netscape bought out its maker, Paper Software) has consistently been the leader in implementing special features. When we began researching this book, only WebFX had collision detection. Now several browsers do, but Live3D is ahead in animation and sound. However, the VRML-browsing market is young and highly competitive. Any feature that distinguishes one browser will quickly be copied in the next version of most of the others.

It's tempting to go for the browser with the latest, hottest features. But remember, as soon as the next wave of updates comes out (in a month or two, usually), some other browser may be the one with the latest, hottest features. Even speed advantages evaporate from one version to the next. VR Scout 1.1 was one of the slowest browsers in December, but version 1.2 was one of the fastest in January.

The interface is another matter. If one browser feels natural to you and another is a chore to deal with, most likely you will feel the same way about all future versions. Our advice: Find an interface you like and stick with it: A year from now, there will be a version that has all the cool features you know about now plus some you haven't thought of yet.

Chapter 2

Plugging into the Action: Live3D and VRML Add-In

*T*his chapter discusses how to install and use the plug-in VRML browsers Live3D and VRML Add-In. A plug-in version of VR Scout is also on our CD, but (because it comes in a helper application version as well) we delay describing its features until Chapter 3.

The general features of VRML browsers are described in Chapter 1. So if you find yourself asking, "What the heck is collision detection?" then go back there. But if you're asking "How do I turn off collision detection in Live3D?" you want this chapter.

Microsoft's VRML Add-In (for Internet Explorer) and Chaco's VR Scout (for Netscape) are on our CD, but Netscape's Live3D (also for Netscape, as you may have guessed) is not. We begged, but Netscape was adamant about wanting you to download the latest version of Live3D from its Web site, which is http:// www.netscape.com/live3d. When you arrive at this site, follow the on-screen instructions for downloading Live3D.

Working with Plug-Ins

If you use either Netscape Navigator or Microsoft Internet Explorer as your Web browser, then you can extend their capabilities with a plug-in VRML browser: Live3D and VR Scout for Netscape, and VRML Add-In for Internet Explorer.

Installing your plug-in

At the moment, none of our three plug-ins has a Mac version. (The only Mac VRML browser on the CD is Virtus Voyager, which is a helper application covered in Chapter 3.) All require at least a 486DX processor (or a 486SX with a math coprocessor), 8MB of RAM, and about 5MB of space on your hard drive. All three work with Windows 95; Live3D and VR Scout with Windows NT; and only Live3D with Windows 3.1. (The helper-application version of VR Scout runs under Windows 3.1.) And of course, you need a Web browser to plug into: Netscape 2.0 or later for Live3D and VR Scout, and Internet Explorer 2.0 or later for VRML Add-In.

If you have the right hardware, operating system, and Web browser, you can install your plug-in from our CD. For installation instructions, look in the OUR_CD file on our CD (of all places). OUR_CD exists in both a text and HTML version.

A given Web browser can have at most one plug-in VRML browser installed at any given time. If, for example, you have installed Live3D, and you decide to try out VR Scout, you will have to uninstall Live3D.

Uninstalling your plug-in

Knowing how to uninstall a plug-in is important because your Web browser is loyal and won't look at any other VRML browser until you do. To uninstall a plug-in:

1. **Open the Windows Control Panel.** In Windows 95 you'll find it on the Start menu. (You may find your plug-in's Uninstall shortcut on the Start menu as well. If so, you can just click it.)

2. **Double-click Add/Remove Programs.**

3. **Select your plug-in's name from the list of removable programs.** If it isn't there, check to see if there is an Uninstall program in the plug-in's folder on your hard drive. Run it and follow its instructions.

4. **Click OK.**

Opening VRML worlds with a plug-in

The odd thing about plug-ins is that you hardly ever deal with them directly. You deal with the Web browser (Netscape or Internet Explorer), and the Web browser deals with the plug-in.

If you want to view a VRML world with a plug-in, and you're already familiar with the Web browser it plugs into, the basic idea is simple:

1. **Install the plug-in.**
2. **Start the Web browser.**
3. **Find the VRML world you want to see.**

   You can either browse the Web until you find a VRML world or open a file that is already stored on your system somewhere.

The Web browser does the rest on its own. It realizes that it has a VRML file, opens the plug-in, and displays the VRML world inside an ordinary Web-browser window. Plug-ins are so integrated that you may at times browse into a VRML world without intending to (no problem: You still have all the Web browsing controls at the top of the screen, so just click Back).

When you're looking for a VRML world on your system (using the File⇨Open File command in Netscape, or the File⇨Open⇨Open File command in Internet Explorer), make sure that the Files of Type window at the bottom of the Open window is set to either "VRML worlds" or "All files."

Opening our welcome message

After you install your plug-in VRML browser, a good first exercise is to find and open our welcome message. For Live3D and VR Scout, the welcome file is `welcome.htm` (an HTML file), while for VRML Add-In, it's `welcome.wrl` (a VRML file).

The Live3D version of the welcome message is shown in Figure 2-1, while the VRML Add-In version is in Figure 2-3. (They differ because Live3D and VR Scout can embed VRML scenes inside an HTML document, while VRML Add-In can't.)

Netscape's Live3D

Back in those nostalgic days of October 1995, Netscape came out with a new beta version of Navigator 2.0, which allowed other subsidiary applications to display windows right inside the Navigator window. The very first of these "plug-in" applications was the WebFX VRML browser created by Paper Software. Later on, Netscape bought Paper Software and renamed the VRML browser Live3D.

Live3D has received a lot of good reviews. It was the only VRML browser to get the top rating (four orbs) in *Grafman's VRML Tools Review* in January 1996 (which may seem like nostalgia by the time you read this). The reviewer particularly liked its ability to load large worlds quickly.

Getting started with Live3D

After you install Live3D, you can open our welcome message, `welcome.htm`. Once you've opened `welcome.htm`, you should see a color version of Figure 2-1 on your screen.

If you're like us, your first reaction is probably "Big deal! This is just an ordinary Netscape page. So there is a picture on top. So what?" But that small difference is actually the point: with a plug-in like Live3D or VR Scout, the 3D VRML images can sit right there inside of normal HTML documents. That "Welcome to VRML" is a full-scale VRML world — once you know how to navigate, you can fly through the "o" if you want.

Figure 2-1:
A plug-in
VRML
browser like
Live3D lets
our VRML
welcome sit
peacefully
inside a
normal
HTML
document.

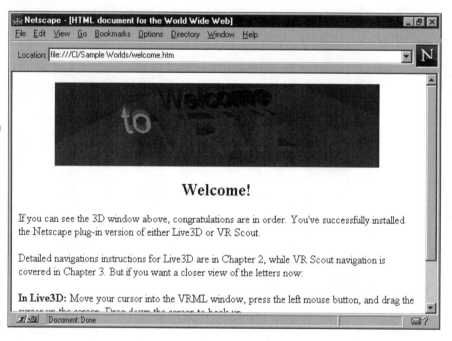

Looking at something interesting

Okay, we admit it: Itty-bitty VRML windows of text in HTML documents aren't very exciting, are they? What you'd probably really like to do is grab your learner's permit and take Live3D out for a spin. And that rectangle on the Welcome page is a bit cramped — let's get a VRML world that fills up the whole screen, one where you can really cut loose.

A good one to try is `netscape.wrl`. You can find it in the Sample Worlds folder on the CD. Open it using Netscape's File⇨Open File command.

You should now be looking at the entry view in Figure 2-2.

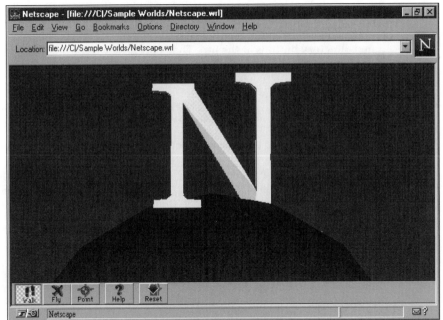

Figure 2-2:
The entry view of `netscape.wrl`. Netscape claims its own virtual planet.

The bar across the bottom of the VRML window is not part of the VRML world; it is the Live3D navigation bar (you always wondered where navigators drink; now you know).

The first three buttons on the left of the bar correspond to the three navigation modes: Walk, Fly, and Point. If you play a lot of computer games, the way things work may seem hauntingly familiar to you: Walk mode (the button with foot-prints) is based on the navigational system used in the game *Doom;* Fly mode (the button with an airplane) is based on the game *Descent.* (If you've never played these games, don't worry about it. We'll explain everything you need to know about the Live3D controls in "Navigating in Live3D," coming up soon in this chapter. Learning how to play *Doom* and *Descent* is a bonus.) Point mode (the crosshairs) is pretty obvious — if you click the Point button and then click an object in the scene, you'll move in for a closer look.

Whichever button on the navigation bar appears to be depressed is the active mode. (It's hard to tell, we know. We're not good at judging the moods of buttons either.) You can change to another mode by clicking its button. Clicking the question mark displays some cryptic instructions about how to navigate. If you already know the Live3D navigation system but are having a momentary mental block, these on-screen tips will remind you. At the far right is the Reset button; clicking it returns you to the Entry view, the one in Figure 2-2.

You might notice that Figure 2-2 doesn't contain the usual Netscape toolbar and directory buttons at the top. That's because we got rid of them using the Netscape Options menu.

Navigating in Live3D

So far, you've looked at some still pictures of a 3D world. Now let's move.

The designers of Live3D must play a lot of computer games. When the question "How do you move in 3D?" came up, the two answers that seemed most natural to them were "The way you move in *Doom*" and "The way you move in *Descent.*" They decided to call one mode Walk and the other Fly.

Walking to your Doom

Remember those basic moves we talked about in Chapter 1, the ones every browser has to let you do somehow? In Walk mode of Live3D, you do them as follows:

- **Charge and retreat:** To move forward, hold down the left mouse button and drag the cursor up the screen; to move backward, hold down the left mouse button and drag the cursor down the screen. You can do the same thing with the keyboard: press the up-arrow key to go forward or the down-arrow key to go backward.

- **Screen motion:** Motion in the plane of the screen (without turning your head to look where you're going) involves the Alt key. Hold down the Alt key, hold down the left mouse button, and now drag the cursor in the direction you want to go — left, right, up, down, diagonally or whatever.

  Or press the Alt key together with the arrow key of your choice.

✔ **Head motion:** To turn your head left or right, hold down the left mouse button and drag the cursor left or right. Or press the left-arrow or right-arrow keys on the keyboard. To tilt your head up or down, drag the mouse up or down while holding down the Ctrl key. Or press the A key to tilt your head down or the Z key to tilt your head up.

✔ **Start/stop and speed:** When you move by holding down a mouse button and dragging the cursor, the motion stops when you release the mouse button, not when you stop dragging. The distance that you drag the cursor controls the speed of the motion — drag it a long way if you want to move quickly and only a little way if you want to move slowly.

When you move by pressing keys on the keyboard, motion stops when you release the key.

With either the mouse or the keyboard, you can go faster by holding down the Shift key.

Flying a Descent path

Fly mode does the basic moves a little differently:

✔ **Charge and retreat:** The mouse and the keyboard are not strictly equivalent in Fly mode. To move forward, push down the left mouse button (no need to drag). No mouse command lets you fly backward, but the keyboard plays no favorites: move forward by pressing the A key and backward by pressing Z. The A/Z keys give you a little bit of momentum, so your motion dies out slowly after you let up on the key. When you move forward with the mouse, on the other hand, motion stops as soon as you release the left button.

✔ **Screen motion:** Just as in Walk mode, hold down the Alt key and the left mouse button; then drag the cursor in the direction you want to go.

✔ **Head motion:** Left/right head motion is the same as in Walk mode. Up/down head motion works according to the joystick model: pressing the up arrow tilts your head down, and vice versa. You can also tilt up or down by holding down the left mouse button and dragging down or up — but with a catch. Remember that pressing the left mouse button moves you forward, so when you tilt up or down with the mouse, you're also moving forward.

✔ **Start/stop and speed:** Just about everything works the same way as in Walk mode. The exceptions are the A/Z keys, which give a small amount of momentum.

✔ **Roll:** Roll left by holding down the Q key and roll right by holding down the E key.

When you are doing complicated maneuvers, sometimes you forget where the cursor was when you first pressed the left mouse button. You can fix this situation by taking advantage of Live3D's Crosshairs option (click the right mouse button to get a menu and then choose Heads Up Display⇨Crosshairs). Now when you press the left mouse button, a set of crosshairs appears at that spot, so you can easily judge how far and in which direction you have moved the cursor. If you want to slow down, just move the cursor closer to the crosshairs.

Standard extras in Live3D

Live3D implements the following standard extras:

- ✔ **Hotlinks:** The cursor changes from an arrow to a hand when it crosses a hotlinked object. Green text appears to tell you what place on the Web the object is linked to. Click with the hand-cursor to go there. (Double-click in Point mode.) Try this example: In `netscape.wrl`, the N is hotlinked to the Netscape home page. (Remember: hotlinks only work when you are online.)

- ✔ **Close up:** Click the Point button on the navigation bar and then click the object you want to move closer to.

- ✔ **Spin:** Spin the scene by holding down the right mouse button and dragging the cursor. Drag in the direction you want to spin; drag farther if you want to move faster. Spinning has an unusual feature — momentum. After you let up on the right mouse button, the spin continues until you choose some other command (just a click of the left mouse button is the simplest way to stop).

- ✔ **Changing viewpoint:** Click Reset from the navigation bar to return to Entry view. Or click the right mouse button (don't hold it down or you'll spin the world) to display a menu, and move the cursor to highlight ViewPoints. A list of the possible viewpoints appears (often the only choice is Entry view — what you saw when you first opened this VRML file). Selecting one of the viewpoints causes you to be teleported there as fast as your processor can reset the scene. Or you can use the Animate to Viewpoints option, described in detail in "Flying to viewpoints rather than teleporting" later in this chapter.

- ✔ **Headlight:** To check whether the headlight is on, click the right mouse button and then move your cursor to highlight the Lights menu. The headlight is on if it has a check mark next to it. Click Lights⇨Headlight to turn it on/off.

✔ **Collision detection:** To turn on Collision Detection, click the right mouse button; then select Collision Detection from the Navigation menu. If a check mark appears next to Collision Detection, the feature is on. If not, it is off. If Collision Detection is grayed out, the designers of this VRML world did not allow for it.

✔ **Help:** The Help button on the toolbar delivers some cryptic instructions about navigation.

Advanced features

Live3D is usually among the first browsers to introduce new features. The current version supports sound, animation, and animated textures.

Changing the moves

The menu you get by clicking the right mouse button has a submenu called Navigation. The bottom half of this Navigation menu gives you a number of options for controlling the way a VRML world works. In each case, the option is on when a check mark appears next to it on the Navigation menu, and off otherwise. Turn an option on or off by clicking it. If it is not active but could be if you clicked it, it will be listed in black without a check mark. If it is not an option in this particular world, it will be grayed out.

Flying to viewpoints rather than teleporting

The ordinary way to switch to a predefined viewpoint is to teleport — you click the viewpoint you want, and the browser redraws the scene assuming you are already there. Changing viewpoint is a great thing to do when you're lost. But sometimes just getting unlost isn't enough because it doesn't answer the question, "Where the heck was I, anyway?"

Live3D has the perfect answer to this question: Click the right mouse button to get a menu, and then select Navigation⇨Animate to Viewpoints. Now when you choose a new viewpoint (by selecting ViewPoints from the same menu) you fly there rather than teleport. Rather than just having the screen redrawn from the new point of view, you get to see a bunch of intermediate views along the way — maybe even enough of them to figure out where you were.

But remember: if you're in a complicated world and/or have a slow machine, your animated trip back to the viewpoint can take a long time. As J. L. Seagull once said, "Perfect speed is being there." Nothing is faster than teleporting.

Banking when flying

When we first saw "Bank when Flying" on the Navigation menu, we had visions of airborne ATM machines. Actually, it's an option for making Fly mode look more realistic. An airplane doesn't just turn, it lowers one wing and raises the other in such a way that the pilot's view tilts. Selecting the Navigation⇨Bank when Flying option tilts the intermediate views when you turn right or left in Fly mode.

Improving the look

Live3D gives you a few options for making a VRML world look better (now, if only they could do something about the real world).

Giving yourself more room

The navigation bar at the bottom of the screen is handy, but it takes up a lot of room. You can make it go away by (or come back) by choosing Options⇨ Navigation Bar from the menu that appears when you click the right mouse button. When the bar is gone, you can still change navigation modes from the Navigation menu. You can also reset by choosing Entry View from the ViewPoints menu.

I've looked at walls from both sides now

One of Live3D's most interesting features is Options⇨Always Generate Back Faces. You see, surfaces in VRML are typically one-sided, a phenomenon completely unknown in nature (see "The Reality behind the Scenery" in Chapter 6). From one side a surface might look like a door, and from the other side it might be completely invisible. This feature is great if you are designing a haunted house — no need for a door to slam shut behind you when it can just appear as soon as you get inside. But in other settings, one-sided objects can be unintentionally disconcerting. (The opening view of Pioneer in Figure 4-1 is a good example. It shows a black cube floating over a complex of buildings, but the cube can't be seen from the inside.)

Live3D will automatically fill in those other sides (a.k.a. *back faces*) if you want. Which option is best depends on the particular world you are viewing. One thing that is certain, though, is that generating back faces requires more processing power. If you need to increase the performance, turn this feature off.

Speeding up Live3D

Speed and appearance work against each other. Most of the choices that improve the look of Live3D also slow it down. (Netscape estimates that Always Generate Back Faces slows Live3D down by about half because it has twice as many surfaces to worry about).

Shading

Smooth shading looks better. Flat shading is less taxing on your processor. Click the right mouse button and then select either Smooth Shading or Flat Shading from the Lights menu.

Detail

The more detail you want, the slower you move. Live3D provides three choices on the Detail menu: Solid, Wireframe, and Point Cloud. If a world is pushing your hardware close to its limits, try switching to wireframe to move around and then back to Solid when you stop to look at something. Point Cloud is a fairly useless option. Instead of giving you a line drawing like wireframe, Point Cloud gives a connect-the-dots picture. You can really move fast in Point Cloud mode, but so what?

Optimize for performance/appearance

You can't do both. Which is more important — to move through the world quickly or for everything to look as good as possible? You decide. Make the choice from the Options menu.

Letting Live3D choose its own window size

Big windows require more processing power. Selecting this option allows Live3D to shrink the window if it needs to. Do so by choosing Options⇨Optimize Window Size.

Microsoft's VRML Add-In

Originally Microsoft named this plug-in *Virtual Explorer,* a catchy title that made a certain amount of sense. But the 1.1 version was renamed VRML Add-In. Version 2.0 is on the CD.

Getting started with VRML Add-In

After you install VRML Add-In, you can open our welcome message, welcome.wrl, which produces a color version of Figure 2-3 on your screen. (The Internet Explorer/VRML Add-In combo doesn't do embedded VRML, so you won't see the VRML window if you open welcome.htm.)

The toolbar at the bottom of the window has seven buttons. The four in the center are labeled Walk, Slide, Tilt, and Spin. The other three are denoted by icons. The button in the left corner is the Menu button because clicking it gives you a menu. (You can get the same menu by right-clicking anywhere.) The two buttons in the right corner are Reset (which returns you to the Original view) and Straighten (tries to reorient you if you've been tilting or spinning).

All the stuff above the image is part of Internet Explorer and really doesn't have anything to do with VRML. (In particular, the Help files are not very helpful. A search for *virtual* or *VRML* got no hits. The Help you want for VRML is on the menu you get if you click the Menu button.)

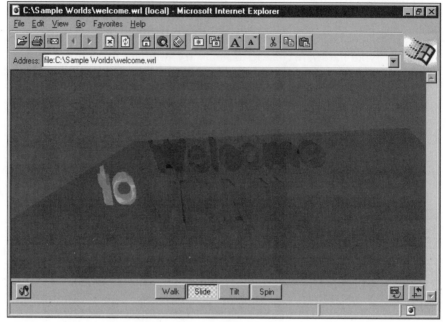

Figure 2-3:
The
Welcome
world as
seen by
VRML
Add-In.

Navigating in VRML Add-In

The navigation system in VRML Add-In is probably the most straightforward of any browser. You move in one of two ways, by holding down the left mouse button and dragging the cursor, or by using the arrow keys on the keyboard. If you ever forget, click one of the center navigation buttons three times. A little help window will pop up to remind you.

Basic moves in VRML Add-In

Move in VRML Add-In by selecting the proper navigation mode (with one of the four center buttons on the toolbar) and then either dragging the mouse or using the arrow keys. You can tell what navigation mode you are in because the corresponding button looks pushed-in.

- **Charge and retreat:** While in Walk mode, hold down the left mouse button and drag the cursor up to go forward, and drag it down to go backward.

- **Screen motion:** In Slide mode, hold down the left mouse button and drag the cursor in the direction you want to go.

- **Head motion:** To turn left or right, hold down the left mouse button and drag the cursor left or right in Walk mode. Tilting your head up or down works according to the joystick model: In Tilt mode, drag the cursor up to tilt down and down to tilt up.

✔ **Start/stop and speed:** Motion starts when you press the left mouse button and stops when you release it. The distance that you drag the cursor determines the speed: drag a long distance to go fast or a short distance to go slow.

✔ **Changing viewpoint:** Clicking the menu button in the bottom far left (or clicking anywhere with the right mouse button) produces a menu that contains the word Viewpoints. Highlighting this option will produce a list of possible viewpoints you can select.

Standard extras in VRML Add-In

VRML Add-In implements the following standard extras:

✔ **Hotlinks:** The cursor changes from an arrow to a pointing finger when it crosses a hotlinked object. Text appears in the lower-left corner (just under the Menu button) to tell you what place on the Web the object is linked to. Click with the finger-cursor to go there.

VRML Add-In does a convenient thing with hotlinks: It provides a list of them, just like its list of viewpoints. From the menu, highlight Shortcuts to get a list and then select one of the hotlinks to jump to the corresponding Web site.

✔ **Close up:** Double-click any object you want to move toward.

✔ **Spin:** In Spin mode, drag in the direction you want to spin; drag farther if you want to spin faster.

✔ **Changing viewpoint:** Click the Reset button on the toolbar to return to Entry view. Or choose Viewpoints from the menu. Selecting one of the listed viewpoints causes you to be teleported there.

✔ **Headlight:** VRML Add-In has no headlight. It also never seems to lack for light. How? They don't explain.

✔ **Collision detection:** If Walk Through Walls is checked on the menu, then collision detection is off, and vice versa. If the world you are in does not support collision detection, you may not be able to move at all if Walk Through Walls is not checked. Toggle this option back and forth by clicking it.

✔ **Straighten:** The Straighten button in the far right corner of the toolbar reorients you if you've been using the Tilt button and can't get upright again. It tries to reorient you if you've been using the Spin button, but it doesn't always succeed.

✔ **Reset:** When Straighten doesn't get you straight, you need its neighbor, Reset. Clicking Reset returns you to Original view (a.k.a. Entry view). Think of it as a panic button.

✔ **Help:** Click the Menu button and then select Help⇨Help Topics.

Advanced features

VRML Add-In 2.0 (the latest version we could find) doesn't support sound, animation, or animated textures. When we try to guess how soon Microsoft will implement these features, a lot of political and business complications enter the picture. Microsoft's proposal for the next version of VRML (VRML 2.0) seems to have been roundly rejected. Microsoft will probably have to choose between implementing the Silicon Graphics/Netscape Moving Worlds proposal and going its own way. (More about VRML 2.0 proposals in Part VI.)

How to change the world

Clicking the Menu button on the far left of the toolbar (or clicking the right mouse button anywhere) displays — betcha can't guess — a menu. The choices on this menu give you a variety of ways to change how a VRML world looks.

Grabbing a little space

Clicking Show Toolbar will make a visible toolbar invisible, and vice versa. Getting rid of the toolbar will make more space for displaying the VRML world, but navigation is difficult. Our advice: Maneuver into position with the toolbar and then make it go away while you admire the view. Or just leave it there.

Picking up some speed

Remember this simple rule: The more options you turn on, the better the image will look; the more you turn off, the faster everything will run. The Options menu allows you to turn off two time-consuming features: Show Inline Worlds and Show Textures.

We'll explain inlining and texture-mapping in more detail in Part IV, but for now you can get by with knowing this: Sometimes a VRML file has placeholders in it that tell the browser to look in other files for complicated objects or images. If Show Inline Worlds and Show Textures aren't checked, the browser doesn't bother to look up those files. The VRML world loses a lot of its detail, but it downloads quickly and doesn't put so much of a strain on your hardware.

In Grafman's Gallery (shown in Figure 13 in the color section), for example, the pictures on the walls are in separate files. If you decided not to show textures or inlining, the gallery would have blank, white rectangles on its walls.

Chapter 3

Helper Applications: Viewing VRML via Virtus Voyager or VR Scout

*W*eb browsers are set up to read a language called HTML (Hypertext Markup Language). When in the course of browsing the Web, a Web browser browses across something written in another language, like VRML, it needs help from an application that specializes in that language.

In this chapter, we discuss how to set up helper applications in general, and how to use two specific helper applications: Virtus Voyager and Chaco VR Scout. Features of browsers are discussed in general in Chapter 1. Look there if, say, you don't know what we mean by "basic motions". Look here if you want to know how to perform the basic motions in Voyager or VR Scout.

VR Scout also comes as a plug-in for Netscape, which also can be installed from the CD. The basics of plug-ins are covered in Chapter 2, while the controls for both versions of VR Scout are described in this chapter.

Configuring Helper Applications

Your Web browser, whatever it is, maintains a little black book of specialists to call in case it runs into something it can't handle. It has a specialist for pictures, a specialist for audio, and a whole bunch of others. Most of the time, you don't need to think about them at all. You just go to a Web page, and your browser recognizes all the non-HTML stuff on the page, calls the appropriate specialists, and assembles their work without you even noticing that it had any problems at all.

The first time you set up a VRML browser, though, you need to worry about your Web browser's little black book just long enough to tell it that this new application is the VRML specialist. Then the little black book can go back into your computer's vest pocket, and you can forget about it again.

What every Web browser needs to know

We'll get into the detailed instructions for configuring specific Web browsers in a page or two, but in general, your Web browser needs to know two things in order to successfully hand off VRML files to a VRML browser:

✔ **That VRML files exist.** Some browsers already knew this before you got them, and some won't know until you tell them. For example, Netscape 2.0 knows, but earlier versions don't. AOL's browser knows, but Prodigy's doesn't.

If your browser doesn't know that VRML files exist, you'll have to *create a type,* which sounds a lot more complicated than it is. Creating a type is geek-speak for telling the browser to put a new line into its black book. The line has the geeky title *x-world/x-vrml.*

✔ **Where your VRML browser is.** Once your Web browser knows that VRML files exist (which means that the list of types in its little black book already has a line *x-world/x-vrml*), you have to tell it which specialist application to call when it sees a VRML file. In other words, it needs to know where on your hard drive to find your VRML browser.

You can tell your Web browser in one of two ways: Either you can type the path name of your VRML browser in some appropriate place (we'll tell you where), or you push a Browse button, which means, "I'm about to go find the VRML browser myself. Watch what I do so that you can do it too."

Specific instructions for configuring helpers

Before trying to configure your VRML browser as a helper application for your Web browser, you need to do the following:

📐 **Make sure that your VRML browser is installed.**

📐 **If you have previously installed a plug-in VRML browser for this Web browser, uninstall it.** A Web browser that has a plug-in won't pay attention to anything you tell it about a helper application (it thinks it knows what to do with VRML files, so it never looks to see if it can call in a specialist). See "Uninstalling your plug-in" in Chapter 2.

A plug-in VRML browser doesn't need to be configured as a helper application. The plug-in's automatic installation program has already told your Web browser everything it needs to know about the plug-in.

With Netscape 2.0 (or higher)

Here's how you deal with Netscape:

1. **Start Netscape.**

2. **Select Options⇨General Preferences from the menu.**

   A Preferences window opens. At the top of the window are several tabs that look like the tops of folders.

3. **Click on the Helpers tab.**

4. **Select x-world/x-vrml from the File Type list.**

5. **From the list of actions near the bottom of the window, select Launch the Application.**

6. **Click the Browse button.**

   Or, if you know where on your hard drive your VRML browser is installed, you can type the path into the box next to the Browse button and skip to Step 8.

7. **Search through your files until you find your VRML browser.**

   The search begins several levels deep into the folder where Netscape is installed. You will probably need to keep clicking on the go-up-a-level icon (the folder with the up arrow next to it) until you reach the top level of folders on your hard drive, and then search downward until you find the file. It will look like PIONEER.EXE or VOYAGER.EXE.

8. **Double-click on the name of the file that contains your VRML browser.**

9. **Click OK at the bottom of the Preferences window.**

With Internet Explorer

The following instructions apply to Internet Explorer:

1. **Start Internet Explorer.**

2. **Choose View⇨Options from the menu.**

3. **Click the File Types tab near the top of the Options window.**

4. **Scroll down the list of file types until you find VRML 3D Geometry. Select it.**

5. **Click the Edit button.**

   The Edit File Type dialog box appears.

6. **Type** x-world/x-vrml **into the Content Type (MIME) box.**

7. **Type** wrl **into the Default Extension for Content Type box.**

   It may already be there.

8. **In the Actions box, double-click on the word open.**

   The Edit Actions for Type dialog box opens.

9. **Click the Browse button.**

   Or if you know the path name of your VRML browser, you can type it in the Application used to perform action box and skip to Step 11.

10. **Find where your VRML browser is installed on your hard drive.**

11. **Click OK.**

    The Edit Actions for Type dialog box closes.

12. **Click Close.**

    The Edit File Type dialog box closes.

13. **Click Close.**

    The Options window closes.

With Mosaic

From Spyglass Mosaic 2.1, do the following:

1. **Select Edit⇨Helpers from the menu.**

   A Helpers box appears, containing a list of all the types of files with which Mosaic might need help. Scroll down the list until you find *x-world/x-vrml*.

2. **Click on x-world/x-vrml.**

3. **Click the Edit button in the Helpers box.**

   A Configure File Type box appears.

4. **Type** .wrl **into the Suffixes box.**

If .wrl is already there, you don't need to do anything.

5. **Next to Encoding, click the Text radio button.**

6. **Click the Browse button.**

If you know the path to your VRML browser, you don't have to click Browse. You can just type the path in the Helper Application box and skip to Step 8. If you do click Browse, a Select Helper Application box appears.

7. **Use the Select Helper Application box to find where your VRML browser is installed on your hard drive.**

8. **When the file containing your browser is highlighted, click Open.**

You return to the Configure File Type box. The path to your browser now appears next to Helper Application.

9. **Click OK.**

You return to the Helpers box.

10. **Click Close.**

With AOL's Web browser

AOL recently signed a couple of high-profile agreements with Microsoft and Netscape to make Internet Explorer and Navigator available to AOL users. But if you are still using the AOL browser:

1. **Select Members⇨Set Preferences from the main menu.**

The Preferences window opens.

2. **Click the WWW button.**

The WWW Preferences window opens.

3. **Click the Helper Applications button.**

4. **Scroll to find Content type x-world/x-vrml on the list of file types (strangely, it is in the Cs). Double-click it.**

A Modify Helper Application window opens. Everything should already be filled in correctly except for the Application Name box.

Just in case anything accidentally gets changed in the other boxes, the correct information is as follows:

- **Description:** Content type x-world/x-vrml. (Actually, this info could be anything as far as the software is concerned. The description is just here for us users.)

- **Content type:** x-world/x-vrml

- **File extensions:** wrl

The Use a separate application option should be selected.

5. Click the Browse button.

Or, if you know the path name of your VRML browser, you can type it in the Application Name box and skip to Step 7.

6. Search through your files until you find your VRML browser. Double-click on the name of the file.

It should have a .EXE ending like PIONEER.EXE or VOYAGER.EXE.

7. Click OK to return to the Modify Helper Application window.

8. Click OK to return to the Helper Applications window.

9. Click Close to return to WWW Preferences.

10. Close the WWW Preferences window and the Preferences window.

With CompuServe

The latest version of CompuServe's software uses Mosaic as its default Web browser. Configure a helper application as follows:

1. Select Tools⇨Options from the menu.

A Tools options property sheet (tabbed box) appears, containing tabs with several options.

2. Choose the File Types tab.

A list of all the types of files that Mosaic might need help with shows up.

3. Scroll down the list until you find application/x-world.

If you find it, go to Step 7. If not, continue.

4. Click on New.

The New Mime Type dialog box opens up.

5. Type application/x-world.

6. Click OK.

7. Make sure that application/x-world is selected.

8. Type .wrl into the Extensions box.

If .wrl is already there, you don't need to do anything. Make sure that you type the period.

9. Click the Browse button.

If you know the path to your VRML browser, you don't have to click Browse. You can just type the path in the Program box and skip to Step 12. If you do click Browse, a Browse for Viewer Program box appears.

10. Use the Browse for Viewer Program box to find where your VRML browser is installed on your hard drive.

11. When the file containing your browser is highlighted, click Open.

You return to the Configure File Type box. The path to your browser now appears next to Helper Application.

12. Click OK.

You return to the Tools Options box.

13 Click OK.

Virtus Voyager

Virtus Voyager has more pluses and minuses than any browser we know. On the plus side, it has a highly intuitive navigation system that you will probably pick up quickly. Voyager is also very versatile — it has both Mac and Windows 95 versions, it runs (sometimes very slowly) on low-end machines, and it works as a helper application with a wide variety of Web browsers.

On the minus side, Voyager is a work in progress. (In geek-speak, it is an *alpha version.* Most of the other browsers on the CD are *beta versions* — closer to being done, in other words.) It doesn't have all the fancy features you find on Live3D or VRML Add-In. When the creator of a VRML world tries something fancy, Voyager often doesn't know what to do with it. Sometimes Voyager displays a less-fancy version of the same scene, and sometimes it just gives you a solid gray screen.

Installing Voyager

Voyager runs under the Power Macintosh, Macintosh, and Windows 95 operating systems. It runs on just about any computer capable of running one of these operating systems, but unless you have at least a Power Mac, a 68040, or a 486, it is painfully slow.

You can install Voyager from our CD. For installation instructions, look in one of the OUR_CD files on the CD.

Using Voyager

Voyager can be used in three ways: as a VRML-reading companion for your Web browser, as a VRML viewer for files that are already on your system, and (in a limited way) as a viewer for VRML files on the Web (without a Web browser).

Voyager as a helper application

If you have told your Web browser to use Voyager as its VRML specialist (see "Configuring Helper Applications" earlier in this chapter), then whenever your Web browser runs into a VRML file, it will open Voyager automatically. Unlike a plug-in, Voyager's display is in an entirely separate window from the Web browser.

Voyager as a VRML viewer for your computer

After you have Voyager installed, you can display VRML files that you have on your computer system (like our welcome message, `welcome.wrl`, which you'll find in the Sample Worlds folder on the CD):

1. **Find the file VOYAGER.EXE on your hard drive.**

2. **Run VOYAGER.EXE.**

3. **Select File⇨Open from the Voyager menu.**

4. **Browse until you find a VRML file.**

   It will have a .WRL extension on its filename.

5. **Open the file.**

Voyaging on the Web without a Web browser

A few objects in the Voyager window resemble pieces of a Web browser: a Back arrow, a Forward arrow, a Home button, and a window for typing Web addresses. These objects control Voyager's Web-browsing capability. (At least they do in the Mac version. In the Windows 95 version 1.00a, most of the Web-browsing features don't work yet. Wait for future versions.)

If you know the Web address (URL) of a VRML file, and if you are online, you can type the URL into Voyager's Web address window and click the Go button.

A good URL to try out is Virtus's object gallery: `http://www.virtus.com/3d/objects/object7.wrl`.

This site is Virtus's collection of household objects in VRML. Object 7, the fireplace we've started you on, appears in Figure 3-1. Each object has a left arrow and a right arrow floating over it. (When viewed from the front, that is. If you get turned around, the left arrow is purple and the right one is green.) The arrows are hotlinks — click the left arrow to go to the previous object and the right arrow to go to the next one.

Navigating in Voyager

You can move in one of two ways in Voyager: Either you can click the buttons on the toolbar (see Figure 3-1), or you can position the cursor inside the scene and hold down the left mouse button. In general, the cursor-positioning method

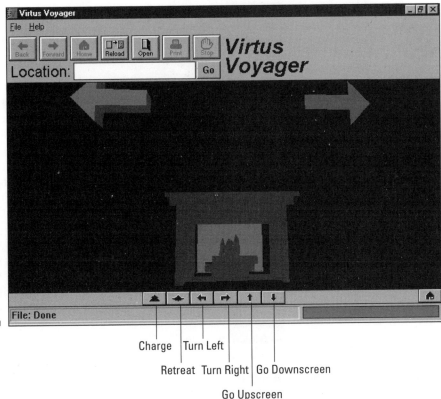

Figure 3-1:
Virtus maintains a gallery of household objects for your viewing pleasure.

Charge
Turn Left
Retreat   Turn Right   Go Downscreen
Go Upscreen

gives you a smoother motion, while the toolbar buttons give a more cautious (or jerky, depending on your point of view), step-by-step motion. Also, you can make some motions with the mouse that you can't make from the toolbar.

Virtus's navigation system is used throughout its product line (you see it again in Virtus Walkthrough Pro), and is quite different from the navigation system of any other company. If you have learned any other browser first, you are likely to be a little disoriented when you try to move around in Voyager. Nevertheless, the system is quite natural, easy to learn, and easy to use.

Basic motions in Voyager

In other browsers, you move by dragging the cursor across the screen — the browser figures out what to do by looking at the direction and distance of the drag. In Voyager, you move by positioning the cursor relative to the center of the screen. Voyager figures out what to do by looking at the direction and distance that the cursor is from the center.

If you are used to using Live3D, you can picture Voyager navigation like this: Holding down the left mouse button in Voyager gives you the same motion as if (in Live3D) you had clicked in the center of the screen and dragged the cursor to where it currently is.

- **Charge and retreat:** Move forward/backward by placing the cursor above/below the center of the screen while holding down the left mouse button. Or use the two leftmost buttons on the toolbar at the bottom of the Voyager window.

- **Screen motion:** Hold down the Option (or Ctrl in the Windows version) key and press the left mouse button to move in the plane of the screen. Position the cursor relative to the center of the screen to determine the direction of motion: left-of-center slides you left, above-center slides you up, and so forth. Sliding straight left or right can't be done with the toolbar. You can slide up or down by using the two rightmost buttons.

- **Head motion:** Turn your head left/right by positioning the cursor left-of-center/right-of-center and holding down the left mouse button. Or you can use the center two toolbar buttons. To tilt your head up/down, position the cursor above-center/below-center and hold down both the Shift key and the left mouse button. Tilting up or down can't be done from the toolbar.

- **Roll:** If you hold down the Shift key and position the cursor left-of-center/right-of-center, you tip your head counterclockwise/clockwise.

- **Start/stop and speed:** When you use the cursor-positioning method, motion starts when you press the left mouse button and stops when you release it. Speed is determined by the cursor's distance from the center of the screen. When you move via the toolbar, a click on a button will move you a discrete distance and then stop. The toolbar has no speed control.

Standard extras in Voyager

Being an alpha version, Voyager is still a little light on standard features. We hope Virtus adds a few as Voyager matures.

- **Changing viewpoint:** Clicking the house icon in the lower-left corner of the screen returns you to the entry view. Other viewpoints are not supported in this version of Voyager. (It is an alpha version, after all. Presumably Virtus will include other features such as viewpoints in the version it finally releases.)

- **Hotlinks:** When an object in a VRML world is a hotlink, the Voyager cursor changes from an arrow to a pair of crosshairs. Clicking your crosshairs on a link transports you to the address the link specifies. If a VRML file is at that address, Voyager displays it. If not, Voyager hands it off to a Web browser. In Figure 3-1, the two arrows are hotlinks.

If you have tried Walkthrough Pro (Voyager's cousin the builder), you no doubt miss those convenient crosshairs in the center of the screen. We have no idea why Virtus didn't include them in Voyager, and we hope they will put them in future versions. In the meantime, though, you can find the boundary between the left and right halves of the screen by tracing the vertical line between the third and fourth buttons on the toolbar. Unfortunately, we have found no easy way to eyeball the boundary between the top and bottom halves of the screen.

VR Scout

VR Scout is an example of how quickly things change in the world of VRML browsers. The December 1995 edition of *Grafman's VRML Tools Review* found VR Scout to be near the bottom of the pack of VRML browsers. The January 1996 edition had VR Scout neck-and-neck with WebFX (now Netscape Live3D) as the best VRML browser available for a machine running Windows. The difference? VR Scout 1.2 replaced VR Scout 1.1. Suddenly all those nasty things people said about VR Scout are ancient history. (You can find Grafman's reviews on the Web at http://www.graphcomp.com/vrml/review.html.)

VR Scout is available either as a Netscape plug-in or as a helper application for a wide variety of browsers. If you run Netscape anyway, you might as well use the plug-in version because it gives a few extra features, such as the ability to integrate a VRML window into a larger Netscape window.

However, we put VR Scout in this chapter because it really stands out in the non-Netscape, non-plug-in category. If you are one of the millions of people using AOL's Web browser or Mosaic from a machine running some version of Windows, VR Scout is your best bet (at least until somebody else comes out with a new version of its browser).

Installing VR Scout

VR Scout requires either a 486DX (or better), or a 486SX with a math coprocessor. It runs under Windows 95, Windows 3.1, or Windows 3.11. To run VR Scout on Windows 3.1 or 3.11, you must have installed the Microsoft Win32s version 1.30 or later. Win 32s can be downloaded for free from Microsoft's home page: http://www.microsoft.com.

You can install VR Scout from our CD. For installation instructions, look in one of the OUR_CD files on the CD.

Using VR Scout

VR Scout can work as a helper application for most Web browsers (see "Configuring Helper Applications" earlier in this chapter). Once your Web browser knows to send its VRML questions to VR Scout, VR Scout will open automatically to display any VRML files you browse across.

You can also use VR Scout without a Web browser to look at VRML files that you have on your system (like the ones on the CD, for instance). In addition, if you know the URL of a VRML file on the Web, or if a VRML file on your system is hotlinked to a VRML file on the Web, you can view it in VR Scout without a Web browser.

Reading VRML files you already have

If you are using VR Scout as a plug-in for Netscape, you can look at your VRML files in the same way you would look at an HTML file (see Chapter 2).

If you're using the helper application version of VR Scout, you don't need to open a Web browser at all to look at a VRML file on your system:

1. **Find the file** `vrscout.exe` **on your hard drive.**

2. **Run** `vrscout.exe`.

3. **Select File⇨Open File from the menu.**

4. **Browse until you find the file you want and select it.**

   It will have a .WRL extension on its filename.

5. **Click the Open button.**

Web browsing without a Web browser

If you should somehow find the Web address (URL — you know, one of those `http://some.junk` sort of things) of an interesting VRML world, you can browse over there with your Web browser, which would then call on VR Scout to view it (or whatever helper application you've configured — see "Configuring Helper Applications" earlier in this chapter). Or if you connect to the Internet via a SLPP or PPP connection, you can eliminate the middleman and just look at the site with VR Scout. Here's how:

1. **Connect to your Internet provider.**

   In other words, do whatever you usually do before you start your Web browser.

2. **Start VR Scout.**

3. **Click the Open Location button on the toolbar.**

   Or select File⇨Open Location from the menu. In either case, an Open Location box makes its appearance.

4. Type the Web address (URL) into the Open Location dialog box.

5. Press Enter.

Various Web-gremlins will go off searching for the VRML file and bring it back to VR Scout, which will display it for you.

Hotlinks

Of course, URLs are a little clumsy to handle. They're long, hard to remember, and you don't get any partial credit for being close. You also hardly ever see "For a good time, browse `http://www.something-or-other`" written anywhere convenient. The best way to find something on the Web is to find something else that knows it so that you can get there with just a mouse click.

If you are in a VRML world and your VR Scout cursor changes from an arrow to a hand, then you have discovered a hotlink. Look at the bottom of the screen to see the Web address of the hotlinked object. If you are online, clicking the object with your hand-cursor sends you to the linked address. If the file at that address is a VRML file, VR Scout will show it to you. If not, VR Scout will send it back to your Web browser.

The layout of the VR Scout helper application

The controls for VR Scout are found in a toolbar at the top of the VR Scout window (see Figure 3-2).

The first three buttons from the left are like the Back, Forward, and Home buttons on your Web browser. If you look at more than one VRML file in the course of your session, you can go back to the previous one by clicking the left arrow. After you have gone back, you can go forward again by clicking the right arrow. The Home button only works if you have designated a home page (which you can do from the Options⇨Preferences dialog box).

The fourth button, whose icon is the world with a folder in front of it, is the Open Location button. It is equivalent to File⇨Open Location on the menu, and it opens up a box into which you can type the URL of a VRML world on the Web.

The next three buttons correspond to the three navigation modes of VR Scout: Walk, Fly, and Examine. More about them in the "Navigating in VR Scout" section later in this chapter.

The next button is a Stop button, which again is similar to a button on your Web browser. If you are loading a VRML file that is taking too long for you, click Stop.

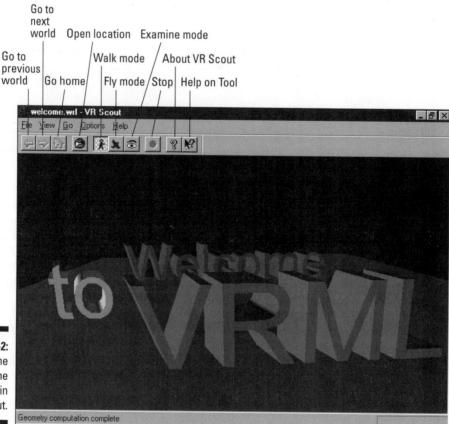

Figure 3-2:
The welcome message in VR Scout.

The layout of the VR Scout plug-in

The Netscape plug-in version of VR Scout differs in screen appearance from its helper application cousin, but functionally, it is much the same. Like fellow Netscape plug-in Live3D, the VR Scout plug-in displays its world inside a Netscape window and gives Netscape the capability to combine a VRML window with an HTML document, as in Figure 3-3. The one major disadvantage of the VR Scout plug-in is that it does not allow you to change viewpoints.

The navigation bar of the plug-in (see Figure 3-4) is across the bottom of the screen, rather than the top. It has no Web-browsing controls (because it uses Netscape's). Six options are spread across the bar. The first three are the navigation modes: Walk, Fly, and Examine, which we discuss in the "Navigating in VR Scout" section coming up soon. Only one of the three is active — the one highlighted in green. The fourth is Headlight, which is on if highlighted and off if not. The fifth, Reset, returns to Entry view. The question mark should open a help index, but at the moment it does nothing.

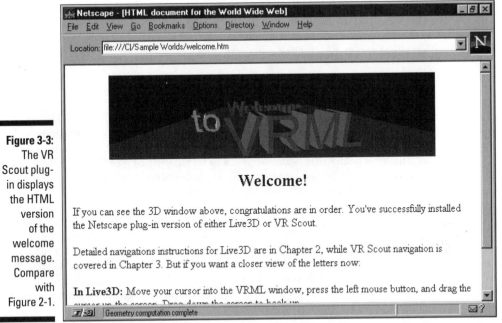

Figure 3-3:
The VR
Scout plug-
in displays
the HTML
version
of the
welcome
message.
Compare
with
Figure 2-1.

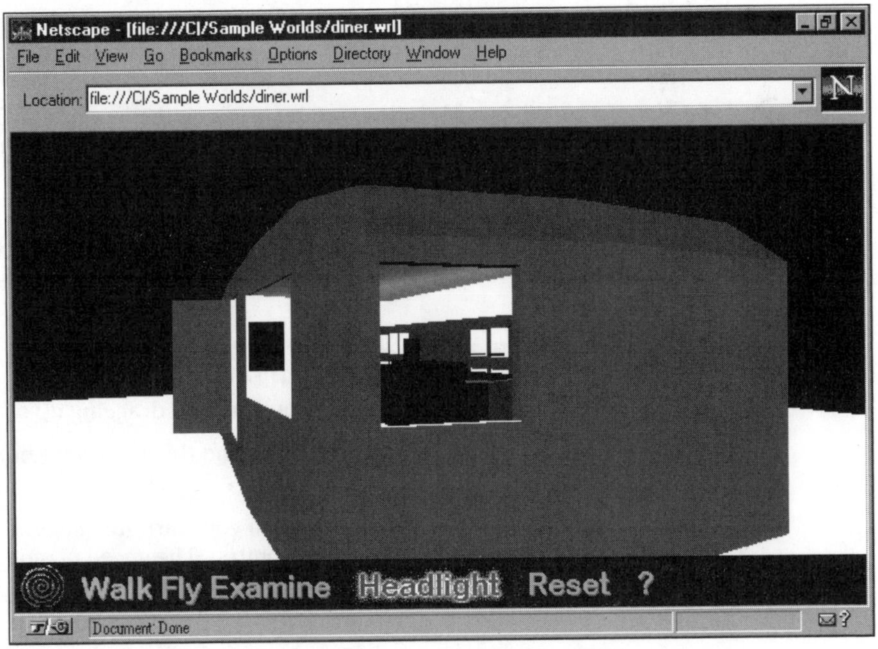

Figure 3-4:
Window-
peeking at
the diner.

Right-clicking anywhere produces a menu. Most of what you can do with this menu you can do more easily with the toolbar. But the Preferences menu command opens up a box that allows you to change the brightness of the headlight and switch collision detection on or off.

Navigating in VR Scout

VR Scout has three navigation modes: Walk, Fly, and Examine. In the helper application, each has its own toolbar button with an icon on it. Walk is denoted by a figure walking (the figure appears to be wearing one of those Chinese sun hats, but it could be our imagination). Fly is denoted by a bird with wings spread. The Examine button has an eye on it.

VR Scout does a trick that is so simple and helpful that surely everyone will copy it soon: When you click the left mouse button, a set of red crosshairs appears where the cursor is. As you drag the cursor, the crosshairs stay in place, and a red line extends out to the cursor's new location. Let's call this the *drag line*. Because VR Scout (like nearly all the browsers) moves according to the length and direction of the drag, you can always see exactly what you're telling it to do by looking at the drag line.

Basic motions in VR Scout

Basic motions are performed in either Walk or Fly mode, using the same mouse or keyboard commands. Fly allows you an additional motion: rolling.

- **Charge and retreat:** Move forward by pressing the left mouse button and dragging the cursor up the screen (the red drag line should point straight up from the crosshairs). Move backward by dragging down the screen.

- **Screen motion:** Screen motion is done with the Shift key. Hold down Shift and the left mouse button and then drag the cursor in the direction you want to go. The way the red drag line points from the crosshairs is the way you're headed.

- **Head motion:** Turn your head left or right by pressing the left mouse button and dragging the cursor left or right. Tilt your head up or down by holding the Ctrl key, pressing the left mouse button, and dragging up or down.

- **Roll:** In Fly mode, hold down the Ctrl key and the left mouse button; then drag left or right.

- **Start/stop and speed:** Motion starts when you start dragging the cursor and stops when you release the left mouse button. The speed of motion corresponds to the distance of the drag (that is, the length of the red drag line).

Standard extras in VR Scout

✔ **Hotlinks:** When the cursor crosses a hotlinked object, it becomes a pointing finger. The URL of the link appears just below the finger-cursor. Clicking takes you to that URL.

✔ **Spin:** Pressing the left mouse button and dragging the cursor in Examine mode rotates the entire scene up, down, left, or right. The scene rotates around its own center, not around the observer. The keyboard commands still move your position, as in Walk mode (see "Keyboard equivalents to mouse commands" later in this chapter). The arrow keys and Shift+arrow keys work in Examine mode just as they do in Walk or Fly.

✔ **Changing viewpoint:** The plug-in version does not have the capability to change viewpoints, other than by using the Reset option on the toolbar to return to Entry view.

In the helper application version, use the View menu. View➪Reset Camera returns to Entry view. View➪Cameras produces a list of the possible viewpoints in the current file. If you don't want to bother making a choice, just select View➪Next Camera repeatedly to scroll through all the preset viewpoints. Want to go back? View➪Previous Camera takes you there. **Note:** Next Camera and Previous Camera are not like the Back and Forward buttons in a Web browser. *Previous* means previous on the preset list, not "go back to the last camera I used."

✔ **Headlight:** The headlight in VR Scout makes a bigger difference than the headlight of any other browser. Without it, almost all scenes are dark. With it turned up full, almost all scenes are overexposed.

In the plug-in, turn the headlight on/off from the toolbar. In the helper application use Options➪Headlight. Set the brightness of the headlight from the Preferences box. In the plug-in, right-click to get a menu and then choose Preferences. In the helper, select Options➪Preferences.

✔ **Collision detection:** VR Scout does partial collision detection. From the Preferences panel, choose between None and Forward in the Collision Checking box.

✔ **Help:** In the plug-in, neither the question mark on the toolbar nor the Help Index choice on the menu work. The helper application's toolbar has two question-mark buttons, one of which may be helpful. The question-mark-by-itself button takes you to the About VR Scout window, which is sort of like the credits at the end of movie. Other than giving you a lead on who to either congratulate or firebomb (depending on how you are getting along with VR Scout that day), it's not very useful. The question-mark-and-arrow button is a Help on Tool feature, a nice idea that is not fully implemented in version 1.22. The idea is that you click on the button, and then your cursor turns into a question mark. Take that question mark to whatever thing on the screen you don't understand and click again. A Help window is supposed to appear to explain the object you clicked. Sometimes it does, and sometimes it's helpful.

Really helpful Help comes from the Help⇨Index on the menu of the helper application. This command opens up a window of Help topics, and you then click on links until you zero in on the thing you want to know. The entries are concise and well written. The Navigation help is excellent, giving you graphical reminders of what all the mouse drags do. Unfortunately, not all the entries are accurate. (Occasionally you run into a description that just doesn't apply — for example, "How to speed up drawing scenes," left over from version 1.1.)

After you've examined a scene and returned to Walk or Fly modes, the Shift+mouse drag commands no longer do what you might expect. Instead of shifting in the plane of the screen, they will shift in the plane that the screen *used* to represent, before you started rotating things. We don't know whether this movement is a bug or a feature, but it can be disconcerting the first time you notice it.

Keyboard equivalents to mouse commands

You can also control VR Scout with the keyboard rather than the mouse. The relationship between the keyboard commands and the mouse drags is very straightforward (see Table 3-1).

Table 3-1	Correlation between Keys and Mouse Movements
Key	*Similar Mouse Movement*
→	dragging right
←	dragging left
↑	dragging up
↓	dragging down

Some motions are obtained by combining a mouse drag with either Shift or Ctrl. The arrow keys interact with Shift and Ctrl in exactly the same way as their mouse equivalents.

Chapter 4

Browsing with an Option to Build

*C*aligari's Pioneer is perhaps the most interesting browser that we discuss in Part I. It is simply chock-full of vision and good ideas. It browses, it builds, it slices, dices, and makes julienne fries. It does a few things we hadn't even thought to ask for, like allowing you to build a *neighborhood* — a 3D scene full of objects that are hotlinks to your favorite VRML worlds.

However, it's a beta version — Pioneer .97. Eventually, a Pioneer 1.0 will come out, in which all these wonderful features work every time, and even work the same way every time. It will happen. We've been following Pioneer since version .9, and a lot of things have been fixed since then.

But not everything. Pioneer still fails to load some VRML worlds that other browsers have no trouble with. It still moves slowly in anything but wireframe mode — too slowly to be useful in some of the more complicated worlds we look at in Chapter 5. And the coolest Pioneer feature of all, the VRML neighborhood, crashes the program about half the time we try to use it. Caligari will fix this.

But the vision is beautiful: One tool, one set of commands to learn. And then you can browse VRML worlds on the Web, build your own, splice them together if you want, and eventually be part of the great VRML Web that will finally put the *space* into *cyberspace*. We want to be there when Caligari gets it right.

Pioneer has a big brother, Pioneer Pro, which Caligari charges real money for. (Pioneer is downloadable free over the Web at http://www.caligari.com.) The CD contains trial copies of both Pioneer and Pioneer Pro. Both are browser/builders, and the differences between the two are entirely on the building side. This chapter is about browsing, so for now, we'll just talk about Pioneer. If you install Pioneer Pro instead (and pay the extra money to keep it after the trial period), you won't notice a difference until Chapter 8.

Installing Pioneer

The current version of Pioneer requires a computer with at least a 486DX processor (or a math coprocessor), running either Windows 3.1 (plus Win32s) or Windows 95. These requirements are firm: No Mac version exists, and when we tried to install Pioneer on a mere 486SX (without a math coprocessor), we failed. Pioneer requires 8MB of RAM. The Pioneer directory takes up about 2.7MB on your hard drive. Pioneer also installs the 3DR rendering software into your Windows directory, filling another 2 MB or so. Pioneer Pro is slightly larger. Both Pioneer and Pioneer Pro use the same copy of 3DR, so installing both uses up a little less than 8MB.

Check out the OUR_CD file on the CD, for instructions on installing Pioneer and Pioneer Pro.

Setting up Pioneer as a helper application

The current version of Pioneer can be set up as a helper application with either Netscape or with Spyglass Mosaic 2.1. For instructions, see "Configuring Helper Applications" in Chapter 3.

The Layout of the Browsing Tools

Caligari has conveniently given us two separate toolbars — a browsing bar and a building bar. Whichever is currently displayed is arranged across the bottom of the screen. You can switch from one to the other by clicking the button at the left end of the toolbar.

Browsing bar button basics

The buttons on the browsing toolbar all have pictures or other icons associated with them, but they're not exactly self-explanatory. Fortunately, they don't need to be. When you pass the cursor over a button (you don't have to click it), a description of the tool appears just above the menu bar.

If you look carefully, you can see that some of the buttons have little colored triangles in their upper corners (see Figure 4-1 or Figure 1 in the color section). Four of the buttons have little (we mean *little* — get out your bifocals and look hard) blue triangles in their upper-left corners and three of the buttons have little red triangles in their upper-right corners. These triangles are not just decoration (it'd be kind of pointless if they were, given that you can barely see them); they tell you something about the tool and how to use it.

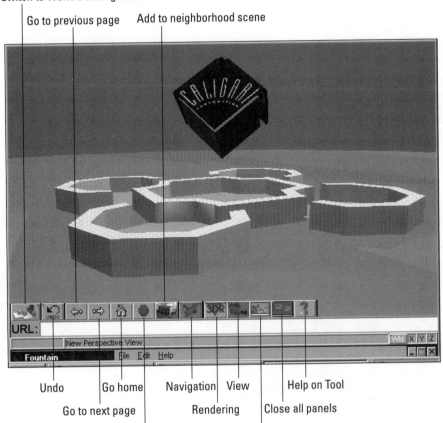

Switch to World Building mode

Go to previous page   Add to neighborhood scene

Figure 4-1:
What you
see when
you start
Pioneer.
More than
just a pretty
picture.

Undo   Go home   Navigation   View   Help on Tool

Go to next page   Rendering   Close all panels

Stop receipt of current page   New perspective view

✔ **A blue triangle means that the tool has a family of variants.** For example, the Cake tool (if there were one) might have the variants "Have Cake" and "Eat Cake." You would see a blue-triangled button on the toolbar with a cake on a platter, representing the current choice (Have Cake). If you moved the cursor over that button and held down the left mouse button, two ghostly buttons would appear above it — one a duplicate of the Have Cake button and another showing an empty platter, representing the Eat Cake option. To change the current choice, you would move the cursor to the ghostly Eat Cake button and release the mouse button. The ghosts would disappear, and the Eat Cake button would be on the toolbar where Have Cake had been. (It must be lunchtime.)

To see what the actual tool variants are, look in the next section, "The browsing bar buttons in brief."

✔ **A red triangle means that the button is associated with a pop-up panel that allows you to make more complicated choices.** These panels control all the subtleties of Pioneer — lights, shading, and so forth. You'll see a lot of them in "Changing the Look of Pioneer" later in this chapter.

The browsing bar buttons in brief

From left to right, the buttons are

✔ **Switch to World Building mode:** Click the left mouse button here to exchange the browsing toolbar for the building toolbar. For an explanation of the building toolbar, see Chapter 8. The red triangle tells you that you can pop up the Object Info panel by clicking the right mouse button.

✔ **Undo/Redo:** The blue triangle tells you that this tool has variants — it is both Undo and Redo. Undo is a good way to reverse a mistake. (Everything in life should come with an Undo button.) Once you've undone something, though, you might decide that undoing it was a mistake, and that you want to un-Undo it. Pioneer has prepared for this possibility: As soon as you use the Undo button, it becomes the Redo button. Clicking Redo undoes the Undo.

✔ **Go to previous page in history/next page in history/home page:** These three buttons work just like the Back, Forward, and Home buttons on your Web browser. Pioneer keeps track of the addresses of the VRML files it has seen, whether they were on your hard drive or from the Web. So if you want to go back to the last VRML file you were looking at, you don't need to remember where it was — just click the leftward-pointing arrow. After you have gone back to a previous VRML file, you can go forward again by clicking the rightward-pointing arrow. The House button returns you to the opening scene of Pioneer.

✔ **Stop receipt of current page:** Just like the Stop button in your Web browser. Sometimes you click a hotlink accidentally when you're rummaging through a VRML world, or you click a hotlink on purpose and discover that the file you've asked to load is much bigger than you thought. Click Stop to avoid waiting a long time for something you didn't want anyway.

✔ **Add to Neighborhood Scene:** A fascinating little tool that allows you to build a *neighborhood* of your favorite VRML worlds by taking an object from each and arranging them all into a new VRML world. Each object becomes a hotlink to the world from which it came. Eat your heart out, Mr. Rogers. (Read more about the Neighborhood tool in "It's a Beautiful Day in the Neighborhood" later in this chapter.)

✔ **Navigation:** The blue triangle tells you that you have a choice of two variants: Fly Through World (represented by an airplane) and Walk Through World (represented by a pair of sneakers). The red triangle tells you that you can open the Object Info panel by clicking the right mouse button.

✔ **Rendering:** The variants here are solid or wireframe. The solid rendering icon is a triangle that says 3DR on it (we assume this stands for 3 Dimensional Rendering). The wireframe icon is three wireframed cubes. Clicking the right mouse button opens the Render Quality panel.

✔ **View:** The variants are View From Object (whose icon looks like a camera) and Perspective View (whose icon looks like a house). To use View From Object, you just select an object (cameras are ideal objects for this purpose) and then click the View From Object button. Just like the name says, you get the view from that object. After you have enjoyed this view long enough, selecting Perspective View gives you a long-distance look at the scene.

✔ **New perspective view:** Opens a small window with a long-distance view of the scene.

✔ **Close all panels:** Just what it says. When the screen gets cluttered up with panels, you can close them all at once by clicking this button.

✔ **Help on Tool:** This feature will be great when they finish it. (If the version of Pioneer on the CD is more recent than the one we're using, it might work fine for you.) Here's how it is supposed to work: Click on the question-mark icon at the end of the toolbar and then click on a toolbar button that you don't understand. A paragraph or two of explanation appears, together with a new scene specially designed to demonstrate the tool as simply as possible. At the moment, though, the demos haven't been written for most of the tools.

Navigating in Pioneer

Pioneer has a Walk mode and a Fly mode, like Live3D and VR Scout. Unfortunately, the similarity only goes so far. Someday we may have a standard Walk mode and a standard Fly mode, but not yet. Pioneer's walk-and-fly are actually not all that different from each other — the main difference is in how you stop.

The basic moves in Pioneer

- **Charge and retreat:** In either mode, move forward by holding down the left mouse button and dragging the cursor up the screen. Move backward by holding down the left mouse button and dragging the cursor down the screen.

- **Screen motion:** Screen motion involves the right mouse button. If you hold down the right mouse button and drag the cursor up the screen, you will move straight up in the scene without turning your head. Ditto for down, left, right, or anything in between. Anytime you hold down the right mouse button and drag, you move in the plane of the screen.

- **Head motion:** Turning left or right is just like all the other browsers — you hold down the left mouse button and drag the cursor left or right. Tilting your head up or down follows the joystick model: hold down *both* mouse buttons and drag the cursor down to tilt up or up to tilt down. You can change this setup if you like: Select File⇨Preferences to open the Preferences dialog box. Then click on Pitch Swap. Now you can drag the cursor up to tilt your head up and down to tilt it down.

- **Start/stop and speed:** The two modes differ here. In Walk mode, the motion is directly connected to the mouse drag: If you want to go a long way, drag a long way. If you want to go faster, drag faster. To stop moving, stop dragging.

  In Fly mode, the mouse drag controls the speed, not the distance. If you want to move fast, drag a long way. If you want to move slowly, drag a little way. The motion will continue until you let up the mouse button(s).

  In general, use Fly mode to cover long distances and Walk mode to fine-tune your position — just as in real life. You'll wear out your arm dragging the mouse if you try to get to the other side of the structure on Caligari's home page in Walk mode.

Standard Extras in Pioneer

Using the standard extras in other browsers is like ordering breakfast at McDonald's — simple because you only have a few choices. Using the standard features in Pioneer is like standing in a kitchen, telling the chef how to make your favorite dish. You can get exactly what you want, but the process is more complicated than just saying "value meal number three."

Hotlinks

The cursor changes when it crosses a hotlinked object. If the object is hot-linked to another VRML world, the cursor changes to a cube that says 3D on it. But if the object is hotlinked to an HTML document, the cursor becomes a chain link that says 2D next to it. In either case, click the left mouse button to jump to the linked location.

Spin

The browsing toolbar has no spin command, but you can maneuver individual objects in every conceivable way with the Object Move tool (and its variants) on the building toolbar. See Chapter 8.

Changing viewpoints

Other VRML browsers let you select from a list of predetermined viewpoints — and if you don't like the viewpoints selected by the authors of the world, too bad. But Pioneer is a builder of worlds in addition to being a viewer of worlds. So if you don't like something, such as the position of a viewpoint, you can change it.

Pioneer represents a viewpoint as a camera. The basic idea behind changing to a new viewpoint is simple:

1. **Find a camera.**

2. **Select it.**

3. **Click the View from Object button.**

Clicking the button is straightforward, and you select a camera just by clicking it — it turns white when you do. But finding the cameras is a little more complicated than it sounds.

Finding the cameras

If you're going to find the cameras, you'd better make sure they're visible. Pull up the Render Quality panel by moving the cursor to the Render button on the toolbar and right-clicking it with the mouse. In the upper-right corner of the Render Quality panel lies an icon that looks like a camera. If the icon is white, the cameras in the scene are not shown; if it is blue, the cameras are shown. Click the icon to change it from one state to the other. Once you have made the cameras visible, they look like the camera in Figure 4-2.

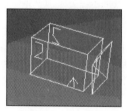

Figure 4-2:
Lights!
Camera!
Pioneer
can make
viewpoints
visible.

Even visible cameras can be hidden behind other objects. But if you switch to wireframe rendering, any surface that might be hiding a camera becomes transparent, while the cameras themselves are the only orange things in the scene, other than lights. (Lights actually work just as well as cameras when you want to switch your viewpoint — View From Object considers a light to be an object.)

Cheating

Changing viewpoint might be a browsing feature, but finding and selecting cameras is easier from the Building toolbar.

1. **Click the Switch to World Building Mode button.**

2. **Click the Object List button on the building toolbar.** It's the second-to-last button on the right. The object list appears. The cameras may be listed as cameras, or (if the designer has given a name to the viewpoint) the viewpoint name may appear. Anything on this list is an object, though, and can be used with the View From Object tool.

3. **Select an object from the object list.** Click its name on the list. The name turns white. In wireframe mode, the object turns white as well.

4. **Click the View From Object button.** It also lives on the building toolbar. The view changes, though it is still partially obscured by the object list. You can see enough to decide whether this view is the one you wanted. If not, select another object from the list and click View From Object again.

5. **Click the Switch to Browsing Mode button.** It has a car on it.

Lights

Pioneer's browsing features don't include a headlight. But the builder half can provide any kind of light you want — any brightness, any color, any location. See "Light It Up" in Chapter 12.

Help

Selecting Help⇨Contents takes you to the table of contents of the Pioneer help document. The subject titles are all hotlinked to more specific subjects, and eventually to a paragraph or two on all the basics.

Help On Tool (the question mark at the end of the toolbar) is a great idea that Caligari hasn't implemented yet. See the discussion of the Help On Tool button in "The browsing bar basics in brief" earlier in this chapter.

Letting Pioneer Browse on Its Own, or What If the Whole Web Were VRML?

Pioneer's opening screen (back in Figure 4-1) is more than just a cute decoration. That black cube that floats over the complex of buildings is a hotlink to Caligari's Web site. If you are looking at it while you are connected to your Internet provider with a SLIP or PPP connection (the former is called a *slip connection* by the cognoscenti), give the cube a click and wait a minute or so.

What's happening? Pioneer is running off to look up a file on the Caligari home computer. When it comes back, you see the futuristic scene of Figure 4-3. Wow!

But wait, there's more. This scene is futuristic in more ways than one: It's a VRML Web. As you wander around in the scene, you discover objects hotlinked to other VRML worlds. If you click on the objects, Pioneer goes off and grabs other VRML files to transport you to other scenes. In the same way that the hotlinks in an HTML document lead you to other HTML documents, the hotlinks in this VRML world take you to other VRML worlds that Caligari has created.

At the moment, the adventure goes just that far, but someday it could go much farther. For more examples like Caligari's, see "Archipelagos in the Net" in Chapter 5.

Figure 4-3: A spider in the middle of its VRML Web.

The URL box near the bottom of the Pioneer window shows the Web address of whatever you are looking at. You do not need to use Pioneer to come here because any VRML browser will do. However, Caligari knows its own worlds best — other browsers won't show you all the details that you see with Pioneer.

Getting more prosaic for a moment, you can use the URL box in Pioneer to look at any VRML file on the Web — if you know its address. Here's how:

1. **Start Pioneer.**

2. **Log in to your Internet provider via a SLIP or PPP connection.**

   A rule of thumb: If you're using Netscape as your Web browser and Eudora to read your mail, you probably have a SLIP or PPP connection.

3. **Type the Web address of a VRML file into the URL box near the bottom of the Pioneer window.**

Changing the Look of Pioneer

Voyager (see Chapter 3) and Pioneer make an interesting contrast. Voyager is simple to use precisely because it doesn't have many features — no bothersome choices to worry about. Pioneer, on the other hand, lets you control all kinds of things. Having options is great — except when you find yourself controlling things that you don't really understand. In this section, we attempt to explain what you need to know to make use of the power that Pioneer gives you.

These issues come up in spades when we talk about the building commands in Pioneer (see Chapter 8). But so long as we are talking just about the browsing commands, you only need to be aware of two centers of power:

✔ **The Render Quality panel:** You can access this panel from the Render button on the toolbar. Just move the cursor to the Render button and click the right mouse button.

✔ **The Preferences dialog box:** Make the Preferences dialog box appear by selecting File⇨Preferences from the menu.

Looks versus speed

The current version of Pioneer is slow compared to, say, Live3D or VR Scout, unless you have a graphics accelerator board in your computer. (This fact could easily change with future versions. VR Scout 1.1 was slow, but VR Scout 1.2 is one of the fastest browsers available.) You can do a number of things to speed up Pioneer. Of course, if that speed-up came for free, Caligari would have made the choice for you. In general, speed-ups come at the expense of appearance.

These trade-offs are made in the Render Quality panel, which you can see in Figure 4-4. The Render Quality panel has six icons across the top and then several lines of text beneath.

Figure 4-4:
The Render
Quality
panel.

Shading

The first two icons on the left give you a choice between two methods of shading — faceted and smooth. Click the first icon on the left for faceted shading and the second for smooth. Faceted is a little faster, but smooth is better looking. The Pioneer Help notes give a description of what the two methods do, but it probably won't mean much until you try them out and see how different they look.

Textures

The third icon from the left toggles the use of textures on surfaces. The easiest way to see the difference between textured and nontextured surfaces is to look at the hanging cube on the opening screen of Pioneer (the one pictured back in Figure 4-1). When texture rendering is on, the hanging cube says "Caligari" on each side. When texture rendering is off, it doesn't say anything. Naturally, turning the texture rendering off makes Pioneer faster.

If you decide to render textures on surfaces, you still have a choice to make about the maximum resolution. The choices are 32x32, 64x64, 128x128, or 256x256. You don't need to know what those numbers mean. All you need to know is that the bigger the number, the better the texture looks. The smaller the number, the faster Pioneer runs.

Make the texture resolution choice by holding down the left mouse button on the box next to Texture Res in the Render Quality panel. The different options are displayed, and you move the cursor to the one you want. Next, release the mouse button.

Again, the easiest way to test the different resolutions is to look at the hanging cube. At the higher resolutions, making out the writing on the cube is much easier.

Scene Detail

This area is where the big trade-offs are made. If you move your cursor to the box next to Scene Detail in the Render Quality panel and then hold down the left mouse button, the various choices are listed for you: Render All, Wireframe, Always Wire, Boxes, and Always Boxes.

Render All means exactly what it says: Give me a fully rendered picture all the time. Pioneer is really slow when you make this choice.

The Wireframe choice gives you a fully rendered picture when you stop moving, but while you are moving, the image is given only in outline, without any color or shading. Always Wire stays in wireframe even when you stop. Both of these choices are pretty fast.

The Boxes choice gives you a fully rendered picture when you stop, but while you are moving, you see only the boxes around the objects. So all you know about an object as you move past is its position and size. Always Boxes stays in Box mode even when you stop. These choices don't look like much, but they really whip.

Constant Frame Rate

If the scene detail choices are like the gears of a car, Constant Frame Rate is like an automatic transmission. If this box is checked in the Render Quality panel, then Pioneer will do whatever it must to keep rendering the scene at the designated speed. Usually Pioneer keeps up by putting most of the scene into wireframe, and it may even go to boxes if it has to.

The default rate is 5 frames per second. You can adjust it by typing another number into the box.

Rearranging the furniture

Back in the '70s, we had a friend who wrote a computer chess program. He was extremely proud of the interface he had written: The program would recognize your moves no matter what notation you used to type them. If you typed in N-K4, the program would figure out for itself which knight could make it to King-4. In fact, if you were in a situation where only one bishop move was possible, you could just type a B and the program would assume that you intended to make that move.

But he had just one small problem: The interface part of the program ate up almost the entire memory of the computer, leaving very little space for the part of the program that figured out what moves to make. The program had a great interface, but it played terrible chess.

You might wonder why we mention this story. Well, the current version of Pioneer is still a beta version, and not all the important features are in yet. It can't always open the files you want to see, the Help On Tool feature isn't done yet, it doesn't load a scene as quickly as some other browsers do, the Neighborhood feature doesn't work (see next section), *but you can rearrange the screen any way you want.*

Take the menu bar for instance. Tired of seeing it at the bottom of the screen? No problem! Just select File⇨Preferences to get into the Preferences dialog box. Click the box next to TopMenu, and presto! The menu bar and toolbar are both at the top of the Pioneer window.

Or consider those panels that pop up when you click the right mouse button on a red-triangled tool button. They have those thin blue strips at the top of their windows, the ones that give you the title of the panel and a click box to close it. Waste of an eighth of an inch, isn't it? Well, you can use the Preferences dialog box to reclaim that space. Just click the Titles click box to make the X go away. Poof! Those title bars are gone.

But wait, there's more! When a panel opens up in an inconvenient place, you aren't stuck with it. You can drag it by its title bar (or some other spot, if you have gotten rid of the title bars) and set it down anywhere you want.

Great work, guys. But can you fix the Neighborhood feature?

It's a Beautiful Day in the Neighborhood

When you're cruising along on the Web and you hit a particularly interesting Web page, what do you do? Add it to your bookmarks, that's what. Your bookmark file is an HTML document that lists a whole bunch of other HTML documents. Click on the name and off you go.

That process is cool enough in its way, but it's so . . . verbal. Words, lists, documents — all that 1-D and 2-D stuff. You can see the names of things, but what's in a name, really? VRML should move us beyond all that.

And it does. Or at least it will if Caligari can make Pioneer's Neighborhood feature work right. Here's what they have in mind: Suppose you happen across a VRML world that you really like and know you're going to want to visit again. Instead of adding the URL to your bookmark list, you do the following:

1. **Click the Add to Neighborhood Scene button on the browsing toolbar.**

   It's the one that looks like a house, to the right of the Stop button. When you move your cursor back into the scene, it changes into a little house.

2. **Find an object in the scene that will really stick in your mind.**

3. **Click on it.**

   The object should turn white to show that it has been selected, and your cursor should return to normal.

Now whenever you want to go back to this particular VRML world, select File⇨Show Neighborhood from the menu. Pioneer looks up your neighborhood file and displays it. Click an object and off you go.

Or at least that's how its supposed to work — and eventually it probably will. This feature was introduced in Pioneer .95, and it crashed our system whenever we tried to use it. In Pioneer .97, Caligari fixed that problem, and now we can't make the Neighborhood feature do anything at all. Our attempts to add the squid from Chapter 8 to our neighborhood have failed. The (squidless) default neighborhood file is shown in Figure 4-5.

Before you close Pioneer, be sure to save your neighborhood (everyone should try to save the neighborhood). Select File⇨Save Neighborhood from the menu.

The Neighborhood file is a VRML world like any other. Using Pioneer's building tools (see Chapter 8), you can rearrange it any way you want.

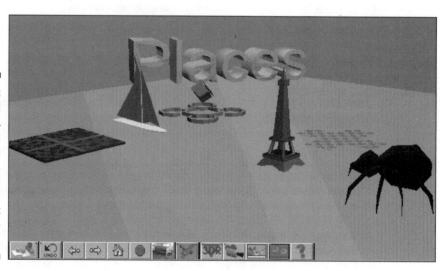

Figure 4-5:
A typical VRML neighborhood: a garden, an Eiffel Tower, a floating cube, and a giant spider — but no squid.

Chapter 5
Oh, the Places You'll Go

● ●

In This Chapter

▶ Finding VRML worlds on the net

▶ Lists of VRML worlds

▶ Worlds that connect you to other worlds

▶ Do-it-yourself VRML sites

▶ VRML as art

▶ Virtual tours of actual places

▶ VRML visualizations of science and math

▶ VRML in MUDs and chat rooms

● ●

So far, we've just told you about worlds you can find on our CD. But VRML was made for the Web, and people put the most amazing work out there where you can look at it for free. Of course, none of these worlds will simply invade your modem. You have to know where to look, and occasionally having some program notes helps explain what you're looking at.

The quantity of VRML on the Web is exploding as more and better VRML-building tools become available. By the time you read this chapter, many new worlds will be out there that were still on the drawing board when we were writing. As is true of the Web in general, a lot of those worlds will be silly and worthless — but some won't. When tools are getting better so quickly, and when the community of people who know about VRML is growing so rapidly, the latest and greatest sites of one week can start to look primitive only a month or two later. So even though this list of worlds will give you a good start, don't limit yourself to it. Get out, look around, and find some of that amazing stuff that didn't exist yet when we were writing this book.

And when you find yourself saying, "Hey, I wonder if I could do something like that?" you're ready to move on to Parts II and III of this book, where we introduce some building tools.

Islands in the Net: How to Find VRML Worlds on the Web

Ever had browser's block? It's like writer's block, but instead of staring at a blank piece of paper, you stare at a blank URL box and can't imagine what to type there. People claim that a thousand or more VRML worlds are out on the Web someplace. But where? And which one should you look at first?

Yahoo!, and other exuberant places to start

Libraries don't just throw their books into a pile and expect you to root through them until you find the one you want. They organize the books according to categories in a system like the Dewey Decimals. If you have a subject in mind and you know the system, before too long, you'll find yourself standing in front of a shelf of books related to your subject.

Several services are competing to be the Dewey Decimal system of the Web. Three that are available to anybody are Yahoo! (`http://www.yahoo.com`), Point (`http://www.pointcom.com`), and Excite (`http://www.excite.com`). If you belong to an online service like AOL, you also have access to their in-house guides to the Web. All the guides work more or less the same way: You start at a top-level collection of categories. After you select one, you are given a collection of its subcategories, and so on, until you reach a list of documents or services that you can jump to. Or, if what you are looking for doesn't fit exactly into one of the service's sub-sub-subcategories, you can type a keyword or two into a box, and have the service search for Web pages that might be interesting to you. Typing **VRML** into the search box in any Web guide service should give you a list of Web sites that will, in turn, lead you to almost any VRML site on the Web.

In both Yahoo! and Excite, you don't have to bother doing a special search — VRML is in the category system. In Yahoo!, you follow the path Computers/Internet/WWW/VRML, and in Excite (after you select the Net Directory tab), it's Computing/Authoring/VRML. In Yahoo!, the VRML category has subcategories of its own, like Browsers and Object Libraries. In Point, pursue Computers/Virtual Reality — the list you get is about half VRML and half other VR-related sites. Point also has a VRML version of its homepage, PointWorld, which we examine more closely in "The MUDdy, Chatty Future" later in this chapter.

Of course, all of these systems of categories are still in flux, particularly in areas as new as VRML. But if you take these paths as hints and follow your nose down any reasonable category tree, you're bound to get to a list of VRML sites.

Our list of lists

Web guides like Yahoo!, Point, and Excite are not the only ones making up lists of VRML sites. Most of the companies involved in developing VRML have lists of sites as well, and some people list VRML sites just for fun. Here's our current list of lists.

✔ **Excite:** `http://www.excite.com/Subject/Computing/Authoring/VRML/s-index.h.html`

✔ **Yahoo!:** `http://www.yahoo.com/Computers_and_Internet/Internet/World_Wide_Web/Virtual_Reality_Modeling_Language`

✔ **Point:** `http://www.pointcom.com/gifs/reviews/coswvi.htm`

✔ **Netscape's VRML Resources List:** `http://www.netscape.com/comprod/products/navigator/live3d/vrml_resources.html`

✔ **Aereal's Serch:** `http://www.virtpark.com/theme/cgi-bin/serchrnd.html`

✔ **InterVista's VRML Resources List:** `http://www.intervista.com/technology.html`

✔ **Virtual Reality VRML Library:** `http://cedar.cic.net/~rtilmann/mm/vrmllink.htm#REFERENCE`

✔ **The Weblynx Ultimate Virtual World Library:** `http://weblynx.com.au/virtual.htm`

✔ **VRML Legit List:** A list of site URLs checked by the VRML Authenticator and found to be legitimate VRML. If you have doubts about your browser, loading one of these URLs is a good way to check. `http://www.geom.umn.edu/~daeron/bin/legitlist.cgi`

Demo packages

Most companies that make VRML browsers also have some demo files on their Web site. Some of them are listed in Table 5-1.

Table 5-1	VRML Browser Demos and Where to Find Them
Company	*URL*
Virtus	`http://www.virtus.com/voydemos.html`
Chaco	`http://www.chaco.com/vrml/links.html`
Silicon Graphics	`http://www.sgi.com/VRML/island.wrl.gz`
Netscape	`http://www.netscape.com/comprod/products/navigator/live3d/examples/examples/examples.html`

The purpose of these sites is to demonstrate cutting-edge stuff — stuff that doesn't always work. Netscape's site in particular (which is trying to demonstrate the VRML 2.0 features of Live3D) tends to give us a lot of JavaScript errors. We come back to this site in the section, "Too cool not to mention," later in this chapter.

Bests, top tens, and other ways to let somebody else sort through the garbage

Are you one of those people who puts off going to movies until the Oscar nominations come out? You may not be living adventurously, and you miss that occasional diamond-in-the-rough that plays for a week and vanishes. But on the other hand, you won't waste six bucks and several hours of your life on a complete turkey, either. The same idea applies to VRML worlds. Why sift through the hundreds and hundreds of VRML worlds on the Web when other people are more than happy to do it for you and tell you where the good worlds are?

Proteinman's Top Ten VRML Worlds

We've never figured out whether Proteinman is a real person or a high nutrition superhero, but he does a great top ten list. Anybody can do a top ten where you just list the biggest, gaudiest worlds — and figure that if people don't have a Cray, that lack is their own fault. Proteinman's list usually has a nice range of sizes, from worlds as small as 20K up to 1 MB or more. You can find the list at http://www.virtpark.com/theme/proteinman.

Like Serch and Boom (two sites mentioned later in this chapter), Proteinman's list is part of the Web site of Aereal, Inc. In addition to these interesting VRML-related features, Aereal's site makes *our* top ten list in the Best Executive Biography category: "Aereal was founded by Adrian Scott, Ph.D. Adrian . . . has performed with the New York City Ballet, sung with Placido Domingo, been a management professor in Hong Kong, traveled around the world, and earned a Ph.D. applying Math (nonlinear optimization) to DNA (the youngest Ph.D. ever from Rensselaer Polytechnic Institute)." But what have you done *today*, Adrian?

The Virtus VRML Site of the Week

Do you think we crawled through all the home pages of all the students from the University of Wisconsin at Stevens Point to find "The Unofficial Star Wars VRML Pages" for you? (Check it out in the section, "Too cool not to mention," later in this chapter.) No way! Virtus found it for us by choosing it as the Site of the Week back in March. We never asked how they found it.

Check out `http://virtus.com/vrmlsite.html` to find the current Site of the Week.

Boom! A habit less fattening than salted nuts

Aereal has created a truly addictive site at `http://www.aereal.com/boom`. Here's the deal: Every time you press the BOOM button, they give you a randomly chosen VRML world on the Web (more than 1,000 possibilities). You look around until you feel like you know the place, and then you give it a rating. The higher-rated worlds are more likely to show up when the next person BOOMs. You get a chance to participate in a collective intelligence with all those other BOOMers out there. Ready to quit? Well, maybe just one more.

"But it's not there!" What to do when you catch us in a lie

Corporate Web sites tend to be pretty stable — we can say with some confidence that Virtus and Caligari will still be at `http://www.virtus.com` and `http://www.caligari.com` when you look for them (of course, all bets are off if either company gets bought by Microsoft or Netscape or someone). A lot of the best VRML worlds on the Web, however, are put out there by hobbyists, many of whom are students. The URLs (Web addresses) of these pages can change whenever the author graduates, or gets a new job, or changes Internet providers. Even a world on a corporate Web site can change its URL if the corporation reorganizes, or just reorganizes its Web site.

We recommend that you not give up if the URL that we give for a site doesn't work. Here are a few things to try:

- ✔ **Keep truncating the address.** If you can't find Proteinman's Top Ten VRML Worlds where we say it is (at `http://www.virtpark.com/theme/proteinman/`), take a look at `http://www.virtpark.com/theme/` or at `http://www.virtpark.com/`. You're hoping to find a more general site description page, one that contains a link that looks like it might lead to a VRML top ten page.

- ✔ **Search for the name of the page.** Go to Yahoo! or some other search engine and have it search for Proteinman's Top Ten VRML Worlds.

- ✔ **Check some of the lists of VRML sites.** They don't call it "the Web" for nothing. Everything connects to everything else in many, many ways. We give a list of online lists in the section, "Our list of lists," earlier in this chapter. One of those lists is bound to be more up-to-date than this book.

Archipelagos in the Net: Worlds That Connect to Other Worlds

A lot of VRML pioneers confess to having been inspired by the cyberpunk science fiction novels, most notably by William Gibson's classic, *Neuromancer*. In cyberpunk novels, cyberspace is not like the Web — a bunch of 2D pages linked together into one big document. It's a bunch of 3D spaces linked together into a virtual world. See "Could VRML take over the Web?" back in Chapter 1.

A lot of things have to happen before Gibson's cyberspace becomes a reality (although people are working on it — look at the section, "The MUDdy, Chatty Future," later in this chapter). But VRML worlds linking to other VRML worlds is already a reality — a primitive sort of reality that future generations will no doubt find highly amusing, but a reality all the same. You've already seen your first example of a VRML-to-VRML link — the Caligari Home World back in Figure 4-3. (What? You mean you skipped that chapter to get here? At least go back and look at the pictures.)

Terminal Reality

One of the cutest of the archipelagos, Ziff-Davis Terminal Reality (http://www.zdnet.com/zdi/vrml/content/vrmlsite/outside.wrl) consists of two linked VRML worlds (inside and outside) that between them (with their various inline files) take up about a megabyte. The metaphor for Terminal Reality is a transportation hub servicing an airplane, a ship, a rocket, and a blimp, all headed for some different VRML world on the Web.

From the outside view, you can see all four of the vehicles surrounding the terminal building. Each of the vehicles is a hotlink to the VRML site it is supposed to be going to. The glass door of the terminal is a hotlink to the inside view.

Inside, you find four gates, one for each of the vehicles. Like the vehicles themselves, the gates are hotlinks to the worlds. When we visited, Gate 1 (the ship) took you to an Intel site, smaller than (but similar to) the inside-your-computer views on the Intel TV commercials; Gate 2 (the blimp) to Intervista's Home VRML World; Gate 3 (the airplane) to Planet 9's Virtual San Francisco (see the section, "Virtual tours of actual places," later in this chapter); and Gate 4 (the rocket) to PointWorld (see the section, "The MUDdy, Chatty Future," later in this chapter). The Departures board is on the wall between Gates 3 and 4. (As in many terminals, the Departures board was wrong when we were there. It said that the rocket was going to Microsoft Games.)

The gates are not the only action inside: The phone booth is a hotlink to Internet Phone. The magazine kiosk advertises four Ziff-Davis magazines, and the ads are hotlinks to VRML-related stories that have appeared in the magazines. The guy inside the kiosk is reading one of the magazines — and yes, the magazine in his hands is a hotlink also.

Terminal Reality takes a long time to load, especially compared to a 2D Web page with the same hotlinks. So the attraction here is novelty rather than utility. TR gives us an idea of how things could be if we had a lot more bandwidth, memory, and processing power.

TIP

Maneuvering in big worlds

No matter how good your hardware is, somebody is going to construct a VRML world to max it out. The first sign of stressed hardware is that your navigation controls start to lag. You tell your browser to turn left, and it thinks about it. By the time it does start to turn left, you've dragged the mouse way, way, way to the left — far enough to spin yourself around a time or two, when the browser gets around to it.

In a big world, you need to change your navigating strategy to keep from wandering uncontrollably hither and yon. In each of the sections on particular browsers, we give tips on how to speed them up. But almost all of those tips trade off appearance for speed. If you came to this big world to oooh and aaah, trading off appearance is crazy. You could probably hike the Grand Canyon more quickly if you didn't waste all that time looking around — but who wants to?

Sometimes you just have to accept the fact that the controls will be slow. When they are, remember these two techniques:

- **Use Point mode:** When the controls start to lag, the difference between near left and far left gets lost. But *that way* is still *that way*. If you want to go towards the green house, get into your browser's version of Point mode and click on the green house. You may still have to wait a bit before you start moving, but at least you know you'll be going the right way.

- **Use viewpoints:** We would like to pound one idea into the heads of the designers of big worlds: *Put in lots of viewpoints.* Even if you can't maneuver through a world with any skill, you can still see the sights if the designer put in enough viewpoints. If your browser has a feature like Live3D's *animate to viewpoints,* you can get a nice guided tour by going to each of the viewpoints in order.

VR Scout presents special problems, because its plug-in version has neither a Point mode nor viewpoints. Nonetheless, we navigated Virtual San Francisco well enough to get the shots in color figures 3, 4, and 5. Here's the trick for VR Scout: *Don't drag the mouse until you see the crosshairs.* The time lag is precisely the time between when you click and when the crosshairs appear. Once the crosshairs show up, drag and release normally, and then wait to see what motion you get before you click again.

The Silicon Graphics Palladio

VRML files at the Silicon Graphics Web site never look quite right on our machine when running any of the browsers discussed in this book. We assume that they are designed to be seen on Silicon Graphics workstations running WebSpace, SGI's browser.

Nonetheless, running Live3D on a machine with an imitation-Pentium chip, we can definitely make out a pavilion of some sort, with a number of objects in it. We're not sure how big the file is because it downloaded in pieces, but the Palladio is sufficiently large that our Live3D controls were too sluggish to be useful. We navigated in Point mode and by using viewpoints (see the sidebar "Maneuvering in big worlds"). The *Arches* view is the one that gives the best look at the various objects on display in the pavilion.

The Palladio is, in essence, a 3D hotlist. The various objects on display are all representations of the sites they hotlink you to: Virtual Vegas is represented by a giant floating V, the Math Zoo hotlink is a dodecahedron, the link to chemical VRML models from Imperial College is a big IC, and so forth. Clicking any of the objects transports you to the site represented by the object (unless you're still in Point mode).

Serch — VRML's answer to Yahoo!

The Serch world (http://www.virtpark.com/theme/serch/home.wrl.gz) is laid out like a town green, with four buildings facing a decorative statue (see Figure 5-1). The buildings have these curious-looking green cones in them, which are hotlinks to various VRML worlds.

All in all, the site is cute but (like the other VRML hotlists we've seen) not terribly functional. The shape of a building (a tent, an office building, a house, a pavilion) seems to have little to do with the VRML icons it houses, and the icons themselves have nothing to do with the worlds they represent. The mailbox is a hotlink to their suggestion box, but otherwise, the three-dimensionality of the world conveys no real information.

Our suggestion: Wander around for a while, and then when you decide you want to find another VRML world to look at, go back to the 2D version of the Serch list at http://www.virtpark.com/theme/cgi-bin/serchrnd.html.

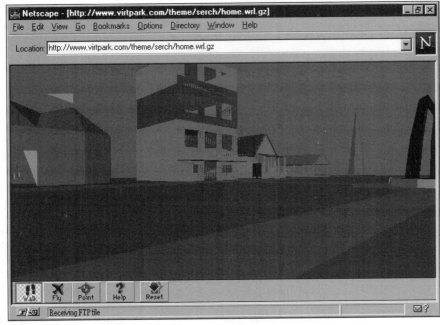

Figure 5-1:
A VRML
hotlist as a
small town:
Aereal's
Serch.

Interactive VRML Sites

Seeing the cool stuff that other people have made gets old after a while, like
spending all day wandering around one of those look-but-don't-touch museums.
Personally, we like the museums where we can turn some knobs, push some
buttons, and make something happen. So not surprisingly, some of the most
popular VRML sites on the Web are those that let you make some choices and
have a hand in creating something.

Glenn's jack-o-lanterns

Go to http://userwww.chaco.com/~glenn/jack to put in your order for a
VRML jack-o-lantern. Choose the shape of each eye, the nose, the mouth, and
the length of the stem, and then submit your specifications to Glenn's jack-o-
lantern constructor. Your choice (from the 3888 possible combinations of
features) gets built while you watch, and after it's done, you can fly around it in
true 3D style. Pictures from inside and outside our jack-o-lantern are in the
color section, Figures 8 and 9.

Glenn Crocker, the Chaco programmer who wrote this simple gadget (in almost no time at all, he claims) to demonstrate the Halloween 1995 beta version of VR Scout, professes to be completely amazed by its popularity. Halloween came and went many months ago, but the jack-o-lantern program keeps carving its virtual pumpkins.

Grafman's snowmen, valentines, bunnies, and so on

Why should Halloween be the only holiday with a made-to-order VRML object? Grafman Productions (http://www.graphcomp.com/vrml/index.html) meets your complete holiday needs with a Christmas snowman (you get to pick the number of body segments), a Valentine heart (pick the color and number of arrows), or an Easter bunny like the one you see in Figure 5-2 (pick the color). No doubt Grafman's designer (Robert M. Free) will have some Fourth of July fireworks up soon.

The choices in these programs don't give you anything like the feeling of creativity you get from the jack-o-lanterns, but they are cute. Well, most of them, anyway. Somehow a 3D heart with arrows through it makes us queasy.

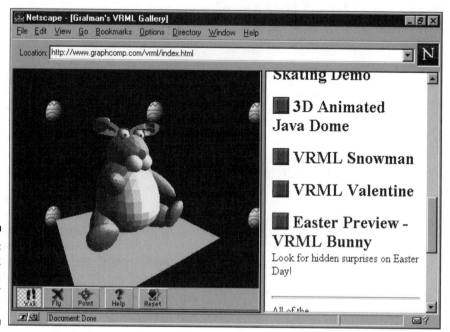

Figure 5-2: A pink Grafman Easter bunny.

It's Cool, It's Hot: A Few of Our Favorites

Surfing around the Web looking for good VRML sites is a little bit like being a tourist. Like anybody recently back from a long tour, we have some slides we'd like to show you. And although our slide show is far from exhaustive, we've tried to put together a representative sample of the kinds of things that people are doing with VRML.

VRML as art

VRML is a new material for artistic expression, as malleable as clay, as reproducible as a photograph, and free to anyone who can access a computer. It also provides a new venue for housing art. Virtual galleries can be any size, have infinitely adjustable lighting, and allow any number of people inside without jostling.

As you look at our examples of VRML art, you may notice that we picked most of them out of the same virtual neighborhood: tcc.iz.net. This node is the site of The Community Company, VRML's answer to the left bank of the Seine.

Grafman's Gallery

After you've seen Grafman's Gallery (`http://www.graphcomp.com/vrml/gallery0.wrl`), you may never put your photos in an album again. Think about it: Why not build yourself a grand virtual hall and display your pictures in style?

Grafman's Gallery is a virtual museum, complete with a high ceiling and airy lighting (see Figure 13 in the color section). Images of great pieces of art hang on the walls. As you might expect, the images start to pixel (look boxy) when you get too close, but unlike the interior of the Castle of Bari (in the section, "Italian tourist sites," later in this chapter), the gallery is big enough that you can back off to an ideal viewing distance. Two exhibits are statues (one of Moses and the other a Pieta). They are positioned and lit in such a way as to give the illusion of three dimensions; in fact, they are photos of statues, not models of them. You have to wonder what the bust of D. Owen Rowley (see "The bust of D. Owen Rowley" later in this chapter) would look like in the gallery.

The basic gallery is 42K, but the full package is actually much larger: Each of the pictures is a texture file that your browser needs to load separately. The full gallery takes a good chunk of memory and download time. (It does demonstrate the advantages of inlining, though. You can enjoy the gallery and the first few pictures while you're waiting for the others to come in.)

The gallery, like all the VRML in the Grafman Web site, is the work of Robert M. Free. He also writes the Grafman VR Tools Review on the same site — well worth checking out while you're there. He tells us that the gallery is due for an expansion soon — don't bump into any of the workmen.

The bust of D. Owen Rowley

If you think that VRML objects have to be cartoonish, look at `http://tcc.iz.net/o15xx.wrl` and think again. With enough effort, enough processing power, and (most of all) enough polygons, VRML artists can make objects of startling realism. At 15,000 polygons and about 100K of memory, the bust of D. Owen Rowley represents the current state of the art in realistic VRML representations of people (see Figure 5-3).

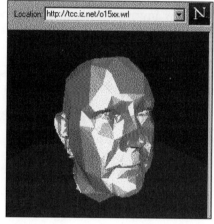

Figure 5-3: The first statue in cyberspace: D. Owen Rowley modeled his own head.

It's still black and white, and it's still static, but remember: Only about ten years lies between the first realistic computer-generated photographs and *Toy Story*. Ten years from now, computer-generated D. Owen Rowleys could be performing *MacBeth*.

Dimensional Graphics

Some of the best VRML art is being produced by C. Scott Young, who displays his work at the Dimensional Graphics Web site (`http://tcc.iz.net/dgraphix/`). The IMAGES2G.WRL file shows you what's available and contains hotlinks to the artworks themselves.

To get a taste of Scott's work, look at Figures 10, 11, and 12 in the color section.

The Jerry Garcia Memorial VRML Park

This simple but appropriate memorial shows the trademark Grateful Dead dancing teddy bear on top of a 3D pedestal. Make your pilgrimage to `http://tcc.iz.net/gdeadwc.wrl`.

Virtual tours of actual places

When you're on tour, eight cities in nine days is a killing pace. But online, you can stop off in San Francisco, England, and three cities in Italy all in one evening, without even getting tired. Virtual cuisine, however, remains a problem.

Virtual San Francisco

Planet 9 Studios has an ambitious project to put San Francisco online. The top-level work has already been done, as you can see in Figure 3 of the color section. Virtual San Francisco (`http://www.Planet9.com/worlds/vrsf.wrl`) allows you to fly over the Bay and pick out such landmarks as theTransAmerica Pyramid, Coit Tower, and the Golden Gate Bridge (see Figure 4 of the color section). The orange cubes are hotlinks, which eventually will connect to VRML worlds that map individual neighborhoods in more detail.

Planet 9's immediate neighborhood is already mapped, street by street, building by building for several blocks. You can see it in Virtual SOMA (`http://www.Planet9.com/worlds/vrsoma.wrl` — or find the right hotlink in Virtual San Francisco) and also in Figure 5 of the color section. Eventually, Planet 9 wants to texture-map each model building with a photo of the actual building it represents, as well as include hotlinks that allow you to tour the inside of several buildings. Delivering that quantity of information over today's 28.8 kbps modems is clearly unreasonable, but as technology marches on, many things become possible.

While you're at the Planet 9 Web site, you can also see VRML's participation in local politics. The proposed site of a new Giants baseball stadium lies within the Virtual San Francisco area, so Planet 9 just added the stadium to its model. VRML-savvy voters who want to get a better idea of how the stadium will fit into the neighborhood need only look at `http://www.planet9.com/ballpark.htm`.

None of these views comes cheap: Virtual SOMA begins as a 332K file and then has countless inlined files. The new ballpark view is 258K. Virtual San Francisco is large but doesn't have as many inlined files as Virtual SOMA.

The University of Essex campus model

We don't know whether or not the University of Essex has a model campus, but it does have a great campus model. Like the Norman-Swebian Castle of Bari (see "Italian tourist sites" later in this chapter), the Essex Campus model (`http://esewww.essex.ac.uk/campus-model.wrl`) is an example of how you can use VRML to make a place more comprehensible. You don't just wander around in the model and say, "Oh, wow!" This baby earns its keep as the front end to the campus information system. You can see one view of it in Figure 14 of the color section.

It works this way: Buildings in the 3D campus model are hotlinked to the Web pages of the campus departments that inhabit those buildings. Click on the Sports Centre, for instance, to find out the hours it is open or to see pictures of its staff. Click on the Library building to get access to the card catalog or find summaries of current periodicals. At most universities, finding a department on the map, finding it in the directory, and recognizing its exterior once you get there are three entirely different processes. But at Essex, they are one and the same.

Italian tourist sites

What is it about the Italians? They have produced many more than their fair share of excellent sites for the virtual tourist, several of which include VRML worlds.

The Norman-Swebian Castle of Bari

The name is a mouthful, but the Web site (`http://www.tol.it/bari`, English translation `http://www.tol.it/bari/uk`) is a wonderful example of how VRML can work together with text and images. Even without the VRML model, this site is an excellent virtual tour of a medieval castle in southern Italy. Text, maps, and pictures present this marvelous old castle from whatever angle you want: history, architecture, military, or just recreating the experience of tromping through it.

But to top it all off, they have the castle modeled in VRML. Interior and exterior are two separate models, and you can move from one to the other via hotlinks. Both files have a number of viewpoints available. Our advice: Look at it in Live3D and turn on the Animate to Viewpoints feature. As you move from viewpoint to viewpoint, you get a pretty good tour of the model (aside from running through a few walls).

For some reason, the entry view of the exterior comes up tilted — the other views are fine. In addition to the views, you'll notice panels of some sort floating about the castle: They are hotlinks to Web pages describing the part of the castle that they hover over. (Unfortunately, they take you to the Italian versions of the Web pages. No problem. Once you get there, look at the URL box on your Web browser. Where you see a `bari/it` in the name, replace it with a `bari/uk`. Most of the time, that substitution takes you to the English version of the page.)

The interior world shows you a hall exhibiting six paintings by Corrado Giaquinto. Again, Animate to Viewpoints is your best bet. Each of the paintings is a viewpoint, and the north and south ends of the hall are viewpoints. Sadly, the hall is not wide enough for the resolution of the photos of the paintings. Just as you are starting to get far enough away for the picture to lose its pixeling effect, you disappear behind a wall.

Planet Italy

Can't afford a trip to Italy right now? Don't sweat it. The folks at Planet Italy have modeled the central square of Siena for you at `http:www.PlanetItaly. com/Spazio/VRML/siena.wrl.gz`. You can wander around or try one of their dozen or so preset viewpoints, including the view from the café, the view from the bell tower, and several other picturesque settings. Not for the memory-limited, the file is 1.1MB, or 85.6KB gzipped.

Rimini

Before you head home, stop in Rimini at `http://www.iper.net/rimini-vrml`. So far they've only modeled the Arch of Augustus, but they're working on other local tourist attractions as well.

Visualizing science and math

Many people have told us that their last agreeable math experience was plane geometry in high school. Why? Because they could draw everything on paper and see what was going on. Now that we can draw in three dimensions, many new possibilities open up. We've picked out two examples, but we could have added many others. If you start nosing around, you'll find VRML models of the solar system, of chemical compounds, and countless other previously mysterious objects of science.

The math zoo

If you're like us, you have a hard time telling your dodecahedra from your icosahedra, and when folks start truncating, stellating, snub-nosing, or doing whatever other cruel things that geometers do to polyhedra, you get completely confused. Lose no more sleep wondering what a truncated cuboctahedron looks like. The Geometry Center at the University of Minnesota has made VRML models of all the Platonic solids, plus many other solids that Plato probably never imagined. Rotate them, fly through them, or examine them any way you like at `http://www.geom.umn.edu/software/weboogl/zoo`.

VR Stats

For years, people have been trying to figure out the best way to present data in two-dimensional charts on paper. Three dimensions put us in a whole new ball game, and the first pitch has been tossed by VR Stats (`http://www. earthnews.com/personal/d.leconte/vrstat/vrs7d.wrl`).

In essence, VR Stats is a 3D bar chart showing the hit rate of a Web site by day and by hour for a week. That amount of data makes a 7-by-24 forest of bars. Behind and to the left of the bars are walls with 2D charts on them, showing what would happen if you averaged over one of the dimensions to get the average hit rate per hour of the day (on one wall) or the average hit rate per day of the week (on the other).

You can look at VR Stats for what it is, or you can look on it as a challenge: VRML means that a Web page is more than just a piece of paper or a screen to project our slides on. How can we use that third dimension to present information in a richer, more coherent way? For now, those presentations are likely to be 3D expansions of 2D ideas, like bar charts, pie charts, and graphs — just as the early movies were filmed plays, and the early TV shows were broadcasts of vaudeville acts. In time, however, the new medium is likely to come into its own in ways we can't imagine now.

Too cool not to mention

Some sites don't fit into any category but are still well worth your time.

The Unofficial Star Wars VRML Pages

Remember those kids in junior high whose basements were full of 10,000-piece models of the Starship Enterprise and the USS Lexington? Add a few years, substitute a Web site (`http://cbzoroms.uwsp.edu/vrml`) for a basement and VRML for plastic, and you've got Brian Zoromski. His *Star Wars* collection is awesome. Want to see what Darth Vader's mask looks like from the inside? Like to examine a 1MB model of the Millennium Falcon? Everything is there. We'd love to show you pictures, but our lawyers would have to have a long talk with George Lucas's lawyers first (George — if you're reading — hire this guy).

Be sure to check the size of a file before you load it. Brian's models tend to the large side, and if you don't have a lot of memory and a lot of time, you probably don't want to look.

For those of you who click the link to Brian's home page, the picture there is not Brian. It's Wacko from *Animaniacs*. We're told the resemblance is uncanny.

The MUDdy, Chatty Future

Someone once remarked that people will pay to see a dog walk on his hind legs, not because he does it well, but because he can do it at all. Many of the early VRML worlds on the Web have that dog-walking-on-his-hind-legs quality. The point is simply to show that something can be done, not to make something that is either beautiful or useful. But the novelty of VRML will eventually wear off, and people will start to ask, "What does this stuff help me do?"

We believe that the usefulness of VRML won't be fully apparent until it is well integrated with other computer media. The first steps in this direction have already been taken: Plug-ins allow VRML scenes to sit inside HTML pages. Models like the Castle of Bari and the Essex Campus are integrated into larger, multimedia information systems.

But the Internet is not just a library for storing information; it is also a communication tool. Many companies and individuals are working on making VRML part of a system in which you interact with other people. So far, we have seen two approaches for making this happen: one based on *Multi-User Domains* (affectionately known as *MUDs*) and the other based on chat rooms. In the MUD approach, people interact in a text-based world from which they have access to the Web in all its forms: HTML pages, images, sound files, or VRML worlds. In the chat room approach, a VRML world supplies the background in which people (represented by cartoonish characters called *avatars*) interact.

The two approaches will probably eventually merge into a Gibson-like cyberspace, but for now, they provide distinctly different experiences. They also embody two different paths for how cyberspace might develop. In the chat room approach, as pursued by Black Sun and Sony, designers create big new worlds that tempt people to enter. In the MUD approach, as pursued by Chaco, existing MUDs are provided with tools for upgrading their capabilities incrementally, bringing their user communities with them.

Chaco's Pueblo: Multimedia MUD

Multi-User Domains (originally Multi-User Dungeons because of their origin as online Dungeons and Dragons games) are virtual places that people anywhere in the world can log in to so that they can interact either with the place itself or with the other people who are there. Originally viewed just as game rooms, the MUD format is showing increasing flexibility: The same software that takes you to the castle of the High King for a medieval adventure can also take you to an online medieval history class or to an online meeting of the board of Medieval Inc., worldwide distributor of fine lances and shields.

Originally, all MUDs were text-based, meaning that communication is in written words: The host computer sends you descriptions of where you are and transcripts of what other people in the room are saying. For example, it may tell you, "You are at the gate of the castle. Three men with spears stand before the gate. One says, 'Declare yourself.'" You, in turn, type commands that tell the host computer what you want to do, such as, "Say, 'I am Prince Ari of Tivoli'."

Text-based worlds have a certain charm, and they will probably never go away completely, just as books have continued to be important even after the advent of radio and television. But Chaco's Pueblo opens up some very interesting new possibilities. In a Pueblo-enhanced MUD, users can not only read words in common, but they can see images, hear sounds, or browse Web pages — even

VRML Web pages. The entire MUD might be modeled as a VRML world. Or the MUD's overall structure might still be described in text, although certain particular objects are available for inspection as VRML files. An online geometry teacher, for example, may bring in VRML models of polyhedra from the Math Zoo for the class to examine. Or an online chemistry teacher may provide a VRML model of a benzene ring. An online business conference may have access to 3D graphs like VR Stats.

We provide Pueblo on the CD, but a detailed description of how to use it would take us a little beyond the scope of this book. Look for answers to your questions on Chaco's home page (`http://www.chaco.com`).

PointWorld as 3D chatroom

PointWorld (`http://www.pointcom.com/vrml/home.wrl`) takes VRML hotlists like Serch or the Palladio one better: It isn't just a VRML world that contains links to other VRML worlds on the Web. No, PointWorld is a VRML version of Point. It's an index of the whole Web, not just of VRML sites.

And what's more, if you use PointWorld's preferred browser, Black Sun's CyberGate, PointWorld turns into a place to hang out. (It also turns into a much prettier place. No other browser does justice to PointWorld's starry night sky. See Figure 6 of the color section.) You can meet another person and chat there, with the icons of the whole Web surrounding you.

You yourself are represented in PointWorld by an avatar — a toy-like icon that shows other CyberGate users where you are. They can hail you, trade notes with you, and so on. Other browsers can see the Web icons of PointWorld but not the avatars of the people who hang out there.

When we first heard of CyberGate, we figured it must be an online political scandal of some sort. But no, it's a VRML browser that you can use just like any other VRML browser (with extra chatting features). The version of CyberGate we played with was still a little buggy, but when it worked, it provided stunningly beautiful renderings. You can download it from Black Sun's Web site (`http://www.blacksun.com`).

Part II
Building Tools and Materials

The 5th Wave   By Rich Tennant

"Of course graphics are important to your Web page, Eddy, but I think it would've been better to scan a <u>picture</u> of your worm collection."

In this part . . .

Until recently, the only way you could create your own 3D world was to actually learn to write VRML. Writing VRML is fun if you happen to like computer languages, but we think most of the fun is in creating 3D worlds. Making 3D worlds by writing them in VRML is sort of like going into the woods with hand tools and building your own house. So we scanned the known universe looking for VRML power tools, and with the help of their creators, we put the best ones on our CD.

In this part, we begin by giving you an overview of how VRML works and by introducing our chosen tools. Our discussion of the language is just enough to show you why you probably don't want to write much VRML yourself, but it gives you enough basics so that you can tinker under the hood of the files that your tools generate. Then we get into the VRML builders in detail. Later, in Parts III and IV, we show you how to build worlds with these tools, and you can use these chapters as reference manuals. Finally, we give you some tips on shopping (or scrounging) for building materials and recycling used parts.

Chapter 6

Getting Oriented in Hyperspace

*I*f you've been lying awake at night asking yourself, "So what exactly is Virtual Reality Modeling Language (VRML) anyway, and how do I write it?" then you've turned to the right chapter. This one will put you to sleep in no time. No, no, we mean, here's where you turn for answers. In this chapter, we give you the big picture behind VRML and an overview of the tools that help you work in VRML.

If you've been sleeping just fine and you're the kind of person who learns best by just doing stuff, you should probably go directly to Part III of this book. Refer back here if and when you need the big picture.

First, let us put one misconception to rest. You don't actually have to understand VRML to create virtual reality worlds. Nope, you can just sketch your "castles in the air." How is this amazing feat performed? Well, by using some equally amazing programs, which we call *VRML builders*. These programs are tools that let you draw 3D worlds on your screen and then save those worlds as VRML files. In theory, you don't have to know diddly about VRML to use these tools. In this book, we're going to rely mainly on those tools to help you build your virtual worlds.

Even if you use these tools, knowing something about how VRML and VRML tools work is useful. VRML builders don't always do exactly what you'd like, and you may even need to do a little tinkering in VRML to make your world a better place. You also may need to use more than one tool to get the results you want, so in this book, we offer three ways to work on your VRML world:

  ✔ Using a builder that is excellent for buildings, rooms, doors, windows, and simple furnishings (Virtus Walkthrough Pro)

  ✔ Using a builder that is noted for being able to deliver complex objects, landscapes, surfaces, and special VRML features (Caligari Pioneer and Pioneer Pro)

  ✔ Using a text editor or word processor and having enough knowledge of VRML to tinker with the VRML file that results from using a builder

The first two ways — using VRML builders — are what we recommend and discuss the most. The third one — editing VRML directly — is for the adventuresome, the highly dedicated, the frustrated, or the just plain geeky at heart. This chapter starts with an overview of the builders used in this book and then gives you a little background on the VRML language itself. Sections of this book that get seriously into the language itself (or into editing VRML files as text) are marked with a Deep VRML icon to warn you.

You've probably heard of "leading edge" technologies — technologies on the forefront of what's happening. Well, VRML is what's called "bleeding edge" technology: so leading edge that you're likely to cut yourself regularly. At this stage in the life of VRML (an adolescent stage, by the looks of it) VRML browsers and builders usually work well, but sometimes they can still be frustrating. This situation is mostly the fault of the VRML specification being so new, and not of the tool vendors. We have tried to relieve some of the pain of using such a new technology, but you will still need patience.

How VRML Tools Work: The Basics

In Part I, we showed you how to explore 3D hyperspace (VRML worlds) with a browser or viewer. The following sections describe what's really going on when you browse, as well as provide information about how to start building and viewing your own VRML worlds.

How viewing VRML works

In Part I, you discovered that you can view VRML either on the Internet or from a file on your computer. When you browse VRML worlds, whether it is on the Internet or on your disk drive, several things happen:

1. You tell the Web browser to show you a VRML world.

  When you have a VRML file on your computer (which of course you do, thanks to our CD), you can view it with your VRML viewer-equipped Web browser just by opening the file with the File⇨Open command. When you are online on the Internet, you click a link to a VRML world with your Web browser, or type an URL, like `http://www.brightleaf.com/ vrml4dum/ squiddy.wrl` into the URL box.

2. **Your Web browser figures out that you want to look at a VRML world, not a regular Web document (in HTML), and calls in the VRML specialist: your chosen VRML viewing tool.**

   If the VRML world is a file on your computer, the Web browser figures this out by looking at the extension (file type): .WRL. If the world is online, the remote computer transmits a special code called a *MIME type* that the browser looks for. For VRML 1.0 files, the MIME type is called "x-world/ x-vrml," but you never see these words during transmission.

3. **The VRML viewing tool begins to read the VRML file and display it — often piece by piece.**

   The VRML world can take a long time to transmit over the Internet if it's a big file, so you have to wait a while before you can explore the world. A special feature in VRML called *inlining* helps by allowing the world to be transmitted a small piece at a time, as separate files. As the VRML viewing tool reads the initial file, it discovers references to these other files and begins to download them. In the meantime, it may display rectangular wire-frame shapes called *bounding boxes* to mark the location where these other objects appear. Surface details called *texture maps* may also take a while to appear when these techniques are used because they are being sent as separate files. Inlining is a feature that the creator of the world has to explicitly implement, and it isn't yet as widely used as it should be. We discuss how to do inlining in Chapter 17.

4. **You explore the virtual world.**

Once the main VRML world file and its associated *inlined* files have been transmitted, exploring that world is not much different from if you had opened the file with File⇨Open. Navigating the world is just as fast, and you can even disconnect from the Internet while you do so because the world is now on your computer.

One semi-mysterious event that you may see during exploration is that some distant objects may initially appear as rather simple shapes and get gradually more complex as you approach them. This is a VRML feature called *levels of detail* (LOD), which reduces the amount of unnecessary work the computer has to do. It's another feature that the VRML author has to explicitly implement, and we tell you how to do it in Chapter 17.

One big difference about exploring online (as opposed to exploring on your computer) is the ability to travel (or "teleport") to linked worlds. The big idea behind VRML is to create a giant, interlinked landscape of virtual worlds. So to accomplish this, the VRML wizards have designed VRML to allow hyperlinks (those things you click to go somewhere else in Web documents). In VRML worlds, however, you click linked objects — say, a virtual croissant — and *poof,* you are touring, say, a virtual Champs-Elysees! Clicking a linked object simply downloads another VRML file (or set of associated files). See Chapter 5 for some examples of these worlds.

All VRML tools, whether they are viewers, browsers, or builders, have a lot of work to do — possibly the most work of any program you run on your computer in terms of how much computer time, speed, and memory they require. VRML tools must construct a two-dimensional image on your screen that represents a three-dimensional world, like a camera does. In the process, they must take into account all the objects, their position and orientation, their properties and surface patterns, the lighting, the type and location of the camera, and more.

This process is called *rendering* and the less powerful the computer, the longer it takes. If it takes too long, you can't move very fast in your VRML world. The tool vendors put a lot of effort into their software so that rendering will run faster. Special hardware can help boost the rendering speed. Therefore, if you use a PC, you really need at least a 486 DX computer because it has a special fast-calculation capability (called a numeric coprocessor) built into its microprocessor. A "graphics accelerator" — a special hardware option that takes over the output of graphics to your monitor — also can make a big difference. Caligari, for example, will render faster if you have a graphics accelerator and driver software that uses Intel's *3DR* system for rendering. Matrox Millennium is one such accelerator.

How building VRML works

You can build VRML worlds by writing in that language with a word processor and saving your work as a text file — but you'd have to be an Einstein to create anything interesting. Humans of normal intelligence use VRML building programs, or *builders* for short.

One of the tasks a VRML builder must do, like VRML viewers, is rendering; otherwise, you can't see what you are creating. But builders' main job is to help you create the three-dimensional world by letting you draw it. They give you tools for creating shapes, modifying them, applying colors and surface patterns (textures), adding and positioning lights, and attaching shapes to each other.

This process is called *modeling,* and different vendors' programs take different approaches to the task. One vendor, Virtus, gives you features that allow you to easily create rooms and put furnishings in them. Another vendor, Caligari, provides features that let you make complex shapes with attractive surfaces and other properties. In either case, once you have created a 3D world using a VRML builder, you output the world as a VRML file.

When you use certain VRML builders, what you see on the builder's screen may not exactly be what you have in the VRML file. "Huh?" you say, and rightly so. Let us explain. Early versions of Virtus Walkthrough Pro, for example, do not read VRML files. They read Virtus files and models. (The version on our CD may be able to do so; we're hoping for a last-minute enhancement.) If you work with such a tool, you must save your work in its own, or *native,* file format if you ever intend to work on it again in that tool. Worlds stored in this format, however, may look a little different after they are converted to VRML. Once you are ready to see what your world looks like in VRML, you export the world to the VRML format and view it in a VRML viewer or browser.

Caligari's VRML builders, on the other hand, do read VRML as well as write it. Unlike many vendors' tools, they are combined builder/browsers: You can use them for viewing as well as building. You may still want to check your work periodically with one or more VRML viewers because they all do things a little differently.

Your VRML For Dummies toolbox

A lot of tools are hyped for creating virtual reality; only a few of them, however, do VRML. As VRML progresses, additional vendors are getting on the band-wagon who are good at things like animation, sound, and multimedia. For this book, however, we've chosen building tools from two vendors, Virtus and Caligari, that we think together offer the best available combination of simplic-ity, capability, and good results.

These tools will make more sense to you if you realize that the main business of both of these vendors is not VRML but 3D modeling and rendering, and some form of animation as well. This is mainly a business of making realistic-looking 2D pictures and videos. Modeling and rendering has traditionally been a very power-hungry and expensive task, and Caligari and Virtus have been pioneers in the lower-cost end of this profession. Both vendors are very different in their approach but extremely good at their main business, and they are adding VRML capability to their products.

The VRML builders on our CD are evaluation copies with a time-limited license and with no support included. (Don't call the vendors' support numbers.) They were the latest versions available when we printed this book, but VRML is moving fast. If you like the products, give the vendors a call and buy the current version. You'll get better VRML results and full documentation and support.

Following is a little overview of Virtus' and Caligari's products.

Virtus

Virtus building tools are fairly easy to use and are available for both Windows and Macintosh. Virtus offers two VRML building products, 3D Website Builder and Walkthrough Pro. 3D Website Builder is an inexpensive, easy-to-use, and generally delightful little builder. It lets you make rooms and furnish them by dragging and dropping furniture with all the carefree *joie de vivre* of the movers that handled your last move, but with less breakage. Walkthrough Pro is the professional-grade modeling and rendering product that Virtus has been making for years, recently upgraded for VRML. It does VRML but can do a heck of lot more that's not VRML, including creating video tours of virtual worlds. It will even do stereoscopic displays (like watching a 3D movie) if you would care to blow some serious money on a special monitor!

Since we're relying on Virtus for the Mac users, we decided to cover the more powerful Walkthrough Pro in this book rather than 3D Website Builder. You'll find a special *Dummies*-only 90-day evaluation copy of Walkthrough Pro on our CD and a great coupon deal for buying the product in the back of the book. (Note that this product is NOT Walkthrough VRML, a laudably early but limited Virtus effort that appeared in the dark ages of VRML — a year or so ago.)

Virtus products come with galleries of objects in Virtus format with which to populate your world, and we've included a small sample on the CD. Virtus products have a particularly easy-to-understand user interface for beginners working in 3D, with features that make both moving around and looking around easy, that help you orient things in space, and that help you control the exact size of objects in your world.

Caligari

Caligari's Pioneer and Pioneer Pro products (which run under Windows only) can read and write VRML, and they also offer advanced capabilities in several areas: complex shapes, surfaces, inlining, levels of detail, and an increasing number of advanced VRML features such as spatial audio.

Pioneer is Caligari's get-you-interested product. It's on our CD (in time-limited form) but can also be downloaded from Caligari's Web site (`http://www.caligari.com`). You can hook it up to your browser and use it for viewing VRML on the Internet — then just click a button and *zap!* It's a builder! (It's a bit better as a builder than as a viewer, though.) Pioneer's ability to read VRML files and import a variety of 3D objects allows you to take advantage of existing 3D resources on the Internet and use VRML-specific features we discuss in this book, such as levels of detail, inlining, and hyperlinks, which make VRML worlds easier and more fun to use on the Internet.

Pioneer Pro is Caligari's VRML product for professional developers. It includes object saving, Boolean adding and subtracting of shapes, additional shape-building tools, more viewing windows, more precise control over dimensions and locations, and other niceties that become essentials when you try to do this stuff for a living. Pioneer Pro is also on our CD in a time-limited evaluation form.

Pioneer and Pioneer Pro let you import shapes in other formats besides Caligari and VRML. These formats include DXF (Drawing eXchange Format, a common 3D format originated by AutoDesk, the makers of AutoCAD); 3D Studio (files with lots of scene information like VRML, also from AutoDesk); Wavefront (a long-time vendor of 3D modeling and rendering software, which mainly runs on

UNIX workstations); LightWave (another popular vendor); and Imagine. Pioneer also lets you use 2D files to enhance your world: You can make 3D shapes by extruding 2D PostScript files into a third dimension, and you can use Windows JPEG (.JPG) image files to create realistic surfaces through texture mapping.

If you want to explore the really jazzy end of modeling, rendering, and animation, check out the demo version of Caligari's trueSpace 2 on our CD. Pioneer and Pioneer Pro are very closely related to trueSpace 2 and are clearly derived from it. This tool can do some of the amazing stuff you see on TV or in the movies, such as dancing credit cards and scenes like those in the movie *Toy Story* (but simpler). The tool has a time-limited license, though, so if you get hooked by it, you'll need to lay out some cash to keep going.

You can use trueSpace 2 to create a scene in trueSpace .SCN format, read it into Pioneer Pro, add VRML features like links, inlining, and levels of detail, and export the scene as VRML.

Deciding which tool you need

Three things determine which vendor's tools you'll want to use:

- ✔ Your computer (PC or Mac)

- ✔ How fancy you need to get in terms of shapes, surfaces, and special VRML features

- ✔ Whether you prefer to work in 3D (perspective) views or in top views and side views

If you are working on a PC, you may want to use both vendors' tools for the best results. By starting with Virtus, creating a VRML file, and then moving on to Caligari for fancier shapes and special VRML features, you can get the best of both worlds. If you are working on a Mac, your choice is Virtus.

For simple shapes and buildings, Virtus' products are easier to use than Caligari's. Virtus' commercial product gives you a nice, well-organized library of furnishings and other objects as well, so you don't have to reinvent the wheel— just load it into your world. Virtus keeps things simple, so your VRML worlds and shapes tend to be simple.

If your imagination runs to things like, say, virtual squid or other complex shapes, or if you want the best control over surface appearances, Caligari has the edge. Caligari also has some of the best support for advanced VRML features. We have included a bunch of prebuilt Caligari objects on our CD, so you don't have to build everything from scratch in Pioneer, either.

Working on 3D shapes in a non-3D environment (your computer screen) is tricky. Some people are comfortable creating objects using a top view and front view — sort of like the views called *orthogonal views* you see on architectural blueprints or floor-plan layouts. Other people prefer creating objects in a perspective view. If you're the engineering type who prefers using orthogonal views and you like to create things with very precise dimensions, you'll probably find Virtus' products more comfortable to use than Caligari's. If you're the artistic kind of person who would build VRML worlds using modeling clay if you could, you'll probably prefer Caligari's user interface, which tends to favor using natural perspective views. Both vendors offer both orthogonal and perspective views in their professional products, however.

The licenses for some of the tools we've included are for personal use only, meaning that you can't use them to do work for commercial Web sites. Also, some of them are early (or even *beta* — meaning "still being tested") copies, so they are not without a few flaws. Read the file OUR_CD.TXT on our CD, or load OUR_CD.HTM into your Web browser, for details.

Writing and editing VRML as text

You can, if you like, just forget about all these cool building tools and create your worlds by writing VRML as text. More likely, however, the only reason you might resort to writing VRML as text will be that you need to edit your VRML files. VRML files are just ASCII text, so you can write or edit them with any word processor or text editor. Write or WordPad on the PC will generally do the job, as will TeachText or other text editors on the Mac. (To examine Virtus VRML files on the PC, Write or WordPad works best.) Just launch your word processor or text editor and then open the VRML file with the File⇨Open command.

After you're finished, make sure that the word processor saves the file as text. Use File⇨Save As if you're not sure how the word processor will save the file; choose Text as the file type in the dialog box that appears, or preferably Text with Line Breaks, if that's an option.

Of course, the tricky part is in the middle: actually knowing how to write or edit VRML. We don't expect most of our readers to do a lot of actual VRML manipulation — and the ones who do are probably already pretty clever about languages in general. So we give you some background, some examples, some tips, and, on the CD, the specification for the language — enough so that the novices can do what's necessary and the experienced programmers can figure out the rest. Where we do delve into the language, you'll see a Deep VRML icon.

Virtual Ingredients

Virtual worlds are the sum of their ingredients. As the virtual chef, you should be aware of the principal ingredients available to build your virtual world, as follows:

  ✔ **Shapes:** Shapes make up the objects in your virtual world. They consist of 3D polygons — some regular shapes like cubes, 2D text, and irregular shapes. By combining and modifying shapes, you can create darn near anything, from coffee mugs to candelabra.

✔ **Surfaces:** Unless you do something to the surfaces of shapes, shapes are boring gray lumps. Who wants to watch boring gray lumps? If we do, we already have congressional representatives on C-SPAN. No, for real visual excitement you at least want to give your lumps some color, some transparency, maybe a little shine, or maybe apply some patterns or other images to the surface. Applying images to surfaces is also called *texture mapping;* using texture mapping is sort of like applying simulated wood-grain shelf paper to your kitchen shelves, but less sticky.

✔ **Lights:** If anything is more boring than gray lumps, it's gray lumps in the dark; so you'll want some lights. Most VRML tools automatically provide some ambient light that lights everything uniformly, but that's not exactly scintillating either. VRML lets you put in several different types of lights, including point sources (radiating uniformly in all directions, sort of like a light bulb), directional lights (radiating in a given direction), and spotlights.

✔ **Camera:** VRML tools are very much like a TV studio: They give you an environment in which you can create and arrange objects, and then they help you generate two-dimensional pictures of those objects. The images that you see on your screen are as they are seen through the camera. In VRML, you can even have a camera that gives you views you'd never see in real life: *orthogonal* views, like what you see in blueprints or engineering drawings. Normally, however, you use a *perspective* view camera, which produces pictures much like those of a real-life camera.

✔ **Action:** VRML 1.0 doesn't let you do action — that is, animate objects, cameras, or viewpoints. Many people are working on animation, and it will be part of VRML 2.0. Right now, some browsers will crudely animate a scene if the animation information is stored in the vendor's own, unofficial VRML *extensions* (additions to the VRML language). But, officially, you can't do animation in VRML 1.0. We discuss animation in Part VI.

✔ **Links:** In the same way that you can have a link to another document or an audio or video file in a Web page, you can have links in a VRML world too. When the person viewing the scene clicks a linked object, that link is activated and the person receives . . . whatever! It could be another VRML world, a Web document, or an audio or video file. If it's another VRML world, this action is called *teleporting.*

✔ **Sound:** VRML allows you to create links to audio files, and in addition, some tool vendors are offering 3D sound extensions, which cause the sound volume to vary with distance and even give directional cues by using stereo speakers.

✔ **Viewpoints:** Viewpoints are locations specified by the world builder (you) from which the user can (but doesn't have to) view the scene. Although viewpoints aren't officially part of the VRML 1.0 specification, they are being used in VRML files and browsers.

✔ **Groups:** Groups allow shapes to be grouped together into more complex objects so that you can do something with all of them at once. For instance, if you create a virtual Mr. Potato Head, you will want to be able to move and rotate the entire head and not leave the eyes, the nose, and the lips dangling in space.

The Reality behind the Scenery

Virtual worlds are made up of files — in particular, they are made up of one or more VRML files plus, occasionally, some image files. (VRML files are also called WRL files because of the three-letter extension, .*WRL,* that appears at the end of the filename).

One of the first things to understand about how VRML files work is that — like certain politicians — they don't actually do any work at all. They just sit there and let your VRML browser or viewer do all the work. VRML files are really *scene description files* that specify the details of what shapes, surfaces, lights, and other elements are present in your world. The browser or viewer has to translate these details into an image on your screen.

VRML — the language

The computer world is a regular tower of Babel when it comes to languages. Most people have used or at least heard of general-purpose programming languages like BASIC or C or FORTRAN. But other, more special-purpose types of language exist as well. VRML is in a class of languages sometimes called *description languages.*

If you have created documents for the World Wide Web, you probably know something about the *page description language* called HTML (HyperText Markup Language). HTML describes a two-dimensional (2D) world: a flat page of text, graphics, and links to other text and graphics. VRML is sometimes called the 3D counterpart of HTML.

Unlike HTML, however, VRML is very difficult to write, at least for scenes of any useful complexity. For that reason, you need VRML builders. In that sense, VRML is actually more like PostScript than it is like HTML. PostScript is a page description language that describes 2D (flat) images line by line and pixel by pixel. This is such a complicated job that no human ever actually writes PostScript. Instead, programs like word processors and drawing programs create PostScript files and send them to printers that can read these files. Few humans ever bother to — or need to — read a PostScript file, although they can.

Likewise, in a perfect world, none of use would ever have to muck around in VRML — we would just use our nifty building tools. The world, however — like virtual worlds — is not a perfect place, so if you want the best results, you may occasionally have to strap on your waders and write a little VRML.

A mercifully brief look inside a VRML file

Just to kill off any lingering curiosity you may have about VRML as a language, let's take a brief peek at it. Inside a VRML file is text (ASCII text, to be precise). You can write, look at, and modify text in a VRML file with any word processor or text editor (like Write or WordPad on the PC or TeachText on the Mac).

Following is a very simple example of a VRML 1.0 file, just to give you a taste. (To really understand what's going on in this sample, you need to refer to the VRML specification on our CD and the Deep VRML sections of this book. But, as we said in the beginning of this chapter, a detailed understanding of VRML is optional.) You can, if you like, write this file with a word processor, save it as a text file with an extension of .WRL, and then view it with a VRML browser.

```
#VRML V1.0 ascii
# Here's a sample file we created. The first line is a
          "header" and every VRML
# file has to have one. Elsewhere, text that follows a #
          symbol is a comment, and
# doesn't affect the scene.
# The Separator statement associates things that appear with
          its curly braces.
# Below, it associates a "material" (a color) with an object:

Separator {
   Material {
      #The Material statement can specify color and other
          surface effects.
      diffuseColor .5 .5 1.0   # The 3 numbers are for red,
          green, and blue
      }              # values. In this case, the color is light
                     # blue.
   Cube {
      # A Cube is one of the shapes VRML supports, although
          it's really rectangular
      # since the sides don't have to be all the same size.
      width 1
      height 1
      depth 1
      }
   }
```

The preceding code is a pretty boring example that creates a blue cube and provides no lights. Your VRML browser may or may not provide lighting automatically — if it doesn't, be prepared for a lot of boring blackness when you try to view this file!

Wading into deep VRML

Okay — see that Deep VRML icon? That should be a warning flag for all you normal folks out there who are content to just build cool 3D virtual reality worlds and leave the technical stuff to the engineers. You guys should skip this section altogether.

For you other folks who — bless your geeky little hearts — intend to understand something about the guts of VRML, here beginneth the deep waters. Put on your waders and keep your eye out for more sections like this one with the Deep VRML icon. To start, we're going to give you an overview of the structure and nomenclature of a VRML file, referring to the preceding simple example.

As we write this, the VRML standard is in its childhood: Version 1.0(c). It is, however, approaching adolescence (VRML 2.0) when we expect it to get surly and start demanding the car keys. We will focus on VRML 1.0 in this book since it's cuter, and most tools will work with VRML 1.0 for the forseeable future. The VRML specification is on our CD, and you can also find it on the Web at `http://vag.vrml.org`. VRML 2.0 will follow a proposal called Moving Worlds, so look for references to that name at `vag.vrml.org` for more information. You can also find it at `http://webspace.sgi.com/moving-worlds/`.

All VRML 1.0 files begin with the same first line: *#VRML V1.0 ascii* — and from there get a lot more complicated. Note that except for that first line, anything that falls between a # sign and the end of the line is a comment for humans to read and doesn't affect the scene.

The building block of VRML language is the *node*. There are different officially-named types of nodes, such as *Separator, Material,* and *Cube* in the earlier example. Each node begins with its type name, which has its initial letter capitalized and has a pair of squiggly brackets (also called *curly braces*) like these: { }. Inside the braces are *fields* that give the particulars for a specific node. The whole set of nodes that define a world is called a *graph*.

The fields within the braces provide detail. For example, you can't just say "display a cube"; you have to say how big it is. Within the Cube node, for example, fields define the dimensions. Another example of fields is within the Material node, where fields define a particular type of color called *diffuseColor*. Field names begin with lowercase letters.

For standard VRML nodes, all browsers are supposed to know what kind of fields go with what kinds of nodes. They are all, for instance, supposed to know that when they see a Cube node, they should look for fields named height, width, and depth. If you use a non-standard VRML node in a WRL file, you must tell the browser what fields to expect. You do this by first defining the name and type of the field in square brackets. So if you see the term *fields* followed by square brackets, that's what's going on: A nonstandard VRML extension is being defined.

Quite often, there are nodes within nodes, just as the Material and Cube nodes are within the braces for the Separator term in our example. When this occurs, the Material and Cube nodes are called *children* of that particular Separator node). This containment is how the VRML browser handles things belong together; in this example, the Material (a blue color) applies to the Cube and not to some other shape that may appear outside of the Separator braces. Some nodes, like Separator, exist for the sole purpose of grouping other terms together and are therefore called *group nodes,* logically enough.

Since there can be many nodes of the same kind in a file, each instance of a node may have a personal name assigned to it by the VRML builder in order to distinguish one node from another. The names are assigned by preceding a node, *Separator,* for example, with the word *DEF* followed by a name, as in *DEF CUBE001 Separator {...}*. This term lets you do things to that cube by name rather than by pointing at the cube. For instance, the object list in Pioneer lets you select objects by their node name rather than by pointing and clicking.

There are three kinds of nodes in VRML 1.0:

- ✓ **Shape nodes:** In VRML version 1.0, the fundamental shapes include AsciiText, Cone, Cube, Cylinder, and Sphere. For more complex shapes, VRML has IndexedFaceSet node (a shape made up of faces or facets, like pieces of cardboard glued together at the edges); an IndexedLineSet node (a shape defined by its edges); and a PointSet node (a collection of points). Future VRML versions may contain other shapes as well.

- ✓ **Properties:** Properties describe what a shape looks like and where it exists in the world. The simplest example of a property is the Material property, which tells what color or surface patterns (like wallpaper) a set of shapes exhibit, and how that color or pattern is attached (or *bound*) to the shape or shapes. (The Material property appears in the preceding example, where it specifies a light blue color.) Other properties specify where a shape is located and how it is rotated in your virtual world, what sort of lighting is present and where, and through what sort of camera the scene is being viewed.

- ✓ **Groupings:** Groupings help connect things together. One of their important roles is to allow VRML to connect a Property (say, color) to a shape (such as a cube). The Separator type of grouping, for example, appears in the VRML code earlier in this chapter, where it connects a color to a cube. Groupings also allow shapes to be grouped together into more complex objects so that you can do something with all of them at once. The Separator node is perhaps the most important and common grouping, as it also isolates one set of objects from another. For example, to keep the rotation or scaling applied to one object from affecting another, the two objects are kept in different Separator nodes.

The VRML browser processes all this stuff in this way:

As the browser reads down the file, it maintains a certain "state" that is made up of all the properties that can be applied to objects. When it encounters an object, it applies that state to the object. So at some point, the state might include, say, the color green, a 45-degree twist around the X axis, and an offset of 5 units in the upward direction. When the browser next encounters an object, it colors it green, twists it 45 degrees around the X axis, and moves it 5 units in the +Z direction. If it encounters another object, it does the same to that one.

If the browser encounters new state information, it just modifies the current state. Some state settings, such as color, are replaced by the new information. Other state settings — in particular the so-called "transform" settings of location, orientation, and scale — are cumulatively modified. So if a new statement adds a Z motion after an earlier Z motion, the two motions add up.

Group nodes help keep this current state under control. Within a Separator node, for instance, any changes to the state (say, color or position) only apply to things that follow within the node. How does that work? First, when the browser encounters a Separator node, it makes a mental note of the current state. When the browser first begins to read the contents of the Separator node, the state is unchanged. So if the current state is "five units in the +Z direction" before the separator node began, any additional movements within the separator add to the situation. This is why child nodes (nodes within nodes) are said to inherit from their parent nodes. After the node ends, the browser consults its mental note about the original state and returns the state to its original condition, throwing away any changes that took place inside the Separator.

Finally, a word about formatting: Even though our example is nicely indented to show which terms are contained within other terms' braces, VRML code doesn't have to look that pretty to work. As with C, C++, and other programming languages, the line ends, spaces, indentations, and other formatting are ignored by the program that displays the scene. The formatting just makes it easier for humans to read.

Chapter 7

Veni, Vidi, Vici — Virtus

*R*emember that famous Roman dude who said, "I came, I saw, I conquered" ("Veni, Vidi, Vici")? Talk about immediate gratification! Although Virtus Walkthrough Pro probably won't give you quite the same thrill, it is big on immediate gratification.

This product is not Walkthrough *VRML*, an early attempt by Virtus to create a VRML tool, which (probably because VRML was so new) suffered from poor VRML export. Walkthrough Pro is a professional-grade 3D modeling and rendering tool, and one of the few to run on both the Macintosh and the PC.

This chapter is your *Dummies* reference manual for Virtus Walkthrough Pro, one of the two main tools we show you for VRML world building (and the only builder in this book for Mac-based folks). This chapter is tool-oriented, in contrast to Parts III and IV of this book, where we take a task-oriented approach to using Walkthrough Pro (and Caligari's Pioneer). This chapter is where to turn when you're wondering, "What's that gizmo for?" or "How do I use that tool again?" when you're in Walkthrough Pro.

About Walkthrough Pro on our CD

The good news is that we've arranged to include the very latest software in this book. The bad news is that because it is the very latest software, as we write we don't know exactly how the installation process will go! So see the file OUR_CD.TXT on our CD or load OUR_CD.HTM into your Web browser to read about installation.

Like most of the software on our CD, the copy of Walkthrough Pro we've included with this book is an evaluation copy, valid for 90 days, and licensed with certain restrictions. Among the restrictions is that you may not call Virtus for support. Read Virtus's license agreement on the CD for more details. But more importantly, we have arranged with Virtus to include a coupon for a substantial discount in the back of the book! Remember that VRML is changing fast. If you like the version of Walkthrough Pro on the CD, you will probably appreciate the latest, fully supported version.

Features Overview

Walkthrough Pro offers a range of different features to help you build a great world in VRML. Among them are the following:

- Multiple views, including views from all six sides and a perspective "walk" view
- A variety of 2D shape-creation tools and multiple ways to "inflate" them into 3D
- "Infinite" light sources
- An Observer that sets the initial viewpoint the user sees when browsing your world
- Painting on entire objects or on individual faces
- Painting of colored shapes on surfaces
- Texture mapping on objects or surfaces and output of "inlined" texture files
- Import of 2D images to serve as drawing guides or "templates"
- Export to DXF, a common 3D format used in computer-aided design
- Linking of URLs to objects

For the Macintosh, Virtus recommends you use a Centris, Quadra, Power Macintosh, or 68040-based PowerBook with 8MB or more of RAM and System 7.1 or later. Any PowerBook will do, however, and System 6.0.5 will suffice.

For the PC, Virtus recommends an 80486-based or Pentium system with 8MB or more of RAM and Microsoft Windows 3.1 or later, plus a VGA or Super VGA grapics adapter. An 80386 PC with 8MB of RAM will suffice, however.

Following is a more detailed look at the principal features of Walkthrough Pro.

Views

Virtus takes the scenic route to VRML building, providing you lots of *views* of your work in progress. Two principal kinds of views exist, each in its own window just as you see in Figure 7-1.

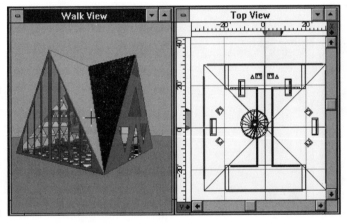

Figure 7-1:
Views in scenic Walkthrough: Walk View and Design View (Top).

✔ **Walk View:** A cool, realistic, 3D-looking perspective view for viewing only (you never create anything in Walk View). The view is what's seen through a virtual camera held by a virtual Observer (whom we sometimes call *Cyrano* because of his long nose), whose position and viewing direction you control.

✔ **Design Views:** So called because these views are where you design the shapes that you want. These views are not in perspective, but, like the views you have probably seen in floor plans and blueprints (sometimes called *orthogonal* views), they show you your world from any of six sides.

Generally, you want one Design View (for example, the Top View) window and the Walk View window open while designing things. You can have as many view windows open as you like, however; each shows the same set of objects from a different viewpoint. Also, a *Tumble Editor* window offers a view from any angle, not just from one of six sides, and a *Surface Editor* lets you view and work on any of the individual surfaces that make up an object.

Tool pads

The Design and Walk Views have their own unique *tool pads,* which appear in sepa-rate windows that float around on your computer screen. Only one tool pad appears at a time: When you switch between a Design window to a Walk window or one of the editor windows, the tool pad changes accordingly (as does the menu bar). The tool pads of both the Design and Walk Views appear together (by special arrangement with their talent agents) in Figure 7-2. The Tumble and Surface editors also have tool pads very similar to the Design tool pad.

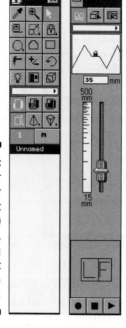

Figure 7-2:
Tools for designing or walking (left to right) appear, depending on what you're doing.

The Design Views have the most tools, naturally, because they are like work-shops where you build your shapes, and any good workshop is full of tools. The Design View tool pad is on the left in Figure 7-2. For details on the tools of this view, see "Tools for industry" later in this chapter.

The Walk View is mainly for looking, not building, so one of the functions of its tool pad is to let you zoom in and out with the Observer's camera. (The Walk View tool pad is on the right in Figure 7-2.) At the top, it also provides buttons that can select an object or work on an individual object surface in the Surface Editor. At the bottom is a so-called Orientation Cube that tells you which sides of the shape you are looking at (left, right, front, back, top, bottom). At the very bottom, the tool pad provides a neat (but non-VRML) feature: recording and playing back animated fly-throughs. For details on these tools, see "These tools are made for walkin'" later in this chapter.

Editors

Editors are special tools for doing special tasks (as authors, we think editors are very special). Walkthrough provides three editors, which you arouse by clicking their icons in the tool pad of any Design View:

- ✔ The Tumble Editor helps you rotate your view around objects in space and lets you chop pieces off them. (The block icon takes you to the Tumble Editor.)

- ✔ The Surface Editor lets you change the appearance of each individual flat surface that makes up a shape, adding color and changing the transparency. (The wall icon takes you to the Surface Editor.)

- ✔ The Lighting Editor lets you add and position light sources of various types and colors. (The light bulb icon brings you to the Lighting Editor.)

Each of these editors works in its own separate window and has its own special tool pad.

Objects

With Walkthrough Pro, life appears hollow — but certainly not meaningless. When you navigate through Walkthrough objects or within them, they appear hollow, as if they were made of infinitely thin cardboard.

Walkthrough objects also live a regulated life, and as their creator, you must be aware of the rules by which they live. The rules are

- ✔ **No dimples:** Objects cannot be concave (although you can create concavity by joining objects at their surfaces). Walkthrough simply won't let you create concave shapes, even though VRML will accept them quite happily.

- ✔ **No flatworld objects:** Every object you make has thickness whether you want it to or not. You can't create lines or planes (except for the planes that Walkthrough Pro uses to form the faces of an object).

- ✔ **Surfaces have independent sides:** Each of the surfaces that makes up a Walkthrough Pro object has two independent sides that you can paint on — just like the real world. Unlike the real world, one of the "paints" you can apply to a surface is transparency, and just because a surface is transparent in one direction does not mean it is transparent in the other direction. Walkthrough Pro's Surface Editor lets you control which side of a surface is transparent.

It's Virtus, but is it VRML?

Walkthrough Pro is a cool tool that gives you great results, fast. It has just a few limitations in terms of its VRML support. Some of the limitations are (in order of how much you probably care) as follows:

- ✔ **Sculpted or concave objects:** Walkthrough doesn't allow concave (dimpled) objects, although they are allowed in VRML. Also, Walkthrough creates 3D objects by "inflating" 2D objects in one of three simple ways: straight, pointed, or rounded. From a practical standpoint, these constraints limit your ability to do complex shapes and surfaces.

- ✔ **Surface attributes:** VRML lets you say exactly how reflective, radiant, rough, and transparent a surface looks. Walkthrough Pro gives you color settings, texture mapping, and three degrees of transparency, but stops there.

- ✔ **Object inlining:** This feature helps you break up larger worlds into a bunch of files to make downloading the world from the Web more pleasant.

- ✔ **Levels of detail:** Used for large worlds, this feature allows simple shapes to represent distant, more complex pieces of the world.

- ✔ **Alternative viewpoints:** You can't currently set up multiple viewing locations that the user can choose while viewing your world. You can, however, set up the important main viewpoint that the user sees when initially browsing your world. It is determined by the location and orientation of the Walkthrough Observer (whom we call Cyrano).

Walkthrough Pro has certain advanced capabilities that work just fine in Walkthrough's Walk view but just won't show up when you export to VRML. Collision detection, for example, is an optional feature of Walkthrough Pro and of some browsers — but it's not part of the VRML file.

Tasty Selections from the Menus

Many of the selections on the Walkthrough Pro menu bar are the same ones you know and love from Windows or your Mac. Some of the selections only appear when you are using certain views or editors, so we discuss those menu selections in those sections of this chapter. Following are a few of the basic menu selections, as recommended by your Maitres d'Software, Doug and Dave (us).

File menu

The File menu has your usual stuff for opening, closing (without saving), and saving a file, and starting a new one. Here are a few special items of note, however:

- ✔ **Save:** Saves your work in a special Virtus format. This format is *not* VRML, but you should save your work in this format anyway because it preserves everything in your Walkthrough Pro world. In the Save dialog box, there is a choice of "linking" or "embedding" textures; we recommend you stay with the default, "Link Textures (use less disk space)".

- ✔ **Import Trace Layer:** If you have a drawing or photograph of some object in a PICT, BMP, 2D DXF, or TIFF file format, you can import it and scale it and then "trace over" it using Virtus drawing tools. This is great for constructing buildings from floor plans, machines from computer-aided design drawings, or complex objects from top-view or side-view sketches or scanned-in photographs.

- ✔ **Export⇨VRML:** Using this command is how you get a VRML file. There are several important options in the Export VRML dialog box:

  - • Do Not Export Textures / Export Textures Links: These alternatives determine whether or not Walkthrough saves your texture mapping in VRML (by generating an inlined texture file). We suggest you choose Export Textures Links.

  - • Export Textures As: This option determines what graphics file format Walkthrough uses to store your texture image. You can choose JPEG or BMP (PICT on the Mac), but we recommend using JPEG. (It doesn't matter what kind of graphics file you used for your texture mapping or where it is located; Walkthrough generates the texture file you need and places it in the same directory as your VRML file.)

  - • Skip Opaque Surface Features: Choose this option only if you want to reduce your file size somewhat by omitting any non-transparent surface features that were applied using the Surface Editor. This option is mainly useful when you have imported complex Virtus models that have lots of detailed surface features, and you consider them unnecessary in your VRML file.

- ✔ **Export⇨DXF 3D:** DXF is a standard format for 2D and 3D shapes that many 3D programs can read; it does not communicate color or surface features, however. (Exporting to DXF 3D is a good way to get a Virtus shape into Pioneer; for multiple shapes, put each shape on a different Virtus "layer.") In the Export Options dialog box that appears, choose Line Termination according to the kind of computer you will use to read the DXF file (choose PC for Pioneer). Other choices in this dialog box are less important, but for Surface Type, sometimes 3DFACE gives better results than POLYLINE.

- ✔ **Snapshot:** Creates a BMP (on Windows) or PICT (on the Mac) file containing the image of the active window.

✔ **Revert to saved:** This command is not a religious instruction for the fallen but simply a way to reload your file as it was (before you messed things up badly).

✔ **Library:** The Library command allows you to open a Virtus model library, a program from which you can select and extract models. Just choose Edit⇨Copy to copy a model you're viewing and then switch back to Walkthrough and use Edit⇨Paste to insert the model.

Edit menu

The edit menu has all the usual stuff for copying, cutting, pasting, and deleting that you know from other Windows or Mac programs. Here, of course, the commands apply to cool 3D objects instead of boring text or flat graphics! Here are a few ringers you may not recognize:

✔ **Duplicate:** Rather than copy and paste an object, just select it and choose the Edit⇨Duplicate command.

✔ **Modify Selected:** If you don't care for the tool pad, use this command to make changes using a menu. It also lets you do a few things that the tool pad doesn't, such as flip things over, undo rotation, skew, scale, and change the number of sides in a regular polygon.

✔ **Hide Selected and Hide All:** When objects get in your way, don't delete them; just select them and use Hide Selected. Use Show All to bring 'em back. If they are all getting annoying, use Hide All.

✔ **Lock Selected and Lock All:** Locking protects you from accidentally changing things you spent hours making. Protect your valuables by locking them. Use Unlock All if you need to change them after all.

✔ **Preferences:** See "Have It Your Way: Preferences and Defaults" later in this chapter.

View menu

You'll be chowing down on the View menu frequently in order to get new Design Views. Some other amusing dishes are here too. The full list appears when your active window is a Design View; Walk has an abbreviated list.

✔ **Change View:** Whatever your active window is, this command lets you change the view that it displays: Walk View or any of the six Design Views — or use Opposite to switch from Top to Bottom, Front to Back, or Left to Right.

✔ **New View:** Opens a new window with your chosen view displayed.

✔ **Home:** Home is not where the heart is, but any point in space you define. Default is at eye level (Z=5' 6") at X=0, Y=0. (Isn't everyone 6 feet tall?) You can (a) set Home or (b) go Home using the following commands:

- **Set Home to Editor:** Places Home at 0,0 in the two axes of your current Design View (the third axis remains unchanged).

- **Set Home to Observer:** Places Home where your Observer is.

- **Home Editor:** Places the center (0,0) of your Design View at Home.

- **Home Observer:** Moves your Observer to the Home position (the Observer's viewing direction does not change, though).

- **Center Observer:** Nothing to do with Home, this command puts your Observer in the center of your active Design View.

- **Reset Origin:** You can move your origin points (0,0) in Design Views; this command sets them to true 0,0 in the axes of your world.

- **Level Observer:** Removes any tilt (up, down, left, or right) from the Observer's head.

Window menu

Walkthrough is pretty window intensive. Because of the multiple views you need for designing things, you often need several windows on your screen at once. Sometimes Walkthrough is a real "pane" as a result (rim shot, please), so you need some Window commands to help you along.

The menu has the usual window controls that you expect in a Windows or Mac program, including the usual list of currently open windows that you can make active, plus the following:

✔ **Tools Window:** Choose this option to turn on or off the tool pad for your currently active window.

✔ **Depth Window:** Choose this option to display a depth gauge for the Design window that's currently active (the gauge lets you specify *inflation depth* for the shapes you create).

✔ **Coordinates Window:** Choose this option for a display of cursor location and measurements.

Walk View

The Walk View is the cool, realistic view of your world. When you first start up Walkthrough Pro, it is one of the two views presented to you. If you close the Walk View window and later need to get it back, choose Window⇨New View⇨Walk View from the menu bar.

Walk this way, please

One of the most fun and useful things to do is to navigate around in the world you are building using the Walk View. To do so, in the middle of the Walk View window, find the skinny crosshairs (sort of a gray plus sign with white tips). Then move around:

Forward and back motions:

- ✔ **To move forward:** Click and hold above the crosshairs.
- ✔ **To back up:** Click and hold below the crosshairs.

Left and right motions:

- ✔ **To turn your view:** Click and hold to the left or right of the crosshairs (like turning your head).
- ✔ **To slide your viewing position:** Hold down the Ctrl key (Option key on the Mac) while clicking and holding to the left or right of the crosshairs. This motion is like shuffling your feet left or right while looking straight ahead.
- ✔ **To tilt your view:** Hold down the Shift key while clicking and holding to the left or right of the crosshairs. This motion is like tilting your head to the left or right.

Up and down motions:

- ✔ **To look up:** Hold down the Shift key while clicking above or below the crosshairs. (Beware of pigeons. Keep your mouth closed.)
- ✔ **To rise up:** Hold down the Ctrl key, or on the Mac, the Option key, while clicking above or below the crosshairs.

Those are the basic moves. Here are a few advanced tips for navigating around in Walk View:

- ✔ **No place like home:** If your cameraperson (the Observer — the little round-headed guy with the long nose who appears in Design Views) gets utterly lost, choose View➪Home Observer from the menu bar. Walkthrough keeps track of a location called *home,* and this command puts the Observer there. You can change your Home to any location by moving the Observer and choosing View➪Set Home to Observer.
- ✔ **Keep a level head:** If the navigation controls seem to move you in the wrong direction, or you end up looking at the sky, try choosing View➪Level Observer. Sometimes Cyrano — the Observer — seems to get a crick in his virtual neck, and this virtual chiropractor straightens it out.

✔ **Speed:** To move faster, click farther away from the crosshairs. If the speed is too slow, choose Walk⇨Fast from the menu bar (choose Faster or Fastest instead if it's still too slow). At faster speeds, Walkthrough gives up transparency, and at the fastest speed, it gives up coloring your drawing (filling it in). It just gives you a skeletal-looking, transparent, "wireframe" view, which is faster to draw. (The little guy with the crayola crayons inside your computer can go on break.)

If you have set Walkthrough to the lowest possible speed and it's still too fast, try setting the Units in File⇨Preferences to smaller units.

✔ **Shift vs. Ctrl:** To remember the difference between using Shift and Ctrl (or Option), just say to yourself, "Sliding out of Control" (or "Sliding is an Option" on the Mac). Just don't say it out loud too often or people will think you have taken up residence in virtual reality!

✔ **Sliding with the mouse:** In Windows, to slide left, right, up, or down you can click on the right mouse button instead of holding down Ctrl.

✔ **Move the Observer in a Design View:** You can drag Cyrano, your virtual cameraperson, around in a Design View, which of course changes what you see in Walk View. See "Moving Cyrano — the guy with the nose" later in this chapter.

These tools are made for walkin'

Whenever the Walk View is your active window (which happens whenever you click in it), a skinny tool pad generally appears somewhere on your screen (see the tool pad in Figure 7-3). You can click on its top bar and drag it around to wherever it's not in the way. If your tool pad does not appear, choose Window⇨ Tools Window from the menu bar. The tool pad does a variety of things, but its most useful functions in life are letting you zoom in and out and letting you select things you want to work on.

From top to bottom, here are what the controls on the tool pad do:

✔ **Walk button:** This button is normally depressed, which means clicking in the Walk View causes you to walk. If you choose the Surface Select or Object Select button instead, you are no longer walking but selecting stuff.

✔ **Object Select:** When you choose this button, you can click on any object in Walk View to select that object. If any Design View window is open, you can see handles around the object, which appears in the center of the Design View. Now you can do stuff to that object. To select multiple objects, hold down the Shift key while clicking on them.

✔ **Surface Select:** When you choose this button, you can click on any surface of any object in Walk View, causing that surface to be selected and a Surface Editor window to appear.

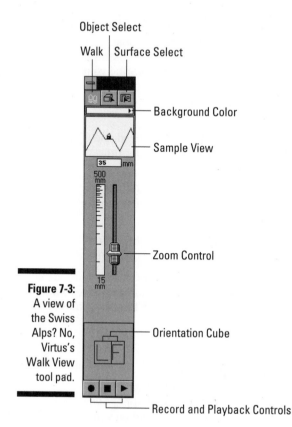

Object Select

Walk | Surface Select

— Background Color

— Sample View

— Zoom Control

Figure 7-3:
A view of
the Swiss
Alps? No,
Virtus's
Walk View
tool pad.

— Orientation Cube

— Record and Playback Controls

✔ **Background color:** Although you can set a background color in Walkthrough, VRML 1.0 does not actually support background colors, so there's no guarantee that VRML browsers will show the color. Live3D does, however, display Virtus' background color.

✔ **Zoom control:** Most of the tool pad is taken up by the zoom control. Dragging the button on the big slider up or down makes the lens of your virtual camera zoom in or out. Although you seem to be moving your Observer forward and back, you're really not. You are just zooming the lens. The little display that looks like a cabin in the Swiss Alps gives you an idea of just how far in or out you have zoomed.

✔ **Orientation cube:** Whenever an object is in the Walk View, this cube tells you which sides you are currently viewing. The orientation cube has letters for each side: R = right, L = left, F = front, B = back, T = top, and b = bottom. Knowing which side is which will help you choose the right Design View.

✔ **Record and playback controls:** These buttons are cool but not VRML. You can record a walk through your world. Click the button with the round dot to start recording, and then navigate around in Walk View. Click the square dot to stop recording. Click the triangle dot to play back. The playback repeats continuously, so to avoid getting mesmerized, click the square dot again to stop.

Walk menu

When you're walking, you need a good take-out menu. Here's what's on the Walk menu selection from the Walkthrough menu bar:

✔ **Button Down:** Nothing to do with shirt collars. Normally, this option is checked off; if it isn't checked off, your Observer moves when the mouse button is up and stops when it's down. Weird.

✔ **Cross Hair:** Not an angry rabbit, the crosshair is the thing in the middle of your Walk window. If you don't like it, click here to remove the check mark.

✔ **Velocity Grid:** A bunch of tic marks helping you see how far out from the crosshair you are clicking.

✔ **Normal Speed, and so on:** Adjusts how fast you move in Walk View. At faster speeds, Virtus gives up handling transparency. At fastest speed, it gives up rendering your drawing (filling it in) and just gives you a wireframe view.

✔ **Record, Play, Stop:** These options allow you to record a walk path and then play it back. Choose Record to start, and then take yourself on a tour. Choose Stop to stop and Play to play. Simpler than your VCR!

✔ **Aspect Ratio:** Adjusts the Walk View height and width according to your setting in Edit⇨Preferences⇨Navigation.

✔ **Full Screen:** Choose this option to have the Walk View fill your monitor. On the PC, press Esc after you're finished. On the Mac, the menu bar is still there but invisible; click and hold to pull down menus until you find the Walk menu. Then reselect Full screen.

Design Views

Virtus uses a very engineer-ish approach to designing — and why not? Who has more experience with designing than engineers? So borrowing from the engineering world, Virtus uses Front, Back, Left, Right, Top, and Bottom views for design work, just as you see in engineering blueprints or floor plans.

These views, called *orthogonal* views by engineers, make everything look flat or two-dimensional. They do not show things in perspective, as in real life. In real life, if you look down into your coffee mug (to pick an example always close to our hands), the bottom looks smaller than the top because it is farther away. Also, you see the inside surface. In a Virtus Top View (an orthogonal view) the bottom of your mug looks just as big as the top, and you can't see the inside walls of the mug.

Why on earth do engineers like this sort of thing? First, because it helps keep them from getting confused about how big things are. Second, it helps them work on only one or two dimensions at a time, a task which is easier than thinking about all three dimensions at once.

Seeing what you want to see

With all these views in Virtus, you can have about as many different views on things as Congress does (unlike Congress, all these views agree!). Here's how to see pretty much anything in a Design View:

- ✔ **Pick a side, any side:** Walkthrough worlds have definite sides to them (left, right, top, and so on), as if you were building within a big transparent cube. You can get a Design View from any side of your world just by choosing View⇨New View and choosing one. To change the view shown in your current window, choose View⇨Change View.

- ✔ **Zoom in and out:** Choose Design⇨Zoom In or Zoom Out. Each time, the scale changes by a factor of two. In Windows, another alternative is to hold down the Ctrl button and press the = or - key on your keyboard.

- ✔ **Slide left or right, up or down:** Use the slide bars along the bottom or side of the window to move your view within a window, just as with any other Windows or Macintosh program.

- ✔ **Have it your way:** To remove or change the colors of grid lines, rulers, gauges, guidelines, origins, or background color, choose Edit⇨Preferences and choose Editor in the Preferences box.

Moving Cyrano — the guy with the nose

In the Top View, you may have noticed a little round shape with a sort of nose. No offense, but that's you! Or, rather, that symbol represents the position of the Observer — the hypothetical cameraperson through whose camera you look through Walk View. His nose (the tiny line that protrudes from the circle) shows which way he goes.

To change his view, first click on the selection tool (the arrow) in the Design View tool pad and then:

- ✔ To change his position, just click and drag him around. (Don't you wish you could change your congressional representative's positions like that?)

- ✔ To change the direction he's looking, Ctrl+click on him (Option+click on the Mac) and drag a line in the direction you want him to look. Note that in anything but the Top or Bottom view, this action results in tilting his head!

All hail the ruler (and gauge)

Every Walkthrough Design View window is a kingdom governed by a pair of benign rulers: one across the top, and one up the side. Each ruler has a shady enforcer, the gauge! You can see them all in Figure 7-4.

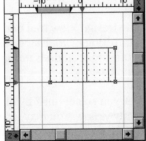

Figure 7-4:
The ruler
and its
shady
sidekick, the
gauge.

We call these rulers benign because they don't do anything; they just sit there and help you measure stuff. You can drag around the little blue triangle at the zero point to move your zero point. To reset the zero points to where they were, choose View⇨Reset Origin.

The gauges are the shady areas within the rulers, and they enforce the *inflation* of objects when you create them or edit them. When you create objects in Walkthrough, you draw a shape in two dimensions (X and Y if you're drawing in the Top view), and Walkthrough inflates the shape in the third dimension (Z, in Top view) — the one you can't see. Here's how to use the gauges:

- ✔ To adjust the gauge for the axis you can't see (Z in Top view), choose Window⇨Depth Window. Or add a view window that *does* display that axis by choosing View⇨New View and adjust the gauge there.

- ✔ The black triangles (endpoints) of the gauge determine the inflation size and position of the object in that third dimension. The letter in gray at one end of the ruler tells you which axis the gauge controls (in Figure 7-4, the vertical gauge is for the Z axis).

- To change the endpoints (the black triangles), just drag 'em. (As in the vertical gauge of Figure 7-4, one or both endpoints may be hiding under the blue zero mark of the ruler. If so, drag the blue mark out of the way.)
- To move the gauge, click on the gray area and drag.
- To see a numerical display of where you are in X and Y and the endpoints of your depth gauge, choose Window⇨Coordinates Window.

To change the inflation of an existing object, set the gauge, select the object, and then double-click on the gauge.

Rulers also offer guidelines to help you position objects. Just click on the dark gray *dock* areas (where the axis letter appears), drag into the ruler area, and a guideline will appear. To remove the guideline, click on its diamond-shaped endpoint in the ruler and drag the guideline back into the dock.

Tools for industry

Whenever you're working in a Design View, the Design View tool pad generally hovers somewhere nearby. If the tool pad is hovering in your face, just click on the bar at the top and drag the pad away. If your tool pad does not appear, choose Window⇨Tools Window from the menu bar.

Each symbol on this pad is a design tool. After you select one (by clicking on it), it is proud and happy and turns a nice sunny yellow. You may also hear a snap if your computer provides sound. Figure 7-5 shows what's initially visible on your tool pad. The most valuable tools, the main object-making tools, are in the third row.

Here are your tool descriptions. Note that some buttons — the ones with tiny triangles near the symbol — are hiding other buttons. Each of these buttons and the shy friends it is hiding represent variations on a tool. You can see the hidden ones by clicking and holding on the button: The variations appear to the right. To select a variation, just drag to the button you want and release the mouse button. The normally hidden tools are marked **(Hidden)** in the following descriptions.

- **Color lifter:** To save a swatch of a surface's color on the Color Bar, for reuse on other surfaces or objects, click the tool and then click on any surface.
- **Magnifier:** Zooms in by a factor of 2 with each click of the tool. Ctrl (Option)+Magnifier should zoom out but doesn't. Alternatively, use Ctrl+= and Ctrl+- or Design⇨Zoom In / Zoom Out.
- **Select:** In order to select an object for editing, painting, or otherwise mucking around, click on this tool and then on any object. To select multiple objects, use Shift+Select, or drag a rectangle around the objects.

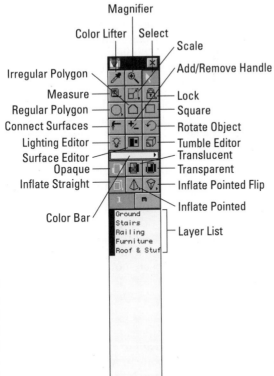

Magnifier

Color Lifter | Select

Scale

Irregular Polygon — Add/Remove Handle

Measure — Lock

Regular Polygon — Square

Connect Surfaces — Rotate Object

Lighting Editor — Tumble Editor

Surface Editor — Translucent

Opaque — Transparent

Inflate Straight — Inflate Pointed Flip

Inflate Pointed

Color Bar

Ground
Stairs
Railing
Furniture
Roof & Stuf — Layer List

Figure 7-5:
It's Tool
Time in
Walkthrough
Pro.

✔ **Measure:** Click on this tool and then anywhere in the Design View window to display your cursor location; or drag a line from anyplace to anyplace else to measure length and angle. See "Getting Coordinated: The Coordinates Window," coming up later in this chapter.

✔ **Scale:** Click on this tool and then double-click on the object and drag to scale it in the dragging direction. Shift+Scale scales all dimensions uniformly. Contents are also scaled unless Ctrl (Option) is pressed. Use Edit⇨Modify Selected⇨Unscale to undo. (**Hidden**) **Skew:** Use the same action as for scale, but Skew distorts the shape by sliding one side and tilting the connecting sides (like a parallelogram); think of a deck of playing cards that you "slide" by putting your hand on the top and pushing the stack so it "tilts." Use Edit⇨Modify Selected⇨Unskew to undo.

✔ **Lock:** To prevent an object or surface from being changed, click this tool and click on the object or surface; to unlock, choose Edit⇨Unlock all. (**Hidden**) **Hide Object:** When objects or surfaces impede your view, hide them: Click the tool and then the object. Double-click the tool to reveal all hidden items.

- **Regular Polygon:** To create an object based on a regular polygon (sides of identical length), click this tool and hold it to see available shapes. To choose a shape, drag to the desired shape button and release — or choose *n* for any number of sides. To set n, double-click the n button and enter a number in the Sides box of the Preferences dialog box that appears. Click and drag in Design View to create your shape.

- **Irregular Polygon:** To create an object based on an irregular shape, begin by clicking this tool. Each click in Design View extends a new side of your polygon; double-click to close the shape. The shape can't have any indentations (concave parts).

- **Square:** To create a rectangular 3D block, click the tool and then click where you want the rectangle to begin and drag to the opposite corner.

- **Connect Surfaces:** Where two objects need to share a common surface (for example, two adjoining rooms with a common wall and a connecting door or window), use this tool to allow transparency, a hole, or a common surface color. Click this tool, and then if the surfaces are touching, click on the line that represents them. If they are not touching, drag one object toward the other (you may hear a snap). To disconnect surfaces, use the Select Object tool and drag the objects apart.

- **Add/Remove Handle (+/-):** To add a vertex (edge) to a shape, click this tool and then click on the point on the edge where you want the new vertex; drag the point if you need to adjust the position. You may need to drag outward slightly to create a point. To remove the vertex, click on it with the Ctrl (Option) button depressed.

- **Rotate Object:** Click this tool and then double-click where you want the center of rotation. Drag a dotted line outward to serve as a sort of wrench, and drag in a circular motion to rotate the object. To undo, use Edit⇨Modify Selected⇨Unrotate.

- **Lighting Editor:** To add lights to an entire world, double-click this tool. To light a single object and any objects it contains, click the tool and then double-click the object. The Lighting editor window appears, together with an associated tool pad containing a series of bars representing individual lights. The top one provides general illumination and the others, directional. Click in the shaded area on the right of a bar to see the position of a directional light source. See "Lighting Editor" later in this chapter for more information.

- **Surface Editor:** To change the color or transparency of a surface, click this tool and then double-click the surface. The Surface Editor window appears together with an associated tool pad. Use the Color Bar and the Translucent and Transparent buttons to change the surface. See "Surface Editor" later in this chapter for more information.

- **Tumble Editor:** To easily view an object from any direction — or to knock a slice off the object — click this tool and then click the object. The Tumble Editor window appears, containing the object, along with an associated tool pad. See "Tumble Editor" later in this chapter for more information.

- **Color Bar:** Click and hold on this bar. A palette box appears: Colors used elsewhere in the scene appear across the top. Click on one of these or one of the many colors below to set the default color for new objects. To color existing objects, select the object and then select a color. In the Surface and Tumble Editors, the Color Bar can color individual surfaces.

- **Opaque:** To make an object fully opaque, select the object and then double-click this tool. You can set the opacity of individual surfaces using this same technique in the Tumble or Surface Editor.

- **Translucent:** Select an object and double-click this tool for a semi-transparent object (no gradations exist). You can set surface translucency individually using this same technique in the Tumble or Surface Editor.

- **Transparent:** Select an object and then double-click this tool for a fully transparent object. You can set surface transparency individually using this same technique in the Tumble or Surface Editor.

- **Inflate Straight:** Click this tool before creating a shape to give the shape straight sides in the inflation direction. **(Hidden) Double:** Inflates a shape in both directions at once along the inflation axis. **(Hidden) Round:** Inflates a shape to rounded ends; Round is the only way to make round shapes in Walkthrough Pro. To make an object straight-inflated after the fact, select the object and then double-click on the tool.

- **Inflate Pointed:** Click this tool before creating a shape to make the shape's sides come to a point in the inflation direction. To make an object pointy after the fact, select the object and then double-click on the tool.

- **Inflate Pointed Flip:** Just like Inflate Pointed, only upside-down.

- **Layer List:** Names listed here indicate the various optional *layers* in your world. The highlighted layer is the one you are currently working on; any new objects you create go into that layer. Use Design⇨New Layer in any Design view to add layers. Click to select a layer; click and hold to choose Hide or other layer options from a menu. Using layers is optional, but it's a way of grouping objects that makes creating complex worlds easier. Layers help you temporarily get a group of objects out of your way. For example, when you are using a Top View, hiding a layer containing the second floor of a house improves your view of and access to the first floor.

As your world gets more and more complex, your access to certain objects can be blocked. Some objects are naturally contained by other objects (furniture in rooms, for instance), and some objects are located behind objects. To make these objects accessible, simply select the object that's in your way and choose Edit⇨Hide Selected. To restore the hidden object, choose Edit⇨Show All.

Design menu

Designer jeans, designer hair, and now . . . designer menus! Imagine the possibilities! This particular menu selection, Design, appears only when your active window is a Design View.

- ✔ **Snap to Grid:** Choose this option to help you create shapes of precise sizes and to align objects and surfaces precisely with each other. When you drag the handles of selected objects or surfaces, Walkthrough only allows you to stop at precise intervals, determined by the tick marks on your rulers. You can also drag entire objects, but if they were not created on the same grid, they may not align precisely.

- ✔ **Zoom In, Zoom Out:** Zooms in and out by factors of two, causing ruler resolution to change accordingly.

- ✔ **Group, Ungroup:** When you're creating a complex object out of many parts (Mr. Potato Head, for example) and you want to move, rotate, or scale the whole potato, create a Group: Select multiple objects by holding down the Shift key while using the Select tool (arrow), and then choose Design⇨Group. Poof, they are all glued together. Choose Ungroup to break 'em up again.

   Grouping does not change your VRML file. That is, it does not result in a grouping node in the VRML. At least, as of this writing it doesn't.

- ✔ **VRML Anchor:** Select an object, and then choose this command to link an object to an Internet URL (like http://www.brightleaf.com) using the dialog box that appears. When people click on that object in a VRML browser, they will go to that URL.

Have It Your Way: Preferences and Defaults

Hold the pickles, hold the lettuce, set your Virtus preferences. (Try singing it! Catchy, eh? Apologies to Burger King.) There are five, count 'em — five categories of things you can change about the way Virtus works for you.

None of these Preferences really change the meat of your VRML design: They have no effect on your VRML file. (Some of them, like camera settings and units, might do so in the future, but as of this writing, they don't.)

Choose Edit⇨Preferences from the menu bar to get a Preferences dialog box, and then choose your category from the Preferences selection box there.

✔ **Editor:** All the stuff that clutters up your windows, plus a few more. Here you can turn on or off rulers, grids, depth gauges, guidelines, and origin points. You can also turn on snapping to a grid, or you can set the colors of these items. One mysterious item is *Tracking*, which has to do with the Coordinates window. See the discussion of that window later in this chapter.

✔ **Rendering:** How things look in your Walk window.

- *Shading* box determines whether or not there appears to be a directional light source (choose Shaded) that makes some surfaces darker than others; choose Unshaded to turn off this source, or White to remove colors.

- *Drawing* box determines if shapes are outlined (choose Frame), colored-in (choose Fill), or both (Fill & Frame).

- *Flash Graphics* turns on special Virtus fast rendering if your computer allows it.

- *Black Frames* checkbox makes outlines black and edges therefore easier to see.

- *Print Fill* lets you see unshaded white surfaces better when you print.

- *Dithering* gives you more precise colors but a grainier image.

- *Blended Translucency* must be on or surfaces don't really look translucent.

- *Openings* checkboxes let you See In translucent or transparent objects (when the Observer is outside), See Out (Observer is inside), or See Through translucent or transparent connecting surfaces (like doors between rooms).

✔ **Navigation:** How you move around and the height-to-width ratio of the camera your Observer uses. Most of these settings just do annoying things once they are changed from the default, so leave them alone. Collision Detection keeps your Observer from going through opaque surfaces, if you care.

✔ **Defaults:** The default depth setting for gauges and the location of home and n for n-sided polygons. *Depth* determines how the depth gauge endpoints are set for each axis, X, Y, and Z. *Home* sets the location of home for View⇨Home Editor and Home Observer. *Sides* sets n for n-sided regular polygons.

✔ **Units:** whether you're working in inches, miles, or angstroms. *Ruler Unit* sets, well, the units on the rulers. You may find that settings other than inches or centimeters cause problems. *Model Unit Size* determines the precision of the rendering in Walk View in ruler units. *World* sets how big your world is in these units.

In all these Preferences settings, the Default button records your settings for posterity, and Walkthrough uses them as the default for future work. The Revert button returns you to the previous settings.

Getting Coordinated: The Coordinates Window

For precise design work, you have to know exactly where you are and how big things are as you draw them. The Coordinates window gives you that information.

To see a Coordinates window, choose Window⇨Coordinates Window. Or, in the Design View tool pad, click the tape measure icon. You can close a Coordinates window just as you do any other Mac or Windows window.

The Coordinates window can work two slightly different ways, depending on an Editor Preferences setting called *Tracking*. Choose Edit⇨Preferences and select Editor preferences to change it. We find that just leaving it set to the default *View* is easier, rather than choosing *World*. View gives you measurements in the horizontal and vertical axes of your Design View, whereas World gives you X, Y, and Z, forcing you to think about whether your View is in X and Y, X and Z, Y and Z, or whatever. In the following description, we assume you've taken our sage advice and stayed with the View setting.

When you're just moving your mouse cursor, not dragging, the box gives the following information:

h = horizontal distance from 0,0

v = vertical distance from 0,0

f = current floor for inflation of shapes (bottom endpoint of inflation gauge)

d = current depth of inflation (top minus bottom endpoints of inflation gauge)

When you drag a line, either while drawing a shape or just for measurement, h and v are the same, but you also see the following:

h° = distance you have dragged horizontally

v° = distance you have dragged vertically

l = length of the line you've dragged

a = angle of the line you've dragged (in degrees)

Surface Editor

Objects that are the same all over are boring — so Walkthrough comes with a tool that lets you color surfaces individually, draw stuff on them, or draw virtual holes and windows by using transparency. You can get to the Surface Editor wherever you see the Surface Editor tool (it's the button on the tool pad with the little wall, door, and window symbol).

✔ From Walk View, click the Surface Editor tool, and then double-click on any surface (the way we got Figure 7-6).

✔ From any Design View, ditto.

✔ From the Tumble Editor, likewise.

Surface Editor tool pad

When you invoke the Surface Editor, the Surface Editor window appears, showing your selected surface and sprouting up a tool pad that looks just like a Design View tool pad. No surprise — it works like one too; except it only works on surfaces (the two-dimensional flat things that make up your three-dimensional objects) or on features you draw on those surfaces. In Figure 7-6, we've colored one of the surfaces of a hexagonal pyramid using the surface editor.

However, a few extra tools are along the very bottom of the tool pad, pointed out in Figure 7-6. These are your (really badly named) *Placement Modifiers* (ugh). They should be named Front Side, Both Sides, or Back Side because they are really just tools that tell Walkthrough whether you are modifying the front side, both sides, or back side of your surface (front is the side facing you in the Surface Editor). Select one of these tools before editing surfaces or making surface features.

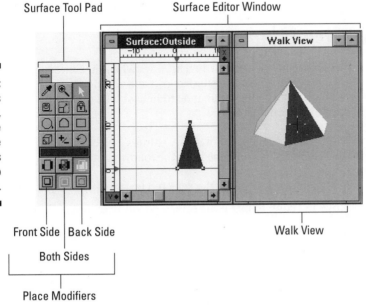

Figure 7-6: Beauty is skin-deep, so the Surface Editor helps keep up appearances.

Surface Tool Pad

Surface Editor Window

Front Side | Back Side

Both Sides

Place Modifiers

Walk View

Here are a few popular tasks and how to do them:

- **To draw a feature (a shape) on a surface:** Use the shape-drawing tools on the third row of the tool pad (square, octagon, and so on). You can alter shapes afterward by choosing the Select tool, clicking on the square dots at the corners of the shape, and dragging.

- **To select the surface or feature** (which makes handles appear around it): Click the Select tool and then click the surface or surface feature.

- **To specify which side you're applying a color, a surface feature, or a transparency to:** Click the surface or feature and then double-click one of the three Placement Modifier buttons (which we call Front Side, Back Side, or Both Sides).

- **To color:** Click the surface or feature, click and hold on the Color Bar, and then click a color in the palette.

- **To change transparency:** Click the surface or feature and then double-click a transparency button (under the Color Bar). Make this change to surface features in order to create doors or windows.

For descriptions of the other tools, see "Tools for industry" earlier in this chapter. Just remember that in the Surface Editor, the tools apply to surfaces or surface features, not entire objects. You can't scale, rotate, or change the number of vertex points in a surface, but you can do those things to a surface feature, like a window.

Surface Editor menu

The Surface menu selection (which appears when the Surface Editor is your active window) has the same snap to grid and zoom selections as the Design menu but also some cute commands to help shuffle overlapping features you may have drawn on the surface.

To change the stacking order of these features, select the one you want to move with the Select tool and choose from the following:

- **Move Forward:** to move the selected feature towards you in the stack

- **Move to Front:** to move the selected feature on top of the stack

- **Move Back:** to move the selected feature away from you in the stack

- **Move to Back:** to move the selected feature to the bottom of the stack

Tumble Editor

Tumble Editor is not only a great name, but also a fun and useful feature. Its main purpose in life is to let you get at any surface of an object by tumbling the object rather than having to walk around (or through) stuff in Walk View. Its other purpose is to let you whittle off chunks of objects to make fancier shapes. The Tumble Editor lets you

✔ See any side of an object

✔ Change the color or transparency of any object or surface

✔ Whittle slices off objects

✔ Select a surface and then invoke the Surface Editor for fancier stuff like adding surface features

The Tumble Editor does not change the orientation of the object in your world. To do that, choose a Design View and rotate the object.

You can get to the Tumble Editor wherever you see the Tumble Editor tool (it's the button on the tool pad that shows the little cube with a slice being taken off it):

✔ From Walk View, click the Tumble Editor tool and then double-click on any object (if the object was already selected, a single click will do).

✔ From any Design View, ditto.

✔ From the Surface Editor, likewise.

The Tumble Editor window appears, showing your selected object and sprouting up a tool pad that looks just like a Design View tool pad.

Tumble Editor tool pad

Figure 7-7 shows the Tumble Editor and its tool pad.

Here's how the tools that are unique to the Tumble Editor work (the others are the same as in the Design View tool pad):

Select tool (arrow): Selects either entire objects or entire surfaces for coloring and transparency adjustment. To select an entire object, click in the Tumble Editor window anywhere not on the object. To select a surface, click this tool and then the surface. To select a surface and rotate it forward, double-click on the surface. To color the selected object or surface, click on a color in the Color Bar palette. To adjust transparency, double-click on one of the Placement Modifiers.

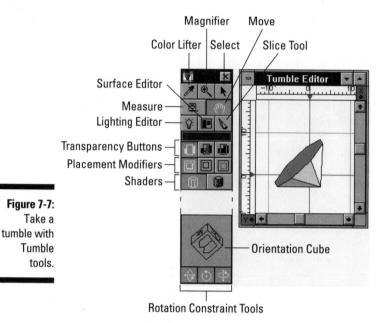

Figure 7-7:
Take a
tumble with
Tumble
tools.

Move tool (hand shape): Rotates and selects. To rotate your view of the object, click this tool and drag in the Tumble Editor window — or on the orientation cube on the Editor's tool pad. To restrict motion to rotation around certain axes when dragging in the Editor window (not in the cube), use the Rotation Constraint tools. To select a surface and bring it forward, double-click on the surface.

Rotation Constraints: To allow rotation around an axis in the Editor window, the corresponding axis button must be depressed. From left to right, the three button icons depict axes horizontal, into the screen, and vertical. Note that rotation is around the selected axis, as if the object is on a skewer and the skewer is the axis. At least one button must be depressed.

Orientation cube: This cube is an alternative way to rotate the object in the Tumble Editor window. It identifies the different sides: T= top, b = bottom, F = front, B = back, L = left, and R = right. Drag the cube with the Move tool to rotate the cube; the object in the Editor window is linked and also rotates. Double-click on a surface to select it and bring it forward.

Slice tool: This tool removes a chunk from an object, creating a new surface. Select the tool and then drag a line through the object. Dragging left-to-right or top-down removes a piece above or to the right. The opposite direction removes the opposite piece. If you drag incorrectly, choose Tumble⇨Reverse Slice from the menu bar.

The Color Grabber, Zoom, Measure, Color Bar, and Surface Editor tools work as they do in Design View. See "Tools for industry" earlier in this chapter. The Placement Modifier tools work just like those for the Surface Editor; see "Surface Editor" earlier in this chapter.

Tumble menu

The Tumble menu shows up when your active window is the Tumble Editor. No surprise there. Most of its commands are identical to commands in the Design menu. The unique one is Reverse Slice, which has nothing to do with golf. If you have accidentally cut off the wrong half of an object using the Slice tool, Reverse Slice solves the problem. Now if they would only make one for barbers!

Lighting Editor

Want to brighten up your world? Walkthrough Pro lets you set lights of any color at any angle. For a more leisurely discussion of how to set up lighting, see Chapter 12. Here, we just discuss the controls.

Walkthrough lets you set lighting for the entire world and also for each object in that world. Objects initially inherit their lighting from the world or the object that contains them (such as a room). You can override this inherited lighting by lighting the object individually.

Walkthrough Pro's Lighting Editor, while it works fine within Walkthrough Pro, may not work well in VRML. In particular, Walkthrough offers an object-by-object lighting scheme that may not translate perfectly to VRML. (Or it may work fine. We can't tell because the pre-release software we are using isn't quite the same as what you have on the CD.) If you stick to lighting the entire world, however, you should make out fine.

To add lights, you use the Lighting Editor tool — the light-bulb icon on the Design View tool pad or Tumble Editor tool pad.

> ✔ To light the entire world (well, your virtual world, anyway): Double-click the Lighting Editor tool.
>
> ✔ To light an object: Click the Lighting Editor tool, then click the object.

The Lighting Editor tool pad comes to your aid, as shown in Figure 7-8, and a Light window appears where you can set lighting angles and get an idea of the results of your efforts.

Omnidirectional Source

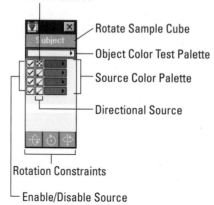

Rotate Sample Cube

Object Color Test Palette

Source Color Palette

Figure 7-8:
The Lighting
Editor
toolpad.

Directional Source

Rotation Constraints

Enable/Disable Source

A light source is represented by a row in the tool pad. The tool pad initially shows four sources, as in Figure 7-8. The first one is omnidirectional — a sort of overall illumination; the remaining sources are directional, like sunlight.

The lighting you set up in the Lighting Editor doesn't apply to your scene or your selected object until you choose Light⇨Apply from the menu bar.

Here is how to control your lights:

✓ To view the effect of a light in the Light window, click the light source's shaded bar. The cube in the Light window represents whatever you are lighting and shows the effect of the lighting on different surfaces. If you click a directional light source, a spotlight symbol appears which you can drag to any angle around the cube.

✓ To rotate the sample cube so that you can see other sides, click the Subject button at the top of the tool pad and drag on the cube in the Light window.

✓ To adjust a light source's color, click and hold on the source's shaded bar and then choose a color from the palette that appears.

✓ To switch a source between directional and omnidirectional, click the box with the arrow or arrows.

✓ To disable a source, click its checkbox to clear the check mark.

✓ To add a source, choose Light⇨New Light from the menu bar.

✓ To delete a source, choose Light⇨Delete Light from the menu bar.

✓ To see the effect of light color on a colored object, you can color the sample cube in the Light window: Click and hold on the white bar at the top of the tool pad and choose a color from the palette that appears.

✓ To see how your scene or selected object really looks, choose Light⇨Apply from the menu bar and view the scene in Walk View.

A set of rotation constraint buttons on the bottom of the tool pad give you more precise rotation control — although we doubt you will need them. They work just like their cousins in the Tumble Editor.

There is no setting for light intensity apart from the color you choose. Also, there is no setting for light location. Light comes from infinitely far away and, although it reflects off objects in its path, it doesn't make any shadows. (Shadows are a feature that VRML browsers may someday provide but don't yet.)

Texture Mapping

Walkthrough Pro allows you to apply images to surfaces in a process called texture mapping. Texture mapping generally involves a repeated pattern, which Walkthrough allows you to specify. For a more leisurely discussion of texture mapping in Virtus and Caligari tools, see Chapter 14. Here, we just discuss the controls in Walkthrough Pro.

- ✔ To apply a texture to an entire object, first select it in any Design view.
- ✔ To apply a texture to an individual surface of an object, first select it in the Surface Editor or double-click on it in the Tumble Editor.
- ✔ To open the Textures window, choose Window⇨Textures Window.
- ✔ To add a texture to the Texture window, click the triangle in the upper-right corner of the Texture window and choose Add Textures from the drop-down menu. Select an image file or Virtus texture file from the Add Textures dialog box that appears.
- ✔ To apply a texture to a selected object or surface, double-click the texture in the list in the bottom area of the Textures window.
- ✔ To remove a texture from an object or surface, double-click "No Texture" in the Textures window.
- ✔ To delete a texture, click a texture in the list and then click the triangle in the upper-right corner and choose Delete Texture.

Texture options control the way in which the selected image is applied across the surface. To use the options, click the triangle in the upper-right corner and choose Texture Options from the drop-down menu. The Texture Options dialog box appears, of which there are three variants, depending on your choice in the Edit box: First Tile, Tile Pattern, and Appearance. All variants of the Texture Options window have these controls in common:

- ✔ The Set button allows you to choose the image file that forms the basis for the texture you are working on.
- ✔ The Name box allows you to give the texture (the image and its associated options) a name.

✔ The Apply button applies the texture to the object or surface.

✔ The Revert button returns the texture to the original conditions you found in this box.

✔ The OK button applies the texture to the object or surface and exits the Texture Options dialog box.

In the box marked Edit:

✔ Choose First Tile to see a variant of the Texture Options window where you can change the orientation of the image. In the "Flip" area, choose Horizontal and/or Vertical to reorient the image.

✔ Choose Tile Pattern to see a variant of the Texture Options window where you can make the texture repeat across the surface in various ways.

✔ In the Mirror area, choosing Horizontal and/or Vertical causes the image to flip back and forth in an alternating pattern as it tiles the surface. This effect can give the appearance of a seamless texture across adjoining tiles.

✔ In the Cover area, the preselected option is Fit tiles, which places an integral number of tiles across each surface of the selected object. Enter the number of tiles in the text box to the right of "Fit tiles." Walkthrough stretches the image as necessary to fit your settings.

✔ If you prefer to set the tiling pattern according to a given number of pixels per unit length, choose the buttons marked H: and V:, enter the number of pixels per unit length, and choose the unit of length you wish in the boxes to the right of the H: and V: buttons.

The third possible choice in the Edit box is the Appearance selection, which controls aspects of texture mapping that work only in Walkthrough Pro and are not exported to VRML, such as transparency of white areas (select Decal) and allowing textures to be shaded by lighting colors (select Shade).

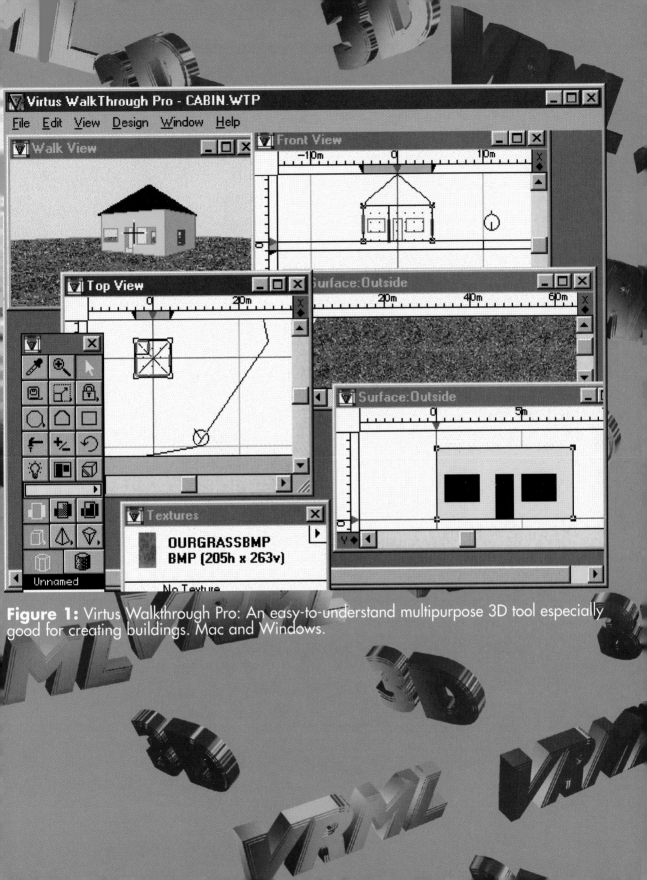

Figure 1: Virtus Walkthrough Pro: An easy-to-understand multipurpose 3D tool especially good for creating buildings. Mac and Windows.

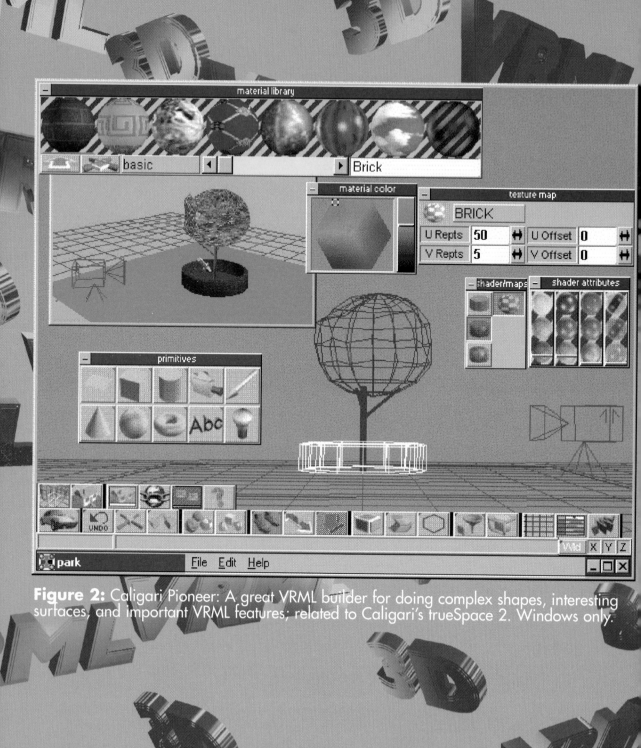

Figure 2: Caligari Pioneer: A great VRML builder for doing complex shapes, interesting surfaces, and important VRML features; related to Caligari's trueSpace 2. Windows only.

Figure 3: Aerial view of Planet 9 Studios' "Virtual San Francisco" (http://www. Planet9.com/worlds/ vrsf.wrl), as seen by VR Scout. The orange cubes are hotlinks to more detailed neighborhood models still under construction.

Figure 4: A virtual postcard of downtown San Francisco seen through the Golden Gate bridge — another view of Planet 9s' "Virtual San Francisco," as seen by VR Scout.

Figure 5: The prototype San Francisco neighborhood model, Planet 9 Studios' "Virtual SOMA" (http://www.Planet9.com/worlds/vrsoma.wrl), as seen by VR Scout.

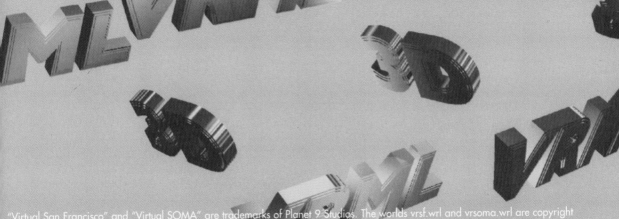

Figure 6: Face-to-face with an avatar in the entry scene of PointWorld (`http://www.pointcom.com/vrml /home.wrl`), constructed by Black Sun Interactive. Any VRML browser can see PointWorld, but the avatars only show up in Black Sun's CyberGate. The yellow cylinders are also avatars.

Figure 7: Inside the Politics building of PointWorld, as seen by CyberGate. The books on the table are hotlinks to subcategory worlds.

Figure 8: One of the 3888 possible Glenn's Jack-o-Lanterns (http://userwww.chaco
.com/~glenn/jack), as seen by VR Scout. Programmer Glenn Crocker had no idea
they'd be so popular.

Figure 9: "And there he kept her very well." The same jack-o-lantern seen from the inside by VR Scout.

Figure 10: VRML in motion: A squadron of paper airplanes circles over a model city by C. Scott Young (http://tcc.iz.net/dgraphix/sing/singmain.wrl), as seen in Live3D.

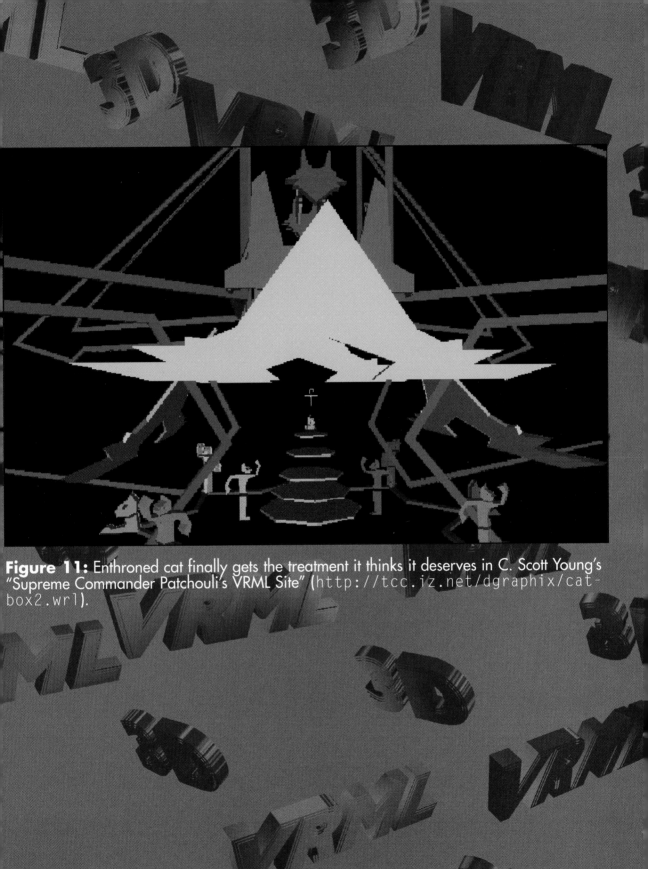

Figure 11: Enthroned cat finally gets the treatment it thinks it deserves in C. Scott Young's "Supreme Commander Patchouli's VRML Site" (`http://tcc.iz.net/dgraphix/cat-box2.wrl`).

Figure 12: Ancient patterns become futuristic architecture in C. Scott Young's "Keltic Pyramid" (http://tcc.iz.net/dgraphix/kelpyra.wrl), as seen in Live3D. A spire extends beyond the range of the picture.

Figure 13: Even 2D images benefit from a 3D display: Grafman's Gallery (http://www.graphcomp.com/vrml/gallery0.wrl), created by Robert M. Free, as seen by Live3D.

Figure 14: England's University of Essex, as seen by Live3D. Adrian and Christine Clark's model (`http://esewww.essex.ac.uk/campus-model.wrl`) is based on a ground elevation survey, and is the front-end to the campus information system.

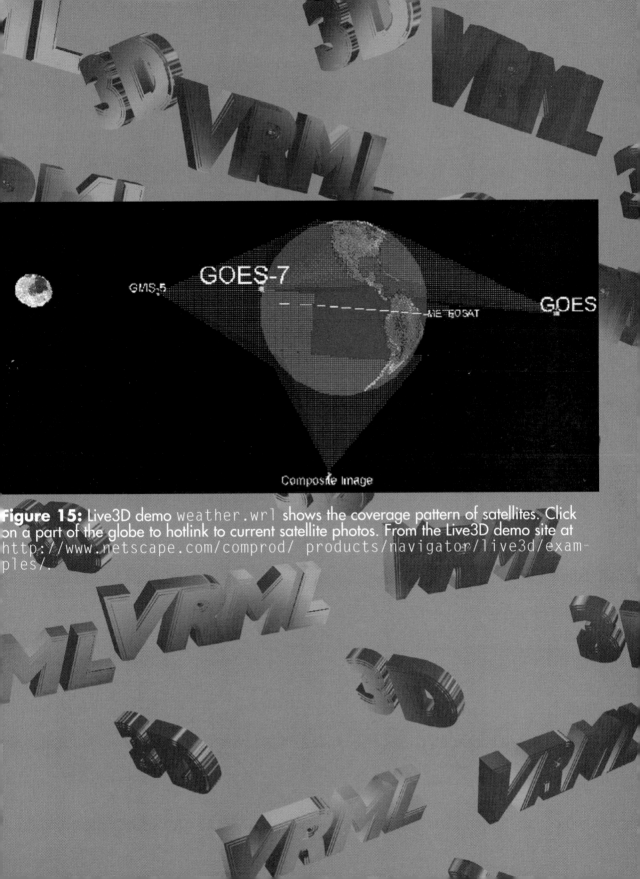

Figure 15: Live3D demo `weather.wrl` shows the coverage pattern of satellites. Click on a part of the globe to hotlink to current satellite photos. From the Live3D demo site at `http://www.netscape.com/comprod/ products/navigator/live3d/exam-ples/`.

Figure 16: Another Live3D demo shows off the animation features of Moving Worlds. The 4x4 drives around in a circle.

Chapter 8

Caligari — Virtual Squid and More

1 f, like us, you have visions of fantastic virtual objects — say, giant squid — dancing in your head, Caligari may have just what you need. No, not a mental health professional (although with the dancing squid and all, we are considering it) — Caligari's Pioneer and Pioneer Pro. These programs are probably the most sophisticated VRML builders available as of this writing. They are a little tricky to learn, but the trade-off is that they can create some amazing shapes (like squid in Figure 8-1), surfaces, and special effects that you can't achieve using Virtus Walkthrough Pro. Pioneer is Caligari's get-you-interested product and Pioneer Pro is the professional-grade product.

One of a family of related products from Caligari, Pioneer is basically a more limited, VRMLized version of Caligari's flagship product, trueSpace 2. (There's an evaluation copy of trueSpace 2 on our CD.) If you get serious about doing VRML, you should definitely consider buying Caligari's Pioneer Pro; it works the same way but gives you more tools. Caligari products are available for Windows only — sorry, Mac users.

Figure 8-1:
Flying
calamari are
a snap with
Caligari.

Our CD contains early (pre-release) evaluation copies of both Pioneer and Pioneer Pro, but in the book we'll focus mostly on Pioneer, since you can get updated evaluation copies of Pioneer from Caligari's Web site. Updated versions of Pioneer Pro are only available by purchasing it in final form. Since the software is in pre-release, or beta, form, you'll find some bugs in its behavior. We'll try to steer you around the ones we know about.

This chapter is your *For Dummies* reference manual for Caligari Pioneer, one of the two main tools we show you for VRML world building. This chapter is *tool-oriented,* in contrast to Parts III and IV of this book. In those parts, we take a *task-oriented* approach to using Caligari's Pioneer products (and Walkthrough Pro), and go more slowly through the complicated stuff. This chapter is where to turn when you're in Pioneer and you're wondering "How do I use that tool, again?" or "Where the heck is that tool?"

Pioneer was called Fountain until about ten minutes before we published this book. So if you see "Fountain" somewhere in this book or on the CD, just think "Pioneer." (Try thinking of Ponce de Leon, a sort of pioneer looking for a fountain.)

About Caligari Products on Our CD

The good news is that we've arranged to include the very latest software in this book. The bad news is that because it is the very latest software, as we write this, we don't know exactly how the installation process will go! So instead of printing up the instructions here, we've put them on the CD. Load the file OUR_CD.TXT into your word processor, or load OUR_CD.HTM into your Web browser to learn more.

Pioneer and Pioneer Pro are changing so fast that the versions we finally put on the CD may have more features than the ones we used to write this description. Caligari provides some nice Help descriptions, so see Help⇨Contents in Pioneer and the Caligari README.WRI file on the CD for the latest info.

Like most of the software on our CD, the Caligari products we've included with this book are time-limited evaluation copies, with certain licenses and other restrictions. Among the restrictions is that you can't call Caligari for support. Make sure you read Caligari's license agreement on the CD. Remember that VRML is moving fast, and although the products on our CD were the latest we could get, it's worth a few bucks to buy the latest from Caligari.

Features Overview

Pioneer is one of the most full-featured VRML tools you can buy. It provides tools for advanced modeling, texture mapping, and VRML-specific features. When you work in Pioneer, the perspectives are natural looking, and you have your choice of many buttons and tools (see Figure 8-2). In other words, we think it's pretty cool, even though the advanced nature of its features requires a bit more work to get used to.

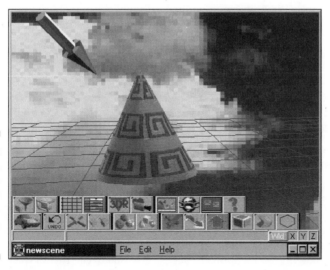

Figure 8-2:
In Pioneer, you work in a natural perspective view, with lots of tools.

What follows are some of the capabilities that Pioneer gives you for VRML building:

- 3D shape creation tools such as 3D primitives, 2D polygons, face editing, lathing, sweeping, tips, and extrusion of TrueType fonts

- "Infinite" and local light sources

- Multiple cameras for viewing and viewpoints within Pioneer

- Painting entire objects or individual faces

- Texture mapping on objects or faces

✔ Import of existing 3D geometry in DXF and other popular formats

✔ Import of existing 2D geometry in PostScript or Adobe Illustrator

✔ Acquisition of VRML worlds from the Internet

✔ Inlining of VRML objects and texture maps

✔ Level-of-detail (LOD) groups for faster viewing of large worlds

✔ Linking of URLs to objects

The minimum requirements for Pioneer are a fast 486 with 8MB of RAM. For large worlds (worlds with over a thousand polygons), Caligari recommends a Pentium processor PC with a 64-bit graphics card (preferably with 3D acceleration).

Tool Basics

Caligari's tools (the buttons along the bottom of the screen) are fairly easy to use once you know their secrets. Here are a few of the more important ones:

✔ **What tool is what:** Caligari uses a dizzying array of buttons; fortunately, you just pause your mouse cursor over a button (don't click), and the button's name appears in the help bar below the buttons. (A feature that will be great if Caligari finishes it is the ability to see a demo of each tool; click on the button sporting the "?" symbol and then on a tool — the Paint Face tool, for instance — and be patient. Pioneer runs a narrated demo.)

✔ **Selecting tools:** Click tool buttons with your left mouse button to select them. Tools that are gray and fuzzy are not available (generally because they don't work with some other tool you are using or action you are doing). If you click on a tool and then change your mind about using it, drag your mouse pointer off the tool before you release the mouse button.

✔ **Variants ("Pop-ups"):** Some tools — the ones with a blue triangle in the upper-left corner — are only one of a family of tools you can access from the same button location. To access any one of the rest of the family (called *variants* or *pop-ups*), click (left) and hold on the variant that is visible. Drag upward along the column of family members that appears and release your mouse button over the tool you want. The help bar at the bottom of the screen tells you what each tool is as you pass over it.

✔ **Property panels:** Some tools — the ones with a red triangle in the upper-right corner — have *property panels* that set the specifics of how a tool works. To see these panels and modify them, right-click on the tool.

✔ **Control panels:** Some tools have control panels that pop up whenever you click on them. The panels for some tools go away when you click on another tool. Panels appear wherever they have room and will try to pack together as closely as possible on the left side of your screen, although you can drag them to a new row. You can close a panel as you do any other in Windows; you can also close them all with the Close All Panels button (the icon shows two rectangles with red Xs in them).

Seeing What You Want

With all the features in Pioneer, sometimes you may have difficulty figuring out how to see the features you are seeking. Here are the basics.

Browsing versus building

Caligari takes the *we do it all* approach to VRML, which is pretty nice. As a result, they have created Pioneer to be not only a builder, but a browser too. Pioneer keeps these two functions separate with two distinct modes — browse mode and build mode, each with its own set of buttons.

Pioneer starts out in browse mode, which we describe in Chapter 4. Click the big button at the far left of the toolbar to switch modes. It's shown to the left of this paragraph.

When you're in the building mode, the button changes to show a sports car icon. (Caligari apparently thinks of you as zooming around in a virtual sports car in browse mode.) Click the same button to return to browse mode.

A last-minute addition to Pioneer was a Publish button in the browse mode. It's supposed to let you transmit your world to Web sites listed in your Neighborhood that are specially designed to accept contributions. Frankly, we don't know of any such sites.

The big view — and the little view

Pioneer does everything in a perspective or *3D* view. No blueprint-like top, front, or side views exist in Pioneer (although they do exist in Pioneer Pro and trueSpace). However, a second window is available, and with it you can see your scene from a different viewpoint than you do in the main window. Unlike most Windows windows, the size of this window is fixed.

To view that second, smaller window, click the button that looks like the one to the left of this paragraph. In Pioneer Pro, you can click and hold on that button and you'll find buttons ("variants") for the top, front, and side views. Just drag up the column of buttons and release to select one.

You navigate in the second window the same way you do in the main window. Close or drag the second window just as you would any other Windows window or panel. The second window always shows things as solids, not wireframes (they are "fully rendered" in geek-speak).

To switch to a camera view in the second window, just navigate so that you can see the camera in the window and then select the camera with the Selection tool.

We suggest you walk or fly to a position in the small window where you can look down upon your work. This position will help you see where things are while you are building them in the main window. In the walk or fly mode, an easy way to do this is to push your mouse away from you, holding down the right mouse button (which moves your viewpoint up) and periodically adding the left mouse button (which tilts your viewing angle down).

Help for the lost

Pioneer has two features for the lost, and they help when you are lost or a particular object is lost. Both features are selected by buttons that are (strangely enough) variants of the Close All Panels button; that is, they share the same location on the tool bar. Click and hold on one, and the other two variants pop up, like you see in Figure 8-3.

Figure 8-3:
The Close All Panels button and its pop-up friends.

— Reset View
— Look at Current Object
— Close All Panels

The top button in the stack is the Reset View button. The middle one is the Look at Current Object button. The bottom button is the Close All Panels button.

If your view has become totally messed up and you can't tell which way you are looking, you can reset to the default viewpoint by choosing the Reset View button. To aim your view at a particular object (we love this one!), select an object and then choose the Look at Current Object button. If you can't see the object at all, click the Object List button and choose objects from the list that appears. (See "Being Selective and Manipulative" later in this chapter for details on the Object List button.)

Beta versions of Pioneer are still a bit unreliable in these view control features.

Views from cameras and objects

 Pioneer provides cameras for your viewing pleasure. A camera is a viewpoint that you can switch to in Pioneer. To add a camera to your scene, use the Primitives tool (see "Let's get primitive: Primitives panel" later in this chapter). To view from a camera in your scene, click on that camera and then select the button with camera icon (technically, the View from Object tool), which looks just like the one to the left of this paragraph.

You can make any object serve as a camera: Select the object and then click the camera button; you are looking along the object's Z axis. As you walk or fly, the selected camera or object moves. Having the small secondary window open helps you see where you are.

 In Pioneer and Pioneer Pro, Caligari tries to turn your cameras into VRML "viewpoints" that can be selected from a browser. Unfortunately, the rules for viewpoints aren't well defined by the VRML 1.0 specification. So in the beta versions we tried, Caligari implemented viewpoints in a way that ought to work, but which other browser vendors don't recognize. The bottom line is that they often don't work unless you edit the VRML file. See Chapter 12 for more about viewpoints and cameras.

Wireframe versus fully rendered

Pioneer offers two ways to view the world: *wireframe* (like the world was made from pipe cleaners) and *fully rendered* (realistic). We call the *fully rendered* way "rendered" for short. Wireframe viewing lets you navigate faster, if speed is an issue for you. It also lets you see through things, a view that is particularly useful when objects are within or behind other objects.

 For rendered mode, choose the render button variant (shown next to this paragraph) where the characters "3DR" appear. (Think of 3DR as standing for 3D Rendering. It's actually a standard developed by Intel that works particularly well for PC graphics accelerators that use Intel chips and works reasonably well on normal PCs too.)

 For wireframe mode, choose the variant that looks like the button to the left of this pargraph.

To switch between the two forms of display, click and hold the rendering button, drag to the variant you want, and release the mouse button. To access the rendering quality control panel (described in "Rendering controls" coming up next), right-click either button.

Rendering controls

If the appearance of your world isn't what it should be, or if the quality of its appearance (rendering) is so high that it slows you down, check out the rendering quality panel.

Right-click on the rendering button (either the wireframe or 3DR variant) for the render quality panel you see in Figure 8-4.

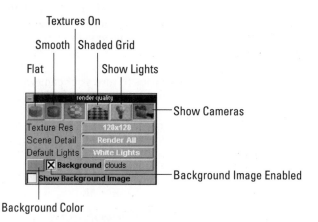

Textures On

Smooth | Shaded Grid

Flat | Show Lights

Figure 8-4:
The render
quality panel
controls the
reality level
in Pioneer's
virtual
reality.

Show Cameras

Background Image Enabled

Background Color

✔ **Smooth/Flat:** Alternative shader types for Pioneer's rendering. Smooth looks better; flat (or *faceted*) is more representative of what you see in other VRML browsers. These shader selections are recorded as VRML *shape hints.* Because they are only hints, they may be ignored by some browsers that can't do smooth shading. Your shapes will appear chunky in those browsers.

✔ **Textures on:** Enables textures to be seen and used in Pioneer. Without this button being enabled, material libraries and paint tools do not apply textures.

✔ **Shaded grid:** Turns the wireframe grid into a checkerboard in rendered mode (the mode you are in when the rendering button displays "3DR").

✔ **Show lights:** Displays light sources that are in your world.

✔ **Show cameras:** Displays cameras that are in your world.

✔ **Texture Resolution:** Determines the resolution of texture maps applied to surfaces and objects. Click and hold to see alternatives; drag and release to select desired resolution.

✔ **Scene Detail:** Provides alternatives to full rendering to allow faster motion. Click and hold to see alternatives; drag and release to select an alternative. Render All renders everything, always. Wireframe displays objects in wireframe during motion and fully renders them once stopped. Always

Wire always shows things in wireframe form. Boxes displays wireframe boxes for objects during motion and fully renders objects once stopped. Always Boxes displays everything as a box, always.

- ✔ **Default Lights:** Replaces current set of lights with a predetermined set, and sets default for starting new scenes. White Lights produces four *infinite* lights, all white, in different directions. Colored Lights produces three point source lights in light blue, light orange, and white. No Lights removes lights.

- ✔ **Background color:** Lets you specify a colored background that appears behind your scene (Pioneer backgrounds work only in Pioneer at this writing). An RGB (red, green, blue) color panel pops up; drag the sliding bar in each color strip, or type in new values to change the mix of these primary colors. The button depicts the color.

- ✔ **Background image enable** (checkbox): Enables Pioneer to use the specified bitmap image for a background. Specify the image by clicking the button to the right of the word Background. (Pioneer backgrounds work only in Pioneer at this writing.)

- ✔ **Background image name** (button): Specifies the name of the image file used as a background. Click the button to obtain a Get Texture Map dialog box that works like any other file-opening box in Windows. Choose a JPEG file (only).

- ✔ **Show Background Image** (checkbox): Enables display of the background image. This checkbox must be selected for the image to appear.

Moving Experiences

Using any VRML building software is a moving experience, and Pioneer is no exception. First you have to be able to move yourself (your view, anyway); then you have to be able to move other stuff.

Walk, fly, or choose

In Pioneer, one button location with three variants determines whether your mouse actions make your view move (walking or flying) or whether the actions choose an object. The three variants you can choose from appear in Figure 8-5.

Just click on whichever of these is visible, drag to the variant you want, and release the mouse button to select that variant.

—— Walk
—— Fly
—— Selection tool

Walk and fly work in build mode exactly as they do in browse mode (see Chapter 4):

- **Walk:** Left-click and push the mouse away from you to move forward, drag towards you for back, and drag left/right to turn. To move up (in the world's Z axis), right-click and push the mouse away from you. To tilt your view up or down, hold down both left and right buttons and drag back (for up) or forward (for down) — as you would with a video-game joystick control. The direction of travel does not angle up or down in a tilted view (you travel as if you were walking while looking up or down).

- **Fly:** Same as walk, but after a brief movement of the mouse, you keep moving as long as you hold the mouse button down. Speed depends on the length of your movement with the mouse.

- **Selection tool:** With this tool selected, click on any object to select it for editing, scaling, moving, or rotating. Right-click to get information on a selected object. See "Being Selective and Manipulative" later in this chapter for more details.

Axes and coordinate systems

Okay, everyone, we're on the cutting edge of technology here, so it's time to sharpen your axes! Of course, by *axes* we mean the plural of *axis.* (Pronounce it *ak-sees* to show off your knowledge of ancient Geek — er, Greek.) Axes are those things you most often see along the horizontal and vertical sides of graphs, generally labeled X and Y. Everything on a graph has a position that can be defined by an X value and a Y value (or *coordinate*), usually written (X, Y). For example, (100, 50) is a point 100 units along the X axis and 50 up the Y axis.

In virtual reality, we deal not in two axes, but in three: X, Y, and Z. Every corner of every shape has a position that can be described by an X, Y, and Z value. The whole set of three axes is called a *coordinate system,* and the 0,0,0 point is called the *origin*.

Every shape or other object in your virtual world can be defined by using a single X, Y, Z coordinate system called a World coordinate system, but having additional coordinate systems is actually useful.

Caligari gives you three main coordinate systems to choose from, depending on what you are doing:

- ✔ **World coordinates:** These coordinates apply to the entire scene you are building. Every object and point in your Pioneer scene shares this common coordinate system, sort of the way North, South, East, and West are the same for everyone in a room. X and Y are along the grid plane that Pioneer displays, and Z is up.

- ✔ **Object coordinates:** Every object has its own coordinate system and axes. This system has no fixed orientation with respect to the World coordinate system, sort of the way everyone in a room has his own left, right, forward, and back directions. If you rotate or move the object, the axes rotate or move too. The origin of an object's coordinates can be anywhere, including somewhere off to the side of the object.

- ✔ **Screen coordinates:** X is along the bottom of your screen, Y is along the left edge, and Z is into the screen.

When does your choice of coordinate systems matter? Generally, when you want to do something precise, like:

- ✔ When you want to move or expand something along an object's axis, regardless of its orientation in space. If you want Mr. Potato Head's nose to get longer, for example, you don't want to have to worry about which way Mr. Head is facing, so you choose Object coordinates (or Pioneer chooses it for you). If you use World coordinates, his nose may go shooting off to the left or something.

- ✔ When you're rotating something. Rotation goes *about* (around) an axis, like a roast pig on a spit. If Mr. Potato head is gazing peacefully off across the fields of Iowa and you want him to lay back a bit and gaze at the sky, rotating him about the world's X axis may well land him on his ear, depending on which way he's facing. Rotating him around his own X, Y, or Z axis is more likely to get the result you want.

Caligari automatically chooses coordinate systems that make sense for the operation you are doing (thereby avoiding getting dirt in Mr. Potato Head's ears).

You can change the coordinate system you are using whenever you see fit. At the bottom-right corner of the Pioneer window, at the right end of the Pioneer help bar, is the *Coordinates panel.* Find the markings X, Y, and Z and the nearby button labeled Obj, Wld, or Scr, which you see in Figure 8-6.

Figure 8-6:
Use these
buttons to
choose a
coordinate
system —
object,
world, or
screen.

To see the other two coordinate system variants, click and hold the Obj, Wld, or Scr button — whatever is visible. To select a different coordinate system, drag upward and release the mouse button. To restrict motion to one or two axes, with a click deselect the X, Y, or Z axis button at the bottom-right corner of the Pioneer window (to re-enable them, click again).

Just to make your life more interesting, Caligari does not show you the axes in Pioneer unless you are selecting objects that are glued-together pieces of larger objects. They apparently believe that since Pioneer is WYSIWYG, you don't need to see the axes. Of course, if you lay out a few bucks for Pioneer Pro, you can display those coordinates by clicking the Axis button. (The button sports a set of three arrows in red, green, and blue.) In Pioneer, Caligari has intentionally left out the capability to display or change the axes. One way to cheat is to build and label your own axes using the cylinder and text primitives (see "Let's get primitive: Primitives panel" later in this chapter).

3D Modeling

Building stuff — that's when the virtual rubber meets the virtual road! And Pioneer does a particularly good job of helping you make nifty shapes. Start with a *primitive* shape, grab it by a face, and you can wrestle it into a slimy slug shape. Make 3D logos with the text tool. Or make a 2D shape of any design and *sweep* it into a 3D one. Taper things to a point or sweep them in circles. Have a ball! Make a squid!

This is a tool reference chapter, so we take a feature-by-feature approach. For a more task-oriented description of how to use these features, read Parts III and IV.

Let's get primitive: Primitives panel

Primitives are simple shapes — plus cameras, text, and lights. You can create them by choosing from the Primitives panel of Figure 8-7, which pops up when you click on the Primitives button (the ball, cube, and cone icon). Primitive shapes only come in one size, but the idea is to scale them.

Figure 8-7:
Have a ball (or cube or cylinder) with the Primitives panel. Pioneer Pro also offers a spotlight.

Cube   Camera
Plane   Cylinder   Directional Light

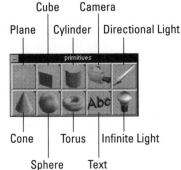

Cone   Torus   Infinite Light
Sphere   Text

Right-clicking a shape button or the text button in the Primitives panel displays another panel. For shapes, that panel controls the number of faces used to make the shape. You can either click and enter new values in the white box areas, or you can drag the double arrows that adjoin the boxes; drag right for a higher value or left for a lower value. Press Enter after changing a value.

✔ Right-click a primitive shape's button to change settings first, and *then* left-click the button to make the shape.

✔ Pioneer always starts with enormous primitives. Click the Object Scale tool and drag down with both mouse buttons pressed to scale objects uniformly.

✔ New objects always take on the appearance of the current "materials." See the section "Materials and Painting," later in this chapter.

The Primitives panel left to right:

✔ **Plane:** Creates a 2D square. To have it composed of multiple faces, right-click and enter a higher resolution (divisions per side) in the panel that appears.

✔ **Cube:** Creates a 3D cube. To have it composed of multiple cubes, right-click and enter a higher resolution (divisions per side) in the panel that appears.

✔ **Cylinder:** Creates a cylindrical solid. Pioneer initially gives cylinders 16 sides. For variations, right-click and enter values in the panel that appears. For more sides, increase *longitude*. For *n* vertical divisions, increase *latitude* to *n*+1. For a conical shape, adjust *top radius,* which is expressed as a ratio to the bottom radius (for example, 0.5 is a top radius equal to 50 percent of the bottom radius).

✔ **Cone:** Creates a conical solid. Pioneer initially gives cones 16 sides. For variations, right-click and enter values in the panel that appears. For more sides, increase *longitude*. For *n* vertical divisions, increase *latitude* to *n*+1.

✔ **Sphere:** Creates a sphere. For variations, right-click and enter values in the panel that appears. For more pie slices, increase *longitude*. For *n* vertical divisions, increase *latitude* to *n*+1.

✔ **Torus:** Creates a torus (or doughnut shape). For variations, right-click and enter values in the panel that appears. For a rounder doughnut, increase *longitude*. For a rounder doughnut cross-section, increase *latitude*. For a bigger hole, increase *inner radius,* which is expressed as a ratio to the outer radius (for example, 0.8 creates a hole radius that is 80 percent of the total radius).

✔ **Text:** Allows you to type 2D text (which can later be swept into 3D). The text appears vertically in World coordinates as you type. To choose a font, right-click and use the Font dialog box that appears; click OK after you're finished.

Caligari's text is not the same as the "text" that is created with the VRML text primitive. Caligari's letters are actually very complex 2D shapes that are defined by TrueType fonts.

✔ **Camera:** Adds a camera to the scene. Pioneer converts cameras into VRML viewpoints, but as of this writing, many browsers fail to read them properly.

✔ **Infinite light:** Adds a light that radiates in all directions, like a light bulb.

✔ **Directional light:** Adds a light that illuminates the whole scene from one direction, like sunlight.

Adding either type of light also pops up a hue and intensity selection panel. Click on a color in the hexagonal color wheel; paler colors are closer to the center. Drag in the vertical intensity bar to change brightness.

✔ Just like shapes, cameras and lights can be moved, rotated, and even glued. Scaling has no real effect on lights; scaling changes the zoom on a camera.

✔ Lights and cameras appear in red until they're selected, and then they turn white.

✔ If your lights are not visible, right-click the button that displays either "3DR" or a wireframe cube (whichever variant is visible) and click the light-bulb icon in the panel that appears.

✔ No more than five lights or cameras are allowed.

✔ To change light properties, click on a light.

Where's Polly? Polygon tools

One way to get the shapes you want in Pioneer is to draw a 2D polygon and then sweep it into the third dimension. Two polygon tool variants share a common space on the tool bar. You can see them in Figure 8-8. In Pioneer Pro, a third variant allows you to make smoothly curved shapes.

Figure 8-8:
The two
polygon
tools.

—Regular Polygon
—Freehand Polygon

As with all variants, click and hold on the visible button to see the other button. Drag to the other button and release to select it.

✔ **Regular polygon** (hexagonal icon): Creates an *n*-sided polygon with identical sides. After you first click on this tool, a panel pops up to allow you to set *n*, the number of sides. Type in a number in the white box or drag the double-headed arrow at the right of the box left or right. Then click and drag in the main Pioneer window (or in the little window) to create the shape.

✔ **Freehand polygon:** Creates a polygon with as many sides as you like, with varying lengths. Click to begin drawing a side, and click again to end that side. Continue clicking at various locations to describe a shape. Right-click to close the polygon. Press Ctrl+Z to undo an incorrect side.

Grab your face: the Face tool

Every scene you make is made up of flat surfaces. A surface can be a plane primitive, a face of a shape, a polygon, or text. All these are also referred to as *faces*. Pioneer helps you make cool shapes by giving you tools to grab any face of an object, scale it, turn it, or move it. The tool is called the Point Edit:Face tool (so named because in Pioneer Pro and trueSpace, additional variants let you edit individual points around the face).

 Click the Point Edit:Faces tool (shown next to this paragraph). The Point Navigation panel shown in Figure 8-9 pops up.

Point Rotate

Figure 8-9:
The Point
Navigation
panel lets
you move,
rotate, or
scale
surfaces.

Point Move | Point Scale

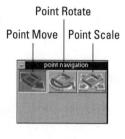

Once you select a face, it is outlined in green. You can manipulate it with the buttons in the Point Navigation panel:

- ✔ **Point Move:** Click this tool and then click any surface. Drag with the left button to move the selected surface(s). Drag with the right button to move in the Z axis.

- ✔ **Point Rotate:** Click this tool and then click any surface. Drag with the left button to rotate around the object's X or Y axis; drag with the right button for the Z axis. Select or deselect axes of rotation (X, Y, or Z) at the far right end of the Pioneer help bar. (For details, see "Axes and coordinate systems" earlier in this chapter).

- ✔ **Point Scale:** Click this tool and then click any surface. Drag diagonally with the left button to scale in both X and Y (Object coordinates); add the right button to uniformly in both directions. Select or deselect axes of scaling (X, Y, or Z) at the lower-right corner of the Pioneer window (for details, see "Axes and coordinate systems" earlier in this chapter).

To select more than one face at a time, hold down Shift while clicking. If Shift doesn't work, try Ctrl; the beta versions of Pioneer are buggy in this area.

Tools for sweeping

To help you make creative shapes, Pioneer gives you tools to *sweep,* to form a *tip,* or to *lathe* a selected surface. A surface can be a plane primitive, a face of a shape, a polygon, or text. All of these surfaces are also referred to as *faces.* To select a face, choose the Point Edit: Faces tool and click on a face. Selected faces are outlined in green.

As you use any sweep tool to sweep a selected face, the Point Navigation panel of Figure 8-9 remains on your screen so that you can move, rotate, or scale the swept face. After that, any subsequent sweeps will duplicate the initial move, rotate, or scale action, creating a continuous skewing, twisting, or tapering effect. (Or at least they *should* do so. Caligari's main product, trueSpace 2, works that way. Pioneer and Pioneer Pro are still a bit buggy as we write this.)

Sweeping tools (in Figure 8-10) are variants sharing a common space on the tool bar.

Figure 8-10:
The sweeping tools; use them to create fun shapes from an object.

 Sweep
Tip
Lathe

From top to bottom, they are Sweep, Tip, and Lathe. Click and hold on the visible one to see the others. Drag to the one you want and release the mouse button to select it.

✔ **Sweep:** Sweeps a selected face through space to create a solid (or to extend a solid)

✔ **Tip:** Sweeps a selected face to a point at the object's center.

✔ **Lathe:** Sweeps a selected face in a circular or spiral motion. First, however, Pioneer displays a control structure: a C-shaped curve starting at the face and ending in a blue tip and a T, as you see in Figure 8-11.

Set the C-curve as described in the next five bullets. Then, to actually perform the lathe operation, click the Lathe tool button again.

✔ The T's crossbar is the central axis around which the face is rotated; to sweep using a smaller radius, click the crossbar at its center point and drag it towards the face. (The face is the shape to the right of the T in Figure 8-11.)

Figure 8-11:
Pioneer uses this structure to control the sweep of the Lathe tool.

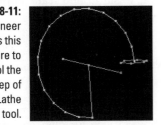

✔ To change the plane of the sweep, click the crossbar at either tip and drag it around the face. For instance, in Figure 8-11, the face is swept around in a three-quarter circle that will create a C-shape on the plane of the page. If you wanted the C-shape going into the page, you can drag the left tip of the crossbar around, behind the face, ending up just to the right of the face. The C would then be oriented into the page.

✔ To sweep in a spiral, click the blue tip of the C that appears just before the T (the last segment of the C), and drag in the axial direction. In Figure 8-11, for example, you can make a spiral by dragging that tip towards or away from yourself in the direction that the crossbar of the T points.

✔ To sweep through fewer or more degrees than the default of 270, click the vertical portion of the T and drag to shorten or extend the C.

✔ To change the resolution (the number of segments in the sweep), click on any of the dots around the C and drag.

Special modeling tools in Pioneer Pro

Pioneer Pro has some fantastic features for 3D modeling that we don't have the space to do justice to in this book. (Since they originated in Caligari's trueSpace product, you can, however, read all about them in IDG's new *Caligari trueSpace2 Bible* by Peter Plantec.) These features let you:

✔ Deform an object (stretch and twist it)

✔ Sculpt a surface (drag a vertex and adjust the surface curvature)

✔ Break up objects and faces into smaller pieces (divide and triangulate them)

✔ Combine objects or subtract one from the other (object subtraction, addition, and intersection)

✔ View, relocate, and rotate the orientation of an object's axes with respect to the object

✔ Return objects to their original orientation, position, and scale (normalize)

✔ Convert objects into their mirror image

✔ Fix flawed object geometry

✔ Reverse the "normal" of object faces so that they are rendered on the correct side

✔ Display object dimensions (using a Dimensioning Tool)

✔ Display and specify, using numbers, an object's size, location, and rotation (using the "object info" panel)

✔ Select not only faces but edges and vertices, and move, rotate, or scale them

  ✔ Delete faces from objects

  ✔ Sweep a face along any arbitrary path to form a solid

  ✔ Bevel a face (taper it) while sweeping it

For more on these functions, you can also check the Pioneer Pro help document (which in early Pioneer Pro beta versions is actually the trueSpace help document).

Being Selective and Manipulative

Software is amazing, and in the case of 3D modeling software, it's amazing how many different buttons you need for selection and manipulation tasks — tasks that in the real world any two-year-old toddler can do. Here are all the buttons you need to select and manipulate virtual objects.

Just pause your mouse cursor over a button (don't click), and the button's name appears in a bar below the buttons. If a button listed here is not visible, it's hiding behind one of its variants; click and hold on the visible variant to see its shyer family members.

  ✔ **Selection tool** (arrow): One of the variants sharing the same location as the Walk and Fly button. We also refer to this tool as the "object select tool." With this tool selected, click on any object to select it for editing, scaling, moving, or rotating. Ctrl+click to select several objects. Selected objects appear white in wireframe mode or with a 3D arrow in rendered mode.

  Right-click the Selection tool for details of the selected object's name, Level of Detail (LOD) distance, and inlining. The Object Info panel in Figure 8-12 opens. Data in the white boxes can be edited; edits will modify the object when you press Enter on your keyboard.

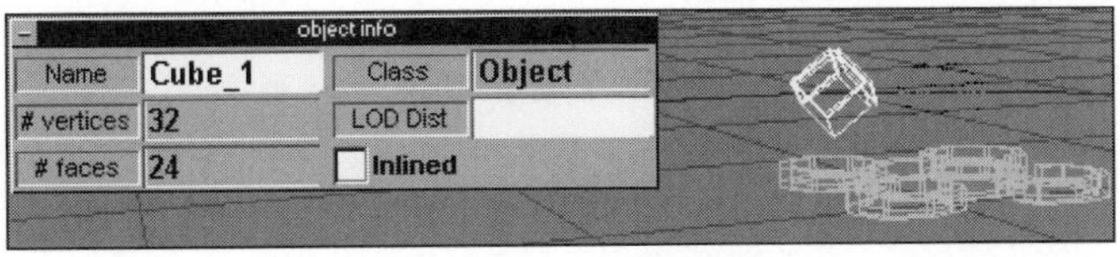

Figure 8-12:
Right-click the selection tool for more details on selected objects.

object info				
Name	Cube_1	Class	Object	
# vertices	32	LOD Dist		
# faces	24	☐ Inlined		

✔ **Deleting an object:** Select the object with the selection tool and press Delete on your keyboard. Zap.

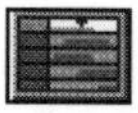

✔ **Object List:** Click on the Object List button, which appears next to this paragraph.

A list appears of all objects, cameras, and lights by name; the currently selected item is in white. Click on any other item in this list to select it.

✔ **Object Scale:** One of the variants in Figure 8-13. (Click and hold the visible button to see all three buttons of that figure.) Allows you to expand or shrink objects in one or more directions by clicking and dragging. Use the left button to scale in X and Y, the right button to scale in Z, or both buttons to scale in all three directions uniformly. To restrict scaling to one or two axes, deselect the X, Y or Z axis button at the bottom-right corner of the Pioneer window. To scale in fixed increments, select the Grid Snap tool (see its description later in this section).

Figure 8-13:
Three variant tools for manipulating objects: scale, rotate, and move.

✔ **Object Rotate:** One of the variants in Figure 8-13. Click and hold the visible button to see all three buttons. Allows you to click and drag to rotate an object about one or more axes. To restrict motion to one or two axes, deselect the X, Y, or Z axis button at the bottom-right corner of the Pioneer window. We suggest rotating in one axis at a time to avoid mental blowout. Click and drag with the left button to rotate around the X or Y axis (left/right for X, up/down for Y); drag up/down with the right button to rotate around the Z axis. To rotate in World or Screen coordinates, choose Wld or Scr in the Coordinates panel. To rotate in fixed increments, select the Grid Snap tool (see its description later in this section).

✔ **Object Move:** One of the variants in Figure 8-13. Click and hold the visible button to see all the buttons. Allows you to click and drag an object (or set of glued objects) in any direction. Use the left mouse button to drag left or right (that is, in the X/Y plane in World coordinates) and the right mouse button to drag vertically (Z). To restrict motion to one or two axes, deselect the X, Y, or Z axis button at the bottom-right corner of the Pioneer window. To move on a grid, select the Grid Snap tool (see its description later in this section).

✔ **Hierarchy Navigation:** Allows you to select individual pieces that have been glued together (the selected piece can then be moved, rotated, edited, painted or fricasseed independently). Select a glued-together object with the Selection tool; then to move down (to smaller groupings) or up (to larger groupings), click on the hierarchy navigation button, which you see to the left of this paragraph.

The selected piece turns white (from stage fright, undoubtedly) in wireframe mode or is marked by a set of red, green, and blue object axes in rendered mode. When you run out of up or down, the button reverses automatically. Instead of the Hierarchy Navigation button, you can alternatively use the keyboard down and up arrows to move down or up the hierarchy. To select among siblings, use the left/right arrows, or click on a sibling.

✔ **Grid Snap:** Allows you to move, rotate, or scale things in increments (see it in next to this paragraph).

Click it once to turn it on and again to turn it off. Right-click on the Grid Snap tool, and a "grid" panel appears in which you can set the increments. A different set of increments is used for move, rotate, and scale. Rotation increments are in degrees. To disable grid snap for a given axis, click the X, Y, or Z buttons *in the "grid" panel* (not the ones at the far right of the Pioneer help bar).

Gluing, Grouping, and Coming Unglued

Anyone who has ever glued together a model airplane will love the gluing tools in Pioneer. You can glue together assemblies of parts and then drag them around as units or glue them to other assemblies. Pioneer also provides a special glue tool for VRML that we haven't seen anywhere else: a *group objects together as a Level of Detail (LOD) object* tool that helps make complex worlds work better in browsers.

The following five gluing tools are variants of each other. (That is, they hide behind each other at a single button location. Click and hold on the visible button to see the others, which appear in Figure 8-14.)

Figure 8-14:
Stick it to
your objects
with glue
tools.

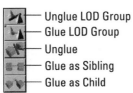

— Unglue LOD Group
— Glue LOD Group
— Unglue
— Glue as Sibling
— Glue as Child

✔ **Glue as sibling/Glue as child:** These tools let you make more complex objects out of sub-objects. Begin with one object selected (the parent-to-be, if gluing children) and then click the tool. Click with the glue bottle cursor on the other object. Click the selection tool after you're finished.

By gluing things together and navigating the hierarchy that results, you can get a lot of control over your objects. If they are glued as *siblings*, you can not only modify each one independently, but you can also modify them together. On a Mr. Potato Head model, the eyes might be siblings, so you can make them bug out (elongate them) the same amount, yet each can be rotated independently. By gluing an object as a *child* to another object, the child is affected by whatever you do to the *parent*. The arms might be a child to the potato, so they can all receive any color changes you might make.

✔ **Unglue:** Unglues glued parts. Use the Hierarchy Navigation methods we described in the last section to select the piece (object or object group) you want unglued, and then click the Unglue tool. To unglue siblings, navigate with the keyboard left and right arrow keys to select any individual sibling and then click the Unglue tool. Only one bond is unglued at a time; multiple siblings require multiple ungluings.

✔ **Glue LOD group:** Lets you assemble a group of alternative — usually simpler — shapes to represent other more complex shapes when viewed from far away. This grouping minimizes the rendering demands on a browser for complex scenes. Create the complex object (the one to be displayed at the closest distance) at the location where the LOD group objects are to appear and then choose this tool. Click on increasingly simpler representative shapes with the glue bottle cursor, ending with the least detailed object. Pioneer moves them so that they center on the first object. Pioneer assigns increasing Level of Detail (LOD) distances to each object, starting at a default of 20 units; you can modify the LOD distances using the Object Info panel of the selection tool (see "Being Selective and Manipulative" earlier in this chapter). See Chapter 17 for details on LOD groups.

✔ **Unglue LOD group:** Ungroups a LOD group into separate objects. Select whichever representative object of the group is visible and then select this tool.

Materials and Painting

One of Pioneer's nicest features for VRML is its capability to apply *materials* to surfaces. A material is made up of various qualities: color, radiance, transparency, shininess, roughness, and texture mapping. Most of these qualities are fairly understandable just from their names, except perhaps radiance and texture mapping. (If you don't think they are understandable, see the upcoming sidebar, "A tribute to attributes.") High *radiance* makes a surface's color less dependent on external light. *Texture mapping* allows you to apply bitmap images (in JPEG format) to entire objects and individual surfaces as if they were wallpaper. Materials are set using the *Materials panels* that arise with the various paint tools.

Paint tools and materials

Pioneer gives you five different tools for painting surfaces with a material; you can see them in Figure 8-15. All five tools are variants, which means they occupy the same space on the toolbar; click and hold on the visible variant to display the others. Drag to the one you want and release the mouse button to select it. As always in Pioneer, the help bar normally found just above the menu bar tells you what each tool is as you pass over it.

Figure 8-15:
Caligari
paint tools
for the
material
world.

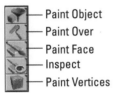

— Paint Object
— Paint Over
— Paint Face
— Inspect
— Paint Vertices

Paint tools apply not only color, but also all the "current materials" that appear in the Materials panels discussed next. Begin by selecting the object you want to paint and then the tool. Then, if you are using a tool to modify an individual face, click on the face.

Changes to surfaces in early versions of Pioneer don't show up until you click the "3DR" button or walk or fly a little. Surfaces don't (and logically shouldn't) appear at all in wireframe mode, only in 3DR (fully rendered) mode.

The paint tools work as follows:

 ✔ **Paint object:** Applies a material to all surfaces of the selected object. If you find that you can't make the Paint Object tool work, try clicking the selection tool, selecting the object again, and re-selecting the Paint Object tool.

   When painting a face or object, something called "UV coordinates" controls the application of bitmap images (texture maps). If a surface is not parallel to the UV projection plane, the image will be distorted. See "UV Projection tool" later in this chapter and Chapter 14 for details.

 ✔ **Paint over:** Click a face on the selected object to replace the existing material with the current material. Repainting extends to any adjoining faces that have the same material. If an object has the same material all over (all its faces), the entire object gets repainted.

✔ **Paint face:** Click a face to apply the current material to a face. Note that if a primitive shape has high resolution (is subdivided into many faces), each face has to be painted separately, even though they are all part of one big, flat surface.

✔ **Inspect:** Click a surface to pick up the material and make it the current material. You can then use the other paint tools to apply that material to another surface. Pioneer displays the material in the Materials panels so that you can review its various ingredients before reusing it.

You can also temporarily invoke the Inspect tool by pressing either Ctrl or Shift while clicking with the Paint face, Paint over, or Paint object tool.

✔ **Paint vertices:** Click on a corner to apply a color (only) to that corner, which then fades with distance from the corner. Click with Shift or Ctrl pressed to remove the color. Painted vertices are a cool idea, and VRML accommodates them, but unfortunately, not very many browsers besides Pioneer can recreate them.

The Materials panels of Figure 8-16 specify the material that the paint tools apply. The panels pop up automatically when you select the Paint face, Paint over, or Inspect tool. You can also right-click on any paint tool to pop the panels up.

Figure 8-16:
Materials panels help you choose what material to paint with.

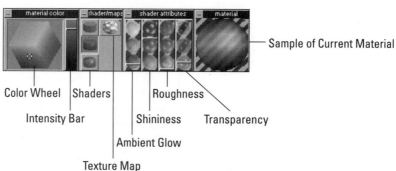

Sample of Current Material

Color Wheel | Shaders | Roughness

Intensity Bar | Shininess | Transparency

Ambient Glow

Texture Map

✔ **Material color panel:** Click on a color in the hexagonal color wheel; less saturated colors are closer to the center. Drag in the vertical intensity bar to change intensity.

✔ **Shader/maps panel:** This panel allows you to apply a texture map and control the smoothness of rendering. To specify the image for a texture map, right-click the texture map button (the checkered ball). To apply the texture map specified in that panel, left-click the texture map button. (The other buttons, Pioneer's shader settings, suggest to the browser where it should perform smooth or flat rendering on a shape. The top button makes all planes of a shape render flat; the bottom, smooth; and the middle button does smoothing at the corners where adjoining planes differ by an angle of less than 32 degrees.)

When you right-click the checkered ball, you get the Texture Map panel that you see in Figure 8-17. Here's how to use it:

- **Get image map:** Click the button to the right of the checkered ball on the Texture Map panel. Select a JPEG image file from the Get Texture Map dialog box that appears. The filename now appears on the button. Pioneer only accepts JPEG files.

- **Pattern repetitions:** For a repetitive *tiling* of your texture map image, enter values in the U Repts and V Repts boxes, or drag the double-headed arrows left or right. U and V are the coordinate system axes, analogous to X and Y, for placing the image map on the surface. See "UV Projection tool" later in this chapter.

- **Pattern offset from edge:** To adjust the position where your texture map image begins, enter values in the U Offset and V Offset boxes, or drag the double-headed arrows left or right. U and V are the coordinate system axes, analogous to X and Y, for placing the image map on the surface. See "UV Projection Tool" later in this chapter.

✔ **Shader attributes panel:** From left to right, these vertical columns control the attributes of *ambient glow*, *shininess*, *roughness*, and *transparency*. Drag the horizontal line up for more of a particular attribute.

The Pioneer attributes (as of this writing) translate into VRML as follows: *ambient glow* in Pioneer = ambientColor in VRML; shininess = specularColor; roughness = shininess (go figure that one out); and *transparency* = *transparency*.

✔ **Material panel:** This displays a sample of the material you have created, with various colors, attributes, or texture mapping.

Figure 8-17:
Putting up virtual wallpaper with the Texture Map panel.

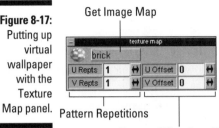

Get Image Map

Pattern Repetitions

Pattern Offset from Edge

Material library

Coming up with the right combination of surface attributes takes work, so being able to store those combinations as a named *material* is nice. Pioneer provides this feature through *material libraries.* Caligari supplies a library with Pioneer, called *basic* (the BASIC.MLB file). You can add to this library or create your own libraries.

Choosing a material from a library makes it the *current material,* which you then apply by using the Paint object or Paint face tool. You can see the current material attributes in the Materials panels.

To do anything with a material library, click on the Material Library button (3 colored spheres), and the Material Library panel opens. The panel is shown in Figure 8-18, displaying eight of the materials in the BASIC.MLB material library.

Chosen Material Indicator

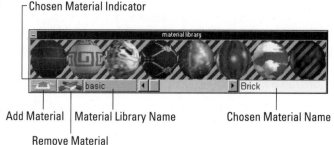

Add Material | Material Library Name | Chosen Material Name

Remove Material

Use the material library for storing surface attributes:

- ✔ **Choose a material:** Click on any of the sample spheres shown to select that material as the current material. Use the horizontal scroll bar to see additional materials.

- ✔ **Add a material:** Set up your material properties as we describe in the previous section, "Paint tools and materials," and then click the Add Material button (the up arrow in the lower-left corner). A new sample sphere displays your material.

- ✔ **Remove a material:** Click on the material to be removed and then click on the Remove Material button (the down arrow at the bottom).

- ✔ **Load, save, or start a new library:** Click the Load/Save Material Library button (the one marked "basic" in Figure 8-18). From the menu that appears, choose New to start a new library, Load to load a library file, Save to save the displayed library with its current name, or Save As to save it with a new name.

UV Projection tool

When you apply an image to a surface, Pioneer applies it according to a set of coordinates called U and V, which are sort of like X and Y axes. The projected image's size is automatically scaled to match the dimensions of the surface or object.

We discuss this subject in more detail in later chapters, particularly in Chapter 14.

Select an object and then click the UV Projection button to see the UV map panel and get a new UV projection grid; see them in Figure 8-19. The UV Projection button looks like it's wearing green sunglasses — undoubtedly to protect it from UV radiation! The grid you see replaces the existing one when you click Apply.

Cylindrial

Planar   Spherical

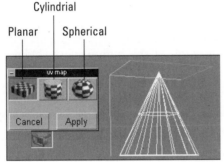

Figure 8-19:
The UV tool,
panel, and
projection
grid.

In the UV map panel, choose one of three projections: planar, cylindrical, or spherical. The UV projection grid is displayed on the selected object. The brown lines indicate the *seam* where the image edge is placed. To adjust the orientation of the image, use the object rotation tool (preferably with rotation limited to one axis). Select the grid tool to get 90 degree or other increments (see "Being Selective and Manipulative," earlier in this chapter).

The projection types are as follows:

- **Planar:** Projects the image in a straight line onto the selected face or object. The image continues *through* to appear on the opposite side of the face or object. The rectangle formed by the brown and blue lines is the plane of projection. The remaining brown line shows the direction of projection. The object need not be planar.

- **Cylindrical:** Projects the image radially towards a center axis; the result is like a label applied to a can. The object need not be cylindrical.

- **Spherical:** Projects the image radially from all directions, towards a point at the center; the image acts like a shrink-wrapped label surrounding an object. The object need not be spherical.

To repaint the object with the new UV coordinates, click a paint tool (see "Paint tools" earlier in this chapter). If a surface is not parallel to the UV projection plane, the image will be distorted on that surface.

Click Apply after you have chosen the UV grid you want and have properly oriented it, or click Cancel to return to the previous UV projection.

Hyperlinks

Objects in VRML can have hyperlinks attached to them, allowing the viewer to click on the object and be linked to a Web page, another VRML file, or any other data type on the web, like sound or video.

To add a hyperlink to an object, select the object with the Selection tool (see "Being Selective and Manipulative" earlier in this chapter) and then click on the *Attach a hyperlink URL* tool — the button showing the world in chains. (We're not crazy about the symbology of this.) (This button may be hiding behind the Attach/Remove 3D Sound button — a green zig-zag icon.) An Attach URL Link dialog box pops up in which you type the linked URL or the path of a file on your PC. You can also add a description of the URL; browsers display this description when the user passes the mouse cursor over the object with the attached link.

If you attach a link to a complex object with a hierarchy of objects glued to it, the child objects inherit the link by default. You may navigate down the hierarchy to subordinate objects and attach different links to them, however. In other words, Mr. Potato Head, as a head, can link to the Idaho or Maine home page, but his mouth (as a child object) can link to the Great Places to Eat Potatoes home page. We refuse to consider what his ears might link to.

Audio

With Pioneer, you can make stereo (or "3D") audio play from any object, although few browsers besides Pioneer can currently play Pioneer's audio.

Select an object and choose the green zig-zag Attach/Remove 3D Sound tool. (It shares a pop-up with the Attach a Hyperlink URL / Description button — the world-in-chains icon.) Here's a description of the buttons that appear in the subsequent dialog box:

- The blank, gray button at the top lets you choose a .WAV file.
- Intensity is the sound's volume.
- Minimum Range defines an inner sphere of constant volume.

✔ Maximum Range defines a sphere of diminishing, stereo volume.

✔ Attach connects the .WAV sound file to the selected object. (Remove disconnects it.)

✔ Enable turns the sound on or off in Pioneer.

See Chapter 20 for details of audio.

Inlined Objects

Inlining of objects is a technique that allows large VRML scenes to work better on the Internet. For the full scoop on inlining and inlined objects, see Chapter 17. Inlined objects are stored in separate files, so they can be loaded incrementally, allowing parts of the scene to be displayed while others are downloading. To mark an object for inlining, right-click on the Object Select tool, and select the Inline option in the Object Info panel that appears.

LOD groups and texture maps are also automatically inlined (see "Gluing, Grouping, and Coming Unglued" earlier in this chapter for more on LOD groups). Objects marked for inlining and textures are normally saved in a separate file, but you can tell Pioneer to include them as part of the main file if you prefer. See "Saving the World," which is next in this chapter.

Saving the World

To save the world you have created, choose File⇨Scene⇨Save from the menu bar. Specify a drive, directory, and filename as you would for any other Windows program (Pioneer automatically adds the .WRL extension). Click OK, and the Export VRML file dialog box of Figure 8-20 pops up.

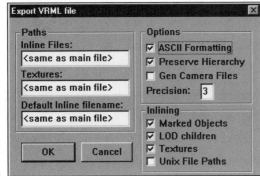

Figure 8-20: Lotsa options for saving VRML files.

Paths

Pioneer normally stuffs all its files (the main file and any inline files) in the same directory, using the same first five characters for the filenames of the inlines. You can change this situation if you see fit:

- ✔ **Inline Files and Textures paths:** Inline object and texture files are normally saved in the same directory as the main file, as you see in Figure 8-20. You can instead enter alternative paths for these files.

- ✔ **Default Inline filename:** You can enter a filename here, or Pioneer will use the name you chose for the main file. Either way, Pioneer will use the first five characters of the filename and append three digits, starting with 000 and increasing by 1 for each inlined file.

Options

The Export VRML file dialog box also lets you set various useful options:

- ✔ **ASCII Formatting:** Indents your VRML text neatly. This makes it easier for humans to read but makes your world unneccesarily large for browsing purposes.

- ✔ **Preserve Hierarchy:** Keeps glued-together objects together. Disabling this option makes more compact VRML files.

- ✔ **Gen Camera files:** Saves Pioneer camera details in separate files. Not particularly useful as far as we can tell.

- ✔ **Precision:** Sets the number of decimal places used for locations and dimensions of objects. Reducing precision creates more compact files but may introduce errors in object locations and dimensions.

Inlining

Check marks next to Marked Objects, LOD children, and Textures cause Pioneer to save these inlined components as separate files. Removing a component's check mark causes Pioneer to save that component in the main WRL file. You should leave these components checked unless they are very small.

Pioneer normally follows the PC convention of using backslashes in paths. Most Web servers expect forward slashes in the paths of inlined files, so for Web server (non-local) use, click to enable the Unix File Paths option.

Preferences

Choose File⇨Preferences to change a variety of miscellaneous behaviors in Pioneer. And the contestants are . . .

- ✔ **Dynapick:** Select this option and you don't have to click once to select an object and again to manipulate it with the current tool. With a tool selected (like move, rotate, or scale), just click and drag.

- ✔ **PitchSwap:** Reverses the control for *look up, look down.* Select this option and instead of dragging up the screen to look down, you drag down the screen.

- ✔ **LoadScene:** Reloads the scene you were working on the last time you quit Pioneer (if saved).

- ✔ **TopMenu:** Puts the menu bar and tools at the top of the window rather than at the bottom. Useful if you accidentally push the window too low and can't see the title bar to raise it up again! (The fact that this accident is even possible is weird, and this problem is not shared by any other Windows program we've ever seen. If it happens to you, press Alt+F, P, and select TopMenu to regain control.)

- ✔ **Titles:** Puts the titles on the panels.

- ✔ **SaveState:** Restores settings at the start as they were when you last quit.

- ✔ **SmallBrowse:** Enables a special, faster, small-screen window for browsing.

- ✔ **Load Inlines:** Determines when inlined files are loaded and displayed. *On Demand* loads inlined objects only when they come into view; *In Background* loads them as quickly as possible, displaying them as they are loaded. *Immediately* effectively cancels the benefit of inlining, waiting until all files are loaded before any are displayed.

- ✔ **Tablet:** Used for drawing tablets running mouse emulation.

- ✔ **Threshold ("Thold"):** When you allow boxes or wireframes during redraw (by right-clicking the render button and setting the rendering quality), a lower value here will cause Pioneer to switch to the simpler representation more readily. This setting allows faster motion.

- ✔ **Home:** The URL for the file or Internet resource that Pioneer tries to load when you start it.

2D and 3D Import Formats

Pioneer provides an exceptionally broad range of import filters, so you can read not only 3D models created by other software (of which there are bizillions on the net), but also 2D *vector* (line drawing) images in PostScript, encapsulated

PostScript, and Adobe Illustrator. These 2D images can then be swept into 3D objects. (Fonts in PostScript will cause problems unless those fonts are installed on your PC and you somehow wrangle the Caligari Adobe Type Manager CALATM.DLL out of Caligari and install it.) The formats that Pioneer can import, in addition to VRML (WRL extension), include the following:

- Adobe Illustrator (AI)
- Autodesk AutoCAD files (DXF)
- Autodesk 3D Studio files (3DS, PRJ, and ASCII)
- Caligari Scene (SCN), Object (COB), and Amiga (SOB)
- Imagine (IOB)
- Lightwave (LWB)
- PostScript (PS) and encapsulated PostScript (EPS)
- Videoscape (GEO)
- Wavefront (OBJ)

Pioneer can also read *gzip* (a compression format) versions of these formats (GZ or WRZ files). Texture maps on these objects may not be included or translated.

To import objects in these formats, choose File⇨Load Object from the menu bar. In the Load Object dialog box, choose the file type from the List files of type box and enter the folder and filename as in any Windows file-opening box. A panel pops up in which you set the following items (PostScript and DXF have different panels):

- **Object Unit Scale:** Tells Pioneer in what units you want the object's dimensions to be; choose meters to equate one object unit to one Pioneer grid unit. Many objects come without unit specifications, allowing you to adjust the scale. Smaller units make the loaded object proportionately smaller.

- **Center Object:** Positions the object at the center of your world, or (0,0,0) in World coordinates.

- **Fix Normals:** Reverses the *normal* of the object's surfaces, so the object's surfaces are visible from the side you wish. (VRML shapes often have only one visible side, the side designated *the normal,* although some browsers such as Pioneer and Live3D can show both sides.)

For more on importing, see Chapter 16.

Chapter 9
Finding Building Materials

● ●

In This Chapter

▶ What VRML building materials are

▶ Buying materials

▶ Getting materials from the Internet

▶ Creating materials from photographs

▶ Compressed files

▶ Recycling VRML components

● ●

*O*ne of the unpleasant surprises of creating 3D worlds is that creating a good-looking virtual world and its furnishings takes an amazing amount of work. Your dreams of building castles in the air can fade as you discover, yes, you really do have to take care of every persnickety detail when you build a chair, house, castle, or animal. You have to create every rung, peg, beam, molding, gargoyle, or eyelash. You work almost as much to build a virtual structure as you do to build a real one.

As in the real world, one way around this problem is to let someone else do the work: to populate your world with some pre-built materials. You can't exactly buy VRML materials at Sears (yet), so in this chapter, we look into ways of finding those materials.

What Are VRML Building Materials?

At the current state of VRML, the main building materials are *models* and *textures* (soon, VRML building materials may also include audio, video, and motion). Models are 3D shapes. Textures are *bitmap* images (made up of dots) used like wallpaper on objects to make them look real. Textures can be any bitmap image that your building tool will read. If you have a scanner and a suitably large ego, you could scan a picture of your face and use it as wallpaper.

Often, however, textures are *seamless* — specially designed to give the appearance of a continuous surface when they are *tiled* (arranged in a grid pattern) like sod on a lawn. Seamless texture edges are crafted so that the left edge of one copy will exactly match the right edge of the adjoining copy, and the top and bottom edges will match similarly. Models and textures are most often found — and most easily used — as independent files, not as part of other VRML worlds.

Models and textures can come in a variety of file types, or *formats.* The trick is to find them in a format that your building tool can read or import. Models tend to come in formats designed for a particular software tool, like Caligari's trueSpace, Virtus's Walkthrough, or Autodesk's AutoCAD or 3D Studio. Usually, other tools from that vendor can also read and/or write those same formats.

Pioneer, for example, can read trueSpace .OBJ files (formats tend to be identified by the three-letter extension used for the file). Virtus Walkthrough VRML can read only models from a Virtus Walkthrough library (.WLB) file. Fortunately (for PC users), Pioneer imports a wide variety of object file formats. Both PC and Mac users get the benefit of Virtus's included object libraries. For a more detailed discussion on importing and exporting files, see Chapter 16.

A lot of models that originate on high-priced workstations are not very suitable for VRML work. People used to do 3D modeling on workstations from Silicon Graphics, Sun, and others. These high-powered workstations can handle objects with many, many faces and very detailed texture maps. PCs and Macs just don't have the graphic power to continuously display these objects as you navigate around. If you use such an object, viewing your world can get very slow.

Buying Materials

Like most problems, the problem of getting materials can be partly solved by tossing money around. Many people create 3D models for a living, and they are delighted to sell you a copy or an entire library of models. You can buy models of vehicles, buildings, animals, plants, people, molecular structures, landscapes, and a variety of fantasy items (assuming the preceding categories do not already fulfill your fantasies). Unfortunately, most of the models are being sold for business purposes such as architecture — uses in which they have a lot more value than they probably do to you. In other words, models can cost a lot. Texture libraries are somewhat cheaper.

Among the people who sell models and textures for a living, a well-known source is ViewPoint Data Labs in Orem, Utah. Give 'em a call at 1-801-229-3000 or set your Web browser to `http://www.viewpoint.com` for more information. ViewPoint was kind enough to provide a sample of 20 really cool models in

Caligari .OBJ format for our CD. (Unfortunately, you folks using Walkthrough can't use them, but then you've got your own sample models from Virtus.) These are pretty complex models for VRML use (they make big VRML files), but hey — "cool" comes at a price.

Another popular vendor is Acuris (1-800-OK-ACURIS) in Menlo Park, California. We have a set of objects from these folks on the CD too.

See OUR_CD.TXT or OUR_CD.HTM on our CD for a detailed list of what we've included, but among them are the following:

- ✔ Animals
- ✔ A human hand and heart
- ✔ An aircraft and a space shuttle
- ✔ Sports cars
- ✔ A palm tree
- ✔ A skyscraper

The models on our CD are licensed to you only for personal non-commercial use.

ViewPoint also manages the extremely useful "Avalon" collection on the Internet. See the section "Getting Materials from the Internet" later in this chapter.

Lower cost sources of material are, logically enough, the vendors of the lower cost tools. In fact, if you buy such a tool, it will probably come with a variety of sample models and textures. The no-charge evaluation copies that are often available on the Internet sometimes come with a few models. On our CD, likewise, there are some sample models for both Virtus and Caligari products. If you lay out the money to buy, say, Pioneer Pro or trueSpace 2 from Caligari or Walkthrough Pro from Virtus, you will get additional models and texture libraries. Virtus also offers model libraries for sale at around $40 a pop, and a tool called Alien Skin Textureshop that creates weird skin-like textures for about $100.

If you go to tool vendors who sell mostly to professionals, expect to pay accordingly. Autodesk (1-800-225-6106), for example, mainly sells computer-aided design (CAD) and professional 3D modeling and rendering tools. They also offer CDs with models and textures: *3D Props,* 300 models in 3DS format, residential or commercial models (about $200); and *Texture Universe* with 500 textures and backgrounds in 24-bit TGA, 8-bit GIF, and BMP format, for about $250. (Pioneer can read 3DS formats, but only JPEG textures, so you'd have to convert the formats to JPEG. Virtus Walkthrough Pro uses its own texture format but can convert Windows .BMP format images in the Windows version, or PICT or QuickTime images in the Mac version.)

Creating Materials from Photographs

If you have a scanner or know a photo-processing service that can also give you your photos on a disk, you can create your own VRML building materials. Textures, of course, are just images; if you can scan them in and convert them to the format you need (usually JPEG), you can do texture mapping with them. You will need to use very low resolution for texture mapping, however. Your texture images should probably be no more than about 200 pixels in either dimension. Set your scanner software to a very low resolution, or use a graphics program such as Lview Pro and reduce the image to 200 x 200 pixels or lower.

The possibility that we're most excited about is creating 3D models from photographs! Just as we were finishing up this book, some companies started offering affordable tools for doing just that. One of these companies, EOS, has a beta version of their latest offering, PhotoModeler LX on our CD. See OUR_CD.TXT or OUR_CD.HTM for details.

The basic principal these tools operate on is the same one your eyes rely on. By using two 2D images of the same subject from two slightly different locations, your brain (or a computer with some help) can figure out the 3D shape. With these computer tools, you can take two photographs, scan them, tell the computer where the tip of the nose, tops of the ears, and other vital points are in Picture A and Picture B, and the computer will output the 3D model!

Getting Materials from the Internet

The lowest cost source of materials is probably the Internet, where public domain models are available. "And what," you say, "about all those VRML models out there? Can I use them?" Well, you can reuse parts from some of them — assuming they are either public domain or you acquire the right to use them.

Finding models and textures

You would think that one place to find models and textures would be in the Web pages of tool and model vendors. For the most part, you would be wrong — at least as far as models are concerned. Not all that many models are available from these folks. One exception is ViewPoint Data Labs, which manages the public domain site called Avalon. Lotsa great goodies there.

Table 9-1 shows a sampling of Web and ftp sites where you can find a few models and textures. Just enter the main URL in the URL box of your Web browser and go. To go directly to the specific directory listed in the third column, append the directory to the URL like this: `http:/www.caligari.com/ ftp/pub/Pioneer/contrib/`. Directories tend to change, though, so if you can't find the specific directory, go the main URL and browse around. Also, new sites are springing up all over.

Table 9-1	Good Stuff on the Internet		
Site	*Main URL*	*Directory*	*What's There*
Avalon/ViewPoint	`http://www. viewpoint.com`	`/avalon/ objects.html`	Buckets of great stuff: Aircraft, anatomy, creatures, landscapes, and more. Nearly all are ZIP files. Don't be fooled by the file extensions of DXF and others. Files ending in DXF are ZIP files of DXF files.
Caligari	`http://www. caligari.com`	`/ftp/pub/ Pioneer/ contrib/`	A few worlds.
		`/ftp/pub/ trueSpace/ objects/`	A few objects (.cob).
Virtus	`http://www. virtus.com; ftp://freedom. interpath.net`	`/textures. html`	40 cool alien skin textures.
		`/pub/virtus/ win/models/`	A few Virtus models.
Graphics BBS	`http://www. graphics. rent.com`	`http://ftp. graphics. rent.com`	Links to lots of 3D objects and other graphics goodies; 3D objects and textures in a multitude of formats, including Caligari COB and DXF.
VRML Models	`http://www. ocnus.com`	`/models/`	VRML models, nearly all gzipped.
VRML Repository	`http://www. sdsc.edu`	`/vrml/`	No models here, but a good starting place for VRML authors.

Compressed files

Many, if not most, of the material and VRML files you will find on the Internet are compressed (some are so large that compression is the only way you can actually download them in your lifetime). The official compression format for VRML is *gzip*, offered by the Free Software Foundation as part of their *gnu* tools. Nonetheless, for files that originate on PCs, the most common compression type is ZIP. For Macs, the most common is StuffIt (SIT). Files originating on UNIX workstations are usually TAR or gzipped files. Caligari's Pioneer, the browser/builder we include on our CD, automatically decodes gzipped files.

If you've been hanging out on the Internet for awhile, you probably already have the programs you need to decompress these kinds of files. If not, you can download those programs. For ZIP files, you can download an evaluation copy of WinZip from `http://www.winzip.com/winzip/download.htm`. Their latest products also handle various UNIX compression formats. To decompress StuffIt files and other Mac compression formats, visit Aladdin Systems at `http://www.aladdinsys.com/` and download some of their shareware or evaluation copies.

To find decompression programs for these and other formats at various sites worldwide, go to any good search engine on the web, such as Yahoo! (`http://www.yahoo.com`) or Alta Vista (`http://www.altavista.digital.com`) and search for *mac compression* or *pc compression*. If you download any programs, check them with a virus detection program.

Recycling VRML Components

You would think that once you had downloaded a VRML file, you could easily reuse its building materials. You would be wrong.

If you have a VRML world in a browser, you can't exactly break that world up and save its parts. A browser can conceivably save a VRML world file, but it won't let you break it up into usable pieces. But, hey, if you have a file in a browser/builder like Caligari's Pioneer, you should be able to do that, right? It loads objects, so it should be able to save objects, even if it saves them in Caligari's own format.

Wrong again. Pioneer is a trimmed-down version of Caligari's fancier products, and one of the functions they trimmed out is the capability to save an object. Now, if you were to buy Pioneer Pro . . .

No, unless you use a fancier tool than Pioneer or Virtus Walkthrough Pro, you have only three hopes for recycling VRML components:

Hope 1: Using Pioneer in the building mode, delete all objects from the scene but the one you want. Save the scene as a WRL file with a new name. Reload the scene and begin to build your new scene around that object.

Hope 2: "Inline" one of your own components to make it reusable. Inlining is something we discuss in more detail in Chapter 17. Following is the cookbook approach to creating a reusable component:

First, take a deep breath. Now, using Pioneer in the building mode, mark the object you want to use as *inline*. That is, select the object, right-click the selection tool (arrow), and click the checkbox Inlined in the panel that appears. (You may have to use the hierarchy navigation tool to select the component if it is part of a more complex object. See "Being Selective and Manipulative" in Chapter 8 for reference material on the navigation tool. See Chapter 13 for more discussion of glued-together components.)

Save the scene as a WRL file, making sure that Marked Objects is checked in the Inlining section of the Export VRML file dialog box. This option causes the inlined object to be saved as a separate file. The first five letters of the filename are the same as the main world filename (say, MYWORLD.WRL), plus a number (like MYWOR001). Put this file in the directory with your WRL scene file.

Having fun so far? Good. Now, using a text editor or word processor, open the WRL scene file to which you want to add the object. Add the following mystical VRML text (all of it, including the final } mark) — and add it immediately before the final } mark of the file, which marks the end of a Separator in VRML 1.0 and the end of a Transform in VRML 2.0:

```
DEF NoName_1 WWWInline {
    name  "calig000.wrl"
    bboxSize 1.000  1.000  1.000
    bboxCenter 0.000 0.000 0.000
    }
```

Instead of calig000.wrl, however, put the name of your inlined object file. The term NoName_1 is this object's name in the WRL scene, so if you add more than one object this way, use your own set of names for them.

If you run into difficulty using this approach, try removing the two lines that begin with "bbox".

Almost done now. Save the edited file (as a text file), and load the scene in Pioneer. You should now find a copy of the inlined object — scaled incorrectly perhaps, but it's there — in the center of your world. Wow! Just move it around and scale it, and there you are: virtual recycling! Now you can exhale.

Hope 3: Inline a component from a downloaded world. Worlds that use inlined objects and textures transmit them as separate files. If you save such a world as a file, you should find a whole slew of inlined files in the same folder as the main world file (they will be the files whose names begin with the same first five letters as the main world file). You can add inlined objects to your VRML scene using the editing technique described in "Hope 2" earlier. If you're a PC user, you can use Pioneer to do the final positioning and scaling of the object. If you're a Mac user, you'll have to go deeper into VRML to position and scale the object with a Transform node. See the VRML specification on our CD for the gory details.

You don't actually have to have a copy of the inlined file or texture to use it in an online world. Instead, you can substitute the URL of that file (its address on the Web) for the filename in the WWWInline statement. The browser of whoever is looking at your world will automatically download the object from that URL. This technique only works when your world is being viewed by a browser connected to the Web, however.

Even if you succeed at recycling a component of a VRML scene, you may not have the right to use that component. People who create software are protected by copyright law, and even if you substantially modify the object or texture, the originator still has rights. Do not recycle any VRML stuff unless you're sure you have the right to use it. You may find a comment in the file indicating its ownership and availability; but to be safe, get permission from the Web site owner.

Part III
World Building 101

IF BOB DYLAN HAD PURSUED A CAREER IN COMPUTERS.

"PUT HIM IN FRONT OF A TERMINAL AND HE'S A GENIUS, BUT OTHER-WISE THE GUY IS SUCH A BROODING, GLOOMY GUS HE'LL NEVER BREAK INTO MANAGEMENT."

In this part . . .

Why should other people have all the fun? You can build simple objects and make rooms to put them in. Add doors and windows, throw in a few off-the-shelf tables and chairs, and you can have yourself a respectable virtual world in a lot less time than you might think.

Chapter 10

Basic Shapes: Let's Get Primitive

• •

In This Chapter

▶ Making cubes, cylinders, spheres, and other simple shapes

▶ Gluing shapes together

▶ Copying objects

▶ Stretching an object in one or more dimensions

▶ Scaling an object uniformly in all dimensions

▶ Building objects that lean

▶ Attaching text to 3D objects

▶ Making 3D text

• •

Making Primitive Shapes and Objects

People used to make stone walls by piling up rocks. Each rock had its own unique shape, and consequently, its own unique place in the wall. A good wall required lots and lots of time and artistry.

Fortunately for those of us who don't have lots and lots of time and artistry, VRML builders don't work that way. Each builder has a few basic shapes — triangles, squares, spheres, cubes, cylinders, and so on — to use. Everything starts with these primitive objects. Once you have them, you can resize them, elongate them, copy them, glue a few together — and before long, you have some pretty complicated beasties, like the virtual squid from Chapter 8. But everything starts with those few primitive shapes.

Who are you calling primitive?

We call an object *primitive* if you can build it with a single command — either one complete instruction in raw VRML or one trip to the toolbar in Pioneer, Pioneer Pro, or Walkthrough Pro. If you have to go back to the toolbar for seconds, the object isn't primitive.

Let there be primitive objects

The first step in creating a VRML world is to learn to make primitive objects.

In Pioneer

Pioneer keeps its three-dimensional primitives on the Primitives panel, where they can discuss all their primitive issues without bothering anyone else. (No doubt CNN will start televising them soon. *The Primitives Panel* could come on right after *The Capital Gang.*) You can find the Primitives panel by clicking on its icon on the World Building toolbar. In addition to the three-dimensional primitives, the World Building toolbar contains a couple of two-dimensional primitives: the Regular Polygon tool and its variant, the Irregular Polygon tool.

Pioneer considers the following three-dimensional objects to be primitive: planes, cubes, cylinders, cones, spheres, and doughnuts (they call the doughnut a *torus*). The Primitives panel also lets you create non-geometric objects like cameras and light sources (which we discuss in Chapter 8), and text (which we clump in with the geometric primitives). Pioneer allows you to make vertical text, while Pioneer Pro gives you a choice of vertical or horizontal text.

You can find a more complete description of Pioneer's modes and their toolbars in Chapter 8. If you're like us, though, just reading a description of the tools doesn't do the trick. You need to get some virtual dirt on your virtual hands and *make* something. In particular, let's make Figure 10-1:

They don't make spheres like they used to

As you start to play around with the geometric primitives, you'll discover that Pioneer has some funny ideas about what a sphere, cylinder, cone, and doughnut are. For example, Pioneer believes that all the objects in Figure 10-1 are cylinders! All the objects in Figure 10-2 are spheres! And how do you think Pioneer would model the Great Pyramid? Well, as a cone, of course.

What's going on here? Pioneer doesn't understand *roundness,* but it fakes it as best it can. To Pioneer, a circle is just a polygon with so many little sides that you don't notice them — it *looks* round, even though it really isn't. All of Pioneer's apparently round objects are like that. For cylinders and cones, the number of sides is the *longitude,* and you can pick any number you want (bigger than 3) on the Properties panel of the Cylinder or Cone tool. A cylinder with a longitude of 20 or so looks round, and one with a longitude of 3 is definitely triangular. The Great Pyramid is a cone with longitude 4.

Spheres are even stranger because they are supposed to be round both horizontally and vertically. In the Properties panel of the Sphere tool, the longitude is the number of sides that the equator has, and the latitude is the number of sides that a meridian has.

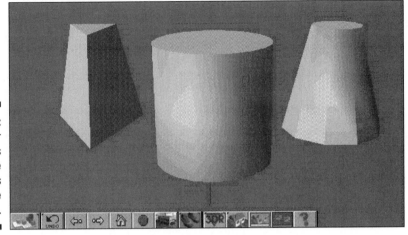

Figure 10-1:
Pioneer
considers
all these
shapes
to be
cylinders.

Figure 10-2:
Three
spheres.
The
latitudes
and
longitudes
of these
spheres are:
2 and 3 (the
sphere on
the left), 12
and 4 (right),
and 12 and
12 (center).

1. **Start Pioneer (or Pioneer Pro) and get into World Building mode.**

   Pioneer normally opens in its Browsing mode. Click the Switch to World Building button to switch over. It should be on the far left side of the toolbar, but if it has moved, you can just move your cursor around the buttons and watch for Switch to World Building to appear in the status line right above the menu bar.

2. **Create a new scene.**

   Select File⇨Scene⇨New. The Caligari building disappears, and you are left with a checkerboard plane.

3. Enter the Wireframe viewing mode.

This step isn't strictly necessary, but it will help you see what's going on. If Pioneer is not already in Wireframe mode, look for a button on the toolbar that says 3DR. Hold down the left mouse button over the 3DR, and the rendering choices appear above it. One button has some wireframe blocks on it — move the cursor there and release the mouse button.

4. Open the Primitives panel.

Click the button with the gold cone, cube, and sphere on it. You are rewarded by getting much bigger pictures of primitive objects.

5. Right-click on the cylinder.

The Properties panel of the Cylinder tool opens. The Cylinder tool has three properties: Longitude, Latitude, and Top Radius. Believe it or not, all the objects in Figure 10-1 are cylinders! Or at least Pioneer thinks they are. Most of them look nothing at all like the cylinder icon, but we're going to make them with the Cylinder tool anyway. We'll start with the least cylindrical-looking objects and work our way up.

6. Set Latitude to 3, Longitude to 3, and Top Radius to .5 .

Type the numbers into the appropriate boxes.

One trick to watch out for: Pioneer doesn't pay attention to any changes you make in a box until you move on to somewhere else or press Enter. Forgetting this fact can lead to a lot of frustration — the right value is displayed right there on the Properties panel, and yet when you click the button, the wrong cylinder gets built.

7. Left-click the Cylinder on the Primitives panel.

Let there be a cylinder! Or rather, this triangular thing that looks very little like a cylinder. It is triangular because the Longitude is 3. It has 3 horizontal layers because the Latitude is 3. The slant is due to the Top Radius of .5 — which means that the triangle on top is half the size of the one on the bottom.

8. Move this so-called cylinder off to the left.

To do so, find the Object Move button on the toolbar and make sure that it is depressed. (You can tell a depressed button because it turns blue. All depressed things have the blues.) Then click on the cylinder to select it. Hold down the left mouse button and drag to the left.

9. Create a second cylinder with Latitude 3, Longitude 10, and Top Radius .5.

Repeat Steps 6 and 7 with these new values. This guy looks considerably more rounded than the first cylinder we made.

10. Drag the second cylinder off to the right.

11. Create a third cylinder with Latitude 3, Longitude 20, and Top Radius 1.

Now *that* looks like a cylinder!

12. Undo Step 3 by switching back to 3D rendering.

Now you should see something similar to Figure 10-1. Did you notice how the 3D rendering helped create the illusion of roundness for the cylinder on the right?

If you want to try your hand at making spheres (or what Pioneer calls spheres), you can adapt these instructions to help you duplicate Figure 10-2.

In Walkthrough Pro

Virtus has what we might call a 2+1 approach to 3D design: Its design windows deal with two dimensions at a time, and then inflate your 2D design into the third dimension. Consequently, you don't create 3D primitive objects just by clicking on a picture of a sphere or a cube, as you do in Pioneer. You make a 2D choice about the *footprint* of the object and then a 1D choice about how that object inflates into the third dimension.

Primitive footprints

The three basic footprint types are: Regular Polygon, Irregular Polygon, and Rectangle. Regular Polygon has variants (hold down the left mouse button on the button to see them): Octagon, Hexagon, Square, Triangle, and N-Sided (a more complete description of the tool pad commands is in Chapter 7).

An obvious question to ask after you look at the footprint types is this: What about circles? Walkthrough Pro (like Pioneer) doesn't really understand the idea of *round*. Pioneer claims to make round things like spheres and cylinders, but as you see in "They don't make spheres like they used to," it really doesn't. Pioneer fakes it by making polygons with a lot of little sides. Walkthrough Pro doesn't claim to make circles, but in fact, you can fake them the same way that round things are faked in Pioneer:

1. Choose the N-Sided variant of the Regular Polygon tool.

2. Double-click on it to reveal its Preferences window.

3. Set the number of sides to be some large number, like 20.

4. Move your cursor to the design window, click, and drag to create an object.

Is that round enough for you? If not, go back to Step 3 and pick a larger number of sides.

Expanding a primitive footprint

The choices for inflating a footprint are Inflate Straight, Inflate Pointed Up, and Inflate Pointed Down. All three have rounded variants: Inflate Round, Inflate Rounded Up, and Inflate Rounded Down. Inflate Straight has the additional variant Inflate Pointed Double. You can find longer descriptions of these tools in Chapter 7.

- ✔ **Inflate Straight** builds a straight wall on the footprint.

- ✔ **Inflate Pointed Up** builds a teepee with a pointed top over the footprint.

- ✔ **Inflate Pointed Down** builds the same teepee but turns it upside down.

- ✔ **Inflate Pointed Double** builds the teepee both up and down so that from the side it has a diamond shape. (**Note:** Double has the same height as all the others — the height specified by the gauge.)

- ✔ **Inflate Rounded Up** builds an igloo on the footprint.

- ✔ **Inflate Rounded Down** builds the igloo upside down.

- ✔ **Inflate Round** builds an igloo both up and down.

The height of these buildings, and how far off the ground they are, is determined by the gauge in the Depth View window.

Example

Here's how to produce a green octagonal tent with a red pointed roof, as you see in Figure 10-3.

1. Find the Regular Polygon tool and select the Octagon variant.

It looks like a stop sign.

2. Select Inflate Straight from the bottom row of the Design toolpad.

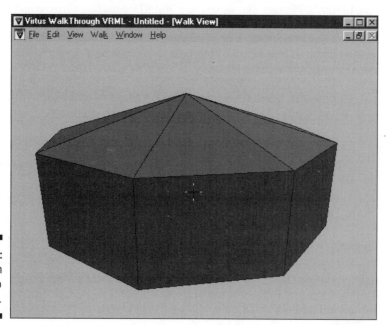

Figure 10-3:
Walkthrough
Pro goes to
the circus.

3. **Check that you are looking at Top View.**

   If not, select View⇨Change View⇨Top from the menu.

4. **Check the gauge in the Depth window.**

   You can open the Depth window with Window⇨Depth Window. The gauge (described in more detail in Chapter 7) is that gray band on the ruler. The default range for the gauge is from 0 to 8. If your Depth window has a different setting, change it back to the range between 0 and 8 by dragging the black triangles on the ruler.

5. **Make the bottom part of the tent.**

   See those blue grid lines in the Top View window? Move the crosshairs so that they sit right on the intersection of two of those blue lines. Then hold down the mouse button and drag one unit sideways to the next intersection point on the horizontal blue line. Walkthrough Pro doesn't care whether you drag right or left — the distance is what counts.

6. **Paint it green.**

   Move to the Color Bar on the Design tool pad. Hold down the mouse button and move the cursor to a green square in the color spectrum.

7. **Click the Inflate Pointed Up button on the tool pad.**

8. **Move the gauge in the Depth window so that it runs from 8 to 14.**

   This way we make sure that the roof is *above* the tent rather than inside of it. Move the cursor to the center of the gauge, hold down the mouse button, and drag it upward so that it runs from 8 to 16. Then move the upper black triangle downward to 14.

9. **Make the tent roof.**

   Repeat what you did in Step 5. Use the same starting and ending points on the blue grid.

10. **Paint it red.**

    Repeat Step 6, but choose a red color this time.

11. **Save the file as CIRCUS.WTP.**

    We'll want to play with this scene later.

In raw VRML

VRML 1.0 has eight *shape nodes,* which are ways of creating primitive objects. One node (AsciiText) creates text. Four others (Cone, Cube, Cylinder, and Sphere) create the familiar geometric objects that their names suggest. The remaining three (PointSet, IndexedLineSet, and IndexedFaceSet) allow you to construct sets of points, line drawings, and more general polyhedra.

We've prepared an easy-to-read VRML file, `primitiv.wrl`, that demonstrates the primitives in action. You can find it in the Sample Worlds folder on the CD. You can open it with a word processor to see the VRML code or with a VRML browser to see Figure 10-4.

TIP

If you ever need to insert some raw VRML primitives by hand (or by word processor) into a VRML file, copy lines from `primitiv.wrl` and paste them into your file. You'll probably have to change the numbers to correspond to specifics of your situation, but at least you'll have the syntax right.

If you do look at the code, be sure to notice the Translation statements: These statements move each object two units from the previous one. The statements that begin with "#" are comments we put there for your understanding; they have no effect on the 3D image.

Figure 10-4:
So raw, so primitive.

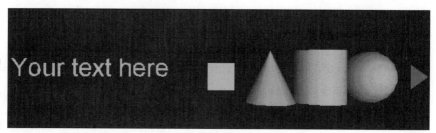

You might think that when Pioneer or Walkthrough Pro creates a VRML file with a cone, cube, cylinder, or sphere in it, it would do so with the Cone, Cube, Cylinder, or Sphere VRML primitives. But if you take a look at the VRML files that Pioneer and Walkthrough Pro produce, you'll see that they create all of these objects as indexed face sets. We can guess their reasons for doing things this way: You can use various tools in either Walkthrough Pro or Pioneer to deform, say, a cube into something very uncubelike. Using the more general IndexedFaceSet primitive makes the object more malleable.

Simple Things You Can Do to Primitive Objects

✔ **Erase them:** In Pioneer, select the object and choose Erase from the toolbar, or press Delete. In Walkthrough Pro, select the object and press Delete.

✔ **Hide them:** If some objects get in your way as you try to make or position others, don't delete them, hide them. Walkthrough Pro's menu provides the Edit⇨Hide Selected command, which does exactly what it says. The hidden object disappears from the Design Views, though you can still see it in the Walk View. After you're ready to see everything again, Edit⇨Show All brings all the hidden objects back. Pioneer doesn't have this feature.

✔ **Move them:** In Walkthrough Pro, select the object in a Design window and drag it somewhere else. This method constrains you to move in two dimensions at a time, but using two or more Design Views, you can drag an object anywhere you want.

Pioneer has two tools for repositioning: Object Move and Object Rotate. Object Move is fairly simple: Click the tool, select an object, and now the same mouse-drag commands that usually move your viewing position work on the position of the object instead. Object Rotate is a little more complicated because now the different directions of mouse drags result in rotating the object around different axes. A more detailed description of Object Rotate is in Chapter 8.

✔ **Rotate them:** Walkthrough Pro has a Rotate Object tool (the one whose button is an arrow going in a circle). Choose the plane you want to rotate in and open that Design window. Select the object to rotate. Click the Rotate Object tool. Your cursor changes — you can imagine that it is carrying around this giant axis. When you click, the tool plants the axis in the ground at that point. Now you move away, and a line appears between the cursor and the planted axis. Turning that line around the axis rotates the object around that point.

Pioneer's Object Rotate is a little more complicated because it tries to handle all the possible rotations with one view window. The different directions of mouse drags result in rotating the object around different axes. A more detailed description of Object Rotate is in Chapter 8.

✔ **Distort them:** You can make cubes and spheres look very un-cubelike and un-spherelike either by scaling them more in some dimensions than others (see "Stretching a Point and Other Sizing Issues" later in this chapter) or by making them lean one way or another.

✔ **Paint them:** In Walkthrough Pro, select the object, move to the Color Bar, and hold down the mouse button. Now move through the Color panel to select a color, as in Step 6 of our construction of the circus tent.

Pioneer gives a variety of painting options: Paint Face, Paint Vertices, Paint Object, and Paint Over Existing Material. Each of these tools opens a Material Color wheel. Drag the indicator in the color wheel to the appropriate shade, and then move the slide bar to adjust intensity. When you take your cursor into the viewing area, it becomes a paint brush. Selecting an object with this paintbrush cursor causes it to change to the chosen color. We discuss the more complicated things you can do with these tools in Chapter 12.

✔ **Punch holes in them:** Pioneer Pro's Object Subtraction tool lets you use one object to define a hole in another. This idea is easier to show than to describe: Look at Figure 10-5. On the left is a cube with a cylinder driven through it; on the right is an identical cube after the cylinder has been subtracted. The Object Subtraction tool is described in Chapter 8.

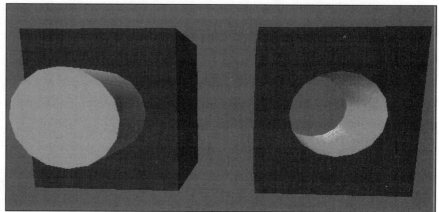

Figure 10-5:
Before and after: Punching a cylindrical hole in a cube with Pioneer Pro's Object Subtraction tool.

Primitive Objects Unite and Multiply

After you have some building blocks, you need to know how to put them together and how to mass produce the things you make out of them. In other words, you need to know how to glue and how to copy.

Keeping your act together: gluing and grouping

After you've worked hard to make a few objects line up in just the right way, you want them to stay put. If you need to move one (or you move one accidentally), you don't want to have to reposition all the others to match it — you want all of the objects to move together, as if they were glued. Pioneer and Walkthrough Pro each respond to this need in different ways.

Two main types of *gluing* are available in the tools we describe here, depending on what you want to accomplish:

✔ **Grouping:** The ability to move, copy, rotate, scale, and (in Walkthrough Pro) save as a library object a whole bunch of stuff at once.

A special kind of grouping exists called *LOD,* or Level of Detail grouping, that has more to do with how objects appear than how to build more complex objects. See Chapter 13 for that sort of grouping.

> ✔ **Attaching surfaces:** Making two shapes share a common face. Of the tools we discuss here, only Virtus Walkthrough Pro does this operation.

Grouping is often a temporary action to help you make some change to a bunch of objects at once. You might temporarily group a coffee table and a sofa together to move or rotate them within a room. Later, you might want to ungroup them in order to lengthen the coffee table.

Walkthrough Pro's groups

If you want only to move the objects once, and don't want them linked for all time (or until you decide otherwise), you can just select all of them at the same time and move them together — their relative positions will be unchanged. Select them together either by dragging a rectangle around them with the Selection tool or by clicking them one at a time while holding down the Shift key. After you select something else, Walkthrough Pro forgets that the moved objects were ever linked.

To establish a more lasting connection between objects (like, say, the tent and its roof in our circus example earlier in this chapter), use the Group command. Select the objects you want to group (either by dragging a rectangle around them or by selecting them one by one) and choose Design⇨Group from the menu. Now Walkthrough Pro will treat all the grouped objects as if they were a single object. Anything you do to one will be done to all.

When you want the grouped objects to behave like individuals again, select the group by clicking on it, and then choose Design⇨Ungroup from the menu.

A few tips for working with groups in Walkthrough Pro

✔ You can select objects in Walk View as well as in a Design View. First choose the Select Object tool (the one with the block-with-an-arrow icon at the top of the Walk View tool pad) and then Shift+click on objects to select them.

✔ You can move, rotate, and scale a group, or save a group to a library.

✔ Objects can't be painted while grouped. To paint a group, select it and then ungroup it with Design⇨Ungroup; the objects ungroup, but all remain selected. Double-click on a color in the Color Bar to paint them all, and regroup them if necessary.

✔ To modify an individual object in a group, including painting it, you must ungroup it first.

✔ Groups can be grouped. Just select multiple groups the same way you would select multiple objects, and then choose Design⇨Group.

Connecting surfaces in Walkthrough Pro

Walkthrough Pro has an interesting feature for combining shapes, which is to let those shapes connect at a surface.

Why connect? The only practical advantage of connecting a surface is to make a door or window between two objects. Do so by making the entire surface transparent, or by painting a transparent feature onto that surface using the Surface Editor. Don't think that connecting two objects makes them a single object; it doesn't. If you want them to act like a single object, group them.

Here's how to connect surfaces of two objects in Walkthrough Pro:

1. **Drag the two objects so that their surfaces are on top of each other (or at least intersect).**

   Use any convenient Design View window.

2. **Select the Connect Surfaces tool. (It's the hammer-and-nail icon.)**

3. **Click where the two surfaces intersect.**

   You may hear a snap, and the two objects align themselves.

That's it. Their surfaces are connected. To disconnect them, drag the objects apart. To make a door or a window, use the Surface Editor. See Chapter 11.

Pioneer's glue

Pioneer gives you a couple of gluing options: You can Glue as Child (which means you get the glue all over yourself), or you can Glue as Sibling (and get the glue all over someone else).

Actually, Pioneer's glue is a way of describing what is related to what and how. If two objects belong together (like, say, needle and thread), then they should be glued as siblings. If one belongs to the other (like the needle belongs to the sewing kit), then they should be glued as child and parent. A hierarchy of objects gets constructed. You can think of this structure as a family tree: Objects on the same level are siblings, and if A is the next object above B on the tree, then we say that B is the child of A.

In the simple constructions we talk about in this chapter, these distinctions aren't very important — when we glue letters on a block (as you see later in Figure 10-8), we could glue them either as siblings or as children, and it wouldn't really matter. But in a more complicated scene, you will find it very convenient to define hierarchies of objects according to their level of complexity. The needle belongs to the sewing kit, which belongs to the sewing table, which belongs to the sitting room, which belongs to the second floor, which belongs to the house. You want to be able to rearrange the objects on the sewing table, and you want to be able to rearrange the floor plan of the second floor, but you want the one to stay fixed while you're dealing with the other.

To work with an object that is glued into a hierarchy of objects:

1. **Select the hierarchy of objects.**

   Click on the object you want to work with — this action will select the hierarchy that includes it.

2. **Move down the hierarchy until you reach the level of the object and its siblings.**

   The vertical arrow icons on the toolbar move you up or down in the hierarchy. At each level, the currently selected object is outlined in white (in wireframe mode) and its siblings are outlined in yellow. If the object you want to work with turns yellow when you move down in the hierarchy, click on it. It belongs to one of the siblings on the current level, and by clicking on it, you select that sibling. You'll know that you have reached the right level when the object is selected by itself — nothing else is wireframed in white.

3. **Do what you want to do to this object.**

   Move it, deform it, erase it, copy it — whatever. You can grant it independence from the hierarchy by selecting the Unglue variant of the Gluing tool.

4. **Select another tool.**

   If you haven't erased the object or unglued it, the altered object now has the same position on the hierarchy that the original object had.

Copying

Making one Mr. Potato Head is hard enough, but what if you wanted an army of them (as in Weird Al Yankovich's "Dare To Be Stupid" video)? Pioneer provides an Edit⇨Copy command, and Walkthrough Pro has Edit⇨Duplicate. They do exactly the same thing: create a copy of the object right next to the original. Pioneer actually puts the duplicate on top of the original so that you can't tell immediately that anything has happened. (Don't be fooled. If you say, "That didn't do anything. Let's try it again," you can wind up with dozens of copies right on top of each other before you catch on.) But if you move the original, you see that a copy has stayed behind.

Walkthrough Pro also provides Cut, Paste, and Copy commands on the Edit menu. They do exactly what you'd expect from using any other program with Cut, Paste, and Copy commands: After you have cut or copied an object, click the cursor somewhere in a Design window and select Paste. A copy of the object appears where you clicked.

Let's return to the circus tent of Figure 10-3, and figure out how to make a small town of circus tents.

1. **Open CIRCUS.WTP (remember saving it earlier in this chapter?).**

2. **Group the two pieces of the tent. Choose Edit⇨Select All and then Design⇨Group.**

3. **Copy the tent. Edit⇨Copy should do the trick.**

4. **Make a second tent next to the first.**

   The easiest view to work with now is Top View (make sure the Depth gauge is set to the range 0 to 12). The tent takes up about a 3-by-3 section of the grid. Click about three units directly to the left of the center of the tent and then do Edit⇨Paste. Poof! A second tent appears.

5. **Group the two tents.**

6. **Copy the group.**

7. **Make two more tents under the first two. Just repeat Steps 3 and 4, but now click about three units below the first two tents.**

8. **Group all the tents.**

9. **Keep going as long as you like.**

   Each time, you group all the tents, copy the group, and then paste a duplicate next to the first. Your village doubles each time you do this. As it grows, you will need to keeping zooming out (Design⇨Zoom Out) in order to see what you're doing. In Figure 10-6, we stopped at 16 tents.

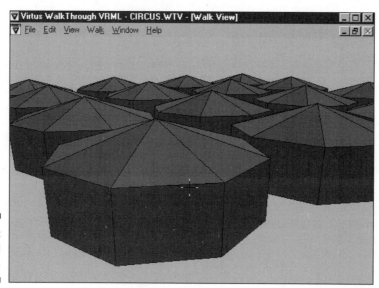

Figure 10-6:
A virtual
village.

Stretching a Point and Other Sizing Issues

Ever want to add just a foot or two to your kitchen? Raise the roof just a smidgen? Ever wish that puzzle piece was just a *little bit* smaller? You're in luck. Both Pioneer and Walkthrough Pro have scaling tools that let you resize things any way you want.

Scaling in one or more dimensions

Both Walkthrough Pro and Pioneer let you scale in any number of dimensions — well, maybe not four, but somebody must be working on it.

Walkthrough Pro

The Walkthrough Pro Scale button on the Design toolbar shows a square daydreaming about getting bigger. It sits right beneath the magnifying glass. To use the Scaling tool, select the object to be scaled and then select the tool. Now click and drag to scale in the two dimensions of the current Design window.

If you think, "I liked it better the way it was," use Edit⇨Modify Selected⇨ Unscale to undo.

Enlarging the kitchen in Walkthrough Pro may enlarge the sink and microwave as well (we won't even think about the roaches). Anything inside the selected object is scaled in precisely the same way, unless you hold down the Ctrl key (Option key on the Mac) while you scale.

Another way to enlarge an object in Walkthrough Pro is to grab a corner and drag it somewhere else. Walkthrough Pro won't let you drag the corner to a place that would make the object non-convex, but otherwise, you have complete freedom.

Pioneer

Scaling in Pioneer is controlled by the Object Scale tool, which is a variant of the Object Move tool. Select the object and then click Object Scale. Dragging the left mouse button controls scaling in the X and Y dimensions (the horizontal, in other words), while dragging with the right mouse button controls scaling in the Z dimension (the vertical).

As with moving and rotating, the most careful way to scale is one axis at a time. Deselect two of the axes (by clicking their buttons on the right side of the toolbar) and scale in the third. You can scale in fixed increments by using the Grid Snap tool.

You almost always want to scale in Object coordinates because they distort the object as little as possible (we discuss intentional distortions in the next few paragraphs). Bear in mind, though, that even Object coordinates distort the object unless you scale in all dimensions at once (see "Scaling uniformly" later in this section). Squares become rectangles, circles become ellipses, and so forth. Check out Figure 10-7 to see a few distorted objects.

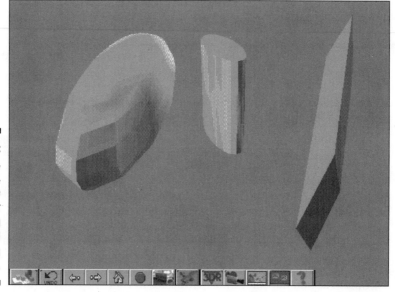

Figure 10-7: A sphere, cylinder, and cube get together the morning after a wild scaling party.

Pioneer has three coordinate sets: World coordinates (which are aligned with the grid), Object coordinates (which are aligned with the sides of the object), and Screen coordinates (which are aligned with the screen). Switch from one to the other by clicking the appropriate button in the lower-right part of the screen.

Scaling in World or Screen coordinates, however, can give you some interesting effects if you know what you are doing (if you discover you don't know what you're doing, there's always the Undo tool). An object that hasn't been rotated since you created it may still be aligned with World coordinates, so scaling in World coordinates may be the same as scaling in Object coordinates. But if the object has been rotated, scaling in World coordinates distorts its shape in some bizarre ways. The effect is particularly pronounced on cubes because the square sides become parallelograms.

Figure 10-7 shows the distortions that scaling can cause. The three objects pictured were originally a sphere, a cylinder, and a cube. The sphere and cylinder have been scaled in Object coordinates. The cube has been rotated and then scaled in World coordinates.

Scaling uniformly

You've spent hours getting an object to look just right. The proportions are absolutely perfect, and then someone says, "That's nice, but could you make it a little bigger?" No problem. Both Pioneer and Walkthrough Pro allow you to scale up (or down) in all dimensions simultaneously. Your object maintains its perfection, but it just gets a little bigger (or smaller).

In Pioneer, select the object, click Object Scale, and then drag the mouse while holding down both the left and right mouse buttons.

In Walkthrough Pro, click the Scale tool, select the object, and then hold down the Shift key while dragging. At least Virtus *claims* that this scales in all dimensions simultaneously. When we try it, our objects scale uniformly in the two dimensions of the current Design window and unpredictably in the third dimension — sometimes not at all in the third dimension and sometimes almost (but not quite) as much as in the other two.

Passing the Text

Unfortunately, Walkthrough Pro doesn't make text. If you want to put 2D text into Walkthrough, your best bet is to make the text with a 2D drawing program like Paint or MacDraw, save the file, and then use it as a texture map in Walkthrough. (You can also do this trick with Pioneer, but for most purposes, you don't need to.) That process is a little too complicated for this chapter — we'll put it off until we introduce textures in Chapter 14. If you want 3D text in Walkthrough, you're just out of luck.

Two-dimensional text is considered primitive in Pioneer and hangs out on the Primitives panel. If you click the Text button on the Primitives panel, your cursor becomes a vertical line. Move that cursor to the place where you want text, click, and start typing. Right-clicking on the Text button opens a window that allows you to change fonts.

Pioneer Pro works with text the same way, but it gives you an additional primitive: horizontal text. You can duplicate horizontal text in Pioneer by making vertical text and tipping it over, but having horizontal text as a primitive saves a little time and effort. Of course, if all you want is 2D text, using a word processor is a lot simpler. The significance of text in Pioneer is that it lives inside a 3D world. You can do a couple of interesting things with text in Pioneer: attach it to the surface of 3D objects or create 3D text.

2D text in a 3D world

Once you create 2D text in Pioneer, you can move it, stretch it, color it, or do any of the things that you do with Pioneer's other objects. For example, you can attach your text to the side of a cube, as we did in Figure 10-8. Look on the CD for a step-by-step description of how we did it.

Figure 10-8:
Cubes and text work together like child's play.

3D text

What could be better than 2D text on a 3D cube? 3D text, obviously. Yes, you too can put your name in 3D, in giant letters that look like something left behind by ancient astronauts. Using the Text tool:

1. **Position the cursor.**

2. **Type the first line of text.**

3. **Click the Sweep button.**

   Your letters suddenly pop into 3D! You can now play with the sweep tools to make the letters angle off in some odd direction, if that's what you want.

4. **Type further lines of text and repeat.**

You can have your letters appear in any font and material that Pioneer knows. Be forewarned, however: It's hard to be modest in 3D. Whatever you type will look as if thousands of virtual slaves spent their lives chiseling it out of some dense material.

Chapter 11

Making Rooms and Spaces

In This Chapter

▶ Making a single room with Walkthrough Pro, Pioneer, and Pioneer Pro

▶ Adding doors and windows to a room

▶ Making several rooms and sticking them together

*W*hat do you give to the person who has everything? A place to put it all. When you come right down to it, you only need to know how to build three things: objects, buildings to put them in, and landscapes to set the buildings in.

We've been making some simple objects, and we'll get to landscapes in Chapter 15. (You can check out a tree under construction in Figure 1 of the color section.) Now let's talk about making a place to display your objects — a room, a gallery, a castle, a cathedral. (Why think small? Real estate is cheap in cyberspace.) In this chapter, we discuss the basics of enclosed spaces: walls, doors, and so forth. The frescoed virtual ceilings and stained-glass virtual windows will have to wait.

Four Walls and a Ceiling

In Chapter 10, we built a few cubes and boxes, but we looked at them from the outside and thought of them as objects. In this section, we build more cubes and boxes, but we look at them from the inside and think of them as rooms — drab, boring rooms in serious need of an interior decorator, but rooms all the same.

Walkthrough and Pioneer are about equally good at building boxes, but Walk-through has a big advantage when it comes to building rooms. Walkthrough's boxes *are* rooms — all that has to change is your point of view. But in spite of appearances, nothing on Pioneer's Primitives panel is a ready-made room. Building a room in Pioneer requires a bit of creativity and a little thought. Pioneer Pro doesn't have any ready-to-furnish rooms either, but it has good tools for building them.

Up to this point in the book, Pioneer and Pioneer Pro have been more-or-less interchangable. In this chapter, we begin to see why Caligari gives Pioneer away free but charges money for Pioneer Pro. Building rooms is much easier in Pioneer Pro than in Pioneer, and adding doors and windows is much, much easier.

What Walkthrough does best

Walkthrough was made for building rooms. Why do you think Virtus named it Walkthrough? You don't walk through objects (except by mistake). You walk through rooms. Nothing could be simpler than to make a room in Walkthrough:

1. **Choose a shape.**

   Use the Top View Design window (just like an architect would) so that the shape is what you would see on a floor plan. Your only restriction is that the room be convex — no little nooks and crannies. (If the word *convex* sounds geeky to you, think of it this way: Every part of the room has to be visible from every other part.) We'll get around this limitation later when we start laying out floor plans, but for now, we have to live with it.

2. **Find a tool that makes that shape.**

   Most rooms are rectangular, so you can make them with the Rectangle tool. But you also have two other choices: the Regular Polygon tools, which let you make any number of sides; and the Irregular Polygon tool, which lets you sketch out a shape line by line (wall by wall). If you use the N-sided variant of the Regular Polygon tool, and if you set N really high, you can get a pretty good approximation of a circle.

3. **Choose a height for the walls and set the Depth window's gauge accordingly.**

   If you've forgotten how to set the gauge, return to Chapter 7. Do not pass Go. Do not collect $200.

4. **Use the tool from Step 2 in the Top View Design window to lay out the room.**

Bang! You have a room. If he's not already there, move your observer inside the room. The Walk View now shows you what the room looks like from the inside: gray. But at least you have a roof over your head. It's a start.

The emperor's new room

We just saw that in Walkthrough, boxes and rooms are really the same things looked at from different vantage points. But a funny thing happens if you try to turn a box into a room in Pioneer: it vanishes. That's right. Build a cube out of brick or wood or some other apparently solid virtual material, and then just as you move inside it, it's gone!

What's going on here? Shifting into wireframe mode only deepens the mystery: You can plainly see the wire frame of the cube all around you, but when you shift back to 3DR, nothing is there.

Another way not to build a room is to draw a rectangle and then use the Sweep tool to make it 3D. Once again, it looks perfectly solid from the outside, but when you move inside it and look around, you say, "Room? What room? Did somebody say there was a room here?"

We've just run into one of the biggest differences between the virtual reality of VRML and ordinary reality. (*The* biggest difference, as every virtual traveler knows, is cuisine. Virtual food is uniformly awful.) *Surfaces in VRML only exist on one side.* Really. We're not making this up. All of Pioneer's 3D primitives are made from these one-sided surfaces, cleverly arranged so that the side that exists faces outward. Viewing from the inside, you can't see any of them.

A two-sided surface in VRML is like plywood — somebody had to glue a couple of one-sided surfaces together in order to make it. Two-sided surfaces are more trouble for the designer and more work for your computer, so the folks at Caligari decided to use them sparingly. The only Pioneer primitives made with two-sided surfaces are planes and text. The following figure shows the view from inside the block of Figure 10-8. The back sides of the letters are visible, but the block is not.

Making a room out of a jigsaw of letters seems a little challenging, but why not make rooms by sweeping a plane up into three dimensions? Nice try, but the most obvious way of doing this construction fails as well: If you make a plane and click the Sweep button, you do get a 3D box — but it also is invisible from the inside. Even the floor and ceiling (which you might think would be copies of the original two-sided plane) are invisible from the inside. Swept letters are also invisible from the inside — otherwise, we might get literal about building A-frame houses.

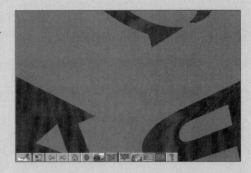

Rooms in Pioneer and Pioneer Pro

You can acquire a virtual room for your Pioneer or Pioneer Pro objects in one of three ways:

- Copy one off the CD.
- Import one from Walkthrough.
- Build one.

Now on CD

We've provided two room files in the Sample Worlds folder on the CD: `room1.wrl` and `room12.wrl`. If you just want a simple box with an inside and outside, room1 will serve the purpose and require very little RAM. If you're using Pioneer (rather than Pioneer Pro) and eventually you want to put in doors and windows, then you want room12, for reasons that we'll explain when we discuss doors and windows later in this chapter.

Prefab housing from Walkthrough

Why not take advantage of what Walkthrough does well? Build a room in Walkthrough, put in doors or windows if you want, and then use the Walkthrough's File⇨Export⇨VRML command to create a VRML file. (Give it a name ending in .WRL.) Now open the file in Pioneer or Pioneer Pro. No problem.

Well, maybe a few problems. Early versions of Walkthrough had all kinds of difficulties creating VRML files. (The most hilarious glitch was that Walkthrough misfigured the transparency coefficients, creating rooms and objects that were completely invisible — more new stuff for the emperor.) Virtus has fixed most of these problems by now, though some minor continuing problems are discussed in Chapter 7. (Check our Web page for workarounds to any problems not mentioned in Chapter 7.)

Also, Walkthrough and Pioneer tend to work on different scales, which can be a nuisance if the Walkthrough room you import turns out to be the size of the Mall of America when it arrives in Pioneer. (The problem is that you'll grow old waiting for Pioneer to move from one end of the room to another.) You can allow for this problem by either:

- **Building very small objects in Walkthrough.** One disadvantage is that motion is too fast now. You'll have a hard time zeroing in on what you want to look at.

- **Rescaling the object in Pioneer (or Pioneer Pro).** The easiest way to rescale massively is in the Object Info window: After you open the file in Pioneer, select the room and then click the Object List button. You'll see a list of objects, with one unnamed object (the room) highlighted. Below the list is the Object Info box. In the box is a line *size* with three numbers in columns labeled X, Y, and Z. Make sure that the Dynaunits box is clicked, and then look at those size numbers. Are they huge? Try repositioning all three decimal points one place to the left (thereby scaling down by 10 in all dimensions).

Room-building in Pioneer Pro

Pioneer and Pioneer Pro were made to model objects, not to build rooms. All the obvious room-building solutions fail (as you can see in "The emperor's new room" in this chapter), so we have to get devious.

1. Make a cube.

Click the Primitives Panel button and then click the Cube button on the Primitives panel. A cube appears.

2. Scale it uniformly just a little bit.

We discuss scaling in Chapter 10. If you use the Object Scale tool and hold down both mouse buttons while you drag, the object grows or shrinks uniformly in all dimensions. You want the cube to become just a little bit larger than it was.

3. Make another cube.

If you look at this situation in wireframe, you'll see that the new cube sits inside the first one, and the distance between them is the same everywhere. That distance is going to be the thickness of the walls, floor, and ceiling.

4. Subtract the smaller cube from the larger one.

Do it like this: Click the larger cube to select it. Now click the Object Subtraction tool. Now click the inner cube. Presto! It's gone.

5. Size and scale so that the room has the dimensions you want.

Very few rooms are actually cubes. Use the Object Scale tool again, but now scale one dimension at a time.

Room-building with Pioneer

Pioneer Pro has a few tools that Pioneer lacks, including the Object Subtraction tool that was so crucial in the Pioneer Pro room-building construction. Consequently, room building in Pioneer is even harder than in Pioneer Pro.

Pioneer Pro gives you ways to cut doors and windows into rooms. But if you eventually want to put doors or windows into your the rooms you build in Pioneer, you have to plan ahead when you build the rooms. Check out "Doors and Windows" later in this chapter.

Planes are visible from both sides. So you can use planes as though they were sheets of plywood and glue them together to build rooms. This technique involves the same kind of maneuvering that we did when we were putting the letters onto the block to make Figure 10-8: There the letters were created vertical, and the third letter had to be rotated 90 degrees so that it could be laid horizontally on the top of the block. Here the planes are created horizontal and have to be rotated 90 degrees to become vertical walls.

1. **Turn on Grid Snap.**

   The grid lets us make 90-degree angles easily and allows us to place the planes so that they fit snugly.

2. **Make a plane.**

   The Plane tool is on the Primitives panel. If you want your room to be any special material or color, either choose it from the Materials panel before you make the plane, or paint it later. If you want to put doors or windows into some of your walls, make sure that the plane has sufficiently high resolution (see the discussion of resolution in "Vanishing cream: doors and windows in Pioneer" later in this chapter).

3. **Copy it.**

   Use Edit⇨Copy from the menu. Nothing appears to change, but actually, Pioneer has made a second plane so completely identical to the first that it is in exactly the same place. The laws of virtual physics are loose enough to allow this.

4. **Drag the duplicate horizontally so that it shares an edge with the original.**

   Use the Object Move tool. As long as you stay away from the right mouse button, your plane can't move up or down. Now you have two planes sitting on the ground like tiles.

5. **Repeat Steps 2 through 4 until you have five horizontal planes making a cross.**

   The original is in the center, and one duplicate is snuggled up to each of its four sides. These planes are going to be a floor and four walls.

6. **Rotate each wall until it is vertical.**

   Use the Object Rotate variant of the Object Move tool. Turn off the Z-axis rotation by deselecting the Z on the right side of the toolbar. Two of the walls will need to rotate around the X axis and two around the Y axis. After you've determined which are which, turn off the rotation axis you don't need. (Open a Perspective View window to help you recognize when the walls are vertical.) The rotation pulls the base of each wall away from the floor, but Step 7 will take care of that problem.

7. **Move each wall into place.**

   Use Object Move again — this time with the right mouse button to move the vertical walls straight up until their bottom edges meet the floor.

8. **Copy the floor and lift the duplicate to make the ceiling.**

9. **Glue the planes together as siblings.**

   After this step, you can treat the room as a single object to resize or paint or mistreat in some other way. And if you start moving stuff into this room later, you won't accidentally knock one of the walls out of place.

It's a room. Or rather, it's a cube that has both an inside and an outside. If you want the room to be a box of different dimensions, you can use Object Scale to make it longer, wider, taller or, conversely, to shrink it in some or all dimensions.

Doors and Windows

Until scientists stop dragging their feet and start building the kind of teleporters we've been seeing for years on *Star Trek,* rooms without doors and windows won't be good for much beyond storing radioactive waste. The virtual world doesn't even *have* radioactive waste yet — don't worry, we're working on it — so you'll probably want to learn how to put doors and windows into your virtual rooms.

Once again, Walkthrough makes doors and windows in a straightforward way, Pioneer Pro has a tool for the job, and Pioneer requires more effort and creativity.

A brief chat with Walkthrough's Surface Editor

We always thought that building doors and windows requires a contractor, a carpenter, and a few hulking workmen, so you can imagine our surprise when we discovered that Walkthrough does it with an editor — the Surface Editor. We picture the Surface Editor standing at the virtual construction site with a yellow hard hat and red pencil, deleting a few bricks, tightening up some molding, and complaining occasionally that the authors could have made the windowpanes more transparent. (Just kidding, editors.)

You can call on the Surface Editor either from a Design View or from Walk View. In either the Design tool pad or the Walk tool pad, the Surface Editor tool button sits right above the Color Bar and looks like a square with a door and a window cut out.

 ✔ From Design View, click the Surface Editor tool and then click a line in some Design window.

 ✔ From Walk View, find the wall you want to add a door or window to, get it in your sights, click the Surface Editor tool, and click the wall in the Walk View window.

In either case, a Surface Editor tool pad appears and a Surface window opens, showing the outline of the surface you have selected. (For more information on the Surface Editor and its tool pad, see the "Surface Editor" section in Chapter 7.)

Use the Surface Editor to make doors and windows as follows:

1. **Find the wall into which you want to cut a door or window.**

   Locate it either in Walk View or in a Design View. In Top View, for instance, a room is represented as a polygon, and each wall is a line (if you want to put a skylight into the ceiling or a trap door into the floor, or make a hole for a stairwell, you would use a side view rather than Top View). We recommend getting the wall in your sights in both Walk View and Top View. A minute or two making sure you have the correct wall is time well spent.

2. **Call in the Surface Editor and point it in the right direction.**

   Click the Surface Editor button on either the Walk or Design tool pads, and then move to the corresponding view window and click the surface you want to edit.

   A window similar to a Design window appears with a 2D outline in it. Unlike the figures in a Design View, though, this 2D figure represents something that really is 2D. You don't have to worry about a Depth window or its gauge. What you see is what you get.

   The Surface Editor window comes with its own toolbar. The top part of this toolbar should be familiar because it duplicates the top of the Design toolbar. The tools of interest to us as door-and-window makers are the ones below the Color Bar. The first row under the Color Bar has three buttons, which let us choose whether the features we add to our surface will be (left to right) opaque, translucent, or transparent. The second row has three more buttons, which let us choose whether the features we add will be (left to right) on the outside of the surface, both sides, or the inside. Remember, even if you invoke the Surface Editor by clicking on an inside wall, the Surface Editor is going to be looking at it from the outside.

3. **Choose to add a transparent feature on both sides of the wall.**

   In other words, we want to blow a hole in the wall. Click the rightmost of the three buttons in the first row under the Color Bar and the middle button of the row under that.

4. **Choose a shape for your door or window.**

   Rectangular is obvious, but we'd hate to inhibit your creativity. Want an octagonal window? Go wild. You have the same choices as you do when you are making rooms in Design View: Regular Polygon (with various numbers of sides), Irregular Polygon, and Rectangle.

5. Draw your feature onto the surface in the Surface window.

A door might be a tall rectangle going down to the floor. A window might be a wide rectangle at about eye level. But, hey, it's your room.

That's all there is to it. If you're looking in the right place in Walk View, the new feature appears instantly. At first, the new feature just looks like something painted onto the wall, but if you place a brightly-colored object inside the room and look from the outside (or outside the room and look from the inside) you see that you have an honest-to-God hole in the wall.

Punching holes in walls with Pioneer Pro

If you want a door or window in a room, the right tool for the job is Pioneer Pro's Object Subtraction. Assume the room is already made by one of the methods given earlier in this chapter.

1. Create a dye.

Figure 10-5 shows you a dye for creating circular holes. The basic idea is that you figure out the size and shape of the hole you want in the wall, and then you create a 3D object so that one end of it has that size and shape. More precisely, suppose you want a rectangular door. Follow these steps:

1a. Create a cube.

1b. Use the Object Scale tool to make one face of the cube door-shaped.

In other words, scale the cube so that, if you look at it from one end, it is tall and thin, like a doorway.

The Object Subtraction process will destroy the dye in Step 5, so if you are going to want to make other identical holes somewhere else, make a copy of the dye and put it off to the side.

2. Move the dye until the end of it passes through the wall at the place where you want a hole.

Picture the dye as a battering ram or a cookie cutter. Use the Object Move tool to maneuver it into the right position and pass the front end of it through the wall. Be careful you don't push it so far that it goes through the opposite wall as well (unless you want a hole there).

3. Click the room to select it.

4. Click Object Subtraction.

5. Click the dye.

The dye goes away and the wall now has a hole in it where the dye used to be.

Vanishing cream: doors and windows in Pioneer

Earlier in this chapter, we gave you three ways to bring a room into Pioneer: You can load one off the CD, you can import one from Walkthrough, or you can build one. If you import from Walkthrough, you can put in the doors and windows there, no problem. But with the other techniques, you will have to install the doors and windows in Pioneer.

Pioneer doesn't have an Object Subtraction tool (which was so crucial in Pioneer Pro's door-and-window construction), and we know no good way to fake one. We do, however, know a way to fake a hole, and if you grew up watching Looney Tunes cartoons, you know it too: You can paint part of a wall invisible.

You still have to worry about one detail: Pioneer can't paint any region smaller than a single face. In other words, the smallest thing you can paint is one of those blocks that you see outlined in wireframe view. So if you want to paint a hole into a wall, the wall can't be one big face. If, instead, the wall is 25 faces, making one of them transparent and calling it a window is no trick.

Remember in Chapter 10 when we were building primitives? Each primitive has a Properties panel, and one of the numbers you can change on that panel is called *resolution.* For the Plane tool, resolution is the only thing on its Properties panel. The smallest possible resolution is 1, which means that your plane is one big face. A plane with resolution 2 is made up of 4 faces in a 2-by-2 pattern. Resolution 3 means the plane has 9 faces in a 3-by-3 pattern, and so forth. Resolution works the same way for cubes: In a cube of resolution 3, each side of the cube is actually 9 faces in a 3-by-3 pattern.

Here's the general rule: If you have more faces to work with, you can do more complicated things. So the important thing to remember with all these methods (other than importing from Walkthrough) is to make sure that you have enough resolution.

- ✔ The room in `room12.wrl` on the CD has resolution 12, so each wall of the room has 144 faces. That should be enough for most purposes.
- ✔ If you build your room by assembling planes of plywood (described earlier in this chapter), you set the resolution of the planes (before you make them) by right-clicking the Plane button on the Primitives panel, typing a new number in the box that appears, and then pressing Enter.

Now you're ready to paint some transparent doors and windows. Assuming that your room (however you got it) is now loaded into Pioneer and on your screen, proceed as follows:

1. **Decide into which wall to put the door/window.**
2. **Open the Shader Attributes panel by right-clicking the Paint tool.**
3. **Set the Set Transparency slider as high as possible.**

   This slider is the rightmost of the four sliders in the Shader Attributes panel.

4. **Select the plane representing the wall into which you want to put the door/window.**
5. **Click the Paint Face tool.**
6. **Paint the squares that are to be part of the door/window.**

   It's invisible! Daffy Duck himself couldn't have done it better.

Expanding Your Domain

Human nature being what it is, you'll probably enjoy your first virtual room for maybe ten minutes before you start thinking about all the neat things you could do with two rooms. Or three rooms. Or maybe Buckingham Palace.

You can build multi-room structures in two different ways:

✔ Build the rooms individually and stick them together.

✔ Build one huge room and start cutting it up by putting in extra walls.

Either approach works in Walkthrough, although in Pioneer and Pioneer Pro, the second is definitely easier.

Multiple rooms in Walkthrough

Walkthrough is well set up to build rooms one at a time and then connect them together with the Connect Surfaces tool. You can also build a large room and cut it up, but you don't get a nice, ready-made tool to help you.

Connecting rooms together

Walkthrough's Connect Surfaces tool allows you to turn a few rooms into an apartment easily, or something even larger. Figure 11-1 shows three rooms connected, with doors between them. (The TV, piano, and bookshelf come from Walkthrough's object library, which we discuss in Chapter 12.)

Connecting two rooms is easy. And once you know how to connect two, why stop?

1. **Make two rooms.**

2. **Move them so that they share part (or all) of a wall.**

   In Top View, the two walls should look like a single line. At this point, the walls aren't connected; they just rest next to each other.

3. **Use the Connect Surface tool to make the shared wall sections identical.**

   After you click the Connect Surface tool (the one with a hammer on its icon), your cursor changes to a hammer. Take that hammer into the Design window and click on the shared portion of wall.

   Now the two walls are identified — only one wall separates the two rooms. The point of connecting the surfaces is so that you can put doors or windows into the common wall, and not have to try to match up doors or windows on each wall. If you weren't planning any doors or windows, you are just as well off if you Group the two rooms. Grouping keeps the two rooms in their relative positions, so that moving one automatically moves the other.

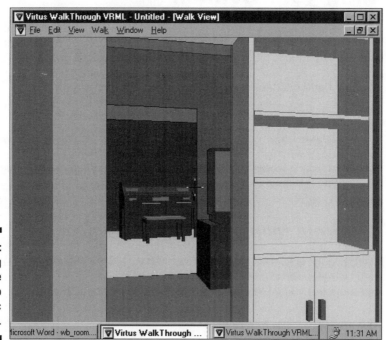

Figure 11-1:
Looking through the TV room to the music room.

4. Use the Surface Editor to put in doors or windows.

The connecting wall is, at this point, just a wall. The Surface Editor works on it the same way that it works on any wall (see "A brief chat with Walkthrough's Surface Editor" earlier in this chapter).

Cutting a large room into smaller rooms

Walkthrough doesn't make 2D objects, so you can't just draw a line down the middle of a room in Top View and expect a wall to appear. But why should walls be 2D? (Mine aren't. They have wires and pipes and oodles of dust inside them.) If you want to subdivide a room:

1. Go to Top View.

2. Click the Rectangle tool.

3. Put long, thin rectangles where you want the walls to be.

If you want these walls to have doors in them, you have a couple of choices.

✔ You can make your wall in two pieces and leave a gap between them to represent the doorway.

✔ You can use the Surface Editor to put a doorway on both sides of the wall (because the wall has width, it has two surfaces, each of which needs a doorway).

If you don't mind having your doorways run floor-to-ceiling, the first way is easier. The second gives you more control, but making the two doorways match up can require a lot of care.

Multiple rooms in Pioneer or Pioneer Pro

Making a big room and cutting it up is much easier in Pioneer than making small rooms and connecting them. Pioneer doesn't have anything like Walkthrough's Connect Surfaces tool, so if you connect two of Pioneer's rooms, you'll have to cut separate-but-identical holes for the doors and windows — possible, but a good trick all the same. Pioneer Pro's Object Subtraction tool, however, is perfect for the job once again. Just copy the dye that you used to make the first hole and use it to make the second. (See "Punching holes in walls with Pioneer Pro" earlier in this chapter.)

If you aren't using Pioneer Pro and really must build rooms one by one and link them together, your best bet is to build them in Walkthrough, save them as VRML files, and then open them in Pioneer.

Using planes as subdividers

Pioneer doesn't have a tool like Walkthrough's Connect Surfaces. But, unlike Walkthrough, Pioneer allows you to make 2D planes, which are perfect for dividing large spaces into rooms.

1. **Make a large room.**

   Use any of the techniques we've discussed, or make up your own.

2. **Create a plane.**

   Use the Plane tool on the Primitives panel. If you're going to want to put a door or a window into this plane, make sure that it has sufficient resolution. (See "Vanishing cream: doors and windows in Pioneer" earlier in this chapter).

3. **Rotate the plane to make it vertical and then move it where you want the wall.**

   Use the Object Move and Object Rotate tools.

4. **Scale the plane so that it is the right size.**

Importing multiple rooms from Walkthrough

Connected rooms make the transition from Walkthrough to Pioneer as easily as single rooms do:

1. **Make the rooms in Walkthrough.**

2. **Connect them in Walkthrough.**

   See "Multiple rooms in Walkthrough" earlier in this chapter.

3. **Insert doors and windows.**

   Use the Surface Editor. See "A brief chat with Walkthrough's Surface Editor" earlier in this chapter.

4. **Export the connected rooms as a VRML file.**

   Select File⇨Export⇨VRML from Walkthrough's menu and give your file a name ending in .WRL.

5. **Start Pioneer.**

6. **Open the file you created in Step 4.**

   Select File⇨Scene⇨Load and then find the file you saved in Walkthrough.

Chapter 12

Decorating and Furnishing Your Rooms

. . . .

In This Chapter

▶ Painting and coloring your rooms and objects

▶ Adjusting the lighting

▶ Importing furniture and other accessories from object libraries

▶ Adding viewpoints

. . . .

Paint Your Wagon

Those gray rooms get awfully dreary. Why make your virtual rooms and objects look like Kansas when they could look like Oz? Walkthrough, Pioneer and Pioneer Pro all give you access to a full spectrum of colors.

Paint the town red at Walkthrough's Color Bar

Whenever something in your world needs a new color, just belly up to Color Bar and place your order. The Color Bar is that short, wide button about two-thirds of the way down the Design toolbar. A glance at the Color Bar tells you the currently fashionable color in Walkthrough-land — anything you make will be that color until you choose a new one. If you click and hold the Color Bar, the Palette Box appears. With it you can

✔ Change the color of existing objects: Select an object of unsatisfactory hue and then click and hold the Color Bar until the Palette Box appears. Click on a color.

✔ Select a color for objects you are about to make: With no object selected, click a color in the Palette Box.

✔ **Change the color of walls, ceilings, or other surfaces:** Click the Surface Editor tool and select a surface. After the Surface Editor toolbar appears, click and hold its Color Bar until a Palette Box appears. Click a color.

The Palette Box displays two kinds of colored squares: a few big ones in the top part of the box and a lot of little ones in the lower part.

The larger colored squares at the top of the Palette Box show the current color scheme of your world — all the colors you've used so far. If you want to go back to making objects that match something you've made already, you need only click on that color — the Palette Box disappears, any selected objects are repainted, and the Color Bar displays the new color.

Sometimes, though, you don't want to go back to making what you've made before. You want to forge ahead and bring new color to your world. In that case, look at the smaller squares in the lower part of the Palette box. Three hundred ninety-six colored squares lie in an 11-by-36 grid in no pattern we've been able to determine. Many of them look identical to us, but this fact should not dissuade you from examining each and every one to find just the right shade for the walls of that walk-in closet. As with the larger squares, a simple click sends the Palette Box away, repaints selected objects, and changes the color of the Color Bar.

If none of the 396 colors (or however many *different* colors actually are on the grid) is quite right, you have another alternative: Click the Palette icon in the upper-left corner of the Palette Box. You are rewarded with the ultimate expression of coloring potency, the Color Box, which you see in Figure 12-1 in none of its spectral glory.

Figure 12-1:
A humble
shadow
of the
Color Box.

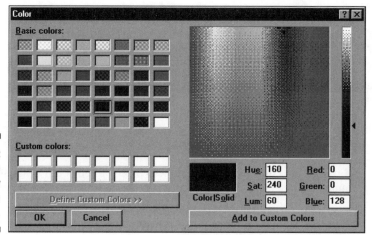

If the Palette Box is like having the big box of Crayolas, the Color Box is like having your own paint store. Forty-eight basic colors are displayed in squares on the left side of the box. But on the right side is real power: custom colors. You can specify a full three dimensions of color in any of the following ways:

- ✔ **Graphically:** Drag the crosshairs in the multi-color square window sideways to set hue, or vertically to set saturation. Set luminescence by dragging the slider on the far right.

- ✔ **Numerically by hue/saturation/luminescence:** Type values between 0 and 240 into the labeled boxes.

- ✔ **Numerically by red/green/blue:** Type values between 0 and 255 in the labeled boxes.

Whichever of the three methods you use to specify a color, the other two adjust automatically.

When you have a color you want to save, click the Add to Custom Colors button, and your handcrafted color appears in a custom color square on the left side of the box. After you have decided which custom color you want to use, click its square and then click OK. As with the Palette Box, the Color Box disappears, the selected items are repainted, and the Color Bar displays the new color.

The many custom color squares in the Color Box are there only to allow you to see candidate colors side-by-side. The colors you decide against are forgotten. The next time you open the Color Box, the custom color squares will all be blank again.

Colors of the wind and other Pioneer painting tricks

The Paint Object tool and its variants can paint a new color on any object in your world, or any of its faces. But the capabilities of this brush go far beyond mere color changes. It can paint an object transparent, paint it brick, or paint it in a sky-and-clouds pattern, to name just a few of the possibilities. In the past, only cartoon characters had this kind of power — now it can be yours as well.

The brushes

When you want to change the color of an object, click a Paint tool. Different Paint tools do different jobs, which we'll describe in a moment, but they all live in the same place on the toolbar, are all variants of each other, and all work the same way. When you click a Paint tool, two major things happen:

- Your cursor changes to some type of Paint tool, like a brush or roller.

- Several panels open, allowing you to make all kinds of choices about what paint to use.

Having made your paint selection, move your paint-tool cursor onto the object you want to paint and click the mouse. If you are in 3DR mode, part or all of the object (depending on which tool you use) changes instantly. In wireframe, you won't see any of the effects of your painting — until you switch back to 3DR. Naturally, we recommend painting in 3DR mode unless you really enjoy surprises.

The different Paint tools allow you to do the following jobs:

- **Paint an entire object at once:** Use the Paint Object tool, whose icon looks like a funnel.

- **Paint a small part of an object:** Use the Paint Face tool because faces are the smallest things that Pioneer gives you any control over. And now we're back to the subject of resolution, last discussed in Chapter 11 when we were making doors and windows by painting part of a wall transparent. The higher the resolution of an object, the more faces it has, and the more complicated the pattern you can paint (see Figure 12-3). The Paint Face icon looks like an artist's brush.

- **Paint a vertex:** The result of using the Paint Vertex tool (whose icon looks like a cube with a painted vertex), is easier shown than described. Figure 12-2 shows a light-colored (yellow) cube with one vertex painted a dark color (blue). Painted vertices only show up if you have selected Smooth shading on the Render Quality panel (which appears when you right-click on the Wireframe or 3DR buttons).

- **Paint over an area:** Suppose you have a plane painted as a black-and-white checkerboard and then you decide you'd rather have a black-and-red checkerboard. You don't have to repaint all 32 white squares individually. Just paint one of the white squares red with the Paint Over Material tool, and all the others will turn red simultaneously.

- **Figure out why an object looks the way it does:** Sometimes you look at an object and say, "How the heck did they make it look like that?" Pull out your virtual magnifying glass and take a look. The Inspect tool, whose icon looks like a magnifying glass, opens all the same panels that open with the other Paint tools. But now when you click on an object, the panel settings shift to tell you the settings of that object. So rather than just wonder why a crystal ball looks that way, you can say, "But of course! High ambient glow, high transparency, low roughness."

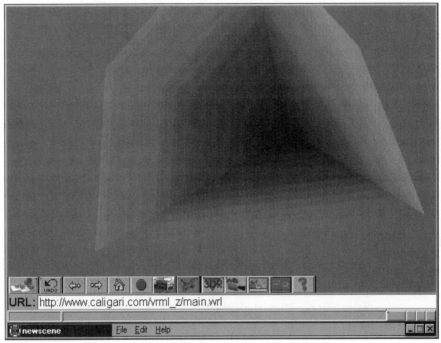

URL: http://www.caligari.com/vrml_z/main.wrl

newscene   File Edit Help

Figure 12-2:
A cube with
a painted
vertex.

The paints

And you thought painting involved just color! Well, color is just one thing you can paint on an object — try shininess, roughness, transparency, and texture maps.

Red fish, blue fish: painting with colors

Colors are handled by the Material Color panel, which opens when you select any Paint tool. When you pick a color, you are actually picking three different things: a hue, a saturation, and a value. The color wheel (well, a color hexagon, if you want to be precise) on the Material Color panel handles hue and saturation. Fortunately, you can make these choices without having to remember what hue and saturation are: You just drag the little circle to the place on the hexagon that most resembles the color you have in mind. Value (or brightness or luminescence) is controlled by the slider on the right of the panel. Bright is up and dark is down.

Having selected your Paint tool and chosen your color, start painting. Move your paint-tool cursor out into the design area and click on anything whose color you want to change.

A strange thing happens when you try to paint an object made of a material like Cloudy Sky or Bullion — nothing. You paint and paint and paint, and still you're staring at a cloudy sky. What to do? When no Paint tool seems to work, check the Shader Maps panel (it shows up when you use any Paint tool) and see if the Use Texture Map button is pushed. If it is, then Pioneer is wall-papering the old pattern over your paint just as fast as you paint it. Click the Use Texture Map button and try your Paint tool one more time.

The Pioneer Help claims that you can set color with RGB (red/green/blue) sliders as well, but we've been unable to find them.

Bright fish, rough fish: painting with attributes

We ordinarily think of painting something green or yellow, but with Pioneer, you can leave an object the same color while painting it shiny or rough or transparent. These sorts of qualities are controlled by the Shader Attributes panel, which opens whenever you use a Paint tool.

The Shader Attributes panel has four sliders: Ambient Glow, Shininess, Roughness, and Transparency. The best way to learn what these qualities look like is to play around with them, making a few objects that have different proportions of the four qualities. High Ambient Glow means that the object always looks like it is in the light, even if none of the scene's defined light sources is shining on it. High Shininess and Roughness make things looks, well, shiny and rough. (Pioneer Help talks about the *intensity of specular reflections* and the *relative size of specular highlights,* which we didn't find all that helpful. Go play with the settings.) High Transparency means that you can see through an object (very high Transparency makes an object invisible, as you saw when we showed you how to paint windows in Chapter 11).

Wood fish, brick fish: painting with texture maps

By far, the strangest way to paint in Pioneer is to get something like Cloudy Sky or Brick or Fabric on your brush and start dabbing it onto an object with a lot of resolution. Figure 12-3 is an example of what can happen if you let the technology get out of control.

Materials like Cloudy Sky are an example of texture maps. You can think of a texture map as being like elastic wallpaper, which Pioneer stretches over whatever shape to which you want to apply it. (A more complete explanation is in Chapter 14.)

Light It Up

Any photographer or movie director will tell you that lighting is a key factor in achieving dramatic visual effects. Our three tools (Walkthrough, Pioneer, and Pioneer Pro) give us varying degrees of control over the lighting of our scenes. All three allow us to decide that light should come from some directions as

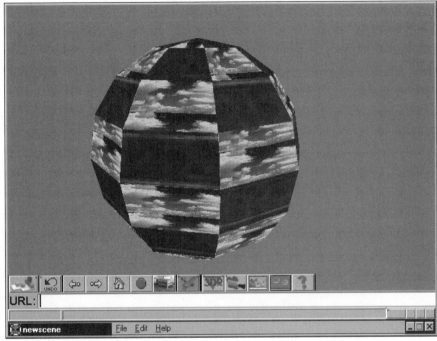

Figure 12-3:
Global
weather:
cloudy,
with a
50-percent
chance of
bricks.

opposed to others, and have a certain color. Pioneer and Pioneer Pro allow certain parts of scenes to be lit differently from others. Walkthrough allows the inside of an object to be lit differently from the outside (though whether any VRML browser is clever enough to deal with this difference is questionable). Pioneer Pro also defines spotlights, which make certain objects brighter than others. None of the three tools constructs shadows — placing one object "upstream" of another object does not block the light.

How these lighting decisions affect your VRML file is a real issue. Caligari's light sources (local light, infinite light, and spotlight) correspond to the three VRML lighting primitives, so Pioneer and Pioneer Pro have a fairly easy time translating their lighting into VRML. Walkthrough's hierarchical light structure is much harder to translate, and early versions of Walkthrough bungled the job. (Things that looked beautiful in the Walk View window looked completely different in Live3D or VR Scout.) The version of Walkthrough on the CD came out too late for us to test its Lighting Editor fully. The tests we were able to do make us optimistic that Walkthrough's lights will translate the way they are supposed to. But if you are counting on Walkthrough to produce a complicated lighting effect, you might want to run some tests yourself before you invest a lot of effort.

Local and long-distance light in Pioneer and Pioneer Pro

Pioneer has two different kinds of light sources: local and infinite. Pioneer Pro gives you a third kind, the spotlight. A local light source is like a light bulb (in fact, the icon on the Primitives panel for creating a local light source is a light bulb). It has a definite location and shines in all directions from that location. The light is weaker the further away you are from it. The only difference between a local light source and a light bulb is that the local light source does not shine. A VRML browser that looks directly at the local light source sees nothing. (VRML lights are modest creatures — they illuminate other objects, but are invisible themselves.)

An infinite light source resembles the sun more than a light bulb. The light seems to be coming from infinitely far away: It doesn't get dimmer as you move away from it, and the angle of illumination doesn't change from one part of the world to the next. An infinite light source doesn't have a location. You couldn't, for example, go to where the light source is or orbit around it. Infinite light doesn't come from a *place; it comes from a direction.*

A spotlight (unavailable in Pioneer) has both a place and a direction. Like its namesake, a spotlight is useful for lighting up an object (or one side of an object) rather than an entire room.

The default lighting

If you start a new scene in Pioneer and then save it immediately without making anything, the VRML file is about two pages long. "How could it take two pages to describe nothing?" we hear you ask (at least, those of you who have never worked for a bureaucracy are asking it). The answer is simple: Pioneer takes for granted that you want to see the objects you make, so it starts every scene out with some default light sources. You arrive on the second day of creation, not the first — somebody else has already made light.

If you click the Object List tool, you notice that your new scene has four infinite light sources. You can see them in World Building mode — four red arrows meeting at the origin, with shafts that go off to infinity. (If you don't see them, the Make Lights Visible option has been turned off. Right click the 3DR or Wireframe button to bring up the Render Quality panel, and click the button with the light bulb on it.) Select one of these sources by clicking on either its name in the Object List or the shaft of its arrow. The shaft turns white, and the Lights panel appears. Between the two of them, the shaft and the Lights panel tell you everything there is to know about this infinite light source: The shaft tells you its direction; the color wheel on the panel tells you the color (white); and the slider next to the color wheel tells you the brightness (maximum).

You may change any of these settings. Change the direction of the light by dragging the shaft with the mouse. Change its color by dragging the square to a different location on the color wheel (as with the color of paint, saturation is increased by moving away from the center of the wheel, and hue is changed by going around the wheel). Change the brightness by moving the slider.

You can get rid of the light source entirely by pressing Delete. (Figure 12-4 shows the effect of deleting three of the four default lights.) But don't get rid of all of your light sources — not if you want to see anything.

Figure 12-4:
On the left: a cone in the default lighting. On the right: the same cone after three of the default lights have been deleted.

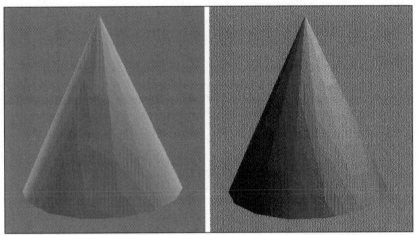

Adding new lights

You can add new lights from the Primitives panel. The Pioneer Primitives panel has two light buttons: the Infinite Light icon looks like a long, white arrow, and the Local Light icon looks like a light bulb. The Pioneer Pro Primitives panel has a spotlight button in addition to the first two. Clicking any of these icons adds the corresponding type of light and opens the Lights panel to let you adjust the color and brightness of the new light.

A new infinite light looks just like the infinite default lights, and a local light looks like a lot of line segments meeting at a point. A spotlight looks like a cone — the light comes out of the wide end.

You can move any light source with the Object Move and Object Rotate tools. Moving the infinite light moves its shaft so that you can line it up better with some other part of the world. But because the infinite light has direction but no location, only Object Rotate has any effect on the scene. Conversely, the local light shines in all directions, so rotating it changes nothing.

A spotlight can be either moved to a new location or rotated to cast its light in a different direction. In addition, the Object Scale tool can either widen the angle of illumination (making the cone fatter) or narrow it (making the cone skinnier). You can adjust the intensity of the cone's hot spot by clicking and dragging on the green circle at the base of the cone with either Object Move or Object Scale.

The natural place to put a local light source is inside a lamp or some other light fixture. If you do, remember that while the light illuminates, it does not shine. The way to make your lamp shine is to give it an ambient glow. See "Bright fish, rough fish: painting with attributes" earlier in this chapter.

The Lighting Editor of Walkthrough Pro

Walkthrough provides two kinds of lights: ambient lights that give the scene its overall brightness and directional lights, which (like Pioneer's infinite lights) have no particular location but illuminate everything that faces in a certain direction.

Lights are controlled from the Light list and the Light menu (seen in Figure 12-5). Open up the Light window and the Light list by double-clicking the light bulb icon on the Design, Surface Editor, or Tumble Editor toolbars.

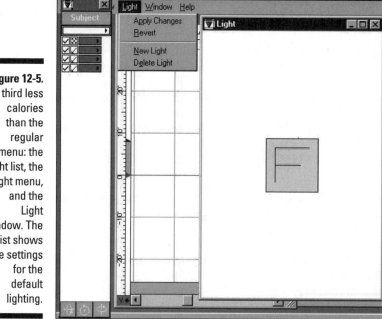

Figure 12-5.
A third less calories than the regular menu: the Light list, the Light menu, and the Light window. The list shows the settings for the default lighting.

The default lighting

A scene in Walkthrough begins with four lights: one ambient light and three directional lights — one in front, one on the right, and another above. All four lights are white. Until you specifically decide to change the lighting of the world or some object, the default lighting applies to all objects in all locations.

The lighting hierarchy

Lighting is defined hierarchically in Walkthrough. Every object inherits its lighting from the object that contains it. Ultimately, everything is contained by the World, which is where the default lighting is defined. Consequently, everything starts out with the default lighting, and any changes you make to the default lighting affect every object in the scene.

But after you change the lighting for a particular object (we'll show you how in a few paragraphs), you give that object — and everything inside it — independence from the lighting of the objects that contain it. Once you have given an object its own lighting, changes in the World lighting no longer affect it.

That description explains the lighting hierarchy from the top down. From the bottom up it works like this: When you create a new object, Walkthrough has to decide how to light it. First Walkthrough checks to see if you have defined a special lighting for this object. If not, it looks to the smallest object that contains this object. If you have defined a special lighting for it, Walkthrough uses that lighting for the new object. If not, it looks to the smallest object that contains the container until it either finds an object with specially defined lighting or it reaches the lighting defined at the World level.

Changing the lighting

To change the World lighting, double-click the light bulb icon on the Design toolbar. To change lighting for an object and all its contents, select the object in the Design window, click the light bulb icon, and then click the object again. These actions will bring up the Light tools — Light list, Light window, and Light menu.

Each light source that applies to the object you have chosen is represented by an entry in the Light list. An entry in the Light list consists of the following:

- **A checkbox to turn the light on or off.** A check indicates on; an x indicates off.

- **A checkbox to change the light from ambient to directional or vice versa.** A single arrow denotes a directional light. Four arrows denote an ambient light.

- **A color bar.** The color of the bar indicates the color of the light. Click and hold on the arrow in the color bar to bring up a color palette. Click a square on the palette to change the color of the light.

As you make changes with the Light tools, you see their potential effects on the sample cube in the Light window. When you decide you like what you see, select Light⇨Apply Changes to alter the lighting for the World or the selected object. *Only then will the effects of your changes show up in the Walk View window.*

To change the angle of a directional light

This change is made from the Light window. After you select a light source by clicking the color bar of its entry on the Light list, the Light window shows a light positioned with respect to the sample cube. The cursor changes to a hand when you move the mouse to the Light window. Use the hand cursor to move the light.

To add or delete a light

Add a light to the scene by selecting Light⇨New Light. A new entry appears on the Light list, which you may then adjust as you like. Delete a light by clicking its color bar on the Light list and then choosing Light⇨Delete Light from the menu.

The subject button

At the top of the Lights list is the Subject button; beneath it is a color bar — press on it to get a full array of color choices. (It works just like the color bar on the Design toolbar.) You might reasonably guess that these two control some kind of light source, but in fact they don't. Instead, they allow you to check how objects of a given color will look under the lighting indicated by the Light list.

To examine how the lighting will affect a given object, click Subject, choose a subject color from the color bar, and then manipulate the cube in the Light window with the hand cursor. The different sides of the cube will be colored and shaded in the same way that an object of the subject color would be under the lighting scheme specified by the Light list.

Check Some Furniture Out of the Library

Good libraries have lots of cushy chairs for reading or sleeping in, but they never let us check out any. That fact is about to change: Virtus and Caligari have put together some libraries of objects that are just sitting there, waiting to be pasted into your VRML worlds. Virtus even has a library of humanoid figures (all named *Brutus*) that can sit in those chairs for you, as you see in Figure 12-6.

Pioneer's libraries

Pioneer doesn't come with any particular library, but because it reads such a wide range of file types, it can use libraries of all sorts. See Chapter 16 for details on importing objects into Pioneer and the Appendix for an accounting of the object libraries on our CD.

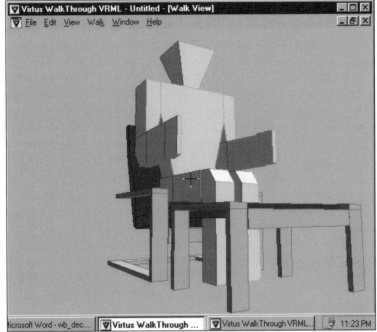

Figure 12-6:
Brutus
never looks
relaxed, not
even in a
lounge
chair.

Three libraries to walk through

Early versions of Walkthrough didn't read VRML, so you couldn't fill your rooms with all kinds of stray objects available on the Web. Virtus claims that the version of Walkthrough on the CD does read VRML — a claim we didn't get the software soon enough to test. If it does, the whole Web belongs to you. But even if not, Walkthrough comes with three object libraries that fill most basic needs.

Access these libraries by selecting File⇨Library from the menu. The Open Library window appears to offer you a choice of libraries: BONLIB1.WLB, BRUTUS.WLB, and SAMPLE.WLB. Both BONLIB1 and SAMPLE are libraries of everyday household objects. BRUTUS is a library of people, or rather, of Brutuses.

Select a library from the Open Library window, and you are presented with a catalog window like the one in Figure 12-7. On the left side is a list of objects, and on the right is a view of the currently selected one. The view window functions just like the Walk View windows you're used to. You can look at your object from every side before you decide whether or not you want it. If you do want it, select Edit⇨Copy from the menu. Then return to a Design window, click where you want the object, and select Edit⇨Paste. As with every new acquisition, finding the perfect location can take a while, but you can move and rotate your new object in exactly the same ways that you move or rotate any other virtual object — without risking your back.

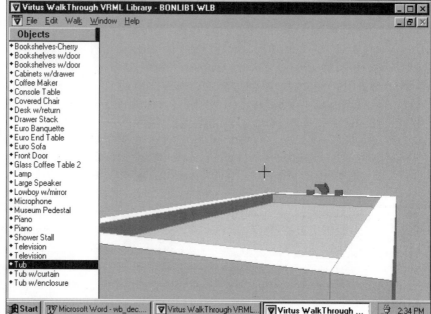

Figure 12-7:
In the
market for
virtual
objects? You
can really
clean up
with
Walkthrough's
built-in
libraries.

Virtus's virtual department store

Furniture, aisle one; housewares, aisle two; bathroom fixtures, second floor.

The libraries SAMPLE.WLB and BONLIB1.WLB aren't quite as complete as Sears, but they have a collection of phones, microwaves, couches, chairs, pianos, and so forth that allows you to populate your rooms with appropriate objects.

Virtual mannequins: the Brutus library

Rooms with furniture, lamps, microwaves, and other accessories may begin to look homey. But a room never gets that lived-in look until it has people in it. And so Virtus provides a library of people — or at least of Brutus — in a variety of poses that, if they are never quite lifelike, are at least life-suggesting.

Brutus is not exactly high art — even calling him a cartoon character is stretching things a little. Nonetheless, Virtus has assembled a collection of Brutus in a variety of positions suitable for plopping in a chair or lying on a park bench. Recognizing the limitations of their art, the folks at Virtus have kept their sense of humor and thrown in a few amusing figures, like the Make-My-Day Brutus in Figure 12-8.

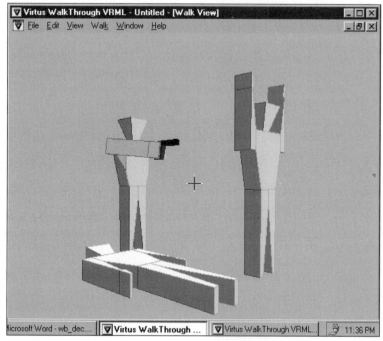

Figure 12-8:
Check out
a murder
mystery
from the
Brutus
library.

Create Viewpoints (Cameras)

If you have created, say, the ultimate house of the future, you probably want people to start touring your house from the front door, not from inside the linen closet. How can you make sure they start where you want them to? In fact, how can you make sure they see all the important sights and don't just spend hours touring the basement?

The answer is to create something called *viewpoints,* also called *cameras.* You can create one or more viewpoints in VRML, each viewpoint specifying a location and a direction to look in. You can even give viewpoints names; many VRML browsers let the users choose a viewpoint by name. These viewpoints serve as starting points for the virtual tourist, who can then look and move around from there.

- If there's only one viewpoint in your world, that is what the VRML browser displays when your world is first downloaded.

- If there's no viewpoint specified, the browser uses the VRML "default". This condition arises in the later section, "Camera problems in Pioneer".

- Walkthrough Pro always gives you one and only one viewpoint: the viewpoint you see in Walk View.

- Pioneer lets you specify several viewpoints. You create them by inserting and orienting camera primitives from the Primitives panel.

The Walkthrough Pro Observer

"The Walkthrough Pro Observer" sounds like a hiking newsletter, but is actually the name of the built-in viewpoint in Walkthrough Pro: the Observer, alias "Cyrano" and "the guy with the nose" that you see in any Design View.

- ✔ To position him, just drag him in any Design View.
- ✔ To orient him, hold down the Ctrl button in Windows (the Option button on the Mac), click on him, and drag a line in the direction you want him to look. To make him look up or down, do that maneuver in any side view.

Cameras in Pioneer

Pioneer lets you create multiple named viewpoints by placing camera primitives.

In the early versions of software we were using to write this book, the non-Caligari VRML browsers did not recognize the way Caligari translated these cameras into VRML. If your cameras don't work, see the next section, "Camera problems in Pioneer".

You can create, position, and delete cameras exactly as you do cubes, cones, or any other Pioneer primitive.

- ✔ Click on the Primitives button (the cone, cube, and sphere) to see the Primitives Panel.
- ✔ Click the Camera button to get a camera primitive.
- ✔ To move the camera, drag with the Object Move tool.
- ✔ To rotate the camera, drag with the Object Rotate tool. To rotate the camera without tilting it, enable only the object Y axis. (See the axis controls at the far right of the help bar.) To angle the camera up or down, enable only the object X axis.
- ✔ To see the view from a camera in the main window, select the camera and then click on the camera icon (the "View from Object" tool). To see this view in the little window, navigate so that you can see the camera there; then click the camera.
- ✔ To name a camera, select it and then right click the Selection tool. In the Object Info panel that appears, enter a name in the Name box and press the Enter key.

Camera problems in Pioneer

In the early beta versions of Pioneer, the cameras just don't work with most browsers. (It's the browsers' fault, however, not Caligari's; Caligari obeys the rules set out by VRML.) As a result of this miscommunication, when displaying Pioneer files, most browsers fail to understand the camera settings and use the VRML "default" viewpoint instead.

Working with default of de camera

One way to deal with this problem is not to use Pioneer's cameras, but instead build your world around the default viewpoint. In Pioneer coordinates, this viewpoint is at X=0, Y=0, Z=0 (the center of the Pioneer grid) looking in the +Y direction. Which way is +Y? When you first start Pioneer after you have installed it, it's away from you and to the right. To find out which way is +Y, try to move something in that direction.

To help you remember where the default viewpoint is, place a camera to represent it. Here's how:

1. **Click the Primitives button and click the camera button on the Primitives panel.**

   A camera appears at world coordinates 0, 0, 0, where objects always appear when they are first created. The camera initially faces in the +X direction.

2. **To turn the camera so that it faces +Y, first turn on the grid mode by clicking the blue grid button; this gives you 45-degree increments.**

3. **Choose the Object Rotate tool.**

4. **At the far right of the help bar, select Wld (world axes) instead of Obj (object axes), and make sure that the Z button is depressed.**

5. **Right-click and drag to the right, turning the camera two increments counter-clockwise.**

Working around de problem

If you really want to be able to control viewpoints and have multiple viewpoints using Pioneer, you will have to edit the VRML file after you are completely done with all other changes in Pioneer. Place your cameras as we describe earlier in this chapter, but avoid tilting them. Then open the VRML file with your text editor or word processor.

First, find parts of the file that look something like the following, near the beginning of the file:

```
TransformSeparator {
   MatrixTransform {
      matrix
         1.000 0.000 0.000 0
         0.000 1.000 -0.000 0
         -0.000 0.000 1.000 0
         3.125  0.000 2.550 1
      }
      DEF Camera1 PerspectiveCamera {
         position 0.000 0.000 0.000
         heightAngle 0.761
      }
   }
```

You will see one such group for each camera. The name you assigned the camera appears after the word DEF (here, it is "Camera1").

For each camera, copy the first three values of the last line of numbers under the word "matrix." Paste them in place of the three sets of "0.000" following the word "position" (shown in bold, here). This places the camera properly.

Rotating the camera is a pain because it is partly a matter of trial and error. Our earlier suggestion that you keep the camera level will help make it easier. Add this line after the "position" line:

```
orientation 0 1 0 radians
```

but replace the word *radians* with a number. That number is the camera rotation you want in degrees divided by 57.3. (It's 180 divided by pi, if that helps.) Use 0.786 for 45 degrees, for instance. Positive values are counterclockwise, viewed from above.

Finally, delete the MatrixTransform "node" that precedes the PerspectiveCamera node: Delete starting with the line "MatrixTransform {" all the way through the next "}" symbol. When you are done with all these edits, the VRML code for each camera should look something like this:

```
TransformSeparator {
      DEF Camera1 PerspectiveCamera {
         position 3.125  0.000 2.550
         orientation 0 1 0 -0.786
         heightAngle 0.761
      }
   }
```

Save the file as a text file, load it into your VRML browser, and try your viewpoint. Keep re-editing the *radians* value, saving, and reloading until you get the rotation you want.

Part IV
Making a
Better World

"Do you think a Web Site with a 3D world like this one will attract or repel customers?"

In this part . . .

In Part III, we show you how to make some simple shapes and build, furnish, and light rooms. In this part, we show you how to put more realism in your virtual reality. Need some realistic-looking paneling for your virtual den or grass for your virtual lawn? Part III shows you how to get more interesting surfaces by texture mapping. Here, we reveal tricks for creating the fancy shapes of your dreams, whether your dreams run to tropical islands, mountains, lakes, or sea monsters. For the fanciest shapes, you may want to import some objects made by someone else with a different tool, so we also discuss how to import alien objects in different formats.

Chapter 13

Making Fancier Shapes

In This Chapter

▶ Breaking and slicing objects in Walkthrough

▶ Moving, twisting, and stretching

▶ Dragging faces

▶ Rotating and tilting faces

▶ Extending (sweeping) faces

▶ Lathing faces

▶ Forming a point

▶ Rounding

▶ Creating concave shapes

S pheres, cubes, cones — phooey! Enough of these primitive shapes. What we virtual world builders want is *serious* shape-shifting: spiral staircases, slimy squid, virtual velociraptors, meteorite-mangled moons, anatomically correct anteaters!

Here's where we plug in the power tools of our virtual model shop. Whether it's lathing, skewing, breaking, or sharpening, you've got the power. It's tool time, folks!

Breaking and Slicing Objects

Ever since Og the Neanderthal knocked a chunk off a rock, thereby creating a better hide-scraper, folks have been making interesting shapes by cutting up boring shapes. Walkthrough Pro is one product that relies on this traditional approach. Pioneer currently doesn't give you any way to break up objects — unless they were composite (glued together) objects from the start. (Pioneer Pro and trueSpace, Caligari's professional-grade products, give you "Boolean" tools that can blow holes in objects, whack pieces off them, and combine them into a single shape.)

Virtus provides an easy way to knock a slice off an object in the Tumble Editor. Here's how to use it:

1. **Open a Design View window (Top, Bottom, Left, Right, and so on).**

   If a Design View window is already open, click in it to make it the active window.

    2. **On the tool pad, click the Tumble Editor tool.**

   (If no tool pad is visible, choose Windows⇨Tools Window.)

3. **In the Design View, double-click the object you intend to mangle. (A single click will suffice if the object was already selected.)**

   The Tumble Editor tumbles into view, looking a lot like Figure 13-1.

Slice Tool

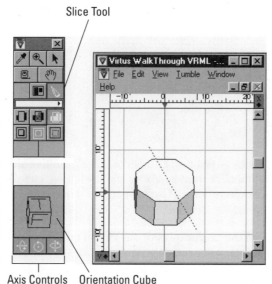

Figure 13-1:
Drag a line, cut a slice. The Tumble Editor makes it as easy as cutting tofu.

Axis Controls   Orientation Cube

Now you need to rotate the object so that you can cut it the way you want. Imagine you are looking down on a chunk of cheese (tofu, if you're a strict vegetarian) on a cutting board. You will be chopping off a chunk by slicing toward the board, so you need to rotate the object until it's oriented the way you want it for chopping.

4. **To rotate the object, drag anywhere in the Tumble Editor window.**

   Your cursor should be a hand shape, telling you that you are using the Move tool (selected automatically after you first enter the Tumble Editor). If your cursor is not a hand shape, click on the Move tool (hand icon) in the tool pad.

You can also rotate the object by dragging the orientation cube at the bottom of the Tumble Editor's tool pad. This cube is linked to your object, and tells you how your object is oriented by showing the initial letters of the words Left, Right, Front, Back, Top, and bottom.

Rotating things in multiple axes at once — which is what the Tumble Editor initially lets you do — can be frustrating. To disable rotation around one or two axes, click to deselect their buttons at the very bottom of the Tumble Editor (selected buttons appear depressed). To rotate only around the vertical axis like a top, for example, deselect the left and middle buttons (across- and into-the-page axes, respectively).

5. **If you want to cut at a precise right angle to a face, double-click that face.**

   That face moves to the forefront, and no other sides are now visible.

 6. **Click the Slice tool on the tool pad.**

   It looks like a chisel.

7. **Drag a line through the object.**

   Dragging a line from left to right removes a piece above the line. Dragging from top to bottom removes a piece to the right. Dragging in the opposite directions removes the opposite piece. If you decide you want the other piece after cutting a slice, choose Tumble➪Reverse Slice from the menu bar. To undo the most recent action, choose Edit➪Undo.

Moving, Twisting, and Stretching in Pioneer

Time for some virtual calisthenics! Get your virtual objects into shape with moving, twisting, and stretching exercises. Stiff, upright, symmetrical shapes are great for buildings, desks, and other manufactured stuff, but more natural objects like rocks, cliffs, arms, and legs call for a little moving, twisting, or stretching of the surfaces (or *faces*) of an object.

Moving object faces around is an area where Pioneer really sparkles. Not only can you skew things by moving a face or two, but you can also tilt, rotate, shrink, and expand faces to create truly complex shapes. For even more interesting (or grotesque) shapes, you can use a face of a shape to grow an extension or appendage by *sweeping* it in a straight line or *lathing* it in a circular or spiral path!

Making faces in Caligari's Pioneer

Every shape in Pioneer is literally multifaceted: it has a lot of faces. Even a *round* shape, like a sphere, cone, or cylinder, is actually made up of flat faces (or *surfaces,* if you prefer). A plane is normally two-faced, a cube is six-faced, and rounder shapes have lots of faces.

This arrangement is generally a pretty satisfactory state of affairs, but what if you want to, say, rough up a cube a little to make it look like a rock? If each side of the cube is made up of a single, monolithic, imperturbable face, the cube will still look pretty cubic no matter what you do to those six faces. What you want is more faces. Figure 13-2 shows three cubes with increasing numbers of faces, from left to right.

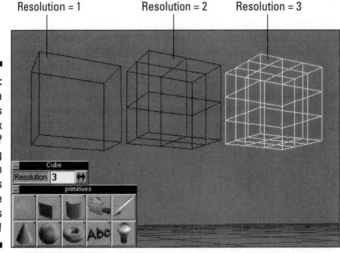

Resolution = 1   Resolution = 2   Resolution = 3

Figure 13-2:
Who says a cube has only six faces? Setting Resolution to 3 gives you nine times as many faces!

To create more complex shapes, start by creating your initial primitive (sphere, cube, cone, cylinder, or torus) with additional faces. Here's how:

1. **To get a panel full of primitive shapes (that you see in the bottom-left corner of Figure 13-2), click the Primitives tool.**

2. **In the Primitives panel, right-click the shape you want.**

3. **Specify the number of faces by using the panel that pops up.**

   A panel pops up, like the one in Figure 13-2, that specifies a *resolution.* That panel sets the number of divisions in the shape. You can either click and enter new values in the white box areas or drag the double arrows that adjoin the boxes; drag right for a higher value, left for a lower value. Press Tab or Enter after changing a value.

Here are the settings you adjust to get more faces:

- **Plane or Cube:** Enter a higher number in the Resolution box.

- **Sphere, Cylinder, Cone, or Torus:** For more faces going *around* the shape, increase longitude. For more faces going *up* the shape, increase latitude (higher latitude in a torus makes the cross-section of the torus rounder). The number you enter should be the number of sides you want plus 1.

  To make a cylinder more cone-like, adjust top radius; for instance, setting the top radius to 0.5 makes the top 50 percent as big as the bottom. This does not change the number of faces, however.

  In a torus, for a bigger hole (skinnier doughnut), increase inner radius; for example, 0.8 creates a hole radius 80 percent of the total radius. This does not change the number of faces.

4. **In the Primitives panel, create your shape by left-clicking that same shape.**

   Pioneer places your chosen shape dead center on the Pioneer grid. Scale it and move it to a convenient size and location, if you like.

If Pioneer is operating in rendered mode, seeing the individual faces is nearly impossible, so switch to wireframe mode (click and hold on the 3DR button, drag up to the wireframe button, and release).

Now that you have a multifaceted cube or other shape, you can fiddle with your faces to make the shape more interesting. Read the upcoming sections on doing various nasty things to your faces. Figure 13-3 shows the difference a greater number of faces makes.

The trade-off of having more faces (or we should say, the *face-off*) is that while having more faces makes shapes more interesting, it slows down the rendering speed of whatever browser people are using to view your world. This slower rendering speed, in turn, slows down the speed at which people can navigate your world, and makes it less interesting. Choose your evil.

Figure 13-3:
The same three cubes as Figure 13-2, with faces shmooshed and a rock-like surface texture applied.

Pioneer's Face tool

The key to Pioneer's shape-shifting capabilities is its Face tool, a button sporting a modest-looking icon, a cube with one colored face. (This tool's formal name is the Point Edit:Faces tool, because in Caligari's other products, other tools in the same family let you edit individual points around the face. We call it the Face tool.)

The Face tool lets you move, rotate, or scale any faces of a shape. Here's how to start:

1. **Select the object you want to work on.**

   Click on the Selection tool — the diagonal arrow — and then click on the object.

2. **Click the Face tool.**

   The Navigation panel in Figure 13-4 pops up. This panel has three gadgets on it: one for moving, one for rotating and one for shrinking and expanding (scaling) a face. The tool for moving faces is already selected.

Figure 13-4:
The Navigation panel contains tools to move, rotate, or scale selected faces.

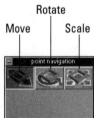

Once you select the object and click the face tool, your next step is to select the face or faces you want to change. Read on.

Selecting your faces

With the Face tool selected, select the face or faces you want to work on by clicking on them. To select more than one, Ctrl+click. Pioneer displays selected faces in bright green.

In early beta versions of Pioneer, the help bar tells you to use Ctrl+click to select multiple faces, but that operation doesn't seem to work reliably. If you find Ctrl+click unreliable, try Shift+click, which seems to work better for us.

A few helpful tips for selecting faces

✔ Pioneer only selects faces that would be visible to you if the shape were rendered. If you must select faces that are on opposite sides from each other, open the small viewing window (click the button with a house icon) and then navigate in that window until you can see the side opposite the one in the main window. You can now select faces from either window using Ctrl+click.

✔ Here's another way to select faces on opposite sides: After selecting faces on one side of the object, choose the Object Rotation tool and rotate the object so that you can see the other side. Continue selecting faces with Ctrl+click.

✔ If Pioneer doesn't select a face at all, try again. Sometimes it takes a few attempts.

✔ If Pioneer selects the wrong face, press Ctrl+Z (undo) and try again. Pioneer's undo feature can undo several steps in a row, so you can back up quite a few steps.

✔ The early (beta) versions of Pioneer have a useful quirk that we're not sure was intended. If you click on another *object* while using the Face tools, you can select an individual edge or point (vertex), instead of a face! Just click on the vertex or edge. If this quirk remains, you can use it to move, rotate, or scale edges and points, just as you do faces. In Pioneer Pro, there are variants of the Face tool available that let you move individual edges or points.

✔ In early versions of Pioneer, the Rotate and Scale tools occasionally refuse to do their jobs — they move the face instead. Click the Selection tool, click the Face tool again, and re-select the face to try again.

Dragging, rotating, or scaling your faces

Once you select a face (or faces), you can move it, turn it, or scale it up or down; it keeps all its connections to the rest of the shape. Click the Move, Rotate, or Scale tool of Figure 13-4 and then click and drag anywhere in your viewing window (see Figure 13-5 for examples of each tool in action).

Moving things around in Pioneer is always a bit mind-boggling, so don't get discouraged if things seem to work weirdly in the beginning. To get the coordinate system straight in your mind, or to get better control over your actions, disable all but one axis (all three axes are normally enabled). Click on any two of the X, Y, or Z buttons at the right end of the Pioneer help bar so that only one button remains pressed; that one is your enabled axis. Try the action you want; press Ctrl+Z to undo the action if it comes out wrong, and try again with a different axis selected.

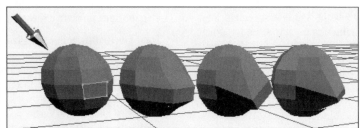

Dragging motions follow Pioneer's normal rules of motion, slightly adjusted for the fact that you are dealing with a face, not an entire object:

✔ Drag with the left mouse button for actions involving the X and Y axes. Drag left-right for X-axis motion; drag forward-back for Y-axis motion. Drag diagonally for motion in both axes at once.

✔ Drag with the right button for actions involving the Z axis.

✔ X, Y, and Z directions are based on the face's own coordinate system, not the entire object's. The Z axis normally points directly out from the face, at 90 degrees to the face. (In beta versions of Pioneer, this isn't always true.) For the other axes, frankly, the easiest way to figure them out is by trial and error.

✔ Rotation is always rotation *around* an axis, as if that axis were a pin through the face.

✔ You can switch freely among the Move, Rotate, and Scale tools while keeping the same face or faces selected. (Beta versions of Pioneer don't let you switch reliably, though.)

✔ You can use the *Object* Move, Rotate, or Scale tools even while you are working with the *Face* tool.

For more precise control over your face operations, turn on Pioneer's snap-to-grid mode. Right-click on the Toggle Grid Mode button (the one with the blue grid), and a panel will pop up so that you can set the grid interval. If the Move or Scale tool is selected, you can set the X, Y, and Z interval (*1*= 1 unit on the visible Pioneer grid). If the Rotate tool is selected, you can set the rotation angle increments in degrees (90 = a right turn). Left-click on the Toggle Grid Mode button to enable the snap-to-grid mode. When this mode is enabled, you have to drag a greater distance to see any results.

Sweeping faces and 2D shapes

Here's a little known fact you can use as an excuse to avoid household chores: Sweeping can turn a face into an appendage! It's not as gruesome a process as it sounds. In fact, it's a lot of fun; Figure 13-6 shows a few examples of the results of *sweeping*.

In Figure 13-6, we've swept a face from a sphere primitive, a text primitive (D for Dummies), and an irregular polygon. On the left are the primitives we started with, and on the right are the cool 3D shapes we ended up with. Notice that a face on the sphere, as promised, has been swept into an appendage!

Starting the sweep

Sweeping causes a plane (any flat, two-dimensional thing, whether it's a face on an object, a letter, a plane primitive, or a polygon) to sprout a third dimension. Repeated sweeping can create beautiful tapering, twisting, and curving shapes.

Here's how to start the sweep process:

1. **Select an object (click on it with the Select tool, the diagonal arrow icon).**

2. **Select a face (click the Face tool and then click on the face) or faces.**

3. **Click the Sweep tool.**

Figure 13-6:
Before and after sweeping faces (a lot more fun than it sounds).

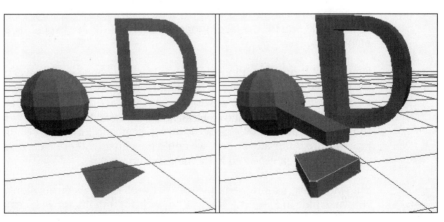

The face you selected now sweeps through space, creating a 3D volume that we call a *sweep*, ending in a new face. Pioneer gives your initial sweep a length of 1 unit, but you can adjust it. In fact, because the end face is now selected (notice the green outline) and the Face tools are standing by, you can do all the moving, twisting, and stretching exercises described in "Moving, Twisting, and Stretching in Pioneer" earlier in this chapter.

If any of the following steps don't seem to work, remember that to take any action involving the X, Y, or Z axis, that axis must be enabled: Its button must be depressed at the right end of the Pioneer help bar. (If that suggestion doesn't help, remember that your copy of Pioneer may be beta-ware and still somewhat buggy.)

- ✔ To change the length of the sweep, move the face in its Z direction: click the Face Move tool and drag left-right with the *right* mouse button.

- ✔ To change the direction of the sweep, move the face: Click the Face Move tool and drag with the *left* mouse button.

- ✔ To make the sweep taper or expand, scale the face: Click the Face Scale tool and drag.

- ✔ To twist the sweep, rotate the face around its Z axis: Click the Rotate Face tool and drag with the *right* mouse button.

- ✔ To tilt the face at the end of the sweep, rotate it around its X and/or Y axis: Click the rotate face tool and drag with the left mouse button.

Repeating the sweep

After the first sweep, things get even more interesting. Each time you click the sweep button, Pioneer sweeps the same face again — but repeats the changes you made using the Face tool. Did you shorten the length of the sweep? Pioneer's next sweep is that same, shorter length. Did you shrink the face with the scale tool? On the next sweep, Pioneer shrinks the face by the same amount. Did you tilt the face? Pioneer continues to tilt the next face the same amount.

Figure 13-7 shows how Pioneer repeats the face changes with every sweep. We selected the top surface of the pentagon and swept it; then we reduced the sweep by moving the face down. We tilted the face and shrunk it using the Face tools. Each time we clicked the Sweep button after that, Pioneer continued those same transformations of the sweep segment, forming a continuous, tapering arc. After any sweep, we could have made other changes, and those would have been repeated in the next sweep.

But wait! There's more! See the faces between each sweep segment? (They are shown in blue in Pioneer.) You can go back and modify those faces with the Face Move, Rotate, and Scale tools. To select 'em, just click on 'em.

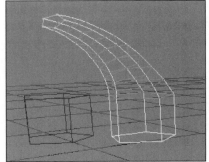

Figure 13-7:
Each click
of the
sweep tool
repeats your
face
changes.

Lathing faces and 2D shapes

Lathing a face sounds even more painful than *sweeping a face,* and — in fact —
it is. But the results are worth the effort. *Lathing* is nothing more than sweeping
in a circular or spiral path. It's a bit more painful than sweeping because you
can adjust so many things: the radius of the circular path, the plane, the length
of the sweep, and any spiraling.

Here's how the lathing process works:

1. **Select the object.**

   (Click the object with the Select tool, the diagonal arrow icon.)

2. **Select a face on the object (click the Face tool and then click on the
   face) — or faces.**

3. **Click the Lathe tool.**

   (The tool is one of the variants sharing a space on the toolbar with the
   Sweep tool and Tip tool. If the Lathe tool is not visible, just click and hold
   on whichever of these family members is visible and drag up to the Lathe
   tool.)

   Pioneer displays a special lathing control: a C-shaped curve starting at the
   face and ending in a blue tip and a T, as you see in Figure 13-8.

4. **Set the lathing controls.**

   In Figure 13-8, we added some 3D arrows and labels to indicate which
   parts of the lathing control to drag to do different things. Here's how to
   set the control. Refer to Figure 13-8 as you read these instructions.

   • The crossbar that forms the top of the T is the central axis around
     which the face rotates during lathing. To sweep in a tighter circle,
     click the crossbar at its center point and drag it towards the face
     you're sweeping. For a larger circle, drag away from the face.

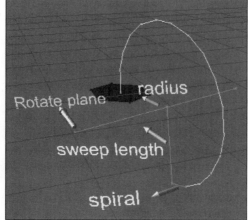

Figure 13-8:
Pushing and
pulling
various
parts of
the lathe
control.

- To change the plane of the sweep, click the crossbar at either end and drag; the entire C shape will move around the face as if it were a strangely-shaped paper clip with one end poked into the face. It's hard to explain with words; just give it a try and you'll see what we mean.

- To sweep in a spiral, click the blue tip of the C that appears just before the T and drag in the axial direction (the way the crossbar on the T runs). This bends the C in a sort of spiral way.

- To sweep more or less than the three-quarter circle Pioneer gives you at first, click the stem of the T and drag it. You can often make Pioneer lathe the face through several rotations if you like.

- To make a smoother or chunkier shape, change resolution (the number of segments in the sweep): Click on any of the dots around the C and drag. More dots mean a smoother shape; fewer mean a chunkier shape.

5. Perform the lathe operation by clicking the Lathe tool again.

Just as for sweeping, when you have lathed a face, the end face remains selected (in green), so you can scale it, rotate it, or move it with the face tools. *The end face must be facing you, however!* If it's hidden behind anything, the controls won't work. Rotate the shape with the Object Rotation tool so that you have a clear view of the face. If you scale or move the end face, the rest of the shape adjusts to follow that change and makes a smooth transition between the original face and the final one. If you shrink the end face, for instance, the lathed shape will taper. Figure 13-9 shows how we spirally lathed a hexagon and then shrunk the end face with the Face Scale tool.

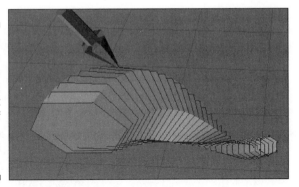

Figure 13-9: Shrink the end face after lathing and you get a nice, if weird, tapering shape.

Lathing also marks the faces between each segment in blue; you can click on any one of these faces and move, rotate, or scale them using the Face tools. Segments preceding or following that face will follow proportionately if you scale or move a segment's face. This whole face-adjustment business can be a little unreliable in the early beta copies of Pioneer.

Making a Point, Getting a Round

If you were wondering when we were going to get *a round* to getting to *the point,* wait no longer. Both Caligari and Virtus offer ways to create a spire, a pencil tip, a fang, or anything else that comes to a point. They both also give you ways to turn boring flat-sided shapes into elegant rounded shapes like baseballs, watermelons, and bullets.

Making points and rounds in Virtus

Virtus's Walkthrough Pro makes points by using a special kind of pointy *inflation.* Remember that Walkthrough makes 3D shapes by having you draw a 2D shape in a design view. It then creates the third dimension automatically (a process Virtus calls *inflation*). Although you are probably used to seeing Walkthrough inflate by extending straight sides up or down, it can also inflate your 2D shape to a point or rounded tip. Here's how to make a pointed or rounded shape:

1. **Make any Design View your current window.**

   (Click on its title bar.)

2. **Choose your inflation type by clicking one of the inflation buttons at the bottom of the tool pad.**

   The icon on the button you choose turns yellow.

Each of the three buttons hides a small family of related tools. The leftmost family gives you symmetrical shapes; the center family gives you upward-pointing shapes; and the rightmost family gives you downward-pointing shapes.

Click and hold on a button to see the other tools in the family; then drag to the right and release the mouse button to choose one of those other tools. The inflation shape is pictured on the tool.

3. **Choose a Shape tool in the third row of the tool pad and drag in the design window to draw your shape.**

To change the type of inflation for any existing shape, first select the shape (click on the Selection tool, the diagonal arrow, and then click on the shape); then *double-click* the inflation button of your choice.

To make your shape more pointed or blunt, change to a view where you can see the shape from the side (use View➪Change View). Click on the dot marking the tip of the point or round and drag that dot up or down.

Pioneer points

To make points in Pioneer, the Tip tool is your pal. Here's how to bring a face or other 2D surface (text, a plane, or a polygon) to a point:

1. **Select the object.**

   (Click the object with the Select tool, the diagonal arrow icon.)

2. **Select a face on the object.**

   (Click the Face tool and then click on the face — or faces.)

 3. **Click the Tip tool.**

   (The Tip tool is one of the variants sharing a space on the toolbar with the Sweep tool and Lathe tool. If the Tip tool is not visible, just click and hold on whichever of these family members is visible and drag up to the Tip tool.)

At this point (pardon the pun), you can drag the point of the tip around. Drag with the left mouse button for X and Y motion; drag with the right button for Z motion.

For more about using the face tool, see the earlier section, "Moving, Twisting, and Stretching in Pioneer."

Pioneer rounds

Considering how many shaping tools Pioneer provides, we're amazed that no tool sweeps a face into a rounded shape. Instead, you use the regular, old straight Sweep tool like this:

1. **Select the object.**

   (Click the object with the Select tool, the diagonal arrow icon.)

2. **Select a face on the object.**

   (Click the face tool and then click on the face — or faces.)

3. **Sweep the face or other 2D object using the Sweep tool.**

   For more about sweeping and scaling faces, see "Sweeping faces and 2D shapes" earlier in this chapter.

4. **Shorten the sweep by right-dragging with your mouse.**

5. **Repeat the sweep (click the Sweep tool) several times, creating a stack of several short segments.**

6. **Click on the blue outline marking the end face of the first sweep segment; then click on the Scale Face tool and drag to shrink that end face slightly.**

7. **Click on the blue outline for the next segment up and shrink that face more than you shrunk the previous one.**

   Repeat this step until you get to the top face, and shrink that face down very small.

8. **Using this click-on-the-blue-outline process, go back and fiddle with the size of all the faces in the stack until you get something that looks pretty round.**

Apples, pumpkins, and dimples

In Pioneer, it's just a small step to go from a rounded shape to a dimpled one, like apples, pumpkins, and belly-buttons. Make a rounded shape using the instructions given in "Pioneer rounds" earlier in this chapter. Then, using the Face Move tool, click the small topmost face and drag it down into the body of the shape. For a smoother dimple, grab the next face down from that one and drag it down too.

In Walkthrough, you just can't do dimples. Walkthrough only does "convex" shapes — shapes that bulge outwards.

Chapter 14

Virtual Veneer: Texture Mapping

● ●

In This Chapter

▶ What textures are

▶ Applying textures in Pioneer

▶ Fine-tuning Pioneer's texture mapping

▶ Textures and Pioneer's surface attributes

▶ Textures and Pioneer's material library

▶ Applying textures in Walkthrough Pro

▶ Texture options

▶ Tiling textures in Walkthrough Pro

● ●

Computers have finally caught up with cabinet-makers. Cabinet-makers discovered long ago that by gluing a thin slice of mahogany onto their pine or particle-board creations, they could get the appearance they wanted and still have easy, low cost, and sturdy cabinets. Today, more often than not, that veneer is a plastic adhesive film with a photograph of wood grain on it.

VRML world builders do the same trick, but it's called *texture mapping*. Texture mapping is nothing more sophisticated than applying an image to the surface of an object. If the image looks like wood grain, the object looks like wood; if it looks like fish scales, the object looks scaly. If you really want to cheat on your model building, you can take a picture of a wall, with a fireplace, bookshelves, framed paintings, and even furniture in front of it, scan it, and texture map it onto a flat wall in your scene. It will look fake close up, but as theatrical set designers (who pull the same sort of trick) say, "From fifty feet back, who's to know?"

It's still in the early days for texture mapping in VRML, and the specification leaves a lot of room for different browser and builder vendors to do things in different and not-perfectly-compatible ways. In other words, texture mapping is still a bit rough in VRML, so don't expect it to work perfectly.

Both of the two main building tools we're covering in this book provide texture mapping. Of course, if you learn some VRML language, you can hack a texture map into your VRML file using a word processor, but hacking a texture map is a bit like do-it-yourself cosmetic surgery.

We're going to start out a little long-winded and give some background on textures in the next section. If you just want to get down to it and start texture mapping, skip it and move on to "Texture Mapping in Pioneer" or "Texture Mapping in Walkthrough Pro."

What Are Textures?

Textures are images; specifically, they are *bitmap* images. The images you see most often on the Web are bitmap images; usually GIF or JPEG files. Bitmap images are made up of tiny rectangular dots of color. (These images are unlike the ones you might create using your word processor's draw program or MacDraw. Those images are generally not bitmap images made up of dots, but *vector* images, made up of lines, shapes, and solid blocks of color. Sometimes, they are combinations of bitmap images and vector images. Programs like Windows Paintbrush and Adobe Photoshop create bitmap files, and some vector graphics programs like CorelDRAW will create a bitmap image file if you ask.)

A texture can be any image at all. If you have a scanner or a bitmap graphics program, you can make your own texture. It can be a logo, a picture of your kids, a close-up of your dog's fur, or a swatch of fabric. We made one from a picture of the grass in Dave's backyard.

Seamless textures are the most popular textures, however. Seamless textures are cunningly crafted images which, if you printed one out and then wrapped, say, the left side around to the right side, you would see no visible interruption of the pattern. Likewise, if you *tiled* them in a nice grid-like pattern like tiles on a bathroom wall, you would see no visible seams. If a strong pattern appears within a seamless texture, however (like a knot in your wood grain), the tiling will be obvious. Seamless textures are popular because your builder can re-use that image several times across the surface of an object, making your virtual world's file size much smaller than if you used one giant image. Most of the textures that come with Pioneer are seamless.

How Textures Are Stored

Textures can make a VRML world much more interesting but also bigger. If you understand a little bit about how textures are stored in your VRML world, it will help you make worlds that are smaller and faster to download. Two aspects of storing textures that you might want to get cozy with are "formats" and "texture inlining."

Formats

A "format" or "file format" is the way that an image is stored in a file. Each format has its own good and bad points. Generally, each format makes a slightly different trade off between quality and compactness. A format that is "efficient" will give high quality but a small file size.

For images that are *realistic,* that is, they look like photographs, the most efficient is the JPEG image (specified by the Joint Photographic Equipment Group, a standards organization). JPEG, however, doesn't deliver quite as high quality as other formats do, particularly for line drawings and text. Hundreds of other bitmap file formats exist; among the most common formats used on personal computers are Windows Bitmap (BMP), Targa (TGA), TIFF, and PICT. The BMP and PICT formats are the most common, but are not very efficient.

In theory, you can use any file format for texture maps in your VRML world. The VRML term that handles texture mapping simply tells the browser software, "Go get this image file and slap it like this on this object." To follow through on this command, however, the VRML browser would have to be able to read all the hundreds of different possible formats that the VRML author might use.

Fortunately, the VRML specification recommends (but does not insist on) two alternative formats, PMG and JPEG. Since PMG is not a very common format among PC and Mac users, you are left with JPEG.

So which file format should you use for textures when you create VRML worlds? The simple answer is JPEG. The folks who make browsers seem to be content to use JPEG for VRML textures. Caligari's Pioneer makes the choice easy — it reads only JPEG textures as of this writing (Pioneer Pro and trueSpace from Caligari allow many more). Virtus' Walkthrough Pro lets you read BMP for Windows and PICT for the Macintosh, and it will output JPEG for VRML work.

Inlining textures

When a VRML world keeps its textures as separate files in some file format, that approach is called "inlining" of textures. The VRML file contains no image data in that case; just a link to the file. Inlining is the most efficient way to store textures, and both Walkthrough Pro and Pioneer perform inlining.

VRML also gives you another way of incorporating textures: Store them right in the world file with everything else. But in order to keep things simple and universally readable, VRML doesn't use any special formats, like GIF or JPEG, for these internal textures. It just stores the image as a bunch of numbers, three for each dot (pixel) of the image. These numbers are written as ASCII text, so anyone can read them with a word processor if they were sufficiently bored to want to do so. Because they are stored as ASCII text, internal bitmaps make VRML files very, very large. A simple world with a block and an inlined wood-grain texture might require a 10K file for the world and a 2K file for the JPEG texture file. If the texture is stored internal to the world file, the whole thing might require 200K!

So, that trade-off describes your choice: If you use inlining of textures, your world doesn't take so long to download, but other people may not see your cool textures because you used a format they can't read. If you use internal textures, your VRML files are universally viewable (the browser doesn't have to read JPEG or any other format) but enormous. We strongly recommend the inlining of textures.

Pioneer lets you choose to inline or not when you save your scene. In the Export VRML panel that pops up during the File⇨Scene⇨Save process, check off Textures in the Inlining area to save your texture as an inlined file. You can also have Pioneer save the inlined texture files to a special directory by entering the path for that directory in the Textures box in the Paths area.

Walkthrough Pro only does inlining; it does not do internal texture maps. It creates texture files (usually in JPEG format) in the same directory as the main WRL file, assigning them names beginning with "TEXTR". For more on inlining, see "Textures in Walkthrough Pro" in this chapter, and also Chapter 17.

Textures in Pioneer

Although texture mapping can get pretty complicated, Pioneer makes the basic texture mapping fairly easy. The complicated part occurs when you want to control exactly how a texture is applied to an object.

Pioneer uses only JPEG files for textures; when you save your scene as a VRML file, the JPEG file is copied to the same directory as your world file.

Applying texture without thinking much about it

You apply a texture exactly the same way you paint colors and other surface attributes: Use the Object Paint, Face Paint, and Paint Over tools of Pioneer. Figure 14-1 shows Pioneer's painting tools.

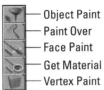

— Object Paint
— Paint Over
— Face Paint
— Get Material
— Vertex Paint

Figure 14-1:
Pioneer's
Paint tools.

The only Paint tool that doesn't work for textures is the Vertex Paint tool.

All the Paint tools share one location on the tool bar, so if you see one of them, click and hold on it to see the others; drag upward and release to select one of the others.

Sometimes the Object Paint tool refuses to be selected. If it does, click on the Selection tool, click your chosen object, and then try again.

Here's how to use the paint tools to choose a texture:

1. **Right-click on any Paint tool.**

   The usual bunch of paint-related panels appears; among them, the Shader/maps panel, the lower of the two panels shown in Figure 14-2. Ignore the other paint-related panels for now.

2. **In the Shader/maps panel, right-click the checkered-ball button, officially called the Use Texture Map button (the names of controls appear on the help bar as you pass your cursor over each one).**

   A Texture Map panel appears (see Figure 14-2).

3. **In the Texture Map panel, click the button next to the checkered ball, called the Get Texture Map button.**

   The Get Texture Map dialog box appears.

Can't see your textures?

You must switch to fully-rendered mode (choose the 3DR button) if you want to see the results of your work. You can, however, apply a texture in wireframe mode (even if you can't see it). In fact, that mode can even make the individual faces that you want to texture map more easy to find.

If you don't see any texture, the texture map display may be turned off in Pioneer. To check, right-click either the 3DR or the wireframe button. If, in the Render Quality panel that appears, the checkered ball is not depressed, click on it. (Like many Pioneer buttons, it's manic-depressive: click once, it's depressed; click again, it's *up*. We sympathize.)

Left-click here to choose texture

Right-click here...

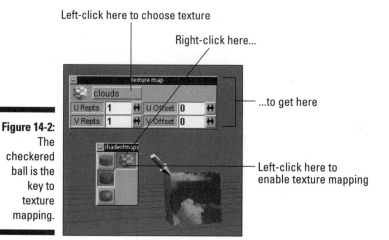

...to get here

Left-click here to
enable texture mapping

4. **Choose any JPEG file (files with the extension .JPG) from any directory on your PC.** A bunch of JPEG files should be in the directory where Pioneer is installed. Click OK after you're finished.

   The name of the texture file now appears on the Get Texture Map button.

To apply the texture you've chosen:

1. **Select the object you want to paint with a texture.**

2. **In the Shader/maps panel, left-click the checkered-ball button. When this button is depressed, it enables texture mapping.**

   If the Material panel is working properly in your version of Pioneer (it isn't in ours), it now shows the texture you've chosen on the sample ball.

3. **Choose your Paint tool: Object (funnel icon), Face (paintbrush icon), or Paint Over (roller icon).** You can see pictures of the tools in Figure 14-1.

4. **If you are painting an object, you're finished.** If you are painting a face or painting over an object, click on the object or face to which you want to apply the texture.

   You may have to click the 3DR button in order for Pioneer to re-render the scene.

When you save your scene using File⇨Save⇨Scene and the Export VRML file dialog box appears, make sure that the checkbox for Textures is selected in the Inlining area. (See the earlier section on "Inlining textures" to find out why.) Pioneer will copy the JPEG file to the same directory as your VRML file (unless you specify a different directory in the Textures box in the Paths area). When you put your world online, be sure to copy both the .WRL file and the .JPG file to your Web site.

Fine-tuning your textures

Applying an image to a 3D object is all very exciting, but that's not the entire game. To fine-tune certain textures, you may need to tell Pioneer how many times to repeat the image, where to start the image, and how to project the image onto the object.

For example, you'll discover that if you apply some of the textures that come with Pioneer, they look rather blurry and not very impressive. The reason is that they are seamless textures meant to be repeated several times across the surface, not just once. And unless you specify otherwise, "once" is all you get. To get more, you need to set *repetitions*. Some patterns, like brick, are downright useless without repetitions.

You may also find that the image starts at the wrong edge and needs to be moved over. To fix that, you need to set *offsets*.

Finally, you may discover that the image is upside-down, on the wrong face, sideways, should run at some angle, or is just plain pasted on funny. To fix these problems, you need to play with the *UV Projection*.

One common problem (or maybe a feature) is the smearing of texture maps at the edges, as the edge colors sort of run down the side. One work-around way to remove this effect is to frame the image in a rectangle of solid color, so at least you get solid-colored sides.

Setting repetitions and offset

Seamless textures, like metal, wood grain, fabric, and other carefully designed patterns are designed to be repeated over the surface of an object. You can control the number of times a pattern is repeated, or *tiled,* on a surface using the same Texture Map panel you used to select a texture.

If the Texture Map panel at the top of Figure 14-2 isn't already on your screen, do this:

1. **Right-click on any Paint tool to display all the various paint panels if they are not already visible.**

2. **In the Shader/maps panel, right-click the checkered-ball button.**

To set repetitions, do this in the Texture Map panel:

1. **Enter the number of repetitions in the U Repts and V Repts boxes.** You can either click in those boxes and type new values, or drag left-right on the double-headed arrow buttons.

U and V are axes sort of like X and Y axes: One goes in one direction and the other in some other direction. Figuring out which is which is rarely worthwhile; adjust one of them, and if you don't like the results, adjust the other one. If you can't get the results you want this way, see the next section, "The UV map."

2. **Choose your Paint tool: Object (funnel icon), Face (paintbrush icon), or Paint Over (roller icon).**

3. **If you are painting an object, you're finished. If you are painting a face or painting over an object, click on the object or face to which you want to apply the texture.**

   You may have to click the 3DR button in order for Pioneer to re-render the scene.

To move the pattern around on the surface, set U Offset or V Offset in the Texture Map panel. An offset of 0.5 means "start the pattern halfway along the axis." (In early versions of Pioneer, offset worked — it changed the VRML file — but the change wasn't visible in Pioneer! If offset doesn't appear to work, try viewing your file in another VRML tool.)

The UV map

We've been talking about textures, but what about the *mapping* part of texture mapping? *Mapping* just means *how the image is projected onto the shape,* as if a slide projector were doing the job.

Unless you tell Pioneer otherwise, Pioneer chooses a map based on the shape of the object. Unfortunately, you have no way to see this default map. But at least if you don't like the way your image is being projected onto the shape, you can create a new map.

The tool for a new UV map is Pioneer's UV Projection tool, which you see in Figure 14-3. The UV Projection icon is a tan cylinder with what appear to be cool, designer green sunglasses.

Cylindrical

Planar | Spherical

Figure 14-3:
The UV
Projection
tool, panel,
and
projection
grid.

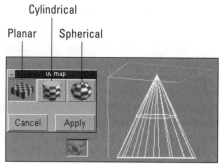

Select an object, click that UV Projection button, and the UV Map panel appears, along with a blue and brown grid around the selected shape, as Figure 14-3 shows (in black and white — sorry). The blue and brown grid represents a suggested *new* UV projection; it doesn't show the existing, default one.

Understanding the UV grid

The blue and brown projection grid, or *wireframe,* as Caligari calls it, confused the heck out of us for a long time. We thought that one color was somehow, mysteriously, representing the U axis, and the other the V axis. This is *not* the case (fortunately — because it makes no sense).

In Figure 14-4, the three brown lines of the UV *planar projection* grid are at the lower-left corner of the cube. (We know the picture is in black and white. Trust us. Better yet, write to IDG and demand that this book be printed in color!)

V axis

U axis ⟶

Here's what's going on in Figure 14-4:

- ✔ The cube in this figure is mapped using the *planar* projection, which only projects in one direction. Two other projections are available. More on that soon.

- ✔ Where the three brown lines intersect is where the image starts (its *origin*).

- ✔ The rectangle bounded on two sides by the blue lines is like the projection screen, and the single brown line is like the direction in which the image is being projected.

- ✔ The brown lines that meet the blue lines are the U and V axes; the U axis is along the bottom of the cube.

✔ Images wrap around at the U or V axis; for example, if you offset the image with a + U value, the right edge of the image wraps around and reappears at the left edge.

✔ The image in Figure 14-4 has a U Repts setting of 3 and a V Reps setting of 2. See the earlier section, "Setting repetitions and offset," for info on repetitions.

Changing how the texture is applied

If your texture just isn't looking the way you think it should, you need to change either the UV projection style or the orientation of the projection. Click the UV Projection tool and the UV Map panel pops up, giving you two types of adjustment:

✔ Changing to another of the three possible styles of projection.

✔ Rotating the projection grid so that the image is oriented correctly.

In the UV Map panel, click on a button for one of three projections: planar, cylindrical, or spherical. Pioneer displays the UV projection grid on the object you've selected.

✔ Click Apply after you have chosen the UV projection you want and after you have rotated it to the orientation you want.

✔ Click Cancel to exit the UV Projection tool without changing anything.

The three UV projection styles are as follows:

✔ **Planar:** Projects the image in one direction; like a regular slide projector, except that the image doesn't get bigger if the *screen* (an object face) is further away. Note that the image goes right through the shape and appears on the opposite side, reversed! (You can fix this effect by painting the other side a solid color, without a texture.)

✔ **Cylindrical:** Projects the image radially towards a center axis; the result is like a label applied to a can (and works regardless of the can's shape). In this case, the blue lines show how the cylinder is oriented, the brown line on the cylinder surface shows where the wrapped image starts and ends, and the other brown lines point towards the central axis.

✔ **Spherical:** Projects the image radially from all directions, towards a point at the center; the image acts like a shrink-wrapped label surrounding an object.

The spherical projection appears in Figure 14-5, with a single image of the *Dummies* guy on a sphere (the shape doesn't have to be a sphere to use spherical projection, but it helps).

In spherical projection, a straight brown line through the center marks the vertical (V) direction. The other brown line (which forms the curving part of a brown D shape) shows where the image starts and wraps around. The horizontal direction (U) is around the sphere.

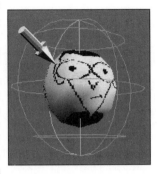

If your texture maps need to be rotated around the shape, tilted, or projected using a different axis than the one Pioneer chooses, rotate the UV projection grid using the object rotation tool (it shares a button location with the object move and object scale tool).

Brightness, shine, and other surface attributes

In Pioneer, whenever you paint an object or a surface, you can give it surface attributes like brightness, shine, roughness, and transparency. Right-click any Paint tool, adjust the four controls in the Shader Attributes box, and then paint.

In theory, you can also apply those surface attributes to an object that has a texture map. And in fact, Pioneer dutifully records those object attributes, along with the texture map, when it creates the VRML file.

Whether or not those attributes actually show up in a browser, however, is up to the rendering capabilities of that browser. In fact, when you have a texture map, Pioneer itself only displays three of those four attributes when it renders the object; it ignores transparency.

Material libraries — reusing your work

After you have gone to all the trouble of getting just the right color, shine, roughness, transparency, and/or texture map, being able to use that combination again in some other project would be nice. Material libraries are a way of doing just that.

Pioneer gives you a material library with a few nice sample materials already in it. You can use these materials, and you can also add your own materials to that library. You can also create other libraries of your own materials.

A few tips for reorienting the UV projection grid

✔ Disable all but one axis before attempting to rotate the UV grid. To do so, click to raise two out of the three axis buttons, X, Y, and Z, at the far right of Pioneer's help bar.

✔ Select the Snap-to-Grid tool to get 45-degree or other increments. Right-click the tool to set the increments.

✔ If a surface is not parallel to the UV projection surface indicated by the blue lines, the image will be distorted on that surface, like projecting a slide at an angle to the screen.

✔ For shapes that are elongated, you can drag and stretch the UV grid by using the Object Move tool.

At any given time, only one library is *current.* To see and to use that library, click on the Materials Library button.

The Material Library panel opens, which you see in Figure 14-6.

Chosen Material Indicator

Figure 14-6:
Material
libraries
include your
textures.

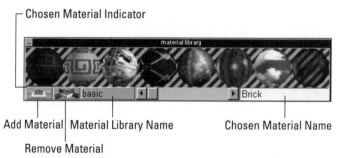

Add Material | Material Library Name   Chosen Material Name

Remove Material

Here are some of the things you can do in the material library (but no loud talking in the library, please):

✔ **Choose a material:** Click on any of the sample spheres you see to select that material as the current material. Use the horizontal scroll bar to see additional materials. Choosing a material from a library makes it the *current material,* which you then apply by using the Paint Object or Paint Face tools. You can see its individual attributes in the Materials panels.

✔ **Add a material to the library:** Right-click on any paint tool and set up your material properties using the Material Color, Shader/Maps, and Shader Attributes panels. On the Material Library panel, click the Add Material button (up arrow). A new sample sphere displays your material.

✔ **Remove a material:** Click on the material to be removed and then on the Remove Material button (down arrow).

✔ **Load, save, or start a new library:** Click the Load/Save Material Library button. From the menu that appears, choose New to start a new library, Load to load a library file, Save to save the displayed library with its current name, or Save As to save the library with a new name.

Textures in Walkthrough Pro

Walkthrough Pro makes texture mapping easy. Even though Walkthrough's texture mapping can't do some of the fancy tricks that Pioneer can (such as different projections, rotations, and offset), it has a few tricks of its own and is more than adequate for most VRML work. You can apply an image to either an entire object or an individual surface of an object.

Basic texture mapping

The basic procedure for texture mapping in Walkthrough Pro is this:

1. **Open the Textures window; this window holds a list of textures that you create and apply.**

2. **Create a new texture by specifying an image file, an orientation, and a pattern for repeating the image.**

3. **Apply the texture to a selected object or surface by double-clicking the texture in the Textures window.**

To start, you will need an image in BMP format for Windows or in PICT format for the Macintosh. If you have a Walkthrough texture, you can use it as well. Windows users can experiment using OURGRASS.BMP on the CD.

Here are the gory details for basic texture mapping:

1. **In any Design view, select the lucky object to be texture mapped.**

2. **To texture map an entire object, skip to Step 3.** To texture map an individual surface of the object, use the Surface Editor: Click the Surface Editor button in the toolbar (the one with a wall, door and window) and then click the surface.

   To texture map a series of surfaces on an object, use the Tumble Editor; double-click a surface to select it for texture mapping.

3. **Open the Textures window by choosing Window⇨Textures Window; the window of Figure 14-7 appears.**

Currently Selected Texture

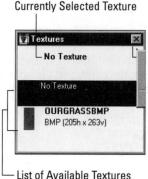

List of Available Textures

4. **Click the triangle in the upper right corner of the Texture window to open a menu.**

5. **Choose Add Textures from the menu.**

6. **Select an image file or Virtus texture file from the Add Textures dialog box that appears.** (If you're using Windows, try the OURGRASS.BMP file on our CD but see the upcoming Warning sidebar.) Your chosen image forms the basis for a new texture, and that texture is now added to the list at the bottom of the Textures window.

7. **To apply the image across the entire selected object or surface, double-click the texture in the list in the bottom area of the Textures window.**

8. **If you change your mind and want to remove the texture from an object or surface, double-click "No Texture" in the Textures window.**

9. **To avoid applying this same texture to new objects, click "No Texture" in the Textures window.** (Whatever texture is currently selected is applied to new objects.)

10. **To see the results of your work, look in the Walk View.**

11. **When you export your world to VRML using File⇨Export⇨VRML, make sure to choose Export Textures Links in the Export Options dialog box that appears.** Also, make sure to set Export Textures As to JPEG.

    These settings tell Walkthrough to create one JPEG file for each texture you used, and put it in the same directory as the main .WRL file. Walkthrough gives each file a name like TXTR0001.JPG. (To avoid conflict when Walkthrough tries to use the same JPEG filenames in the next world you create, put each world in its own directory.)

12. **When you copy your world to your Web site, make sure to copy all the JPEG files as well as the .WRL file.**

To solve these problems and also to achieve certain effects, see the next section, "Texture options."

The 90-MPH lawn

We thought Live3D had gone nuts when we loaded a Walkthrough-created VRML world that used OURGRASS.BMP. The lawn in our world looked like it was zooming by at 90 miles per hour.

What happened? Walkthrough Pro likes to round off the image size of its JPEG texture maps, and the adjustment can sometimes create the exact dimensions that cause Live3D to "animate" its texture maps! If the width of an image in pixels is a power of two, like 128 or 256, and the height is an even multiple of the width, Live3D will treat the image like a strip of movie film! See Chapter 19 for more on this effect.

If you need to adjust the dimensions of your texture image (either to avoid or to achieve this animation), use a graphics program like Paintbrush or MacPaint.

The steps we just gave you will spread a single image across an entire object or surface. Sometimes, that's exactly what you want; but two problems often arise:

✔ For images used like billboards (text, for instance) where there is definitely a right way to orient the image, you may need to flip the image over horizontally or vertically.

✔ For grass or other images designed to create a realistic-looking surface material, the result often looks like the "lawn" in the following figure. The image is spread over too wide an area, and the individual pixels of the image are obvious. The solution is to repeat ("tile") the image across the surface of the object.

Texture options

To make changes and refinements in the appearance of your textures, click on the texture you want to change in the Texture window list and then choose Texture Options from the Textures window menu. The Texture Options dialog box appears, in one of its three forms:

✓ First Tile — for flipping the image

✓ Tile Pattern — for setting up repeating images

✓ Appearance — which doesn't affect your VRML file at all

You can switch between forms by clicking the down-arrow on the Edit box in any of these forms.

Flipping the image

The First Tile form of the Texture Options dialog box in Figure 14-8 is mainly useful for flipping the image horizontally or vertically. If, for instance, your image uses text and it's backwards, you can flip to the mirror image by checking the Horizontal checkbox.

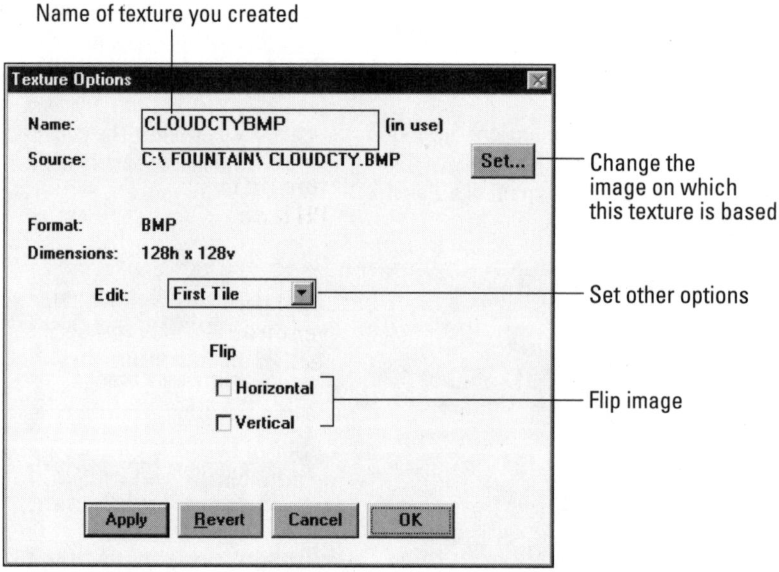

Name of texture you created

Figure 14-8:
The "First Tile" form of the Texture Options dialog box is mainly useful for flipping the image.

Change the image on which this texture is based

Set other options

Flip image

All the forms of the Texture Options dialog box let you change the image (using the Set button), rename the texture (using the Name box), apply the current settings to the texture (Apply button), revert to previous settings (Revert), or apply the settings to the object and exit Texture Options (OK).

Setting up a tiling pattern

One of the nice features of Walkthrough Pro's Texture Window is the ability to set up a tiling pattern.

To make the image repeat across the object surface, open the Texture Options dialog box, click the down-arrow on the Edit box, and choose Tile Pattern. This gives you the form we show in Figure 14-9.

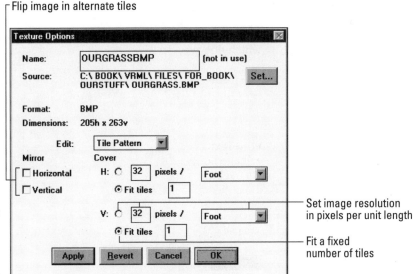

Flip image in alternate tiles

Figure 14-9:
Tile Pattern
settings.

Set image resolution
in pixels per unit length

Fit a fixed
number of tiles

To improve the resolution of your texture (to fix problems like the chunky lawn in the figure in the sidebar, "The 90-MPH lawn"), use the controls in the "Cover" area of Figure 14-9.

There are identical controls for horizontal patterns (labeled "H:") and for vertical patterns (labeled "V:"). In either direction, you can set resolution either by specifying how many tiles or by specifying how many pixels (color dots) you want per unit length of the surface.

  ✔ To repeat the pattern a given number of times across the surface, choose Fit tiles and enter a number in the adjoining box (where you see a "1" in Figure 14-9).

  ✔ To specify pixels per unit length, click the button next to H: or V: and enter the number of pixels in the adjoining text box (where you see a "32" in Figure 14-9). If you want, you can specify pixels per foot, or meter, or any other unit by clicking the down-arrow where you see "Foot" in Figure 14-9, and choosing a different unit.

  ✔ In the Mirror area, choose Horizontal and/or Vertical to make the image flip back and forth in an alternating orientation as it tiles the surface. This effect can give the appearance of a seamless texture across two adjoining tiles.

Click the OK button when you are done and check your work in Walk View.

Chapter 15

Making Landscapes

· ·

· ·

*A*h, the great virtual outdoors. So virtually rich with earth, water, sky, and plants. So virtually . . . *large*, for one thing! And complicated! Nature perversely refuses to come in nice regular shapes with straight sides. How can anyone even come close to simulating the natural world using a bunch of flat-sided shapes?

Well, 't ain't easy. So we wrote this chapter.

Earth

Ya gotta have earth. Castles in the air are fun but kind of disorienting unless you expect to spend all your time indoors. No matter what scene you're creating, you should be well-grounded in earth sciences.

Size

How big should your Earth be? Size is one of those issues that the VRML gurus don't have a lot to say about. They do say, "A VRML unit is 1 meter," but nothing says how many units or meters across the world should be. The plus side of this lack of guidelines is that you can make a world any size from sub-atomic to intergalactic. The minus side is that you don't know how big your sub-atomic or intergalactic world will appear. Some browsers may adjust for the scene's size and zoom in or out as necessary; others may simply show a tiny microscopic spec if the scene is, say, an ant farm. Most worlds today seem to range from a few units to a hundred units on a side.

One confusing issue about size is how VRML builders translate units such as inches, feet, and meters into VRML. Dimensions in Pioneer are, um . . . dimensionless (it has no meters or feet or inches — just units). As a result, one unit in Pioneer is one unit (and therefore one meter) in VRML. Simple, yes?

Walkthrough Pro uses the units you choose using Edit⇨Preferences. For example, if you make something that appears to be 10 feet long, it comes out 3.05 units (meters) long in VRML.

Shape

What shape should your Earth be? You could make an entire, spherical planet, or you could make just a flat square to put a house on.

Making an entire planet is probably not such a great idea, although it's been done. (You can ask God; it's a lot of work, and the results are not in yet.) First, no gravity exists (yet) in VRML, so you can't go very far in a straight line without drifting off the surface of the planet. Second, to have very much of interest on the planet, it will have to be huge and very complex. Complex scenes and large shapes are slow to render and will slow down navigation. Some tricks exist for making these scenes work, however. For that information, see "Making Big Worlds Work" in Chapter 17.

Starting with a thin, mainly flat slab or two-dimensional surface is probably the easiest approach. In Walkthrough Pro, you can't create any two-dimensional surfaces, but you can make a slab out of any shape, just by setting the depth very small. In Pioneer, you can create either a 2D or 3D Earth.

Breaking ground in Walkthrough Pro

To have any fun with terraforming in Walkthrough Pro, you have to do it in chunks. Walkthrough only permits convex objects — no valleys or depressions. The only way to get a real valley (without resorting to tricks like turning hills upside down and making their bottom sides transparent) is to put two hills next to each other.

Here's one approach to creating a landscape with Walkthrough Pro, which we used to make Figure 15-1:

Create a single slab to underlie your entire landscape

1. **Start in Top View: Choose View⇨Change View⇨Top.**

2. **Decide how thick your ground will be and set your depth gauge accordingly: Choose Window⇨Depth Window and drag the two black triangles in the gauge to mark the bottom and top of your slab, placing the top at zero.**

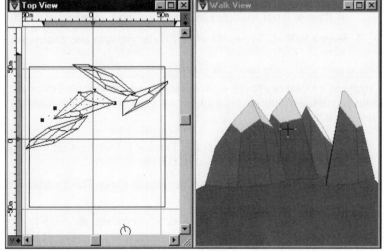

Figure 15-1:
A scaled-
down world
100 meters
across, with
stage
scenery
mountains.

3. **Zoom out (Ctrl+-) until you can see a large enough area to make your slab.**

4. **Be sure your inflation shape is set to square: At the bottom-left corner of the tool pad, choose the square icon.**

5. **Click on any shape tool (in the third row of the tool pad) and drag in the Top View window to create the shape.**

Decide between real mountains and stage scenery

If you put mountains of realistic scale in your scene, people will have to navigate their slopes and move around them to see stuff. You'll also need a really large slab of earth to put them on. If that's what you want, fine — but quite often, we just want a scenic backdrop of mountains around an otherwise level scene. If that's the case for you, plan on creating your mountains as skinny vertical slabs arranged around the outside of your Earth slab.

Build mountains on top of the slab

For mountains, place shapes on top of the slab that are *inflated* to a point. Here's how:

1. **In Top View, choose Window⇨Depth Window.**

2. **Set the bottom black triangle of your depth gauge at zero and the top black triangle at the height for your mountain peak.**

3. **Set your inflation shape to an upward-point: Click the button with the up-pointing icon near the bottom the tool pad.**

(For a more rounded hill, choose the up-pointing dome icon.)

4. **Finally, click on any shape tool and drag to create shapes. Use a variety of shapes, from triangles to hexagons, and a variety of heights.**

5. **Switch to Walk View (Window⇨Walk View) to see your work.**

Make more interesting mountain shapes

To avoid a forest-of-church-steeples look, use the Tumble Editor to whack chunks off the mountain tops and down their sides (makes you feel powerful, doesn't it?).

1. **In any Design View, select the Tumble Editor icon on the tool pad (the block with the chunk taken out of it).**

2. **Double-click the mountain you want to chop. The Tumble Editor window appears.**

3. **In the Tumble Editor window, drag across the shape to tumble it.**

4. **Click the slice tool (looks like a wedge) and drag a diagonal line across the top of the shape.**

Other surface features

With Walkthrough's surface painting features, you can apply snow-capped peaks, splashing blue rivulets, green forested areas, and waterfalls by using the Surface Editor to paint surface features onto your mountains. With texture mapping, you can even apply a photograph of a mountain slope. (If you want to do texture mapping, see Chapter 14.)

Here's how you paint features:

1. **Walk View is the most fun to work in, so switch to that view.**

2. **Click the Surface Editor button in the Walk View tool pad (the icon depicts a wall with a door and window).**

3. **In Walk View click the surface you want to paint. The Surface Editor window appears.**

   You may want to zoom in a bit (choose Surface⇨Zoom In) to make drawing easier.

4. **Click and hold on the color bar in the middle of the Surface Editor tool pad, and when the color palette appears, click a color.**

5. **Make sure the "opaque" surface attribute is selected on the tool pad (the left-most button under the color bar).**

6. **Make sure the "front" surface attribute is selected too (the button under the one in Step 5).**

7. **Choose a shape-drawing tool from the tool pad and draw the feature on the surface in the Surface Editor window.**

We prefer the Irregular Polygon tool (the one with the icon sort of like a house's profile). Click to mark each corner of the shape; remember that Walkthrough won't let you draw any shapes with indentations (concave sides).

8. **Adjust the shape by clicking the selection tool (arrow) and dragging the points at the corners.**

To move the shape, click in the middle of the shape and drag.

Breaking ground in Pioneer

Pioneer lets you do some ground-breaking work in landscapes. You can shape your virtual Earth like clay (well, lumpy clay), creating mountains, valleys, cliffs, gentle rolling hills, or a just a challenging golf course sort of terrain. You can also add individual landscape elements by using fancy 3D shapes.

For those of you who are already cruising securely in Pioneer, here's the process in a nutshell:

1. **In wireframe mode, create a plane or thin-rectangular primitive with a resolution of about 8 or higher; scale it to the size you need.**

2. **Use the Face tool to raise, lower, tilt, and scale various faces, creating a cool terrain.**

3. **Paint and apply textures to the various faces.**

Figure 15-2 shows how to make mountains *rise from the planes.*

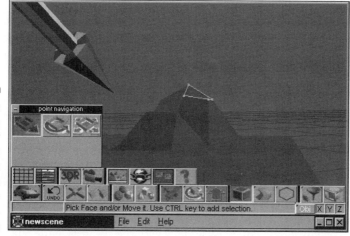

Figure 15-2: By dragging a face or two, you can turn molehills into mountains.

Here's the blow-by-blow, if you're still a bit uneasy with Pioneer:

1. **Put Pioneer in wireframe mode if it's currently showing you rendered views.**

   Click the 3DR button, drag to the wireframe icon, and release. Wireframe makes seeing what you're doing easier.

2. **Click the Primitives tool (the sphere, cone, and cube icon).**

3. **Right-click the Plane-Primitive button (in the upper-left corner of the Primitives panel).**

4. **In the panel that appears, set Resolution to 8 or higher.**

   Double-click the number there, enter a new number, and press Enter.

5. **Left-click the Plane-Primitive button to insert a plane into your scene.**

   Notice that it is made up of many faces. (You may need to tilt your view down to see the plane: Click the Walk or Fly button and drag your mouse forward with both buttons pressed.)

6. **Click the Face tool (the cube-with-orange-face icon).**

   A Point Navigation panel appears with the Point Move button selected.

7. **Click on a face of the plane to select it. Ctrl+click to select a bunch of faces.**

   Use Shift+click if Ctrl+click doesn't work.

8. **Drag with the right mouse button to raise or lower that face.**

   The Z axis button at the far right of the Pioneer help bar must be depressed to allow this action. If it's not depressed, click on it. Drag with the left mouse button to move the face side-to-side (the X and Y axis buttons must be depressed to allow this).

9. **To tilt a face, click the Point Rotate button in the Face Tools panel.**

   Restrict rotation to one axis at a time by making sure only the X or Y button is depressed at the far right of the Pioneer help bar. (Click to raise or press any button.) Drag to tilt the face.

Repeat Steps 7 through 9 until the terrain looks convincing to you. Remember that you can use Ctrl+Z at any time to undo the most recent few steps. Now you're ready to dress things up.

To paint your entire landscape (for example, to start with everything green), use Pioneer's object painting tool (the funnel icon). To paint individual parts of your landscape, use Pioneer's face painting tool (the paintbrush icon). Both tools share a button location with Pioneer's other painting tools. Click your chosen tool, click a color in the Material Color panel that pops up, and then paint a face by clicking on it. By fiddling with the controls in the Shader Attributes panel, you can also adjust the brightness, shininess, reflectivity, and transparency of the surface. For more on painting surfaces, see Part III.

For a more realistic landscape appearance in Pioneer, choose smooth rendering (this is also a choice in some browsers). Right-click the 3DR button, and then in the Rendering Quality panel that appears, find the two buttons with gray cylinder icons; click the smoother-looking one. This setting doesn't change your VRML scene, just its appearance in Pioneer.

Caves

Caves are fun features but are tricky to implement. Creating an apparent hole into a mountain is easy enough by making a face transparent. The main trouble is, inside surfaces are rendered as transparent in many browsers, so from the entrance or from within the mountain you can see right through all the walls: The mountain doesn't appear to have an inside. (A smaller problem is that if someone tries to go through your apparent hole using a browser with collision detection enabled, that person will smack head first into the transparent face. Of course, the person can turn collision detection off and not have this problem.)

As we say, blowing an apparent hole into the mountain is easy. If that's all you want to do, try this:

In Walkthrough: Using the Surface Editor, paint a rectangular surface feature transparent from both sides. Starting from any view, select an object, choose the surface editor tool (click the wall-with-door-and-window icon), and then double-click the surface where you want the cave entrance. Now, in the Surface Editor, choose two-sided surfaces (click the center tool on the bottom row of the tool pad), choose full transparency (click the rightmost tool on the next row up), choose a shape tool, and drag on the surface.

The case of the vanishing face

Terraforming (making terrain) in Pioneer can introduce some weird effects. As you walk or fly around the scene, chunks of landscape may randomly wink in and out of transparency! What's behind this mystery? As you pull and tilt faces, you end up distorting some of the adjacent faces so that they are no longer flat, and you introduce some acute angles between other faces. These changes can confuse Pioneer and some other browsers or viewers.

You may be able to solve some of these problems by starting with triangular faces. Triangles can't be bent *out of flat* like rectangles can. Unfortunately, Pioneer gives you no way to make

triangular faces — but we do. Check the Appendix and find where we've put EARTH1.COB and EARTH2.COB on the CD. Using File⇨Load Object, load one of these files into your scene (EARTH2 has higher resolution). We made these rectangular planes in trueSpace 2, which allowed us to subdivide faces in a triangular pattern. Use these models instead of creating a plane yourself.

Even with our models, you may occasionally see strange shapes appearing in Pioneer. You can often get rid of them by using more gentle angles between faces. Also, they may not be visible in other browsers.

In Pioneer: Using the Paint Face tool, set the transparency to maximum in the Shader Attributes panel, and then paint a face. Poof — you have a hole. (Well, an apparent hole, anyway. The surface is still there.)

Depending on the browser you view your scene in, you may or may not be able to see inside surfaces. WebFX, for instance, offers Options⇨Always Generate Back Faces as a solution.

Some viewers don't offer this option. Besides, relying on the user to turn on a viewer option takes some of the fun out of things. So you might try to pull one trick by editing the VRML file, as follows (it might help or might not, depending on the browser).

Open the VRML file with a word processor (import it as text if your word processor asks how to open the file). Search for the words

```
shapeTypeSOLID
```

and if you find them, delete them. Save the file as a text file (using the original name and WRL extension), and reload the file into your browser.

Even if you succeed in making a non-transparent mountain, having a hollow mountain is still kind of weird, because it's not a real shaft into a mountain. For a more realistic cave, you'll have to use Pioneer. The trick here is to make a seriously deep dimple into the surface of a 3D shape. Here's how:

1. **Use a 3D mountain.**

   Don't use a 2D surface for your mountain, like a plane or our EARTH1 or EARTH2 objects. Instead, create a 3D object for a mountain and place it on the Earth's surface. For practice, use a cone primitive; right-click on the cone icon to increase the latitude to, say, 8. See Chapter 13 for more details on fancier shapes.

2. **Select a face for the entrance.**

   Click the Face tool (the cube with an orange face) and then click on the face you want to turn into a cave entrance. The Navigation Panel pops up, showing the Point Move, Point Rotate, and Point Scale tools.

3. **Sweep the face *into* the mountain.**

   Click the Sweep tool (just to the right of the face tool). Pioneer probably sweeps the face the wrong way — out away from the shape, as in Figure 15-3! No problem, though. Just drag sideways while pressing the right mouse button. One direction, either left or right, will sweep the face back into the mountain — creating your cave. To shift the face around and thereby change the direction of the cave shaft, drag with the left mouse button. To make the shaft smaller or larger, choose the Point Scale tool on the Point Navigation panel, and drag. To make a bend in the shaft, rotate the face with the Point Rotate tool, and go on to Step 4.

Figure 15-3:
Sweep a
face to start
the cave,
even though
it goes the
wrong way
at first. Drag
with the
right mouse
button to
sink a shaft.

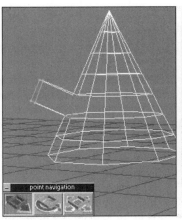 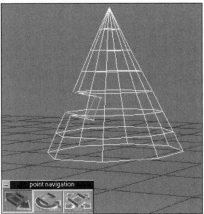

Figure 15-3:
Sweep a
face to start
the cave,
even though
it goes the
wrong way
at first. Drag
with the
right mouse
button to
sink a shaft.

4. Extend the shaft deeper into the mountain by clicking on the Sweep tool again. Your mountain looks something like Figure 15-4.

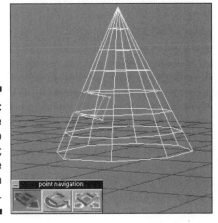

Figure 15-4:
Repeat the
sweep to go
deeper;
rotate the
face to turn
a corner.

5. To create a side shaft off the main shaft, sweep an interior face of the cave wall.

Navigate yourself (or rotate the scenery) so that you can see the inside of the cave shaft. Click a face on the side of the shaft and then click the sweep tool. Drag to extend the face into the mountain.

Here are a few tips for virtual cave builders and spelunkers:

✓ Like real caves, virtual reality caves can be dark — so add a light! Click the Primitives button and then click either the Local Light or the Infinite Light button. Move it to your cave.

✔ As in real caves, cave-ins can occur in which the walls do unwanted, apparently random and inexplicable things. They are sometimes caused by using very acute angles between surfaces; try adjusting the faces to reduce the angles.

✔ Make sure your cave is big enough that people can navigate it easily. Unless the browser expands the scene automatically, small caves tend to require very fine mouse movements to navigate. Folks quickly tire of bumping into walls or going through them like Casper the clumsy ghost.

Water

Virtual water is mostly a matter of setting color, partial transparency and shininess. (For realism, we'd love VRML to allow you to specify *refraction* — the ability of water to bend light — but in VRML 1.0, it doesn't. Computing refraction takes *lots* of computer power, so don't expect to see it for a while.) Color alone will often do the job, if you paint the surface blue.

Both of the two principal VRML builders we're covering in this book offer transparency. Walkthrough offers one level of transparency (or *opacity*); Pioneer offers a range of transparency, and shininess as well. How realistic the water actually looks in a viewer depends on the viewer. For instance, no viewer that we've encountered so far shows reflections, no matter how shiny the surface. (Reflections take lots of computer power.) Some viewers don't even show transparency well. As viewers and computer power improve, however, this should change.

Walkthrough water

The easiest way to simulate water using Walkthrough Pro is to simply paint a blue polygon onto the surface of your Earth using Walkthrough's Surface Editor. See Chapter 11 for details of painting.

If you absolutely must have a pool of water that you can see or move into, try the following:

1. **Before you make your Earth, create a shape for your pond in Top View: Put the top black mark on the depth window at zero, and the bottom below that, so the pond's top surface is at zero.**

   The pond can be any shape, as long as it has a flat top, and works best if it's blue.

2. **Lower the top black mark on your depth window by a small amount, and lower the bottom black mark by a slightly greater amount.**

This action lets you make your "Earth" shape thicker than your water is to be deep, which will leave the water sticking out slightly from the top, so you can grab it easily.

3. **In Top View, drag an earth shape around your pond shape.**

   Your scene will look odd in Walk View because the pond will stick out from the Earth, and intersecting shapes are technically not allowed in Walkthrough.

4. **Switch to Front View, select the Connect Surface tool (the hammer) and drag the top surface of the pond down to the top surface of the Earth until you hear a click.**

   You may have to reposition the pond with the selection tool and try again to succesfully connect the two top surfaces.

5. **Using the Surface Editor, draw a light blue translucent shape on the Earth's surface, right over the pond.**

Pioneer water

You would expect a pioneer to be resourceful in obtaining water, and Caligari's Pioneer is no exception. For simplest simulation, all you need to do is to paint a face blue — an easy job in Caligari's Pioneer.

For more realism, you can make faces transparent, shiny, and smooth. Keep in mind that the only reason to bother making a transparent surface is to see objects below the surface, so unless you're going to populate your body of water with fish, plants, divers and other submarine life, skip the transparency. Shininess helps the surface pick up color from your light sources; smoothness makes the surface brightness change as you navigate the scene, just as real water does.

Your Earth must be made up of squares or other faces in order for you to create a body of water. For instance, if you create the Earth surface from a plane primitive, right-click on the Plane-Primitive tool and set the resolution high (say, 20 or so) before making the plane. Make sure you have enough faces to make a natural-looking outline.

Here's one approach. Try it in the rendered (3DR) mode rather than in wireframe mode — it's easier to see.

1. **Make your Earth from a high-resolution plane primitive.**

   Click the Primitives tool to open the Primitives panel. Right-click the Plane-Primitive button and set resolution to 20 or more; press Enter, and then left-click the button to create the plane. Click the Object Scale tool and drag to adjust the Earth's size.

2. Create a depression in your Earth.

Choose the Face tool (cube with an orange face) and select a group of faces, and then drag with the right mouse button to depress those faces below the Earth surface. See the resulting depression in Figure 15-5.

Figure 15-5:
To make a pond, create a low spot in the Earth and cover it with water — just like you learned in kindergarten.

3. Cover the depression with a transparent, blue plane, just below the surface.

Choose the Object Paint tool to open the usual paint panels, which include the Material Color and Shader Attributes panels. Choose an intense blue in the Color panel and set the four bars of the Shader Attributes panel roughly like this, from left to right: 50 percent Ambient Glow, 100 percent Shininess, 0 percent Roughness, and 30 percent Transparency.

Right-click the Plane-Primitive button and set Resolution to 1; press Enter. Left-click the button to create the plane. Click the Object Move tool and drag the plane into position. For the most natural look, position the plane just below the Earth surface. In Figure 15-5, the plane is just about to be lowered onto the depression.

4. Glue the blue plane onto the Earth.

With the plane still selected, choose the Glue as Sibling tool, and click on the Earth. Click the Selection tool to put away the glue tool.

To get the nicest effect when you're viewing the scene in Pioneer, turn on smooth rendering. Right-click the 3DR button and click the Smooth button (second from the left) in the Rendering Quality panel that appears.

Early versions of Pioneer are a little inconsistent on transparency. If you've placed an object in your pond and can't see it through the surface, try opening the second (little) viewing window and selecting the Earth there while you observe the main window. The submerged object should eventually show up. Weird!!

Sky

Unless you're a serious science fiction fan and plan on setting all your worlds in space, you're eventually going to want some sky. In the 3D modeling and rendering field (the field of which you're now nibbling the edges by doing VRML), the sky is part of the *background*. Usually, it's simply an image that appears behind everything else, never moves, and which always looks like it's infinitely far away. It's great for distant mountains, too.

VRML 1.0 offers no official way to do background. Some browser, viewer, and builder companies started offering background features, but none of them have been standard. So if you put such a background into a scene, you have no assurance it will actually show up. Some tricky half-way fixes for this problem are out there, and we've given you one on the CD that we call the *skydome*. More about that in a minute, in "The skydome approach."

VRML 2.0 proposes a way to do backgrounds. The browser and builder companies will soon be busily implementing it in their tools, we're sure, so in "Backgrounds," later in this chapter, we tell you how Walkthrough and Pioneer do backgrounds, in the hope that they will work the same way once VRML 2.0 backgrounds are implemented.

The skydome approach

First, a few words about a VRML 1.0 trick for background. Some browsers let their users set the background for their viewing pleasure. See Part I of this book for more details about that; what we want to do here is to force *your* viewing pleasure on your audience!

To have a background in VRML 1.0, the background has to be on an object. You can either give the object a color or apply a texture-mapped image to it. This procedure is exactly like creating a background for a theatrical production. The trouble here is that your audience can get up and wander through the set, so the best you can do is to surround them with background. And the only way to do that is to put the entire scene and its viewpoints inside something, sort of like a planetarium.

The problem with putting your scene inside a container is that, in many browsers, the inside surfaces of a shape are perfectly transparent. Once you are inside, no *there* is there. In geek-speak, your shape needs its *normals* reversed, or needs two-sided rendering. In other words, it needs to be turned inside out.

Neither Pioneer nor Walkthrough can do this trick, but Caligari's trueSpace can, so we used that tool to create an inside-out dome for you (in Pioneer, you can create a sort of extended cave, but it's an immense pain to do so). Check the Dummies directory on our CD for the Caligari object SKYDOME.COB. To load it into Pioneer, choose File⇨Load Object. Scale it up or down and color it or texture map it to your heart's content. Add a few lights near the top for illumination. It's far from ideal because people can go right up to it or through it, and it slows down rendering speed. Figure 15-6 shows the skydome from outside (little window) and inside (big window).

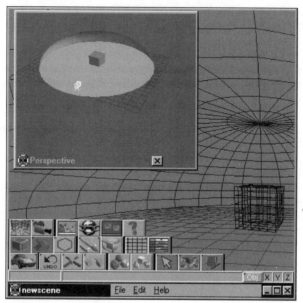

Figure 15-6:
Our
skydome.

Backgrounds

Both Virtus's Walkthrough and Caligari's Pioneer let you set the background color while you are browsing. Pioneer also lets you apply a background image, like sky and clouds. We're guessing that Virtus and Caligari will also wire these features up to create VRML 2.0 backgrounds at some point, which gradually other browsers will start to read. Right now, backgrounds can't be written in standard VRML.

In Walkthrough, in the Walk View tool pad, find the horizontal bar that appears just under the buttons on top of the tool pad and just above the zoom control (the sketch of the cabin in the mountains). Click and hold on that bar, and then click any color in the palette that appears. The bigger color swatches to the right of the palette icon are colors that are currently in use in the scene, in case you want to use them again.

In Pioneer, right-click the 3DR button (or the wireframe button that lives at the same location). A Rendering Quality panel appears. To set the background color, click the gray button just *left* of the word *Background.* In the Background Color panel that pops up, drag left to right in each of the three color bars to mix your background color. The button shows you your chosen color.

To choose a background image in Pioneer, click the gray button just *right* of the word *Background* in the Rendering Quality panel. Choose a JPEG image (such as CLOUDS.JPG, which you may find in the Caligari Pioneer directory) from the Get Texture Map dialog box that appears. To turn on the background image, click the Show Background Image checkbox. For higher resolution, click and hold the button to the right of the words Texture Resolution, and then choose 256 x 256.

Plants

Plants — at least realistic plants in any profusion — are a real problem for the modeling and rendering world, and for VRML in particular. Plants have lots and lots of complex faces, all turned every which way, which take rendering software eons to figure out. Also, all those faces can take a long time to download — not to mention the effort of creating them in the first place.

You have to ask yourself, "What am I doing all this work for?" Unless you intend for your audience to examine every leaf, you don't need the umpteen thousand faces of every leaf on a tree. No, what you want is the general appearance of leafiness. What you want is texture mapping. For the full skinny on texture mapping, see Chapter 14; for some leafy tricks that only work in Live3D, see Chapter 19.

For trees and shrubs, we suggest that you create basic shapes for the leafy areas, like the lollipop-style trees you drew in kindergarten. Rough 'em up a little using Pioneer's Face tool and then apply a leafy JPEG image to them. For a forested area of a distant landscape, rough up the terrain a bit by dragging faces and tilting them to form points, and then apply a mottled green texture map.

Of course, you may need the occasional plant that survives close-up scrutiny. For these plants, your best bet is to try to find some existing models; they are really tricky to make. If you do decide to create your own plants, use the fancy shape making capabilities of Pioneer, which we describe in Chapter 13. Here's an example of how to make a palm tree:

1. **Make a short, tapered cylinder with the top slightly skewed.**

2. **Sweep the top, adjusting height and taper and rotating the top slightly.**

3. **Repeat the sweep several times to make the trunk; Pioneer should repeat the taper and rotation as you do. Paint the trunk brown. Figure 15-7 shows the trunk.**

4. **To start the top, make a short cylinder primitive with five sides (a pentagon).**

5. **Select and shrink the top face slightly, which tilts the sides upward.**

6. **Select one side face and sweep it to start a palm frond.**

Figure 15-7:
Growing the trunk of a palm tree.

7. **Widen the resulting face and tilt it slightly downward.**

8. **Sweep that face; the frond extends, widens, and droops downward. See Figure 15-8.**

Figure 15-8:
Virtual agriculture: Ag-sense makes the heart (of palm) grow frond-er.

9. Sweep once or twice again, narrowing the face each time to finish the frond.

10. Select the entire object and duplicate it.

11. Choose the object rotation tool and drag with the right mouse button to rotate the new, copied frond into position.

12. Keep duplicating and rotating fronds until you have five.

13. Glue all the fronds together as siblings.

14. Paint the frond-set object green.

15. Position your frond-set at the top of the palm trunk and glue as a sibling. The result appears in Figure 15-9.

Figure 15-9:
Topping off
the palm.

Chapter 16

Importing from Alien Worlds

· ·

In This Chapter

▶ Importing DXF files

▶ Importing 2D Adobe Illustrator and PostScript files

▶ Importing other foreign file types

▶ Importing inlined files

· ·

*W*hy build when you can buy? Or for that matter, when you can get it for free? A lot of cool 3D stuff is out there — you might download it, buy it, or get it from your brother-in-law — but unfortunately, it's all in different file types *(formats)*. See Chapter 9 for more on where to find stuff.

After you've found some 3D objects, how do you use them? A number of programs are available on the Internet for converting files from one type to another. For most practical purposes, however, Caligari's Pioneer will do the conversion for you, and that's what this chapter is mainly about. Just remember that no conversion will be perfect, especially in the bleeding edge world of VRML.

2D images or drawings can also be useful. Pioneer will import 2D Adobe Illustrator and PostScript files, which you can then sweep into 3D shapes. Walkthrough Pro allows you to import PICT, BMP, or 2D DXF files so that you can use them as guidelines for drawing. For example, if you have a floorplan of a building and can scan it or otherwise capture it as an image file, you can import it into Walkthrough, scale it to the size you need, then trace over it in Top View.

Importing DXF Files

Mechanical engineers and architects have been working in 3D for a long time, often using one of the pioneer PC computer-aided design (CAD) tools, AutoCAD. Autodesk, who makes AutoCAD, years ago created one of the first *open* standards for storing 3D information, Drawing Exchange Format, or DXF. Because the standard was open, meaning that Autodesk publishes the standard and lets anyone write in that format, a lot of other 2D and 3D tool vendors could and did build DXF-output capability into their tools. The format only works for shapes, not for colors or other surface features.

The result of all this nice, cooperative effort is that a lot of DXF files are hanging around out there. If you visit any of the online sources for objects, you will find buckets of DXF files. DXF files come in several different varieties:

- ✔ 2D only
- ✔ 3D with some 2D stuff
- ✔ 2D or 3D in ASCII format
- ✔ 2D or 3D in binary format

Don't overlook the possibility of using 2D stuff. If it uses closed shapes (polygons) and not just a lot of lines, you can *sweep* it into 3D in Pioneer. In Walkthrough Pro, you can import 2D DXF files as Trace Layers. If you have a drawing program, you might find that it can output 2D DXF files. The ASCII form of DXF is more common than the binary files, and the ASCII form is what Pioneer and Walkthrough Pro can read.

Loading options

To load a DXF file into Pioneer, choose File⇨Load object, and the dialog box in Figure 16-1 pops up, asking you to select from a bunch of arcane settings.

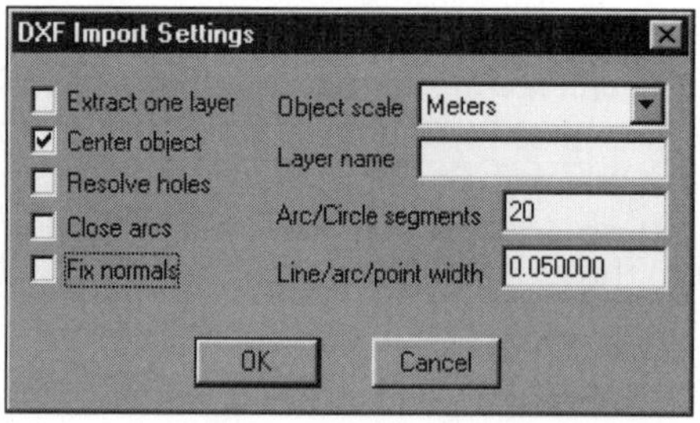

Figure 16-1:
DXF Import
Settings
make you
ponder the
possibilities.

DXF Import Settings

☐ Extract one layer   Object scale [Meters ▼]
☑ Center object   Layer name [ ]
☐ Resolve holes
☐ Close arcs   Arc/Circle segments [20]
☐ Fix normals   Line/arc/point width [0.050000]

[OK]   [Cancel]

Generally, the best approach is to just click the OK button and see what happens. Then, if things come out screwy, go back, fiddle with the settings and try again. Here are what the various selections mean:

✔ **Extract one layer:** Mechanical and architectural drawings in general are done on several *layers*. One layer might contain all the text and dimensions; another might contain the walls; another the electrical system, and so on. Usually, however, the DXF files you encounter will have everything on one layer. If you know the name of a layer, you can select Extract one layer and enter the name in the Layer name text box. Layers turn into objects in Pioneer, and every object in that layer becomes a sub-object (a glued object).

Walkthrough Pro is great at creating certain types of objects, which you might later want to load into Pioneer. Exporting to 3D DXF is a good way to pull this trick off. In Walkthrough, choose File⇨Export⇨DXF 3D. If you want to export more than one object at a time, put objects on individual layers in Walkthrough before you export. When you load the DXF file as an object in Pioneer, you can extract one layer; otherwise, the objects will be imported glued together.

✔ **Center object:** Select this option to place the so-called *center of the object* at the center of the Pioneer grid, at X=0, Y=0, Z=0. Now, why did we italicize *center of the object?* Because the object's center is arbitrarily determined by the program or person who created the DXF file, and it can be very, very far away from anything you would think of as *center.* If you try to import a file and can't find the object, you may, in fact, be better off with Center object unselected.

✔ **Resolve holes:** This option is one of those "if it didn't work right the first time, try this" selections. If the holes in your DXF file don't work out, try again with this option selected.

✔ **Close arcs:** Arcs are usually handled fairly well by Pioneer without this option selected. If for some reason you want to turn arcs into pie-slice shapes, select this option.

✔ **Fix normals:** Here they are, those troublesome *normals* again. Makes us glad we're not normal. Anyway, if some surfaces seem transparent that shouldn't be, or if very weird shapes appear that shouldn't be there, try importing with this option selected. This option reverses normals, so if you are trying to show the interior side of an object (which doesn't show up in many VRML tools because the *normals* are on the outside of the shape), this can be a very useful selection.

If you are trying to import a room in DXF, normals can be very troublesome. If the walls look okay from the outside, they look transparent from the inside. Before doing anything else about the problem, save your file in VRML and test it in a VRML browser; it may look just fine. If not, try importing two copies of the room — one with normals fixed and the other not. Shrink the one where the walls look okay from the inside and center it inside the other room!

✔ **Object scale:** Usually, Pioneer's default selection, Screen fit, works just fine. If you think you know the original scale and want to be truer to that scale, choose a specific unit from the list of alternatives. The smaller the unit you choose, the smaller the object will be.

✔ **Layer name:** Works with the Extract one layer selection, described earlier in this section.

✔ **Arc/Circle segments:** This setting is very much like the longitude settings for Pioneer primitives: it tells Pioneer how many segments to use for arcs and circles.

✔ **Line/arc/point width:** When Pioneer converts 2D files into 3D, it uses this setting to specify the third dimension. Lines are converted into planes of the width that you specify here.

Working with DXF objects

If you are fortunate enough to have a DXF drawing with each object on a separate layer, Pioneer will turn the drawing into a composite (glued-together) object, with each layer a separate sub-object. Unfortunately, most often, DXF files are on a single layer, so you end up with one, huge, monolithic object.

If you are using Pioneer Pro, however, there is a solution. Select the object and choose the Decompose into Surfaces tool to break the object up into sub-objects. The icon for this tool looks like a little stick-figure guy with an arm being disconnected (there are some twisted minds at Caligari); the tool is a variant (pop-up) of the Triangulate Object, Smooth Quad Divide, and Quad Divide tools of Pioneer Pro.

If you do succeed in converting the objects into sub-objects, use Pioneer's hierarchy navigation to select individual sub-objects, which in turn lets you to paint the sub-objects individually, delete them, move them around, or unglue them to turn them into separate objects. Just select the big, monolithic object and then use your keyboard's navigation keys to select individual sub-objects. Up and down arrow keys move up and down in the hierarchy between parent and child objects; left and right arrow keys move between the siblings. As you navigate, Pioneer displays the main object in brown lines (in wireframe display mode) and the selected sub-object in white lines.

Choose the Object List tool (the icon that looks like a spreadsheet) to help you keep track of which object is currently selected. As you navigate the object hierarchy, an Object Info panel gives you the object's name and other details.

Importing 2D Adobe Illustrator and PostScript Files

If you are a graphic designer, you're in luck. Your logos and illustrations can now make the jump to 3D — maybe. Unfortunately, if you are using fonts, Pioneer requires some software that (as of this writing) isn't included: the Caligari ATM (Adobe Type Manager) dll file, CALATM.DLL. Drawings should import — although we can't confirm that possibility because the early version of Pioneer is rather buggy on importing these files.

To import an Adobe Illustrator (AI) or PostScript file (PS or EPS), choose File➪Load object, and the dialog box in Figure 16-2 pops up, asking you to select a bunch of settings.

Figure 16-2: The dialog box for both AI and PostScript files.

- ✔ **Curve Resolution:** This setting is like the longitude settings for Pioneer primitives: It tells Pioneer how many segments to use for curves. The Low setting is fine for most work.

- ✔ **Data Types to Convert:** By selecting or deselecting these options, you can control how much of the file is imported.

  - Standard text is the sort of text you would find in a word processor document, not fancy text created graphically, as in a logo.

  - Filled curves are solid arcs, ellipses, and circles.

  - Stroked curves are outlines or individual lines.

- ✔ **Inter-Object Step:** This setting controls the space between loaded objects.

- ✔ **Object Scale:** Usually, Pioneer's default selection, Screen fit, works just fine. If you think you know the original scale and want to be truer to that scale, choose a specific unit from the list of alternatives. The smaller the unit you choose, the smaller the object will be.

✔ **Inter-Page Step:** For multi-page PostScript files, this number is the amount of space between the pages.

✔ **Center object:** Places the graphic objects at X=0, Y=0, and Z=0 in Pioneer.

Importing Other Foreign File Types

Pioneer imports a whole bunch of foreign file types besides DXF, AI, and PostScript formats. Here's what they are and a little background about how Pioneer is supposed to import them.

✔ **Amiga Caligari:** Pioneer imports all object information.

✔ **3D Studio:** As with DXF, all the objects in a 3DS file become glued-together sub-objects in Pioneer; no hierarchy information is converted. Colors come from the 3DS diffuse color. Pioneer looks for texture maps first in the directory the 3DS file is in and then in Pioneer's own directory.

✔ **Imagine:** As with DXF, all the objects in a 3DS file become glued-together sub-objects in Pioneer; no hierarchy information is converted.

✔ **LightWave:** All surface information, except surface details and weird things called *one and two-point polygons,* are converted.

✔ **Video Scape:** All surface information, except surface details and weird things called *one and two-point polygons,* are converted.

✔ **Wavefront:** Material colors are converted as well as possible, provided that they are named. Wavefront object groupings are not converted.

Importing Inlined Files (Not)

Many WRL worlds are made up of *inlined* objects, which are transmitted as separate files. Being able to use these objects would be nice. One of Pioneer's failings is that it doesn't give you any way to import the inlined objects of downloaded worlds. This fact is particularly surprising because it *does* give you a way to make inlined files. Oh, well.

We have come up with a procedure for you to edit in inlined files, however, if you don't mind mucking around in VRML code. Check out Chapter 9. The procedure might just work for you.

Part V
Worlds on the Web

In this part . . .

It's fun building 3D worlds, but it's even more fun to put them on the Web where other people can live in them. In this part, we show you how to become a virtual realtor by putting your world on the Web. Just as in the real realty business, however, there are some tricks of the trade to learn. Here, we discuss special VRML features that help your world fit through the skinny computer pipelines that connect people to your Web site. You don't have a Web site? We'll give you tips on getting one and installing your world there. Soon you'll be ready to hang out an "open house" sign and prepare some virtual punch and cookies for visitors.

Chapter 17

Making Big Worlds Work

In This Chapter

▶ Inlining
▶ Bounding boxes
▶ Levels of Detail
▶ Reusing objects and textures
▶ Removing formatting
▶ Lowering precision
▶ Compressing

onsider for a second just how absurd is the whole idea of transmitting entire virtual reality worlds over the Internet to people hooked up mainly by modems. Talk about ridiculous. The whole setup is like trying to chug a McDonald's Thick 'n' Frosty shake through a straw.

Of course, Any Day Now, Real Soon, we'll all be using our 28.8 kbps modems as coffee cup warmers because we'll have high-speed connections through the cable TV wires or ISDN lines, or whatever comes out of the whole telecommunications mess. Until then, the only people who aren't trying to suck thick 'n' frosty data through a skinny straw are the professional software developers whose companies have special, high-speed Internet connections.

So unless the only people you care about seeing your cool Web world are professional software developers who are taking time out from work to shmooze the Web, you're going to have to worry about the straw problem. Fortunately, the Web and VRML gurus have been doing some worrying for you. They've come up with a bunch of schemes that — if people use them well — will help make VRML work on the Internet as we all know it and love it today. Among these schemes are *object inlining, texture inlining, reusing, Levels of Detail, removing formatting, lowering precision, and compressing.*

First the bad news: This stuff is all rather technical in concept. Also, few builders support all these features. Walkthrough, for instance, doesn't support any of them except texture inlining. And neither Pioneer nor Walkthrough does your compression for you.

The good news it that by using the techniques in this chapter, you can reduce the size and speed up the downloading of your world by a factor of 5, 10, 20, or more. More good news: Even though this stuff is conceptually pretty technical, Pioneer gives you easy ways to do inlining and Levels of Detail (LOD), remove formatting, and lower precision. Pioneer doesn't do reusing, but we do provide a Deep VRML work-around solution for the brave to try. Pioneer also provides decompression of files in the VRML-standard *gzip* format, although it doesn't provide compression.

An Object Inline Saves Time

Inlining simply means "Some stuff is in separate files." If you've ever written HTML, you are probably familiar with the concept from putting images into Web documents. In HTML documents, you see lines that look something like <IMG SRC="nicepict.gif"> saying, in effect, "Display the image that's in this file called nicepict.gif." In geek-speak, you have *inlined* your images. A similar feature has been built into VRML that lets you store objects, textures, and other things in separate files.

In this chapter, we only discuss object inlining; for information on texture inlining see the texture mapping chapter, Chapter 14.

The VRML inline idea

Here's the VRML inline idea. Instead of one big WRL file, with all the objects jammed into it like this:

> Gigantic WRL file:
> palmtree1palmtree2palmtree3oceanbeachloungechairsailboatvolcano

You might create a world using one main WRL file and separate inlined WRL files like this:

> Main WRL file: palmtree1palmtree2beachocean
>
> Inline file 0: palmtree3
>
> Inline file 1: loungechair
>
> Inline file 2: sailboat
>
> Inline file 3: volcano

The main WRL file contains references to the inlined files. As your VRML viewer or browser reads the main file, it finds those references and asks the Web server to transmit the inlined files.

"That's all very nice, but really, what good is it all?" you say, and rightfully so. In a nutshell, inlining avoids wasting people's time. Consider the way inlined graphics gradually appear on Web pages. You've undoubtedly viewed many pages where the text appears well before the image does. This sequential transmission is kind of nice because the image takes so long to download, and you can be reading the text in the meantime. (You have to set up your browser correctly — *display images after loading* is the Netscape Preferences setting — for this sequence to work correctly.)

In VRML, inlining provides a similar benefit. If some objects don't have to be seen immediately — say, objects that are far away from the initial viewpoint or behind the camera — you can inline them. That way, the person viewing the scene can enjoy your main scene while waiting for the details to show up. The distant sailboat and volcano in our hypothetical beach scene, for example, can probably wait the longest.

Just so the person knows something will be arriving later, however, VRML defines *bounding boxes* in the main WRL file to temporarily represent the inlined shapes. These boxes appear in wireframe form in a VRML browser or viewer.

Besides inlining objects, VRML can also inline textures. Inlined textures have two benefits: they allow the VRML viewer to display a shape while it's waiting for a texture map; and they let you offer textures in a nice, compact, binary image format, like JPEG, instead of nasty, gigunda ASCII bitmaps internal to the WRL file. See Chapter 14 for more on this issue.

How well inlining does its job of not wasting people's time depends very much on the VRML browser/viewer. If the browser/viewer is very stupid, it doesn't show you anything until everything has been downloaded. You see lots of bounding boxes but not much else. If it's very clever, it first downloads things it thinks you would be able to see right away, and then downloads the other stuff.

The object inlining two-step

Object inlining is conceptually a bit tricky, but easy to do in Pioneer. If you're using Walkthrough Pro or some other builder that doesn't provide object inlining, you need to do your inlining in Deep VRML (see the sidebar later in this section).

You have only two steps in Pioneer:

1. Mark objects as inlined.

Select the object, and then right click the Selection tool. In the Object Info panel that pops up, click the Inlined checkbox.

2. **Save the scene with inlines enabled.**

Choose File➪Scene➪Save; give the file a name in the Save Scene dialog box. Then, in the Export VRML file dialog box that appears (see Figure 17-1), make sure that the Marked Objects checkbox is selected (in the Inlining area).

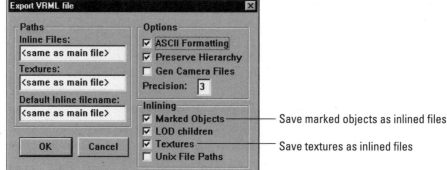

Figure 17-1:
How to keep
your rowdy
virtual
worlds
in line.

Save marked objects as inlined files

Save textures as inlined files

Unless you tell it otherwise, Pioneer saves inlined object files using the first five letters of your main file name, and it appends a serial number to the name. If you call your main file BEACHSCN.WRL, your inlines will be BEACH000.WRL, BEACH001.WRL, and so forth. Pioneer also saves your inlines in the same directory as the main file. Within the main file, Pioneer automatically creates bounding boxes for your inlined objects.

If for some reason you want to use different names or a different directory for the inlined files, edit the Default Inline filename or Inline Files text boxes in the Export VRML file dialog box (see Figure 17-1). You should definitely give different names for your inlined files if you have other scenes beginning with the same first five letters, like BEACHNUT.WRL for instance. Otherwise, the BEACH000.WRL file for BEACHSCN.WRL will replace the BEACH000.WRL file for BEACHNUT.WRL.

Details, Details: Levels of Detail

Half the fun of virtual reality is in the details: the eyeballs on the gargoyle, the phaser arrays on the starship. The other half of the fun is being able to move around in the world at some reasonable rate of speed. Unfortunately, the more details you see, the slower you go. Until we're all running Pentium 500s with graphics accelerators, this trade-off requires your attention if you're going to create a big VRML world.

The inline: the mighty mouse of VRML

The inline is one of the smaller, simpler *nodes* of VRML, and also one of the more powerful. Here's an example in VRML 1.0:

```
DEF Palm1 WWWInline {
    name   "palms001.wrl"
    bboxSize 0.832 2.846 0.800
    bboxCenter -0.826 -0.511
0.052
}
```

(At this point in time, the VRML 2.0 version apparently will be similar. Things are changing even as we write. Check these Web sites for details on the state of VRML 2.0: http://www.wired.com/VAG and http://webspace.sgi.com/moving-worlds/.)

The first line defines (DEF), an object called Palm1. That's the name we gave our object, which happens to be a palm tree. (You can name an object in Pioneer by selecting it, right clicking the Selection tool, and editing the Name text box in the Object Info panel that appears.) The term WWWInline tells the VRML viewer/browser that the object is inlined.

The second line gives the name of the file that contains the inlined object. Don't be fooled by the humble appearance of this line. Instead of a filename, you can alternatively use a URL. If you know where an inline object exists *anywhere on the Web*, you can put its URL here and (here's the good part) the viewer/browser fetches it and *displays it as part of your world*! (Although you are not copying the object, you might ask for permission to inline it to be polite; maybe even to be legal.) This capability is the power of the inline concept.

In HTML Web documents, you can do similar inlining with graphics: Use remotely-located graphics by giving the URL of a remote GIF file in an <IMG SRC="*remotefile*"> statement, where *remotefile* is the URL of a remote GIF file.

The *bbox* lines define the size and location of the bounding box for this shape. The three numbers in each line are X, Y, and Z. In *bboxSize*, they are the dimensions of the box; in *bboxCenter*, they are the (world) coordinates of the center of the box.

The big idea

The VRML gurus came up with a scheme that helps solve the big world problem: Levels of Detail, or LOD. When a world uses LOD, distant objects appear as simpler shapes, like spheres or cubes. Simpler shapes are easier and faster for a VRML viewer to render, and when shapes are far away, who needs details anyway? Why not use a simple shape?

To use LOD, you need to create the shapes that are going to represent your distant starship or gargoyle, lump them together, and specify at what distances from the viewing camera those simpler shapes take effect.

In Figure 17-2, for example, we've created three shapes. The leftmost shape is the detailed one (nearly 300 faces) that appears for close-up viewing; the middle is the substitute shape (about 50 faces) for the middle distance, and the cylinder on the right (18 faces) is the substitute for very distant viewing.

Figure 17-2:
The palm tree and its two stand-ins.

You can make as many different shapes as you like, one for each distance that you wish to represent differently. The trade-off is that each shape adds to your VRML file, so the file takes longer to download. Three shapes is a reasonable number.

We wish we could remember who in the VRML community originated the following idea so that we could give that person credit. It's really cute: Use LOD to "animate" parts of your world. For instance, if you wanted a door to open as you approach it, you can use a series of LOD objects: a closed door for far-away viewing, with increasingly open doors as you move closer. Or as Doug — the one of us with the more twisted mind — suggested, you can really frustrate someone by doing it the other way around: close the door as people approach!

Gluing the LOD shapes together

Now, how do we lump these shapes together? By gluing them into a single *LOD group,* using a special glue bottle (cute, no?). Just select the most detailed shape and then click on the less detailed shapes with the LOD Glue tool. They all become joined together in one location.

Here are the instructions in detail:

1. **Select the most detailed object, the one for close-up viewing.**

2. **Choose the Group-several-objects-together-as-levels-of-detail tool (what a name!), which we call the LOD Glue tool (see Figure 17-3):**

The details of levels of detail

VRML accomplishes LOD by means of a *group node*, where objects are grouped together by a pair of curly braces. The LOD group node in VRML is very simple, although if the objects in the LOD group are complex, the group covers so much real estate that the boundaries of the node are hard to find. So in the following example, we use inlined objects; inlines are nice and compact, so we can show you the whole group.

If you expect to be editing VRML, we recommend you inline your LOD group too (see "Setting LOD distance and inlining" later in this chapter). If you do, you will find the LOD node below in a separate inlined file, not the main WRL file. For instance, if your world filename is PALMSCN.WRL, you'll find the LOD node in PALM000.WRL.

The example below represents a three-object group, moving from a palm tree to a simpler palm tree, to a cylinder, as distance to the observer increases.

```
LOD {
            range [
            20.000, 30.000,
            ]
            DEF Palm WWWInline
{
                        name
"inlin000.wrl"
                        bboxSize
1.998 2.007 3.157
                        bboxCenter
0.023 0.057 -1.453
                        }
            DEF SimplePalm
WWWInline {
                        name
"inlin001.wrl"
                        bboxSize
0.838 0.838 1.375
                        bboxCenter
0.000 0.000 -0.688
                        }
            DEF Cylinder
WWWInline {
                        name
"inlin002.wrl"
                        bboxSize
0.838 0.838 1.375
                        bboxCenter
0.000 0.000 -0.688
                        }
            }
```

The term *LOD* identifies the group node as a Level of Detail node, and everything between the first and last curly braces belongs to that node. The term *range* gives the distances at which the shapes change. Here, the first object appears for any distance up to 20 units, the second for any distance between 20 and 30, and the third for any distance over 30. The number of *range* values is always exactly 1 less than the number of objects in the LOD group.

Figure 17-3:
The LOD
Glue and
Unglue
tools.

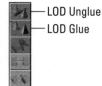

— LOD Unglue
— LOD Glue

The LOD Glue tool is part of the glue family (a family that sticks together). Click and hold on any of the Glue tools, drag to the LOD tool, and release.

3. **With the glue bottle icon, click on the second object, the one for the middle distance.**

In our example, that object would be the middle shape. The shape moves over to join the first shape, but you only see one of them. If you're close up, you just see the first shape as in Figure 17-4; if you're far away, just the second shape.

Figure 17-4:
The middle
shape has
become part
of the palm
tree LOD
group.

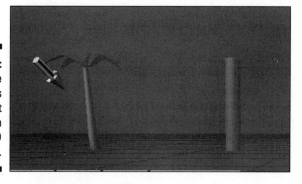

4. **Again with the glue bottle, click on the third object, the one for the farthest distance.**

That object now joins the LOD group.

After you're all finished creating your LOD group, click the selection tool to clear the Glue tool so you don't accidentally glue stuff together. To unglue an LOD group, select the LOD Unglue tool and click whichever object of the group is visible.

Figure 17-5 shows you the transition as you move closer. We put a non-LOD cube in the scene to show you the scale.

Sailboats in the sky

One little problem that arises in Pioneer is that the LOD substitute shapes sometimes stick out to one side or up in the air, compared to the detailed shape they are representing. You'd probably consider a scene rather uncool if the cone you're using to represent a distant sailboat is floating up in the sky.

The source of the problem is that Pioneer aligns these shapes at their internal *centers* (at the *origin* of each object's coordinate system). Call the original shape *A* and the substitute *B* for a moment. If shape *A*'s center is at its top, and shape *B*'s center is in its middle, shape B is going to float in the air when Pioneer aligns the two. Now, in Pioneer Pro, you can simply move the

center within a shape so that the shapes line up properly (select the object, click the Axis tool, choose the Object Move tool, and drag the axes). In plain old Pioneer, you can't do that.

What you can do is adjust the center of shape B by sweeping a face of the shape. Shape B is probably a primitive, like a cylinder or cube. If you sweep a face, say, the top of the cylinder, the cylinder gets taller, but the center doesn't change. Scale the shape back down to the size you want, and *voila!* You've moved the center farther down. If you need to create a shape with its center at the bottom, start with a polygon and sweep it upward. Glue any other objects you need as children to this object.

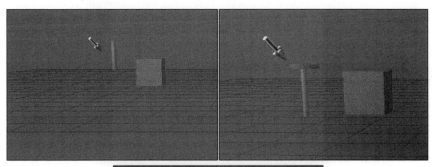

Figure 17-5: Moving towards the object gradually reveals its detailed shape.

Setting LOD distance and inlining

Pioneer arbitrarily assigns distances to each of the objects in an LOD group. It uses intervals of 10 units. The first shape is shown for distances under 10, the second for distances under 20, and so forth. These intervals are fine, but you can change them if you like using the Object Info panel. (The VRML specification suggests that you use distances great enough that your audience can't easily see the difference as the shapes change.) Here's how to do it:

1. **Select the LOD group (click whichever object is visible).**

2. **Right-click the selection tool to get an Object Info panel.**

3. **Walk or fly, or move the LOD group, until you see the object whose LOD distance you want to change.**

4. **In the Object Info panel, edit the LOD Dist figure and press Enter.**

Repeat Steps 3 and 4 until you have assigned distances for all shapes.

You can also inline the entire LOD group while you're at it. While you're looking at the Object Info panel in Step 4, just click the Inlined checkbox; this operation makes the group itself and all objects in the group inlined. When you save your scene with File⇨Scene⇨Save, when the Export VRML panel pops up, make sure that the checkbox "LOD Children" is selected.

Miscellaneous Ways to Trim File Size

To trim 25 percent or more ugly fat off your VRML file, practically for free, just make two changes in the way you save your VRML files. See Figure 17-6. That panel appears when you save your scene. Simply deselect the ASCII formatting checkbox and choose a lower number for precision; a setting of 2 usually does just fine.

The difference between inlining and Levels of Detail

All this stuff begins to rattle around in your skull after a while, and you can easily get confused between these two ways of dealing with large worlds, especially because you can combine them by inlining LOD objects. Here's the difference in a nutshell:

- ✔ Inlining lets worlds be delivered in pieces. It saves downloading time.

- ✔ LODs provide simple shapes for distant objects. They save rendering time.

Remove this check mark

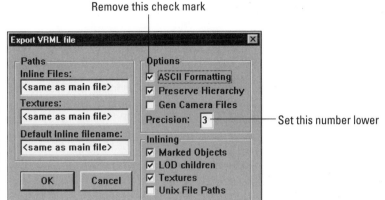

Set this number lower

Figure 17-6:
Two ways to
lose ugly fat
in your
VRML file.

What you have done is remove formatting (extra characters that make the file more humanly readable) and lowered *precision*.

What happens when you remove formatting? Happily, nothing changes in your VRML world. The only change you see is when you examine the file with a word processor or text editor: all the indentations are removed. Without indentations, the VRML file is very hard for humans to read, but computers are just as happy.

Lowering precision actually affects your VRML world, although if you do it carefully, the change is usually too small to matter. *Precision* is how many decimal positions are used in the numbers that describe your world in the VRML file. If you are using a precision of 3, all dimensions and positions are specified by numbers like 2.488; if you set precision to 1, that number would change to 2.5.

For objects down to 1 unit across, a precision of 2 is probably fine because it produces an error of less than .01, or 1 percent, in shape and location. Precision affects colors as well as shape and location, and lower color precision reduces the number of different colors possible. This lower precision may mean that colors that were close but not identical in the original scene turn out exactly the same after you have reduced precision. Also, texture maps may be positioned less precisely on the shape (although their color precision is not affected, even if they are internal to the WRL file).

If you are going to put teeny, tiny objects in an otherwise full-scale world, you may have to raise precision. If you want folks to be able to explore the ant farm in your virtual apartment, you need to set precision high enough throughout the entire world for ant legs to be visible. A more practical solution is to create a separate ant farm world at an expanded scale (many meters across) and link it to the apartment world. Viewers can then click on the ant farm object in the apartment to enter the ant farm world.

Reusing

One of the absolute best features in VRML is the capability to reuse objects. It's sheer poetry. Say, for instance, you want to make a forest. Joyce Kilmer ("only God can make a tree") notwithstanding, you make a tree. Trees being what they are (really, really big and complex), that tree requires 20KB in VRML. A small grove of these beauties, let alone a forest, is going to blow anybody's byte budget! Nobody is going to download your 5MB file to stop by your woods on a snowy evening.

Well, don't get Frosted (yet). VRML lets you reuse that tree! In other words, a VRML file can say to the VRML viewer, "Here's a tree; now put a short copy of it over here, a tall one over there, and one sticking sideways out of the cliff over there." Only one copy of the tree has to be downloaded; the VRML viewer does all the work of duplicating it and mutating it! Great deal, right?

Okay, now you can get frosted because none of the tools we've seen to date let you do this. They will let you copy shapes all you like, but not reuse them. Until Caligari or some other tool vendor gets its act together (probably two days after we print this book), you'll have to get into the dreaded Deep VRML to do any reusing. (If you get a fresher version of Pioneer than the one on our CD, check the help file to see if this feature has been added. It will probably be a special copy tool.)

If you decide to use this Deep VRML technique, you can't do any further editing of your world in Pioneer or Walkthrough. Pioneer, for instance, will read your world okay, but if you then save the file, Pioneer will put actual copies of the object into the file instead of reusing the object, defeating the whole purpose of the exercise.

What follows is the process for reusing objects in a nutshell. We discuss using Pioneer, because that's the tool on our CD that allows inlining. The same concepts hold for whatever builder you are using:

1. **Do everything else you want to do in Pioneer (or whatever builder you're using) first because you won't be able to go back into it for editing.**

2. **In Pioneer, create the object (or various objects) you want to reuse.**

3. **Mark the object(s) for inlining and save your scene.**

4. **In a text editor or word processor, insert *USE nodes* that call upon the inlined object file, together with scaling, translation, and rotation for each use.**

Each of the following sections gives you the details for the above steps.

Create an object for reuse

You can make any kind of object, but you'll make your life easier if you observe a few precautions:

- ✔ Put the object near and at the height where you will want the copies. This placement makes positioning the copies easier.

- ✔ Try to make the object's center at its bottom. This precaution avoids your having to adjust the position of the objects up or down to get them to sit on the ground. This last precaution is a little hard to do. Here are a few tips:

  - Create the object by sweeping a 2D polygon upward with the Sweep tool. The base of the shape is then where its center is located.

  - If the object is a composite object made up of glued-together objects, start gluing from the object that sits on the ground, and glue the subsequent objects as children, not siblings.

Save the object as an inlined file

Reusing is a lot easier if you inline the object you want to reuse. An inlined object takes up only a few lines in the main .WRL file, so you can see it in its entirety. Non-inlined objects can be so enormous that you can't find where they end. Here's how to make your object inlined:

1. **Mark the object as inlined.**

   Select the object, and then right-click the selection tool. In the Object Info panel that pops up, click the Inlined checkbox.

2. **Save the scene with inlines enabled.**

   Choose File⇨Scene⇨Save; give the file a name in the Save Scene dialog box. Then, in the Export VRML file dialog box that appears, make sure that the Marked Objects checkbox is selected (in the Inlining area).

Add USE nodes and positioning terms

Load your main WRL file into a word processor or text editor, and you'll find some VRML code that looks something like the following, fairly near the end of the file. Just search for the term *WWWInline* in your file.

```
DEF Palm2 WWWInline {
    name  "palms000.wrl"
    bboxSize 1.451 3.157 1.406
    bboxCenter 0.050 -0.356 -0.055
}
```

(We have put the official VRML terms and punctuation in bold; the rest is particular to our example.) This chunk of code, called a *WWWInline node,* tells the VRML viewer to define an object — called Palm2 in our example — and to find its definition in a file — called PALMS000.WRL in our example. Your object and filenames will be different. The *bbox* lines define the bounding box that go with an inlined object.

We're talking about VRML 1.0 here. VRML 2.0 is shaping up to be similar, but with subtle differences in punctuation.

To reuse the inlined object in our example, we simply add a term (a *USE node*) that looks like this:

```
USE Palm2
```

You substitute your object name for Palm2. The USE term tells the VRML browser, "Remember that thing we called Palm2? Well, make a copy."

Now, you need to move the copy created by USE, or else the two objects will be superimposed. Put the USE node in a Separator node and scale, rotate, or move the copy, by adding lines similar to the following example:

```
Separator{
    Scale {scaleFactor 0.4 1 0.4}
    Rotation {rotation 0 1 0 0.5}
    Translation {translation 1 0 1}
    USE Palm2
}
```

Now, where do you place this USE node and its Separator node? Well, that question is a bit tricky because the answer depends on your individual file. For a Pioneer-generated file, try inserting it just after the final } of your WWWInline node, so the two together look like this:

```
DEF Palm2 WWWInline {
    name  "palms000.wrl"
    bboxSize 1.451 3.157 1.406
```

```
       bboxCenter 0.050 -0.356 -0.055
   }


Separator{
    Scale {scaleFactor 0.4 1 0.4}
    Rotation {rotation 0 1 0 0.5}
    Translation {translation 1 0 1}
    USE Palm2
   }
```

For multiple copies, just copy and paste the combined Separator and USE node, each with its unique Scale, Rotation, and/or Translation terms, one right after the other.

Putting a copy after the WWWInline node should work well; if it doesn't, try putting the copy at the end of the file, just before the very last } mark of the file (in Pioneer this location places the copied object within the big Separator node that contains all other objects in the scene).

Here's how the positioning and scaling terms work if the copy immediately follows the original (the stuff you fill in is represented by terms in italics):

✔ **Scale {scaleFactor** *x y z*}: Give three scale factors, one each for the object's X, Y, and Z axes. For example, to make the copy half as high but the same in width and depth, use 1 1 0.5 for *x y z*.

✔ **Rotation {rotation** *x y z rotation*}: Put a 1 or 0 for *x, y,* and *z*: 1 enables rotation on that axis and 0 disables rotation. For *rotation,* give an angle in radians (1 radian = 57.3 degrees). The object is rotated in that many degrees from the original in each axis that is enabled.

✔ **Translation {translation** *x y z*}: Give three distances (with no dimensions, such as feet). If the USE node is immediately after the WWWInline node that it is copying, this distance will control the distance between the two objects.

Check and edit your world

After you've inserted your first USE node, check your world in a VRML browser or viewer to see how it worked. You can view it in Pioneer, but don't save the file! (Pioneer will overwrite your USE nodes with separate object nodes. At least, that's how it works as we write this section.) If you need to edit the file, you *must* use a text editor or word processor. Here are some troubleshooting tips:

✔ **Floating or sunken copies:** The original object's center was not at its base. You have to adjust the Translation Z value or reconstruct the object. See the sidebar, "Sailboats in the sky," earlier in this chapter for some alternatives.

✔ **No or too few copies:** You may not have given each copy a unique location, so a copy is superimposed on the original. Fiddle with the Translation X and Y values to move the copy.

✔ **Bizarre appearance or orientation:** You have somehow grouped the USE node with another object that is being scaled or rotated. Try a different location in the file.

Compressing

Compressing is a final step that can make a big difference in the size of your world, although you won't find it used everywhere. More and more browsers and viewers are able to un-gzip files automatically, however — a development that should spur developers to use compression. You should only compress .WRL files, not inlined texture files.

The official compression standard of VRML 1.0 (and probably 2.0) is *gzip.* Pioneer does un-gzip most gzipped files (but not all). Tools are available on the Internet for *gzipping* and un-*gzipping.* The most recent version of WinZIP, a popular shareware package for the PC, does not gzip but does un-gzip.

We've provided some URLs for downloading gzip programs using your Web browser or FTP program. You would think we would include gzip on our CD, but the fact that it is offered for free without signed paperwork worries the lawyers. Go figure.

Many of the programs that you download are self-decompressing executables, meaning that you should put them into a separate folder and run them, and they will unbundle (install) themselves into the actual programs, documentation, and other files.

✔ gzip for the PC is downloadable from `ftp://prep.ai.mit.edu/pub/gnu/`.

✔ A gzip utility is also available for the Mac, *macgzip,* through `ftp://mirrors.apple.com/mirrors/mac.archive.umich.edu/util/compression`.

✔ For gzipping utilities for the Mac or for DOS, check `http://crusty.er.usgs.gov/ gzip.html`.

✔ The most recent versions of WinZIP are downloadable from `http://www.winzip.com`.

At the moment, gzipping worlds that use inlined files is not always a success. Early versions of VRML browsers don't always handle them properly. See the sidebar at the end of this section for an editorial comment.

Here's how to gzip a single WRL file under Windows, using GZIP.EXE or GZIP386.EXE (which is the faster of the two). We assume the file is in the folder C:\GZIP for the following instructions.

1. **Make a copy of your WRL file(s) for safety.**

    Give the copy a slightly different name; for example, give it an extension like BAK instead of WRL.

2. **Run the gzip program under MS-DOS.**

    For Windows 95: Choose Start➪Run... from the Windows 95 button bar. The Run dialog box appears. In the Open text box, type the following line, substituting your file's name for *yourfile*:: `c:\gzip\ c:\yourfile.wrl`

    For Windows 3.1: Double-click the MS-DOS icon, usually located in the Main program group of the Program Manager. Type the preceding line of code and press Enter. After gzip runs, type EXIT and press Enter.

This process gives you files with an extension of WRZ. That's okay, but WRZ is not quite as widely recognized as the GZ extension, so we suggest you change the file extension to GZ.

A brief editorial about gzipping inlined files

At the moment, gzipping inlined files doesn't work consistently among the viewers and browsers. Live3D and a few others appear to handle it. When gzipping inlines does work, you have two ways to pull it off:

✔ The best-performance way: Edit the VRML file to replace the filename extensions of *.WRL* with extensions of *.GZ*. Then gzip the main file and the inlined files individually. The browser or viewer ungzips the main file and then downloads and ungzips the inlined files in sequence.

✔ The less-work-for-you way: gzip the main file but not the inlines. The browser or viewer ungzips the main file and downloads plain old uncompressed WRL files.

Chapter 18

Becoming a Virtual Realtor

● ●

In This Chapter

▶ Getting a Web site

▶ Installing your world

▶ Showing off your world

▶ Linking to other sites

▶ Taking pictures for HTML documents

● ●

So far in this book, you have just been building and playing in your own private hyperspace. The real fun, however, is letting other people play in your yard — and for that, you have to get it on the Web. Now is the time to put your virtual real estate on the map.

If you already have a VRML-ready Web site and know your way around HTML and URLs, the basics are easy: Just transfer your files to your site and tell the world. If you'd like to link your world to the rest of the world, though — or if you're new to setting up your own Web site, read on.

 Before you start putting your world on a Web site, make sure you browse Chapter 17 and Chapter 14. These chapters give important information on *inlined* objects and texture maps, compression, and other techniques to make the size of your world acceptable to the Web community.

Getting a Web Site

For the world to see your world, you need a Web site — a place for your files to reside on a Web server. What exactly is a Web server? It's nothing more (or less) than a program running on a computer that is permanently connected to the Internet. Most Web server software runs on UNIX workstations, or PCs running Windows NT or UNIX. So unless you want to pay for a big-time operating system and a full-time Internet connection, and install and learn a whole lot about Web servers, let someone else provide the Web site.

Many Internet access providers let you "site" your files on their server in your own directory. AOL and CompuServe offer users Web space too. If you're on AOL, check out the Internet Center for information. Some companies provide space for their employees' home pages on a company Web server, although they may not be too happy about putting VRML files there because the files are often large.

Your current Internet access provider is probably the most convenient source for your Web site, although you might want to shop around for good rates. Rates for using a Web server vary from free-with-your-account to pay-by-the-megabyte. You may be charged a flat rate for Web service, plus a fee if you store a lot of data (say, over 10MB), plus a fee based on how much data is transferred from your directory every month. If you create a really popular VRML site, you may end up paying for everyone's pleasure!

If you want a special domain name of your own, like *dummies.com,* you need to submit a name and get it registered by an organization called Internic. Registration now costs $100 per year (your Internet access provider can probably handle the registration). But wait, there's more! Even if you've already paid for a domain name and are receiving e-mail at it, you may receive another one-time or even monthly charge from your access provider to have that name attached to your Web site, as in *www.dummies.com!* (This feature of having your domain name attached by your Internet access provider is sometimes called a *virtual server* or *virtual Web site.*)

MIMEs: silent, but important

You gotta wonder what sort of world we have when MIMEs become so important — but in Web work, they are. MIME stands for Multimedia Internet Mail Extension. It's a scheme that allows things other than plain old text to be sent across the Internet. It was originally intended for sending things by mail, but it's been adopted for the World Wide Web, and it's a tiny but essential key to using VRML on the Web.

You don't really have to understand MIME to make it work for you. All you have to know is this:

Your Web server must have the VRML MIME type set or enabled. The Webmaster (the person who runs the Web server) has to set the type for you.

If other people have VRML worlds on Web sites you are trying to use, then you're all set. If not, ask the Webmaster, "Does the Web server support the x-world/x-vrml MIME type?" If the answer is "no," ask the Webmaster to add the x-world/x-vrml MIME type to the server. (If you don't know who the Webmaster is, call your Internet access provider, or try e-mailing to "Webmaster" at the company address.)

If, after you have installed your world on your Web site, all you see is text when you try to browse it, the MIME type is probably not set properly.

(Note: When VRML 2.0 finally arrives, the MIME type may change to "model/vrml".)

Installing Your World

Okay, you've called your Internet access provider, checked for VRML MIME-type support, and forked over some cash for a Web site. You now need three things:

- A directory (folder) to install your software in on the Web site. Your access provider tells you what and where this directory is.
- Instructions from your provider on how to log on to the site and access your directory.
- A program called FTP or some other way to copy your files to your directory.

You may have received FTP with the software your Internet access provider gave you, or they may offer FTP online. If not, you can find FTP software on the net with your favorite search engine, or try setting your Web browser URL to http://www.shareware.com and search for ftp. FTP programs all work differently, so we won't attempt to tell you how to use yours here.

You can't use the FTP capability of your Web browser to install your files. Browser FTP only works for receiving files, not sending them.

Now you can transfer your files to your directory. If you don't inline your textures or objects but make them integral to a single world file, your life is simple: Just FTP that sucker. If you do use inlined textures or objects, you have multiple files to FTP.

Make sure you use the right *transfer mode* in FTP. Usually you see a button somewhere in the FTP window to change transfer modes. If you're using the FTP mode of NCSA telnet on a Mac, look in the File menu for a binary mode setting to check off. Our FTP software looks like Figure 18-1.

- To send plain, old, unzipped WRL files, use the *ASCII* transfer mode of FTP; don't forget to include all inlined files.
- To send gzipped files (GZ or WRZ), or to send texture images (like JPEG), use the *binary* transfer mode.

When you transfer files by FTP, the best procedure is to enter the filenames and extensions in lower-case letters for the files on the Web site. Most Web sites run under UNIX, which cares about upper- and lowercase, and the people who are trying to view your world are most likely to type the filename in lowercase letters.

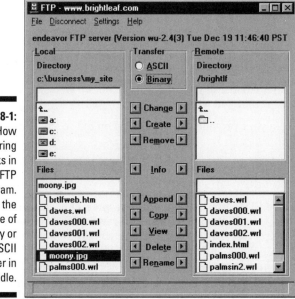

Showing Off Your World

Once your world is on your Web site, the next question is, how do you show it to people? Good question! But in order to answer it, we have to assume you know something about editing HTML documents to talk about this topic. If you don't know about HTML, try *HTML For Dummies* by Ed Tittel and Steve James.

There are three ways that people can view your world:

- You can just tell everyone what the URL for the world is and have them enter that URL in their VRML-equipped Web browser. For instance, if your Web site is `www.vermin.org` and your VRML world is `mickey.wrl` in the `/mouse` directory, the URL would be `http://www.vermin.org/mouse/mickey.wrl`.

- You can link to your world from any text or picture on any document of your Web site. When folks click on the text or picture with a VRML-equipped Web browser, they will see your world. Get your friends to put links from their Web documents to your world too.

- If you want to impress people who have Netscape 2.0 browsers equipped with VRML plug-ins, you can create a window on your world "embedded" right in your home page.

The coolest solution and (since Netscape is the most popular Web browser so far) the solution that will make most people happy is the last one. Unfortunately, it excludes the folks who don't have Netscape 2, who don't have a plug-in style VRML browser, or don't have any VRML browser at all. We suggest you use both linking and embedding.

A nice way to provide for the non-Netscape people is to put a separate hypertext link to your main WRL file, like this:

```
See my <A HREF="carlsbad.wrl"> VRML representation of
Carslbad Caverns</A> You need a VRML browser to
see it, though.
```

Or better yet, you can capture a screen image of your VRML world (see "Taking Pictures for Web Sites" later in this chapter) and place it in your Web document with a link, like this:

```
<A HREF="carlsbad.wrl"><IMG SRC="carlsbad.gif"></A>
```

Now, what about those folks who do have Netscape with plug-in VRML browsers? If you have done much VRML browsing in Netscape, you have seen Web documents in which the VRML world appears in a rectangle, like a picture. The secret to this trick is a special HTML extension, EMBED.

First of all, a little warning about this term. EMBED is an HTML term invented by Netscape, who would like the HTML language to move faster than the official standard does. As a result, the company invents new terms, called *Netscape extensions,* that its browsers recognize. Other browsers may eventually come to recognize them too, but we have no guarantee that they will. Also, the HTML standards folks have a lot of similar proposed terms to choose from, so EMBED may not even end up as official HTML. What a mess.

Netscape intends the EMBED term to be used for files that are recognized by its plug-in programs, like Live3D, so you will see it used for other things besides VRML files, like Adobe Acrobat and QuickTime files.

The official form for the embed term is this:

```
<EMBED SRC="yourwld.wrl" HEIGHT="height" WIDTH="width"
OPTION1="something" OPTION2="somethingelse" ...>
```

(The stuff in italics is what you fill in.)

In this statement, *yourwld.wrl* is the name of your VRML file (the main file if you're using inlines). It can also be a URL for any world on the Web!

The *height* and *width* terms give the size of the window in which your world appears. They are integers, in pixels, like 600 or 480.

We use the placeholder *OPTION* here to represent special options that are recognized by the Netscape browser or the plug-in. Also, although they aren't documented in Netscape's description of the EMBED statement, apparently Netscape software interprets terms you might use in an IMG statement in Netscape HTML extensions, such as *align, center, border, vspace,* or *hspace.*

A simple example is the following:

```
<embed src="main.wrl" width=480  height=280>
```

This statement creates a 480-pixel wide, 280-pixel high, 3D picture in your Web page.

The strict interpretation of EMBED is so unclear at this point that you will find lots of variations in the way it is used and the options it includes. Also, the behavior of EMBED is very quirky, especially when you start using it with a lot of other Netscape formatting extensions. *Keep it simple* is our advice.

Linking to Other Worlds

No man is an island, but at the moment, a lot of VRML worlds are. This state of affairs isn't the way it's supposed to be. The Big Vision that Tim Berners-Lee (one of the principal founders of the World Wide Web and VRML), Mark Pesce, and their colleagues have for virtual reality is that, among other things, it will turn the Web into one, big virtual landscape. For this to happen, VRML worlds need to start linking up.

But we're not making a pitch for social responsibility to create a unified virtual world; no, we're just making a pitch for fun. To "knock" (click) on a door in one world and land in another is kind of cool. Even more cool is traversing a continuous landscape from one virtual world to another.

This kind of fun even lends itself to useful work, like learning biology: Imagine being inside a VRML model of a plant or animal and then being able to click on a model of a cell, explore the cell, zoom in on the nucleus, and then a chromosome, and then — who knows — maybe the DNA model and genome mapping data! The linked worlds don't have to be someone else's worlds. You can link together a whole set of your own interrelated worlds.

When VRML worlds are linked together, jumping from one to another is sometimes called *teleporting.*

In the simplest form of linking, the person viewing the scene clicks on a linked object and moves to another world. This process works just like the text hyperlinks you find in Web documents. The link can go to anything on the Web too — not just other VRML worlds. You can link to a Web document, a sound, or a video. You insert the links when you build your world.

Here's how it goes in Pioneer:

1. **Switch to the building mode.**

2. **With the Selection tool, select the object to be linked.**

3. **Click on the Attach Link tool (the world-in-chains icon).**

   The Attach URL Link dialog box appears.

4. **Type any valid URL into the URL to Jump to text box.**

5. **Type a description of whatever you are linking to in the URL Description box.**

   This description shows up on people's browsers when they pass their cursor over the linked object.

6. **Save your world with File⇨Scene⇨Save.**

In Virtus Walkthrough, the procedure is as follows:

1. **Switch to any Design View, such as Top.**

2. **Select an object with the selection tool.**

3. **Choose Design⇨VRML Anchor from the menu bar.**

4. **Type any valid URL into the Anchor URL box.**

5. **Save your world with File⇨Export⇨VRML.**

In either builder, the link you type in Step 4 doesn't have to be to a URL of the kind you normally see on the Web — with all the `http://www.blah.blah/blah.wrl` stuff. If you want a link to any HTML or VRML file on your Web site, just use a *relative path*. Since relative paths don't contain the http:// prefix, they don't require a Web server to work. As a result, by using relative paths, you can debug your links on your own computer before you move it to your Web site.

Here's how to use a relative path:

- ✔ For a file in the same directory, just enter the filename, like **second.wrl**.

- ✔ For a file in a subdirectory of the directory that your main world is in, give the subdirectory name, a slash, and then the filename, like this: **morewrls/second.wrl**.

> ✔ For a file in a parallel directory, start with two periods and a slash, like this: **../morewrls/second.wrl**.
>
> ✔ For a file in the next higher-level directory, start with two periods, a slash, and then the filename, like this: **../second.wrl**.

Most browsers display some text when you pass the cursor over a linked object, a feature that provides a hint about the link's destination. The text that the browser displays is stored in a special field in the VRML code that neither Pioneer nor Walkthrough Pro currently writes. If you want to display special text, you'll need to edit the VRML file and change the "description" field of the WWWAnchor node. If you don't care to edit your VRML file and you are only concerned about Live3D users, there is a trick you can do using Pioneer. If Live3D doesn't find special text for a link, it displays the name of each object instead! (We don't know if this is a bug or a feature!) In Pioneer, you can assign short names to objects. Just select the linked object, right click the selection tool, and enter the text you want in the Name box of the Object Info panel.

Taking Pictures for Web Sites

For people browsing your Web site who aren't equipped with a VRML browser or viewer, you can still give them a sense of your site's excitement by using some plain old graphics: snapshots taken of your world. The simplest way to do this is to capture a screen from your browser or builder.

In any Windows program, use the PrintScreen key or Alt+PrintScreen to capture to the Windows clipboard. Pioneer needs a little help with this procedure: Drag somewhere in the Pioneer window in order to capture the screen. Then paste the image into a bitmap graphics program such as Paintbrush and crop out all but the image. Use your favorite graphics program to convert the image into GIF (we like Lview Pro; send mail to `mmedia@world.std.com` or check the site `www.shareware.com`), and put the result on your Web site.

Walkthrough has a nice snapshot feature. Set up the view you want in the Walk window, Choose File⇨Snapshot, and you can capture the Walk window to an image file. Afterwards, convert the file to GIF format with your favorite graphics software, and there you are.

Sometimes "a picture is worth a thousand worlds."

If you decide to spring for some cash and buy trueSpace or Walkthrough Pro, both of those programs offer ways to make videos as you cruise through your hyperspace. The trueSpace program also provides animation tools, so you can do your own *Toy Story!* (Assuming you have about 500 friends to help, that is.) Although a video file is a big space- and download-time-consuming file, unlike virtual reality, it lets you have the ultimate in artistic control.

Part VI
The Part of Tens

The 5th Wave   **By Rich Tennant**

"Awww jeez- I was afraid of this. Some poor kid, bored with the usual chat lines, starts looking for bigger kicks, pretty soon they're surfin' the seedy back alleys of cyberspace, and before you know it they're into a file they can't 'undo'. I guess that's why they call it the Web. Somebody open a window!"

In this part . . .

*O*ur publisher told us that every *Dummies* book is
supposed to have a "Part of Tens" — a part containing
chapters comprised of lists of ten items, usually things like
someone's ten favorite shortcuts, ten favorite shareware
programs, and stuff (or is it fluff?) like that. In this part,
however, we talk about the future of VRML, animation, and
audio, (information that's actually useful), so how can we
justify calling this part "The Part of Tens"? Well, consider
this:

- ✔ In the next *ten* minutes, the language of VRML will
  change.

- ✔ In the next *ten* weeks (if you keep at it), you will have
  mastered making simple 3D worlds and will be
  looking for ways to jazz them up.

- ✔ Over the next *ten* months, you will hear that the
  techno-elite are adding sound, animation, and other
  really cool stuff to their VRML worlds.

So in this part, we take our best shot at helping you survive
the trauma of these "tens." Because we can't tell you about
tools or language features that haven't been built yet, we do
the next best thing: We describe how, using the custom
features provided today by vendors such as Netscape and
Caligari, you can add sound and animation to your VRML
worlds. So while the techno-elite are busily arguing about
how to add these features to the official VRML language, you
can actually have some fun.

Chapter 19

At Least Ten Things to Know about Animation

. . . .

In This Chapter

▶ Live3D SpinGroup

▶ Live3D sprites

▶ Live3D animated textures

▶ Live3D collision detection

▶ Animation in VRML 2.0

▶ Non-VRML animation in trueSpace 2

. . . .

*A*fter you've been creating 3D worlds for a while, you realize that one of the big yawns of VRML 1.0 is that — as cool as 3D worlds are — they just sit there. Bo-o-o-oring. "So, what are you going to do for me *now,* VRML?" you might just ask.

If you ask the VRML hotshots, the answer you may get is, "Just wait until VRML 2.0; you're really, really gonna love it. All you have to do is learn Java, Javascript, C, or QuickBasic." Yeah, right. Sorry, guys, we "Dummies" don't write programs. Unless, of course, we want to. We have bigger fish to fry.

The truth is, for real, serious animation and other special effects, you *are* going to have to wait for VRML 2.0 — but you probably won't have to write programs if you don't want to. The nice folks who make 3D animation software today will probably at least protect their turf by offering VRML 2.0 animation. We world-builders won't even have to look under the hood of the VRML file, just drive. For example, although Caligari isn't saying, we imagine they will adapt the animation capability of trueSpace to output Java, C, or whatever is necessary to do animation in VRML 2.0.

The really good news for people who hate waiting around is that, if you are willing to build worlds that only move in Live3D and don't mind doing a little Deep VRML editing, you can do some simple animation and other special effects today. Live3D offers features we discuss here, in particular animated texture mapping, the SpinGroup, sprites, and collision detection.

We begin with the Live3D tricks that simulate motion. To use these tricks, fire up your word processor, your favorite drawing program, Netscape with Live3D, and follow along.

✔ Live3D is in its early stages, and later versions may change the way some features work (including making some of them work as they are supposed to). If you download a new version, check the documentation for changes.

✔ Don't use Pioneer or Walkthrough to edit a world after you have modified it with Live3D extensions. It will remove your modifications. Of the Live3D tricks here, animated texture mapping is the only feature that allows you to edit the world in Pioneer safely.

Movies on the Wall in Live3D

The Live3D folks have a cute trick up their sleeves for giving you a little more zip in your VRML world when it's viewed in Live3D. This one lets you display a rapid-fire sequence of images, texture maps actually, on any object — just as a movie projects a series of images on the screen. It's a bit of a kludge, frankly, but it works. It's called *animated texture mapping*. Remember, it only works when the world is viewed in Live3D.

First you make your movie: a *filmstrip* that is actually one very tall, skinny bitmap image. It has to have very precise dimensions, or it won't be animated. Here are the rules:

✔ The width in pixels must be a *power of two:* for example, 2, 4, 8, 16, 32, 64, 128, and so on.

✔ The height in pixels must be an even multiple of the width. So if your filmstrip image is 128 pixels wide, it can be 256 pixels (for a strip of two images), 512 pixels (for a strip of four images), or 767 pixels (for six images) high.

Keep in mind that it's all one image; Live3D looks at the unique dimensions and says to itself, "Hey, I bet they want me to animate that, not display the whole thing at once," and delivers it one chunk at a time. Figure 19-1 shows our simple film strip; it's on our CD as ANIMTEXT.JPG, and you can see it in action in ANIMTEXT.WRL.

As we discuss in Chapter 14, you have two ways of storing texture maps in VRML, internal to the WRL file or as external files. This animated texture map has to be of the externally-stored or *inlined* variety (which uses the Texture2 node if you want to be technical about it). Pioneer and Walkthrough Pro normally do texture maps this way, so you don't have to do anything special.

Figure 19-1:
Animated
texture
mapping is
as simple as
ABCD in
Live3D.

You don't have to do any deep VRML editing to use an animated texture map in Live3D; just apply a texture that follows the two rules. You can apply the texture in Pioneer or Walkthrough Pro. The image won't look animated in those programs, of course, because they are not Live3D; you see the whole image smooshed onto the object at once. But load the file into Live3D, and the images will zip on by, looping continuously from top to bottom.

Walkthrough Pro, by a truly strange coincidence, will sometimes round off the dimensions of texture map images to exactly the right dimensions to produce animation in Live 3D! See Chapter 14 for details.

If you want something to appear to fly through space, say a cartoon of a superhero, one cute trick is to use GIF images with transparent backgrounds. Place the GIF texture map on a simple rectangle wherever you want the animated image to appear.

"Spinning" the Web in Live3D

As long as you are happy with animating things in circles, Live3D has an animation solution for you, short of waiting for VRML 2.0: the *SpinGroup node*. It looks simple, and it's fairly simple to use for basic rotating motion. You can also do some complicated motions with it if you are very, very clever and careful. You can see a simple example in the Live3D folder on our CD, the file PLANE.WRL.

Early beta versions of Live3D are extremely buggy in this area. We've seen some models change behavior in utterly unpredictable ways. But hey! It's beta software.

Creating an object for spinning

If you are using a VRML builder to make your scene and you want to include a moving object using the Live3D SpinGroup, we suggest you place the object dead center in your world, at 0,0,0. In Pioneer, this is at the center of the 20 x 20 grid. In Pioneer, you can also make your life a bit easier by inlining the object.

Having done that, save your file and load the main world file into a word processor or text editor. Use that WWWInline object as the object in the discussions that follow.

The SpinGroup turntable

The SpinGroup is like a turntable; everything on it rotates. To put any object on a SpinGroup turntable, edit your VRML file and enclose the object of your choice between the curly braces of the SpinGroup starting after the SpinGroup's two fields, *rotation* and *local*, like this:

```
SpinGroup{
You may need something here. See the following "Tip"
rotation 0 1 0  -0.1
local FALSE
...things to be rotated here...
}
```

The *things to be rotated* are objects. A complete VRML file containing a simple example of a cube being rotated might look like this:

```
#VRML V1.0 ascii
Separator{
   SpinGroup{
   rotation 0 1 0  -0.1
   local FALSE
      Cube {
         height 0.5
         width  2
         depth  1
      }
                  }
   }
```

For a more complex object, you would see a Separator node in place of the cube node. (The objects you create in Walkthrough VRML or Pioneer are made this way.) All the parts are collected by the Separator node, appearing between the Separator's curly braces.

The axis of rotation and speed

The SpinGroup is controlled by two fields, *rotation* and *local,* which you can see in our example. To determine the axis your turntable rotates around (which way the spindle of your turntable points) and its speed, use the rotation field. The rotation field is the term *rotation* followed by four values that represent *x, y, z,* and *increment*, as in:

```
rotation 0 1 0  -0.1
```

In this example, the spin is around the Y axis, and the increment is 0.1 in the clockwise direction.

The first three numbers are *x, y,* and *z* values that describe which way your spindle points. To imagine the spindle, imagine an X, Y, Z coordinate system in space. Then imagine a line starting at the point 0,0,0 (the center of your turntable) and ending at the point *x, y, z*. That line is your spindle, or axis.

The fourth number is the increment of rotation, but you might as well think of it as speed. The higher the number, the faster the object rotates. It's actually the amount of rotation the object goes through (in radians) each time Live3D redisplays the scene. A positive number is counter-clockwise, as seen from the top.

TIP

Playing by the rules — maybe

The SpinGroup is an extension to VRML that is recognized only by Live3D and whatever other viewers or browsers choose to recognize it. Standard VRML browsers and viewers have no idea what the heck this SpinGroup is, so when you use it in a file, in theory, you should define it to the VRML browser/viewer. Otherwise, the browser/viewer may get confused and refuse to display the world at all. Besides, the VRML 1.0 rule states that you should define any non-standard extensions. (Things will change with VRML 2.0.)

Unfortunately, as of this writing, Live3D doesn't appear to live by the rule. In fact, if you try to play by the rules, it won't load your world at all. Just in case this problem gets fixed, someday, here's what you are *supposed* to do:

To define the SpinGroup, insert a fields definition just after the opening curly brace, as you see in bold in the following:

```
SpinGroup {
    fields [SFRotation rotation,
    SFBool local]
    rotation  0 1 0  -0.1
    local     FALSE
}
```

The local field is supposed to work like this:

- ✔ local FALSE means rotate around the center of the world.
- ✔ local TRUE means rotate around the center of the object.

In beta versions of Live3D, this field works rather inconsistently. We have left it set to FALSE and achieved local rotation just fine. When we set it to TRUE, all kinds of trouble happens: Shapes go spinning into space, perform epicycloids (without a helmet), and otherwise misbehave. If you're just making bizarre whirligigs, however, feel free to set it to TRUE.

Positioning objects on the turntable

So far, we just have an object spinning about its center on a turntable. To get it to move around in a loop (a far more interesting behavior), it needs to be moved off-center. To move the object, add a Translation statement just before the object, like this:

```
Translation {
    translation 3 0 0
}
```

```
Cube {
    height 0.5
    width  2
    depth  1
}
```

The numbers following the *translation* term are x, y, and z values. This example moves the object 3 meters in the X direction — the cube's X direction, that is (the direction of its width). If you want to raise the object above the turntable, increase the *y* value.

Orienting objects on the turntable

In order to give the illusion of something moving, like a car or spaceship, you not only need to position it on the turntable, but you also need to orient it so it's facing forward (or backward). To orient the object, add a Rotation node *just before the object,* like this (shown in bold):

```
#VRML V1.0 ascii
Separator{
    SpinGroup{
    rotation 0 1 0  -0.1
    local FALSE
        Translation {
        translation 3 0 0
        }
        Rotation {
            rotation    0 1 0  1.57
        }
        Cube {
            height 0.5
            width  2
            depth  1
        }
    }
}
```

The rotation field is followed by values for x, y, and z, defining the axis of rotation just as they did in the rotation term of the SpinGroup. In this example, the axis of rotation is around the object's Y axis (in that x=0, y=1, z=0). The amount of rotation is given in radians. To compute radians, divide degrees by 57.3; the rotation in our example is 90 degrees, or 1.57 radians.

If you also need to tilt the object — for instance, if the object should look like it's skidding, doing a wheelie, or leaning or banking as it turns, add another Rotation node *just before the object*. For example, when we add

```
Rotation {
rotation    1 0 0 .72
}
```

just before the cube in our example, the cube then leans away from the center of rotation. Which way it leans in your world depends on how the object is oriented along its own axis.

The order in which Translation and Rotation nodes appear is important! If you change the order from the way we describe, you can get some very strange effects.

Spinning parts of an object

Can you make the propeller spin on an airplane? Sure. You have to enclose the propeller object in a spin group. Try inlining the propeller, which makes it easier to find in the WRL file. In theory, you should also set the variable *local* to TRUE, but this setting may not work in beta versions of Live3D.

For a detailed discussion of dealing with objects made up of parts, see "Pioneer's glue" in Chapter 10. For details of inlining, see Chapter 17. But if all you need is a reminder, here's the basic procedure. Select the propeller by selecting the airplane in wireframe mode and navigating the object hierarchy: press the down and/or right-left arrows on your keyboard until the propeller is selected. Right-click the selection tool to get the Object Info panel, mark the propeller as an inlined object, and give the object a name. Save your file, load it into your word processor, and search for the object name. You should find a WWWInline object with that name. Enclose that sucker in a SpinGroup and play with the rotation axes until you get it right!

Multiple spinning

Can you make the propeller spin on an airplane while the airplane circles a mountain?! Whoa, Nelly! Pretty exciting stuff here, but the answer is yes! You can have more than one SpinGroup in a world, and they can be nested within each other. Think of this feature as a turntable on a turntable.

You can also have two separate SpinGroups going on — a simpler affair. You can animate a square dance, with different groups of people dancing around, simulate the multiple gears of a machine, or — if you're a real party animal — have Mr. Potato Head's eyes spinning in opposite directions.

Faking 3D with Live3D Sprites

Sometimes making real 3D is just not worth the effort (this fact has kept painters employed throughout the ages at the expense of sculptors). Real 3D shapes take a lot of computer power to render and display (virtual-real 3D shapes, we mean, not real-real 3D shapes). If you use 3D shapes as just sort of window dressing shapes, they waste valuable computer power and time.

Objects that dress up your scene, but which you don't expect anyone to spend time navigating around — like trees, birds, and distant mountains — are good candidates for fake 3D using a technique called *sprites*. Sprites are simply 2D shapes, with or without texture maps, with one unique characteristic: They always face the observer. They are like flats on a theatrical stage being constantly turned by annoyingly persistent stage hands as you wander about on stage. They aren't perfect substitutes for 3D because they do look flat, and they don't change as you walk around them (this is a little annoying because after a while you really "want to see the other side!"). But they're not bad.

In the early beta versions, Live3D has two VRML extensions for doing spritely things: one that works reliably and another that doesn't. Like all extensions, they only work for one specific browser, in this case, Live3D.

✔ The *Sprite* node is the one that doesn't work reliably yet. It lets you display rectangles with a texture map, a technique that is useful for doing trees and bushes.

✔ The *AxisAlignment* node seems to work fairly well at this point. It works for text and 3D shapes.

We'll deal with the Sprite node because someone will probably eventually get the thing working. We can't tell you much about it because nobody's telling. Here 'tis:

```
Sprite {
fields [SFString texture]
texture "c:\book\vrml\files\for_book\leaves.gif"
    }
```

The node that does the job for us is the *AxisAlignment* node. *AxisAlignment* makes the Z axis of whatever text or object (2D or 3D) that follows *AxisAlignment* constantly face the observer.

To put any object under the influence of AxisAlignment, edit your VRML file and insert the following magic incantation immediately before the object of your choice, like this:

```
AxisAlignment {
    fields      [ SFBitMask alignment ]
    alignment   ALIGNAXISXYZ
}


your shape or text node here
```

Here's a WRL file with a simple square sprite:

```
#VRML V1.0 ascii
Separator {

    AxisAlignment {
        fields      [ SFBitMask alignment ]
        alignment   ALIGNAXISXYZ
                        }


    Cube {
        width   1
        height  1
        depth   0
    }
}
```

If you are using a building tool, like Pioneer, most of your shapes are going to be represented not as primitives, like Cube, but as IndexedFaceSets or other more complex things. You may want to turn such objects into sprites, but they can be hard to find in the blizzard of stuff in a VRML file. One helpful trick in Pioneer is to give the object a unique name that you can search for in your word processor or editor. To do so, select the object and then right-click the selection tool to get an Object Info panel. Type a name in the Name text box, press Enter, and then save your file. Now, when you load that file into your text editor or word processor, just search for that name and insert the AxisAlignment node before it.

AxisAlignment is great for making text labels that are always visible. Here's an example:

```
Separator {
AxisAlignment {
    fields      [ SFBitMask alignment ]
    alignment   ALIGNAXISZXY}

FontStyle {
    size    1
}
}
AsciiText {
    string           "This label is always visible"
    justification    CENTER
}
}
}
```

Collision Detection in Live3D

After a while, the ghostlike capability to move through solid objects in a VRML viewer or browser gets a bit tiresome. Live3D lets the user decide whether to allow this effect, or turn on *collision detection,* which simply prevents the user from going through stuff. (To turn it on, the user right-clicks in the Live3D window, chooses Navigation, and enables Collision Detection.)

Collision detection only works going forward. The user can still step sideways or move backwards through walls. For the sake of virtual high-rise dwellers, we hope that they change this behavior before some version of VRML introduces gravity.

You can turn on collision detection for the user by adding some terms to your VRML file. To enable collision detection for the whole scene, insert the following magic incantation immediately before the master Separator statement that encloses the entire scene:

```
DEF CollisionDetection Info
    {
        string  "TRUE"
    }
```

Tips for 3D effects

✔ See our example, SPRITEX.WRL, on our CD. Spin it around in Live3D using the right mouse button to see most clearly how it works.

✔ If the object you want to turn into a sprite is inlined, put the AxisAlignment node in the inline file, preceding the shape itself, not in the main WRL file preceding the WWWInline statement.

✔ To create a tree or bush, try using the transparent GIF texture map that Live3D allows. See Chapter 14 for more info.

✔ The sun, moon, and other heavenly bodies are good things to do as sprites, rather than 3D objects, and if you're feeling brave, you can even make them orbit using Live3D's SpinGroup node (personally, we rather enjoy having heavenly bodies facing us all the time).

✔ Sprite-like objects will probably get more attention in VRML 2.0, where they are also being called *billboards*.

In theory, you can selectively turn on or off collision detection for specific objects by placing this magic incantation before the nodes for those objects:

```
CollisionDetection {
        fields [SFBool collision]
        collision    TRUE
}
```

In reality, however, in the early beta versions of Live3D, this is one of those may-work-someday features. It does not seem to work reliably.

Setting collision to FALSE turns collision detection off.

Animation Overview for VRML 2.0

As we said in the beginning of this chapter, for the real animation excitement, you have to wait for VRML 2.0. You may not have to wait long for the specification to be finalized, but if you draw the line at actually writing VRML from scratch, you'll have to wait even a bit longer for Caligari, Virtus, or whoever else jumps on the bandwagon to make the tools you need. We are having a hard time telling who among the software vendors is going to do a good job.

A lot of competing ideas have been put forth by different companies, groups, and individuals for the VRML 2.0 specification. At least four major proposals have been kicked around. At the moment, however, the proposal that has received the most votes is called *Moving Worlds,* put together by the same folks at Silicon Graphics who were most instrumental in getting VRML 1.0 off the ground.

To get an idea of the sort of thing you might expect from VRML 2.0, take a look at the VRML 2.0 Moving Worlds specification. Using your Web browser online, enter this URL: `http://webspace.sgi.com/moving-worlds/`.

When that document appears, click the link for the Moving Worlds Overview, and when the Overview appears, scroll down to the Example.

To summarize the *Moving Worlds* document in more *Dummies*-like terms, here's what's going on. It's sort of like a play on a stage, but with robots.

- ✔ Objects are like actors that are controlled by a certain set of *scripts* written in some programming language such as Java or C.

- ✔ Things called *sensors* report the state of the world; they detect certain changes and signal the scripts that care about those changes. They serve as eyes, ears, and skin for the scripts.

- ✔ Sensors signal the passage of time, mouse clicks and motions, proximity of one object to another, or just about anything that changes. Sensor signals (events) are "routed" to a script.

- ✔ Scripts are the "brains" behind the VRML scene that decide what aspects of the objects are to be changed based on what the sensors have signaled. Scripts generate *events,* such as an instruction to move to a new position, and communicate those events to certain objects by means of *routes.*

- ✔ Likewise, objects that have changed also generate *events* that can be routed to something that responds to that change.

- ✔ Simple or incremental changes in objects that don't warrant all the work of programming are controlled by *interpolators* that specify just how an object moves to its new location, or how its color makes a transition.

Clearly, all this new stuff involves some pretty fancy additions to VRML. Scenes in VRML 1.0 are like simple descriptions of a room. In Moving Worlds, they are like a room that has been wired with sensors to provide input to a computer, and where all the furniture is now motorized and under that computer's control!

VRML, as before, still serves as the scene description language. Now, however, it also provides sensors (sensor nodes), wiring (routes), and motors (variables instead of fixed locations, dimensions, and other fields for objects). The controlling computer runs Java, C, or some other language that reads the input from the sensors and sends out new values to the various objects.

Chapter 20

At Least Ten Things to Know about Sound

● ●

In This Chapter

▶ Hyperlinking to sound files

▶ Putting sounds in Pioneer

▶ Sounds in Moving Worlds VRML 2.0

▶ Sound extensions in VRML 1.0 for Pioneer and Live3D

● ●

*1*f a tree falls in your VRML forest, can anyone hear it? Well, officially, not until VRML 2.0. In fact, your tree can't even fall until VRML 2.0. But if you want to offer sound in your VRML world today, you can take one of three approaches:

✔ Use Pioneer to build your world because it uses a custom VRML extension. Hope that a lot of people use Pioneer for VRML viewing. Pioneer's way of doing sound is a lot like the Moving Worlds (MW) proposal for VRML 2.0, so conceivably, other software might someday be able to read these files.

✔ Enter the world of Deep VRML. Hand edit your VRML file to use the sound extensions for Live3D and hope that a lot of people use Live3D to view your world. Live3D's way of doing sound is very much like Pioneer's, so the two may someday be compatible.

✔ Add a hyperlink from an object in your world to a sound file. The sound file simply downloads and plays whenever people click on that object (assuming they have audio capability in their browser or an audio helper application).

The first two alternatives, when they work, are *kewl* because the sound originates at some location in your world and is directional! It diminishes with distance, and if you have stereo speakers on your computer, it moves from one side to the other as you wander around. As a result, you can make splashing waterfalls, singing birds, roaring stock cars, or ringing telephones. Of course, the only place anyone can currently hear the sound is in Pioneer or Live3D; but probably other vendors will start adding one form of audio or another. The last alternative, adding a hyperlink to a sound file, has the great advantage of being supported under VRML 1.0, and so it should work for any browser that can deliver audio!

Hyperlinking to Sound Files

The most reliable way to get sound into a VRML world is to hyperlink from an object to a sound file. The link doesn't require any fancy or unreliable extensions to VRML 1.0. Of course, it's not virtual reality, either: the sound doesn't fade with distance or move between your stereo speakers. When people double-click a hyperlinked object in your world, their browser will either play the sound or (if they've configured their browser to do so) launch a helper application that can play the sound.

Hyperlinking is a good way to actually give people useful information in a 3D world, not just create a virtual reality. If you want to create, say, a VRML guide to bird identification where you double-click a 3D chickadee to hear its call, this route is the way to go.

To create a link to a sound file in Walkthrough VRML, just select an object, choose Design⇨VRML Anchor, and in the Anchor URL dialog box that appears, type the filename (for example, CHICKADI.WAV). You can alternatively type the URL of any sound file on the Internet.

To create a link to a sound file in Pioneer, select the object, click the button with the world-in-chains icon, and in the Attach URL link dialog box that appears, type the filename of a local file or the URL of any sound file on the Internet.

Unless you're using a sound file located on somebody else's site, make sure that the path of the file you're using is still correct when you move your .WRL file from your computer to your Web site. The easiest way to do so is to put the sound file in the same directory as the .WRL file in both places.

The Sound of Pioneer

Pioneer is the first VRML building tool we've encountered that offers support for sound. Pioneer's sound is kind of a fun feature to use, even though (at the moment) it only works for the elite: people viewing your world in Pioneer. Here's how to add sound:

1. **Select an object to be your sound source.**

 2. **Choose the Sound tool.**

   Click the button with the green, zig-zaggy line icon. It's probably hiding behind the world-in-chains (Attach a hyperlink URL) button. Click and hold on the world-in-chains button, drag to the zig-zaggy button, and release. The Audio Info panel of Figure 20-1 appears.

Figure 20-1:
Attaching
audio to an
object in
Pioneer.

3. Choose a sound file to attach.

Click the unmarked rectangular button at the top of the Audio Info panel. This button gives you a file selection dialog box, where you choose a .WAV file for your sound. (A few .WAV files are always in your WINDOWS directory, if you just want to test this feature.)

4. Enter an Intensity value (sound volume) between 0 and 1.

5. Enter a small value for Minimum Range.

In this box, Pioneer is asking you to define a spherical zone around the object in which the sound doesn't vary with distance. A value between 1 and 5 often works well.

6. Enter a larger value for Maximum Range.

In this box, you tell Pioneer the maximum distance at which anything can be heard at all. Volume goes down to zero at the distance you specify. Best of all, this setting gives you the stereo effect: If the object is, say, off to your left, you hear sounds from the left speaker.

7. Click the Attach button to attach the sound to the object.

If you later change your mind about having sound attached to this object, just repeat Steps 1 and 2 and click the Remove button in the Audio Info panel.

8. Make sure that the Enable checkbox is selected.

Now your selected sound file will repeat *ad infinitum, ad nauseum*. Adjust the Intensity and Maximum Range as you move about your world.

At this writing, Pioneer is a principally VRML 1.0 tool but borrows heavily from an early version of a proposed VRML 2.0 feature for sound. We're not sure whether any other browser/viewer vendor will accept this particular implementation, although it appears that Live3D may. Right now, the only tool we are certain will understand Pioneer's audio feature is Pioneer.

Sounds in Deep VRML

No official VRML 1.0 code exists for doing sound, so tool vendors are borrowing from VRML 2.0 and creating custom extensions to VRML 1.0 that look a lot like the VRML 2.0 terms. However, VRML 2.0 and Moving Worlds, (the VRML 2.0 proposal likely to be the winner) are works in progress, and Pioneer, Live3D, and other tools will probably attempt to follow that progress, so take everything we say in this section with a very large grain of rock salt. Consider this section to be a snapshot of the evolution of sound features in VRML. Check `http://webspace.sgi.com/moving-worlds/` for the latest information.

As we write this, Pioneer and Live3D are lagging behind VRML 2.0 a bit (by about a month) and use an early version of the Moving Worlds sound specification to do their audio work. This situation will undoubtedly change, but because the versions you have of these tools may be of this era ("eras" lasting about a week in VRML), we describe the Deep VRML for sound in those tools. If you download new versions of this software, you will probably find that it looks more like the VRML 2.0 specification — which is why we're providing that specification here.

First, we give you the current Moving Worlds/VRML 2.0 specification for sound (as of Thursday, April 18, 1996). Then we describe how sound was implemented in Pioneer and Live3D on this date.

Moving Worlds (VRML 2.0)

Following is a description of the VRML 2.0/Moving Worlds node for sound as of this writing. We provide it here because we expect that tool vendors will start borrowing from it and writing custom VRML 1.0 extensions that are similar. This way, if you download new versions of Pioneer or new audio example files and decide to peek inside the files, you may be able to understand what the fields are for and write your own code.

```
Sound {
        source some audio clip or other VRML 2.0 "source"
    intensity value from 0 to 1 controlling volume
    priority value from 0 to 1 specifying how important this
    sound is
    location x y z
    direction x y z
    minFront see minFront in Pioneer/Live3D description
    maxFront see maxFront in Pioneer/Live3D description
    minBack  see minBack  in Pioneer/Live3D description
    maxBack  see maxBack  in Pioneer/Live3D description
    spatialize   TRUE or FALSE; spatialization provides vol-
    ume-by-distance and stereo effects.
}
```

Sound for Pioneer and Live3D

At this writing, Pioneer and Live3D have adopted (and implemented as custom extensions to VRML 1.0) an early Moving Worlds proposal for VRML 2.0 that includes two features for sound. They will probably change to something closer to the Moving Worlds specification in the preceding section. For now, following are the two ways that the audio magic is done in these products:

- ✔ **Point sound:** Equal volume in all directions. Two concentric spherical sound zones center on a sound source. In the inner zone, sound volume doesn't diminish at all with distance; in the outer zone, it diminishes to zero at the limit of the zone.

- ✔ **Directed sound:** Volume is higher in one direction. Inner and outer zones exist, as in point sound, but they are elliptical, not spherical. The sound source sits at a common *focal point* of both ellipses. (The ellipses are *confocal* in geek-speak. Ellipses have two focal points, one near each end, inside the ellipse.)

Both Pioneer and Live3D *almost* exactly duplicate these early Moving Worlds features. Pioneer has cloned the point sound feature, and Live3D has cloned both the point sound and directed sound features.

Because Live3D uses for point sound VRML code that is a lot like Pioneer's, you may be able to use Pioneer to create your initial file and then just edit the file as necessary to make it work in Live3D.

Pioneer's and Live3D's point sound extensions

Here is an example and explanation of the way Pioneer and Live3D do their point sound extensions as of this writing:

```
PointSound {
    fields [ SFString name, SFString description,
    SFFloat intensity, SFVec3f location,
    SFFloat minRange, SFFloat maxRange ]
    name         "beep.wav"
    description  "Annoying beeping noise"
    intensity    1
    location     0 0 0
    minRange     10
    maxRange     10
    loop         TRUE
    start        0
    pause        0
}
```

The **name** field gives the URL or path and filename of a sound file. The Moving Worlds specification doesn't say what types of sound files should be used, but .WAV is what Pioneer currently plays.

The **description** field provides text that the browser/viewer can display if it's designed to do so. This field is optional.

The **intensity** field gives the relative loudness of the sound, ranging from 0 to 1.

The **location** field gives the X, Y, and Z coordinates of the place the sound is coming from.

The **minRange** field gives the radius of the inner zone of sound, where intensity doesn't vary with distance from the source.

The **maxRange** field gives the radius of the outer zone, where intensity does vary.

The **loop** field determines if the sound plays just once (FALSE) or repeats endlessly (TRUE).

The **start** field indicates when the sound is to begin playing, and the **pause** field makes the sound stop some time after it began.

> ✔ For Pioneer, you currently must omit the **loop**, **start**, and **pause** fields that appear in the preceding definition.
>
> ✔ In the field definitions, Live3D uses **MFString** for **name**, where Pioneer uses **SFString**.

Live3D's directed sound extension

As of this writing, Live3D has based its directed sound feature on the original directed sound in the Moving Worlds proposal for VRML 2.0. Directed sound is a more realistic but more complicated kind of sound than point sound. However, it uses many of the same fields as the PointSound node. Here it is:

```
DirectedSound {
fields [MFString name, SFString description,
   SFFloat intensity, SFVec3f location, SFVec3f direction,
   SFFloat minFrontRange, SFFloat maxFrontRange,
   SFFloat minBackRange, SFFloat maxBackRange,
   SFBool loop, SFFloat start, SFFloat pause ]
   name   "beep.wav"
   description   "Directed annoying beeping noise"
   intensity1
```

```
    location 0 0 0
    direction0 0 1
    minFront 10
    minBack  10
    maxFront 10
    maxBack  10
    loop   FALSE
    start 0
    pause 0
}
```

The terms **minFront** and **minBack** take the place of minRange in PointSound, defining the limits of that inner ellipse of sound (the one in which volume does not vary with distance). The terms **maxFront** and **maxBack** define the limits of the outer ellipse.

To visualize the ellipse, start at the **location** and go in the direction described by the **direction** values (+X, +Y, and +Z). That line gives the central axis of the ellipses. For each ellipse (min and max), the Front value gives the distance from the **location** to one end of the ellipse, and the Back value gives the distance to the other end.

Appendix

About the CD

An Introduction to Our CD

You load the CD by placing it in your CD-ROM drive and taking one of the following steps: On Macs, double-click the VRML For Dummies icon that appears on the desktop. On PCs with Windows 3.1, from File Manager, double-click the icon near the top of your screen that represents your CD-ROM drive (usually drive D). On PCs with Windows 95, in the My Computer folder, double-click on your CD-ROM drive's icon (probably drive D).

When you load the CD, the *first* thing you need to do is read the OUR_CD document. This file comes in two file formats: plain text (OUR_CD.TXT) and HTML (OUR_CD.HTM). You can open the OUR_CD.TXT file in any word processor or text editor. OUR_CD.HTM is a file you can load into a Web browser, such as Netscape or Internet Explorer, using the File⇨Open command.

We've taken some pains to make sure that this CD is *not* shovelware. Shovelware is a bunch of stuff mainly intended to fill out a book's CD and make the list of included software on the back cover look really impressive. Generally, shovelware has little or no explanation in the book and often has important capabilities removed. In addition, some shovelware licenses are tied to a fixed expiration date, which may have expired by the time you buy the book. We don't do that.

We explain the operation of all the principal tools on CD in this book. Specifically, we explain in detail how to use the VRML browsers and builders. We made sure that no important VRML features were left out. And we negotiated custom terms with our cooperating vendors so that any software that expires has a useful lifetime starting when it is first installed.

If you read OUR_CD.HTM on your Web browser, you can click on highlighted text to move to the subject we're talking about. You can also find additional notes, corrections, and other stuff on our Web site: http://www.brightleaf.com/vrml4dum/. You can send us e-mail at vrml@dummies.com. In fact, please do; we'd love to hear comments or corrections — but unfortunately, we can't promise to respond to questions or problems.

About Evaluation Software

The principal tools on this CD are evaluation versions (*evals*), included with the book to save you the time and trouble of obtaining evals from the vendors. Because VRML is so new, many of the evals are beta software (not yet for sale and still being tested) — which means they are not bug-free.

The tools on this CD include all of the VRML features of the for-sale versions, so if they weren't restricted in some way, the software vendors would go broke. (Some of these tools are worth hundreds of dollars!) As a result, the tools come with special license restrictions, so please read and respect the licenses. The licenses for some tools on our CD are time-limited, so the licenses expire a given number of days or hours of usage after you install the software. Beyond that point, the software no longer operates.

The following table lists the usage times for the evaluation software on CD:

Software	Evaluation time
Pioneer	30 hours of use or 60 days, whichever comes first
Pioneer Pro	10 hours of use or 30 days, whichever comes first
trueSpace 2	30 days after installation
VR Scout (Plug in and Helper)	30 days after installation
Walkthrough Pro	90 days after installation

Some of the license terms, such as the 90-day trial of Walkthrough Pro, are exclusive to this CD. In some other cases, your license allows you to download new versions of these products from the Web. We give you the URLs of each software vendor (in the OUR_CD file), just in case you want to try to download software or check for troubleshooting information.

Eval software doesn't include post-installation support, so please don't try to call the vendors for support. You'll waste your time and money making long-distance calls. Instead, read the tools' Help files and check the vendors' Web sites for additional tips or frequently-asked questions (FAQs).

The CD at a Glance

The following table lists the contents of the CD:

Software	*Folder Path*	*Mac or PC*	*Description*
Pioneer	Build/Caligari/Pioneer	PC	VRML browser/ builder (Windows 95 only)
Pioneer Pro	Build/Caligari/PioneerP	PC	A more feature-filled version of Pioneer (Windows 95 only)
trueSpace 2	Build/Caligari/TrueSpc2	PC	Professional-grade 3D modeler and renderer (Demo version)
Walkthrough Pro	Build/Virtus/WalkTPro	Both	VRML builder (90-day evaluation)
Photomodeler LX	Build/EOS	PC	Creates 3D models from photos (Demo version)
Textures and Models	Material/Acuris	PC	Models and textures
Models	Material/ ViewPt	PC	Models in Caligari object format
Voyager	Browse/Virtus	Both	VRML browser (on PCs, requires Windows 95)
VR Scout Plug-in Viewer	Browse/Chaco/Plugins	PC	Plug-in VRML viewer for Netscape (requires Windows 95)
VR Scout Helper Application	Browse/Chaco/Helpers	PC	VRML helper application for Web browsers (for Windows 3.1/32s and Windows 95)
Pueblo	Browse/Chaco/Pueblo	PC	Special-purpose 3D browser
Internet Explorer for Windows 95	Browse/Microsft	PC	Web browser from Microsoft

(continued)

Software	Folder Path	Mac or PC	Description
VRML Add-In for Internet Explorer for Windows 95	Browse/Microsft	PC	Plug-in VRML viewer for Internet Explorer for Windows 95
OUR_CD.TXT	Root	Both	Text file describing the contents of the CD; also includes installation information.
OUR_CD.HTM	Root	Both	Same content as the OUR_CD.TXT file but in HTML format; open in your favorite Web browser
vrml10c.htm	Appendix	Both	The VRML 1.0c specification in HTML format; open in your favorite Web browser
Stuff from the authors	Ourstuff	Both	Notes, samples, objects, textures, and videos
VisMenu (index.html)	VisNet	Both	Web page that tells you where can download the VisMenu interface, which makes it easier to install the software on the CD

By the way, we used Lotus ScreenCam to shoot the videos on the CD (in the Ourstuff folder), so we'd like to acknowledge Lotus as the creator and owner of the ScreenCam technology:

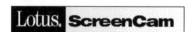

Installing Software

As with any software, each tool comes with the manufacturer's own unique installation process. In general, to install a tool on a PC, just run Setup.exe in that tool's directory. On Macs, you just need to double-click on the program's installer icon to run the installer program.

Each tool has its own unique hardware and software requirements or preferences, which you will generally find in the manufacturer's instructions or in our notes in the OUR_CD document. Some tools are for Windows 3.1 (and will therefore work under Windows 95); others are only for Windows 95. Some will work faster when your PC is equipped with accelerated graphics, especially graphics that run a special system from Intel called 3DR. A few also offer some audio capabilities, so if your PC has stereo audio, you're in luck.

We suggest that you do *not* try to install all the software immediately. In some cases (Netscape plug ins in particular), the result will be that only the most recently installed software will be operational. In other cases, you may accidentally start the clock running on the software before you are ready to use it, thus wasting the time allotted to you for using it. Instead of installing all the software immediately, refer to the appropriate chapter in our book before you install a program to see if it's what you want. Then install and try programs one at a time. It's okay if you end up with multiple programs installed — just install them and try them one at a time.

The VisNet folder on the CD was supposed to contain software (called VisMenu) that would allow you to install the tools on the CD by clicking on objects in a 3D world. But because so many of the tools changed at the last minute, we weren't able to include this neat interface. If you open the VisNet folder, however, and open the index.html file in a Web browser, you will find information on how to download the VisMenu software from the VisNet Web site.

Index

• U •

Special *VRML & 3D On The Web For Dummies* offer!

VIRTUS
CORPORATION

Has your copy of Virtus Walkthrough Pro timed out?

Would you like to get back to building cool
3D worlds for the Internet?

Would you like to save $246 just for
having bought this book?

If you answered "YES!" to any of the above questions . . .

Call 1-800-847-8871 ext. 3050 and get your copy of
Virtus Walkthrough Pro
for only $249 (regular $495).

IDG Books Worldwide, Inc.
End-User License Agreement

● ●

4. Restrictions on Use of Individual Programs. You must follow the individual requirements and restrictions detailed for each individual program in the "About the CD" Appendix of this Book. These limitations are contained in the individual license agreements recorded on the disk(s)/CD-ROM. These restrictions may include a requirement that after using the program for the period of time specified in its text, the user must pay a registration fee or discontinue use. By opening the Software packet(s), you will be agreeing to abide by the licenses and restrictions for these individual programs. None of the material on this disk(s) or listed in this Book may ever be distributed, in original or modified form, for commercial purposes.

5. Limited Warranty.

(a) IDGB warrants that the Software and disk(s)/CD-ROM are free from defects in materials and workmanship under normal use for a period of sixty (60) days from the date of purchase of this Book. If IDGB receives notification within the warranty period of defects in materials or workmanship, IDGB will replace the defective disk(s)/CD-ROM.

(b) **IDGB AND THE AUTHORS OF THE BOOK DISCLAIM ALL OTHER WARRANTIES, EXPRESS OR IMPLIED, INCLUDING WITHOUT LIMITATION IMPLIED WARRANTIES OF MERCHANTABILITY AND FITNESS FOR A PARTICULAR PURPOSE, WITH RESPECT TO THE SOFTWARE, THE PROGRAMS, THE SOURCE CODE CONTAINED THEREIN, AND/OR THE TECHNIQUES DESCRIBED IN THIS BOOK. IDGB DOES NOT WARRANT THAT THE FUNCTIONS CONTAINED IN THE SOFTWARE WILL MEET YOUR REQUIREMENTS OR THAT THE OPERATION OF THE SOFTWARE WILL BE ERROR FREE.**

(c) This limited warranty gives you specific legal rights, and you may have other rights which vary from jurisdiction to jurisdiction.

6. Remedies.

(a) IDGB's entire liability and your exclusive remedy for defects in materials and workmanship shall be limited to replacement of the Software, which may be returned to IDGB with a copy of your receipt at the following address: Disk Fulfillment Department, Attn: *VRML & 3D On The Web For Dummies,* IDG Books Worldwide, Inc., 7260 Shadeland Station, Ste. 100, Indianapolis, IN 46256, or call 1-800-762-2974. Please allow 3-4 weeks for delivery. This Limited Warranty is void if failure of the Software has resulted from accident, abuse, or misapplication. Any replacement Software will be warranted for the remainder of the original warranty period or thirty (30) days, whichever is longer.

(b) In no event shall IDGB or the author be liable for any damages whatsoever (including without limitation damages for loss of business profits, business interruption, loss of business information, or any other pecuniary loss) arising from the use of or inability to use the Book or the Software, even if IDGB has been advised of the possibility of such damages.

(c) Because some jurisdictions do not allow the exclusion or limitation of liability for consequential or incidental damages, the above limitation or exclusion may not apply to you.

7. <u>U.S. Government Restricted Rights</u>. Use, duplication, or disclosure of the Software by the U.S. Government is subject to restrictions stated in paragraph (c) (1) (ii) of the Rights in Technical Data and Computer Software clause of DFARS 252.227-7013, and in subparagraphs (a) through (d) of the Commercial Computer—Restricted Rights clause at FAR 52.227-19, and in similar clauses in the NASA FAR supplement, when applicable.

8. <u>General</u>. This Agreement constitutes the entire understanding of the parties and revokes and supersedes all prior agreements, oral or written, between them and may not be modified or amended except in a writing signed by both parties hereto which specifically refers to this Agreement. This Agreement shall take precedence over any other documents that may be in conflict herewith. If any one or more provisions contained in this Agreement are held by any court or tribunal to be invalid, illegal, or otherwise unenforceable, each and every other provision shall remain in full force and effect.

CD Installation Information

You load the CD by placing it in your CD-ROM drive and taking one of the following steps: On Macs, double-click the VRML For Dummies icon that appears on the desktop. On PCs with Windows 3.1, from File Manager, double-click the icon near the top of your screen that represents your CD-ROM drive (usually drive D). On PCs with Windows 95, in the My Computer folder, double-click on your CD-ROM drive's icon (probably drive D).

Please see the Appendix, "About the CD," for an overview of the contents of the CD as well as brief installation instructions. For more detailed information, please read the OUR_CD file on the CD. This file comes in an HTML version (OUR_CD.HTM) and a text version (OUR_CD.TXT). You can read the HTML version in a Web browser such as Netscape or Internet Assistant. You can read the text version in any word processor or text editor. Many of the manufacturers of the software on the CD include separate README files and documentation. Please read these files for installation instructions as well as license agreement information. Please remember that the licenses for some of the software tools on our CD are time limited. In other words, some of the tools on the CD are evaluation versions that will cease to function after a given number of days or hours of use. Again, please read each program's documentation on the CD for more information.

❏ YES!

Please keep me informed about IDG's World of Computer Knowledge.
Send me the latest IDG Books catalog.